MODERN SOCIAL WORK THEORY

Modern Social Work Theory

SECOND EDITION

Malcolm Payne

Consultant editor: Jo Campling

LYCEUM
BOOKS, INC.

5758 S. Blackstone Ave.
Chicago, Illinois 60637

To Susan

© Malcolm Stuart Payne 1991, 1997

Published by

LYCEUM BOOKS, INC.
5758 S. Blackstone Avenue
Chicago, Illinois 60637

Tel: 773 643-1902
Fax: 773 643 1903

First edition 1991
Second edition 1997

ISBN 0–925065–15–3

Library of Congress Cataloging-in-Publication Data
Payne, Malcolm, 1947–
Modern social work theory : a critical introduction / Malcolm
Payne. 2nd ed.
p. cm.
Includes bibliographical references and index.
ISBN 0–925065–15–3 (alk. paper)
1. Social service—Philosophy. I. Title.
HV40.P33 1997
361.3'01—dc21   96–53614
                                                          CIP

Printed in Great Britain

Foreword

This second edition of *Modern Social Work Theory* continues to provide the reader with one of the more thorough and complete reviews of social work practice theories. Beyond being an excellent review, the text also provides a framework within which the reader can think critically about and evaluate the practice implication of each theory. This text continues to be one of the most readable and intellectually stimulating treatments of contemporary social work theory. It should be required reading for all social work students at both the undergraduate and graduate level. The text provides the reader with perspectives not only from other Western countries, but also from non-Western countries, non-Christian cultures, and Third World countries.

The first two chapters have been significantly rewritten to provide a clearer framework for understanding and thinking about each of the practice theories. Chapter 1 presents a discussion of the importance of examining practice theory within the social context in which it is practiced. In particular, this chapter emphasizes the political, cultural, and national issues that influence both the selection and the implementation of practice theory. Chapter 2 provides a rich discussion and critique of positivist and postmodern views of theory in social work practice. In addition, the chapter examines the relationship between theory and practice and presents a comparative analysis of social work theories. Readers will find the material in this chapter well referenced and helpful in identifying the major literature in the field.

Chapters 3 through 12 review social work theory as grouped into differing theoretical perspectives. The author's basis for including these theories is their current usage. The theoretical perspectives that are covered include: psychodynamic models, crisis intervention and task-centered models; cognitive-behavioral theories; systems and ecological perspectives; social psychological and communication models; humanist and existential perspectives; social and community development; radical and Marxist perspectives; anti-discriminatory and anti-oppressive perspectives; and empowerment and advocacy. The major changes in this edition are the combining of the cognitive and behavioral theories into one chapter and the addition of two new chapters that deal with social and community development and anti-discriminatory and anti-oppressive perspectives. The author has updated each chapter to reflect current materials and has reorganized them to provide the reader with an understanding of the broader perspectives and social contexts of each theory. The richness and uniqueness of *Modern Social Work Theory* is contained in the presentation, discussion, and critiques of the differing social work theories. The strength of the text rests in how the preceding is directly connected with social work practice on a global basis. The international scope provided is most stimulating, and challenges readers to broaden their thinking about the 'what' and 'whys' of their practice.

The last chapter (Chapter 13) addresses factors and issues in assessing social work theories. It is a thoughtful finale that challenges all of us, whether students or seasoned professionals, to work towards the development and strengthening of social work theories that will better guide our practice in effectively meeting the needs of our clients in an ever-changing world.

The second edition of *Modern Social Work Theory* offers a stronger and more reflective treatment of contemporary social work theory. As with the first edition, this edition also provides an extensive bibliography reflecting current literature published both in the United States and abroad. Again, Professor Payne has provided a stimulating contribution to our profession.

Stephen C. Anderson, Practicum Coordinator
The University of Oklahoma

Contents

List of Figures and Tables

Figures

Tables

Preface and Acknowledgements

It has been a surprise to me that in an apparently slow-moving topic such as theory I have been obliged only five years after the publication of the first edition of *Modern Social Work Theory* (and seven years from starting its writing) to make such extensive changes to this new edition. Part of this may have been the hot pace of change in social work ideas in the early 1990s. I am not sure whether this is a continuing feature of social work of which I was naïvely unaware or whether everything will calm down, with social work theory becoming a quiet backwater. I suspect it may have been my ignorance and lack of sophistication in such matters when, in the enthusiasm of returning to academic life from agency management in 1987, I allowed Steven Kennedy to persuade me that I should give rein to my long-standing interest in the application of theories of social work practice. He remembered this had been an ambition during my former bout of academic life in the 1970s, and probably judged that I was now experienced enough to write such a book and still inexperienced enough to believe I could do it.

Anyway, since the publication of the first edition, I have found out how much I did not know and understand. The success of the first edition has led to many comments from people with different perspectives and opportunities to meet and speak about social work theory across Britain and the world. As a result, I have gained a much broader perspective and deeper understanding of many of the things I have written about. I should like particularly to thank the following individuals and organisations:

Gurid Aga Askeland for detailed and extensive criticisms and for lengthy arguments and advice which have improved particularly Chapters 2 and 13 in spite of my aggressive resistance;

Edward R. Canda for materials and information particularly about Eastern philosophies and spirituality in social work;

Inger Glesnes, who took the trouble to pass on to me an extensive critique, which has helped me to improve several parts of this edition;

Charles Guzzetta for help with matters concerning social development;

Gerd Hagen and her colleagues at ØKS, the social work school of the Oslo College, for arranging a seminar for staff and advanced students and other colleagues at the Diakonhjemmets Høgskolesenter Sosialhøgskolen, allowing me to work with some of her advanced students and conveying some of her own thoughts derived from her experience of using the book with students;

Laksiri Jayasuriya for materials and information about social work in Asian cultures;

Diana Mak and colleagues at the Hong Kong Polytechnic University, who invited me to give some seminars on social work theory, helped me with thoughtful critical comments and enabled me to use their library;

Stefan Morén, who gave me written and verbal comments and invited me to give a seminar for Swedish PhD students at the University of Umeå which helped to test out my ideas;

Eric Olssen and *Jenny Ljunghill*, who discussed their ideas with me and sent me information and English translations of their work;

Shula Ramon, the *Soros Foundation* and the *Russian Ministry of Higher Education*, who invited me to give two seminars to Russian social work teachers on social work theory, and the people in the audience and other speakers who made useful critical comments;

Inger Siiriainen, *Tom Sandlund* and *Georg Walls,* who enabled me to give public lectures and work with students at the social work unit and the Swedish Institute of Social Science, University of Helsinki, through a readership there;

Elka Todorova, who invited me to the Balkan Schools of Social Work Summer School at the University of Varna and enabled me to give a public lecture and hear the comments of practitioners and academics on my ideas;

Mait Widmark and *Thomas Lindstein*, who kindly arranged for me to work with students at the University of Stockholm.

All of these people, by making criticisms or by enabling me to work with a broader range of students, and many more who phoned me or spoke to me at conferences and meetings, together with the reviewers of the book in various journals, have helped me to see the weaknesses in the first edition and to develop this new one. I am sorry if I have failed to acknowledge anyone explicitly, but I have experienced so much interest, criticism and kindness that I cannot always trace where an idea or point came from. Please accept my grateful thanks for the personal support and for being saved from so many errors of judgement or fact. I also acknowledge that I have many times ignored advice and comments (sometimes because they were conflicting), so none of these named or unnamed supporters and critics should be burdened with any responsibility for this edition's failings. I am frequently told that this book is too difficult (to which I reply that it is difficult to understand and work with theory) or that it is too simple (to which I reply that any abbreviated general review can only form an introduction to the complexities and full glories of the real thing).

The publishers and author wish to thank the following for permission to reproduce copyright material:

Colin Whittington and Ray Holland (1985) 'A Framework for Theory in Social Work', *Issues in Social Work Education*, 5(1), published by the Association for Teachers in Social Work Education, and David Howe (1987) *An Introduction to Social Work Theory*, published by Wildwood House, for Figure 2.2.

Every effort has been made to trace all the copyright-holders, but if any have been inadvertently overlooked the publishers will be pleased to make the necessary arrangements at the first opportunity.

This new edition contains substantial changes throughout. There are two completely new chapters (9 and 11), and the general chapters 1, 2 and, in this edition, 13 are substantially new, reflecting a considerable advance in my thinking, influenced strongly by colleagues at the Department of Applied Community Studies, Manchester Metropolitan University, over the past few years, whose experience and knowledge I gratefully acknowledge. New 'example' texts have been substituted for or added to those originally discussed in Chapters 5, 6, 8, 10 and 12, and new editions covered in Chapter 3. Significant updating and recasting of the argument has taken place in every chapter. There are more than 400 new references and many references have been retained so that the book remains, I hope, a useful bibliographic resource. In spite of all this new work, I have tried to restrain the size of the volume, so that it remains accessible. I am aware that this reduces the breadth of coverage, and means that to any expert in a particular theory my account of it is inadequate. I also know that my judgements about inclusion and exclusion and my, at times heavy, condensation are disputable and disputed. Nevertheless, I try in this book to give access to a range of ideas useful to those who would know social work more fully. I can only repeat with emphasis the final paragraph of the acknowledgements in the first edition:

> Clearly, any writer of a review of social work theory relies on the ideas of other writers, and I commend any reader to progress from this introduction to the comprehensive accounts to be found in the books and articles referred to. I have found them stimulating and full of ideas for practice and understanding. I am sure you will do so, too.

MALCOLM PAYNE
Edgworth

1

The Social Construction of Social Work Theory

What this book is about

At this moment, somewhere in the world, 'clients' are struggling into an office to meet with a 'social worker'. Perhaps the worker is visiting the client's home, or works with clients in groups, in residential or day care, or in community work. In most societies, this something called 'social work' goes on. It is widely enough spread for international associations of social workers and a shared language and literature of social work to exist.

This apparent shared understanding across many societies raises questions. Is social work a single entity, the same thing, in all those societies? In this chapter, I argue that those workers and clients construct social work within the context of their agencies. Yet it is not constructed anew whenever worker and client come together in an agency context. This is because each worker, client and agency context are themselves constructed by the society in which they exist. What they do is formed from expectations taken up from that society. And they contribute to some extent to that society's expectations by their own thinking and doing. That is the process of social construction. People in different social contexts create a shared reality of some set of social relations which they know as social work.

This book is about one aspect of that construction – social work practice 'theory'. I put 'theory' in inverted commas at this stage because it is a contested idea; that is, people argue about what a 'theory' is or ought to be. Chapter 2 discusses ways in which we understand social work 'theory' and how it might be used. Chapters 3 to 12 each discuss a group of 'theories' which are current in social work at the time of writing. Finally, in Chapter 13, I look at how we might evaluate these groups of 'theories' in use.

I wrote above that this book discusses *one aspect* of the construction of social work. The 'theories' we are going to consider have the following features:

- They are contained in professional writing mainly by social workers.
- Such writing tries to give organised guidance for practice, based on sets of ideas which seek to explain how human beings respond in social relations.
- The guidance is given to workers on how they should act when doing social work.

As a result, we are not concerned here with ideas which try to explain or describe what social work is or what it aspires to be, or with its history, or agencies and the policies they are trying to implement and how these are created. Neither are we concerned with many relevant ideas outside social work, such as the psychological or counselling literature, which some social workers borrow but which are mainly outside *social work* literature. Because we are concerned with guidance from social workers to other workers, we are not concerned with clients' views and contributions to the construction of social work, influential though these ought to be, except where they are relevant to considering the value of 'theories'. Some writing about social work attempts to describe its process, such as the suggestion that it solves problems by starting with assessment or diagnosis, moves on to intervention, action or treatment and is then terminated. Morén (1994) comments that defining social work through such processes can be mechanical. He prefers to see social work, more creatively, as a process of making visible new possibilities of interpretation and action. Berglind (1992), similarly, sees social work action as a process of deciding action from among a variety of alternative positions.

Again, we do not start from such process views because we are dealing with ideas affecting social work which try to *explain* why human beings respond in social relations. These other aspects of social work writing and thinking all help to construct social work. It is useful and interesting to study them, but they are outside this book's focus. Here, I explore practice 'theories' which exist in social work with three aims:

- To try to understand for myself, and contribute to others' understanding of, the uses of these 'theories' and the distinctions between them.
- To offer workers and students a guide to different groups of 'theories', so that they may gain access to knowledge which might help them practise.
- To contribute to understanding how 'theories' may be used in social work practice and professional debate.

This book aims to *review* social work *practice* 'theories', to offer an assessment and arrive at an understanding of them and their value in modern social work practice. It is a *review*, not an attempt at constructing a new 'theory'. Therefore, I reflect what is available rather than extending it where it has not yet gone. It is about social work *practice* 'theories', which try to explain, describe or justify what social workers do. Many such 'theories' have connections with wider social and psychological theories. Each chapter therefore contains some account of wider ideas in a section entitled 'wider theoretical perspectives'. A 'connections' section in each chapter acknowledges links and connections with other conceptions of social work practice. Then, each chapter describes how we have applied the basic principles of the 'theory' in social work practice 'theory'. There is also a more detailed account of 'example texts' showing how writers have used the 'theory' in a comprehensive prescription for social work activity. I have excluded 'theories' unless I can find a coherent attempt to apply the 'theory' to a wide range of social work activity. This is because unless social workers have used a set of ideas fairly comprehensively to prescribe practice, I consider that they have not yet become a social work practice 'theory'. Each chapter also contains some account of the politics and debates which exist around the 'theory'.

In this chapter, I try to show how 'theory' is part of a *politics*. By that I mean particular 'theories' have interest groups within social work seeking influence over our understanding of the nature and practice of social work by gaining acceptance of their 'theory'. In this way, struggle for acceptance of a 'theory' intends to gain a greater contribution for it in the overall construction of social work, by gaining greater impact for it in workers' actions within social work as they daily construct it with their clients in their agency contexts. So in selecting a 'theory' to use, workers contribute to how social work is constructed, because *what they do* in social work *is* or *becomes* social work. These are complicated ideas to get hold of, so I expand on them at some length here.

The politics of social work and its practice 'theories'

I have argued elsewhere (Payne, 1996a) that there are three views of social work:

- *Reflexive-therapeutic views.* These see social work as seeking the best possible well-being for individuals, groups and communities in society, by promoting and facilitating growth and self-fulfilment. A constant process of interaction with others modifies their ideas and allows them to influence others. This process of mutual influence is what makes social work reflexive. In these ways, people gain power over their own feelings and way of life. Through this personal power, they are enabled to overcome or rise above suffering and disadvantage.

This view is basic to many ideas of the nature of social work as an activity, but two other views modify and dispute it:

- *Socialist-collectivist views.* These see social work as seeking cooperation and mutual support in society so that the most oppressed and disadvantaged people can gain power over their own lives. Social work facilitates by empowering people to take part in a process of learning and cooperation which creates institutions which all can own and participate in. Elites accumulate and perpetuate power and resources in society for their own benefit. By doing so, they create oppression and disadvantage which social work tries to supplant with more egalitarian relationships in society. Seeking personal and social fulfilment, as in reflexive-therapeutic views, is impossible because the interests of elites obstruct many possibilities for oppressed peoples, unless we achieve significant social change. Merely accepting the social order, as reflexive-therapeutic and individualist-reformist views do, supports and enhances the interests of elites. It therefore obstructs the opportunities of oppressed people who should be the main beneficiaries of social work.
- *Individualist-reformist views.* These see social work as an aspect of welfare services to individuals in societies. It meets individuals' needs and improves services of which it is a part, so that social work and the services can operate more effectively. Trying to change societies to make them more equal or create personal and social fulfilment through individual and community

growth may be reasonable ideals. Nevertheless, they are unrealistic in everyday practice. This is because most practical objectives of social work activity refer to small-scale individual change, which cannot lead to major social changes. Also, stakeholders in the social services which finance and give social approval to social work activities mainly want a better fit between society and individuals. They do not seek social changes.

Each view says something about the activities and purposes of social work and also criticises or seeks to modify the others. However, they also have affinities. For example, both reflexive-therapeutic and socialist-collective views are centrally about change and development. Also, reflexive-therapeutic and individualist-reformist views are about individual work rather than social objectives. Generally, therefore, most conceptions of social work include elements of each of these views. Alternatively, they sometimes acknowledge the validity of elements of the others. For example, socialist-collective views oppose some social purposes implied in individualist and therapeutic views. Nevertheless, most people who take this view of social work accept helping individuals to fulfil their potential within present social systems.

The nature of social work, therefore, is ambiguous and debated, but we can see the fundamental elements of that debate. These are insoluble problems, and we cannot make final decisions about them. The answers vary according to the time, social conditions and cultures where we ask these questions. Nonetheless, taking part in social work requires a view about your aims – your own construction which guides the actions you take. It includes values appropriate to doing social work, and 'theories' about the nature of social work; for example, sociological theories about its role in society, or its relationships with other occupational groups.

Practice 'theories' appear to form alternatives which compete for attention, and exclude one another. Thus, the image of the politics of social work 'theory' is of competition for territory. Part of this competition represents a politics of support for a view of social work which emphasises one or other of the views on social work discussed above. Radical, anti-oppressive and empowerment perspectives, for example, implement – and exemplify the possibility of acting in – a socialist-collectivist frame of action. Existentialist, humanist and social psychological represent a more reflexive-therapeutic emphasis. Task-centred and systems 'theories', say, are more individualist-reformist in their assumptions.

Sometimes, views are called *paradigms*. This concept means a pattern or template, something which is commonly reproduced in an activity. Kuhn (1970) uses 'paradigm' to describe a general view of the nature of physical or natural phenomena in science. His influential book on the history of science suggests that such paradigms arise. Scientific activity (theory-making, experimentation, methods of research, debate and so on) builds on them, until, in a scientific revolution, a completely new world view of phenomena is constructed. This changes the conception of those phenomena.

Using 'paradigm' as Kuhn uses it, I argue that there is a paradigm of social work, which is socially constructed and into which all current 'theory' and practice may be fitted. It is in practice accepted since most social workers recognisably do similar sorts of things in interactions with their clients. However, the balance among the three views within it is constantly modified and debated. Generally, we accept that the different views are present within the social work discourse, because we debate them all the time. Kuhn questions (1970: 15) whether parts of the social sciences are enough developed to have acquired a paradigm, let alone to have experienced a paradigmatic revolution. Yet some writers (such as Fischer, 1981) argue that such shifts in social work conceptions have occurred. Kuhn (1970: 49) accepts that minor paradigms grow up in what he calls the ramshackle structure of specialities. He gives these paradigmatic status before they have found wide agreement. This seems to me to be the status of the three views in social work. I think, therefore, that debates between 'theories' which fall mainly within each view are in essence debates between these 'minor paradigms'.

'Theoretical' ideas are an important pillar of mutual understanding and identity among social workers. In this way, they form an element in the *social*, that is, *shared*, construction of social work. Taking them up also helps in practice, because specifying what we should do, and why, is an important purpose of 'theory'. Anyone trying to help human beings needs such guidance. It is particularly crucial if we use practical amalgamations of ideas from different sources, instead of one set 'theory' for all our practice. Doing this without understanding is likely to risk confusion and possibly damage to clients. Understanding connections and disparities among the ideas we use can avoid such problems.

I refer to 'modern' social work 'theory' because I argue that understanding a social phenomenon such as social work can only be for this time. Also, we can only consider social work 'theory' within a limited cultural frame, although I have tried to broaden my frame as far as possible. Rein and White make this point in an important paper on the development of new understandings of how we seek and use knowledge:

> the basic movement of knowledge gathering is to provide for contexts in transition. The knowledge that is gathered – the perceived utility or relevance of the knowledge – is bounded in time, place, and person. (Rein and White, 1981: 37)

Cultural differences in social work 'theories'

Differences in cultural frame are important. There has been controversy about whether social work and 'theories' of it may be considered global or restricted in their use. They arose, historically, in Western democratic countries, and their value-base has Jewish/Christian origins. Three sets of arguments support the claim that we should not apply them too widely.

First, *value and cultural bases of different societies may be incompatible* with assumptions and prescriptions within Western social work. For example, writing on social work in Chinese and other Eastern countries claims that the individualistic assumptions of much Euro-American social work would not hold true in societies which give importance to interdependence within families and respect for authority. Chow (1987), considering Chinese and Western philosophies of care, points out that Western social work is based on the importance of the individual, with an associated concept of individual rights. In Chinese social assumptions, individuals' rights are not emphasised. Rather, the responsibilities of being part of a network of family relationships are central. So Western assumptions that the aim of work with young people is to prepare them for independence from families, rather than continuing interdependence, might be inappropriate. Ko (1987) shows how conceptions of the family altered as political and social change affected mainland China. Chan (1987) comments on conflicts arising from attempts to maintain traditional parental authority in changing social climates, and the emphasis given to harmonious, non-conflictual relationships between children and others. Fong and Sandu (1995) argue that Chinese values prefer hierarchical to egalitarian behaviour in authority figures, external to internal controls, controlled rather than uninhibited self-expression and prescribed rather than free roles. Roan (1980) proposes, using Taiwanese experience, that workers should assesss traditional attitudes to authority and status, whether working with families rather than individuals is the preferred cultural approach and what traditional mutual aid systems a particular society has. Canda (1988) argues that social work must take account of diverse spiritualities, including religious and non-religious views, since these are found in a wide variety of ethnic groups in all societies. In a study of Korea, Canda *et al.* (1993) identified a range of personal and social objectives which influence ethnic minorities in Western societies but might usefully influence Western thought more. Examples are the value of cultivating one's mind and thoughts for the benefit of society and contributing to others' learning and the richness of the social fabric, the importance of effort to improve oneself alongside seeking to help others and keeping harmony between oneself and 'spirits' representing personal and social pressures.

There is considerable discussion of these issues in India. Wadia (1961) proposes the Hindu notions of dharma (concern for society as a whole and help for others) and karma (according to Karnik and Suri, 1995, a value that our human condition sums up all past actions which lead to material and spiritual well-being in life and the afterlife) as actual and potential influences on Indian social reform and social work values. However, karma inhibits the development of social work because it promotes inaction as the basis for ultimate spiritual development, since no action can be without selfish social purposes (Kumar, 1994: 6; Karnik and Suri, 1995). This means that understanding how families interpret karma is crucial in social work with Hindu people. Kumar (1994) shows how Indian traditions promote doing good deeds without reward, not being attached to worldly affairs, emphasising social as against personal interests and interdependence in society, which makes charity a right, not a favour. However, some philosophies which might be relevant to social work remained as tools for spiritual rather than social services development. Also, the development of a rigid caste system, including untouchability, interfered with interdependence in reality, and the development of ideas of segregation and chastity for women prevented women from contributing to or receiving help (Kumar, 1994; Karnik and Suri, 1995). There are also attempts to locate a different philosophy of social work in India in the ideas of leaders like Gandhi and Nehru on the welfare of untouchables, women and rural areas (Muzumdar, 1964; Howard, 1971). Gangrade (1970) argues that India requires more concentration on the responsibilities of the family network for maintaining contacts throughout life than the individualistic Western social work model, in which the role of the family is to prepare people for separation and independence from it. Similarly, Western social work encourages plurality and diversity through competition, whereas Hindu philosophy is to try to build connections and avoid conflict. Although casework services exist in urban areas, they adapt Western non-directive techniques to a more culturally acceptable authoritarian approach (Kassim Ejaz, 1989). Verma's (1991) study of Indian psychiatric social work shows how its development responded to the introduction of British mental hospitals in the nineteenth century and American concepts of social work in the twentieth. Neither had much relevance to Indian views of mental illness, which is often interpreted as a family misfortune where one member is possessed by evil spirits. The traditional ayurvedic system of medicine permits psychotherapeutic and drug-treatments, and religion promotes charity and caring services. However, Western psychiatry has limited the social work potential of these advantages, by introducing stigmatised hospitals, separating patients in poor conditions from the community.

Related to this, religious and social philosophies may be incompatible to the extent that at least some parts of many communities would reject Western thinking. As a result, methods of practice aimed at Western problems, such as individualistic, therapeutic casework by workers with individual clients or groups, may be inappropriate. For example, Silavwe (1995), discussing social work in Zimbabwe, argues that a model of work involving the whole family and community in resolving problems is more appropriate to a tribal setting than individual work between worker and client.

Second, *societies face differing problems and issues*. Euro-American social work assumes that a range of welfare state services is available in a relatively rich, economically developed country. Often, it focuses on the social problems of urbanised societies. Mainly rural, undeveloped societies where subsistence and basic health and survival needs are an issue probably cannot use Western social work methods. Something else is required. The failure of Western social work to offer viable models and appropriate training has been criticised, particularly in matters of rural development and social change (Nagpaul, 1972; Nanavatty, 1981; Ghosh, 1984; Ilango, 1988). Even here, Bryant (1985) argues that theoretical and practice needs in different countries are not necessarily the same. African and Asian rural development work varies due to different economies and approaches to farming.

Third, there are *concerns about cultural imperialism and the history of oppressive colonialism.* The countries where most social work ideas come from achieved economic development through exploitative colonial power over countries which remain poor. They dominate the transmission of knowledge and information. As a result, Western ideas gain influence because poor countries have had their own cultures and systems destroyed by colonial influence. This continues through oppressive influences from dominant cultures. The media of such influences are control of language (English and other European languages being widely used for transmitting information) and of journals, television and radio.

Colonial powers were little concerned with welfare matters, since they tended, according to Asamoah and Beverly (1988), to split different aspects of human and social problems rather than seek comprehensive social provision. Political and economic issues were treated as important, rather than social needs. So, colonialists sought to reduce the importance of traditional (for example, tribal) structures which provided a base for welfare (such as in Sierra Leone; Jarrett, 1991) and made decisions for short-term expediency rather than long-term benefit for the colonies. This meant that services and ideas associated with them were underdeveloped, and made the assumption that Western 'theories' would be transferable. Provision by international agencies can be poorly integrated with local services (Schenk and Schenk, 1987; Whang, 1988) and often focused on children rather than other client groups (Dixon, 1987; Dixon and Scheurell, 1989; Onokerkoraye, 1984). Early development often came from problems created by colonial powers themselves. Gargett's (1977) study of pre-independence Zimbabwe, for example, shows that social work grew up to combat the consequences of the breakdown of tribal life arising from colonial-inspired urbanisation. The first services to appear were individualistic probation and truancy services. Groupwork in youth clubs responded to problems with disaffected youth. The individualistic bias of social work in the 1950s and 60s when most colonies became independent was inappropriate where major social and economic problems existed. Yelaja (1970) noted around this period that broader concepts of social work were required, taking in social change and social policy development. Sometimes, economic problems have been so severe (such as in many African countries; Dixon, 1987) and ideological considerations and other priorities have been so important (as in mainland China; Starak, 1988) that forms of social work recognisable to developed Western countries are inappropriate.

Arguments like this have led writers (for example, Midgley, 1981; Osei-Hwedie, 1990, 1993) to identify the need of many Third World countries to avoid the effects of cultural imperialism from rich, economically developed countries. They created more radical and practical approaches to social development (Hardiman and Midgley, 1989; Midgley, 1995).

However, these arguments are not wholly convincing. Conflicts and difficulties about transferring ideas internationally in social work are not a conflict of two incompatible blocs of ideas. First, countries are, these days, ethically and culturally pluralist. So most countries must create services and practice methods to meet needs among different ethnic and cultural groups. This allows us to transfer ideas between cultures. Ideas from non-Western countries may gain influence as Western countries become sensitive to minorities' needs. Chapters 9 and 10 show how the reconceptualisation movement in Latin American and Third World social development has had influence in Western social work.

Second, cultural imperialism and colonial history are not monolithic or all-powerful. Heisler (1970) suggests, for instance, that British colonial traditions often led to reliance on local, decentralised and informal initiatives for social welfare. French colonies, on the other hand, reflected centralising and coordinating tendencies. In turn, the reaction to these trends by governments and people after decolonisation also varied. Although Christian influences were important in European and North American developments (for example, Philpot, 1986), their impact in colonial countries was entirely different. This is because they were part of a missionary effort to convert a subject population to the dominant culture of the colonists. In some places, this was kept astutely apart from conflicting local pressures (as Haile Selassie achieved in Ethiopia in the 1930s; Schenk and Schenk, 1987). In others, there was an uneasy coexistence of cultures. For example, in India legislative attempts were made in the nineteenth century to change conflicting cultural practices such as widow sacrifice and thuggery, but few social reforms were attempted (Chakrabarti, 1987). Other countries, including many in Africa (Dixon, 1987), found that what social provision there was largely comprised Christian missionary and voluntary services. There was little attempt at organised public provision until the late 1940s. Also, while English language 'theories' are pervasive, different forms of service organisation and professional education in various countries led to different sets of ideas which are not widely available in the United States and

Britain. For example, in France, a range of welfare workers exists, all of whom have roles which are related to but different from social work as we know it in Britain and the United States (Birks, 1987). Similarly, Western European ideas about social pedagogy (see Chapter 9) are not widely used in Britain and the United States.

Euro-American cultural dominance may lead to resistance in other cultures. This may help to create explicit responses which generate alternative philosophies and models of practice, rather than repressing them. These may then have influence on Western cultures. Schiele (1994), for example, argues that Afrocentric world views emphasise interdependence, collectivity and spirituality and may be a better basis to promote equality through social work than Western individualist models of humanity. There may also be links between related groups from different cultures. For example, Christian, Muslim, Sikh and Jewish fundamentalists may have more in common with one another than with liberals within their religion (Adibi, 1992). Midgley and Sanzenbach (1989) argue that fundamentalism is opposed to individualist, humanist traditions. Another point is the existence of a variety of media through satellite channels, easier worldwide travel and easy desk-top publishing. These make it economically and technically more rather than less possible for minority interests to gain a voice. Countries and cultures do not stay where they are, and have never done so. They are always changing. Many economies which were underdeveloped, for example Korea and Singapore, are now economically rich. As a result there may be changing needs for different models of social work.

Third, following from this point that cultures are not monolithic or exclusive, there is evidence that useful mutual exchange can be achieved. Development of locally appropriate forms of social work may draw on and adapt Western models. Walton and El Nasr (1988) use the example of Egypt to propose a parallel process. Indigenisation alters imported ideas to make them appropriate to local conditions (Osei-Hwedie, 1993). Authentisation develops local ideas alongside imported 'theories' to form a new structure of ideas. Similar processes occur even among Western countries. For example, American 'theories' have been adapted for use in Britain and other European countries with a more bureaucratic and governmental system of social work. See Chapter 4, for example, on Doel and Marsh's (1992) British adaptation of American task-centred practice. Another point is that models from different cultures may meet a wish within a country to develop services which reflect desired Western values. Some

Eastern European countries have developed social work at least in part in order to liberalise bureaucratised and oppressive welfare services. For example, mental health services in Russia were often used during the Communist period as an instrument of political repression. Apparently different countries may share issues. For example, Chan (1993) studied community-based help in towns in the People's Republic of (that is, Communist) China. She found that claimed systems of neighbourhood mutual help had been idealised and did not in fact exist. Experience of Western community care services might make a contribution to developing ideas for meeting need. Certainly, Britain also faces the issue that neighbourhood help was presumed to exist, but was negated by social and economic pressures (Bulmer, 1987). There are direct parallels in the myth of the availability of community-based help.

Fourth, there is an international structure of organisations (see Payne, 1996a) related to social welfare which take in an eclectic range of approaches, including social development models relevant to non-Western countries. There is, therefore, a structure of communication and organisation to facilitate the construction of a social work or kinds of social work which are more widely relevant than Euro-American models.

This book, therefore, seeks to reflect worldwide literature and developments as far as they are available in the literature. If this policy were widely followed, non-Euro-American models and ideas might increasingly influence the world social work literature. Making available materials about Euro-American social work in more adaptable ways is also important. The approach taken in this book is, therefore, to present ideas relatively generically. Writing material shorn of all cultural specificity is not possible; it would anyway be a bland diet. Writing about social work ideas can, however, reflect an awareness that they might be used in and adapted to a range of cultural and social environments. It should seek, therefore, to avoid aggressively specific materials if we are to develop a worldwide set of ideas within social work.

Constructing social work

If social work is complex and varies in different cultures, as we have seen, we can only understand it in the social and cultural context of the participants. 'Theories' about it must be products of the context in which they arise. They must also influence that context, because 'theories' affect what people do and say within social work. That affects social attitudes towards the people within social work and their ideas and values. To understand what social work is, therefore, we have to look at its social construction. Rein and White make this point forcefully:

> the knowledge that social work seeks cannot be made in universities by individuals who presumptively seek timeless, contextless truths about human nature, societies, institutions, and policy. The knowledge *must* be developed in the living situations that are confronted by the contemporary episodes in the field... it is necessary to enlarge the notion of context to include not only the client's situation but the agency itself and more broadly the institutional setting of practice. This involves the intersecting network of offices, agencies, professionals, government structures and political pressure groups that all act together on the agency. (1981: 37; emphasis original)

The idea of social construction comes from the work of Berger and Luckmann (1971). They maintain that 'reality' is knowledge which guides our behaviour, but we all have different views of it. We arrive at shared views of reality by sharing our knowledge through various social processes which organise it and make it objective. Social activity becomes habitual, so we share assumptions about how things are. Also, we behave according to social conventions based on that shared knowledge. So we institutionalise these conventions as many people agree about understandings of that aspect of society. Then, these understandings become legitimised by a process which attaches 'meanings' which integrate these ideas about reality into an organised and plausible system. Social understanding is, in this way, the product of human understandings. For those humans, it is also objective, because the knowledge of reality is widely shared. Since people grow up within those social understandings to accept their reality, they are in a sense the product of society. So there is a circular process, in which individuals contribute through institutionalisation and legitimation to the creation of social meaning within the social structure of societies. In turn, societies through individuals' participation in its structures create the conventions by which people behave. We can see a spiral of constantly shifting influence, creating and re-creating structures and these changing structures re-creating the conventions by which people live within them.

Accepting that this goes on in society in general, we must also accept that it goes on in social work, which is one of those complexes of social structures and individual participants influencing each other.

Our focus, in this book, is on one aspect of the spiral of influences in social work: the 'theory' that guides workers' practice. This interacts with other aspects of the social work spiral of influence, and that similarly interacts with wider spirals of social influence.

At the beginning of this chapter, I suggested that in spite of cultural and national differences, social work was always constructed from three elements: worker, client and context. So, general statements about social work and its 'theory' must reflect understanding about how that construction takes place. The next three sub-sections of this chapter look at how each of these is socially constructed by patterns of behaviour, expectations and cultural norms. The argument is as follows. We create social work 'theory' within social work, out of an interaction with social work practice, which in turn interacts with wider social contacts. Three sets of forces construct social work: those which create and control social work as an occupation; those which create clienthood among people who seek or are sent for social work help; and those which create the social context in which social work is practised. Social work is a special activity where people interact in special social roles as 'social worker' and 'client'. Those roles thus partly define its nature. Understanding social work involves examining the factors which establish the social positions of these actors in a complex of social relationships. Shulman (1991) researched this process in detail, looking at contexts which create both client and worker. These interact over time and in a power context. There are process outcomes (for example, caring and trust between the participants) which make the interaction effective in achieving desired results. These desired results in many cases produce the outcomes of social services within which practice takes place.

Creating a social worker

Social workers in encounters with clients are constructed by occupational expectations, that is, the organised statements and understandings which say what a social worker is, and the social processes which define someone as a social worker. The various histories of social work, and its relationships with other occupational groups and social institutions, define its nature as an occupation. That nature changes, grows, perhaps declines, in response to social changes. So, knowledge and ideas that workers use also respond to social changes.

To identify a complete list of every factor influencing the development of social work is not possible, but we may identify some features. Many social forces which are nothing to do with the academic and practice development of the occupation influence social work practice and 'theory'. Changing social needs, the influence and needs of related occupations, political and legislative changes are just some examples.

Political and public perceptions of social and personal need condition those social forces and the way in which services should be organised to meet such need. Thus, political debate and media coverage of social work and its activities influence the climate of perceptions which create social work's tasks and interests. This is because public perceptions influence services and because workers are themselves part of the public and are influenced by media and political change.

The organisation of services and agencies, and the legislation, economic capacity and managerial techniques which underpin that organisation affect how social work can do its job. If social work is part of a powerful independent agency, there is likely to be freedom to develop social work techniques independently. This is less likely where social work is done in agencies dominated by other occupations (such as hospitals and medicine). However, the status and influence of the dominant profession may offer benefits as well as disadvantages. Industrial organisation may be particularly important. Where trade unions control to some degree the negotiations for conditions of employment (as in many European countries), they also affect the nature of the work. This differs where employers or members of occupational groups themselves define the task and methods of work.

Many of these social groups and institutions are in conflict either actually or potentially. The academic development of social work 'theories' and techniques may conflict with the wishes of other occupational groups (for example, medical resistance to the independent establishment of social work). It might also conflict with employers' definitions of the social work task (for instance, complaints from employers in several European countries that the theoretical approach of training courses for workers is not practically applicable), or with political objectives for the services. These and other groups may contend for control of the social work 'theory' and practice. Each applies influence in public perception, organisational structure or political systems and legislative change.

From this point of view, social work is part of a network of related occupations. We need to see how it has been established and controlled, and how it relates to the network around it. Part of such an understanding requires us to see how its 'theories' have grown up and exerted influence on it, and how they relate to the network of 'theories' around social work in related occupations. See Payne (1996a) for a more detailed discussion of professional networks. Such 'theories' are themselves social influences which help to position social work among the networks of other services, occupations, professions and agencies. I also argue that those social factors which create the social worker partly construct the 'theories'. This must be so as people within the socially constructed occupation create social work 'theory'. The socially defined purposes and origins of that occupation shed light upon the 'theory'. Equally, the 'theory' as we create it affects the occupation and thence the social influences which form the context of practice.

Creating a client

Much professional writing ignores clients' influences on social work. They are merely the objects of an activity which 'theory' has defined. In fact, I argue, they partly construct the activity through the process by which they become the special people called 'clients'. The client-making process is itself socially constructed, because it relies on general social understandings of the nature of social work. As they bring the outside world into social work activity with them, clients change the nature of social work. In this sense, social work is a reflexive process in which client changes worker *and* the nature of social work *and* therefore also changes the 'theory' of social work. The aim of this argument is to dispute the conception that social work is a catalytic process in which an unchanging worker and agency change the client. Instead, I propose that clients change worker and agency.

Clienthood is not an invariable or absolute *state*. Generally, people are socially defined as clients if they are interacting with social workers. However, this is not always an accurate representation of their position, as they, the worker, or as others involved might see the situation. For example, workers acting as advocates for clients are more colleagues than helpers. Foster carers may have an ambivalent relationship with workers, being treated as colleagues and as needing help. Parents of children with learning disabilities may be colleagues of the worker in helping the child, the object of the worker's help in coping with the child or part of families being helped as wholes.

Clienthood is partly a matter of perception, so that if others see a person as a client, they may treat them as such. People's own definition of their status affects, but does not determine, whether they are seen as clients. Formal designation is also relevant, so that official categorisation as a client may set off or reinforce perceptions of clienthood. Such perceptions may be held by clients, by workers, by officials in the worker's agency, by people in other agencies, by the client's family or by others in the client's social environment. Once we ascribe clienthood to someone, it often persists even if social work activity is intermittent or has stopped.

Clienthood may be associated with certain sorts of people; for example, those of a particular social class, or those living on a particular housing estate. Agencies and observers are more likely to define such people as clients than people from another group. Stigma often comes with being a client because others may disapprove of people who need help in managing their everyday lives. If they are in some way held to blame for their dependence, disapproval will be stronger.

All these factors may interact or conflict. So for example, an agency and its worker may see Albert as a client. To outsiders that might be reasonable, but he may see himself as a friend of the worker. If so, is what the worker does with Albert social work? It is intended to be, but if its client sees it as something else, has it failed and become something else? This example shows how people's definitions of clienthood may affect how we understand the nature of social work.

Since different people's perceptions of clienthood vary, we must see where those perceptions come from. It is likely that the social institutions and their history that we examined as originators of the definition of a social worker are also influential in defining clienthood. This brings us to defining clienthood as a process.

Since clienthood is hard to understand as a state, understanding it as a *process* is more appropriate. People are becoming, acting as and moving away from being clients of social work (Payne, 1993). That process occurs when clients come into contact with a social work agency which gives them services from social workers. Since, as we saw in the previous section, the nature of social work and therefore its agencies is socially defined, so is the process of attaining clienthood. Attitudes to particular human conditions such as alcoholism will define whether they are seen as relevant to social work, and so might become clients. They might, for example, be seen as candidates for prison, or medical intervention or for help from a priest.

The *route to clienthood* only begins when someone becomes aware of some issues in their lives which need resolution; often this arises from coming to see these issues as a problem. Awareness, together with various social pressures may create an *impulsion* towards receiving help. At some point consciousness of the availability of the agency arises, and leads the client to arrive at the agency, where interaction with the social worker begins.

Up to this point, the decisions made may not have been subjected to any professional influence. The definition of a problem, the social pressures, the route to the agency and options which were closed off on that route which led to the selection of this agency, all these may arise from general social perceptions about a problem and the agencies available. Wikler (1986) researched pathways to help followed by Jewish clients in New York, confirming that self-referral and referral from non-professionals was the most significant route.

Then begins the process of *intake*. The aim is to explore clients' circumstances and establish a definition of them as relevant to the agency, including, often, an assessment of their motivation. Specht and Specht (1986a) see the point at which assessment begins as the beginning of the route to clienthood, although I think they pitch this at too late a stage in the process. Certainly at this stage clienthood is not final. We often describe people as 'applicants' or potential clients (Pincus and Minahan, 1974). They are investigated to see whether they may be defined as clients suitable to the agency according to agency policies. Other factors affecting this decision are the training and social institutions which form the social worker's view of appropriateness, and professional, personal, public and political trends. We might not define a caller as a client, for example, if we offer only advice.

All this assumes that visiting the agency is a matter of choice, but in fact many clients are *involuntary*. They are forced to visit the agency by court order, or by being investigated through one of the agency's policing functions such as an investigation for child abuse. Rooney (1992) argues that clients are also involuntary where people feel forced to remain or make coerced or constrained choices in relationships. This is because they will feel some loss, perhaps personal, financial or emotional, if they leave it. They are also involuntary if they feel disadvantaged or oppressed in a relationship, even though they retain it because they get something out of it. More involuntary clients come from groups which are oppressed in other ways in society than from successful or valued groups. Cingolani (1984) argues that workers continually negotiate acceptable relationships with clients. Workers also mediate and negotiate between unwilling clients and their social environments. Rooney (1992) argues that because clients participate involuntarily workers may still give them choices in other matters. The aim should be to reduce the extent to which clients' freedom to act is limited and constraints are used. Incentives, encouragement and empowerment may be more helpful. Sometimes workers act paternalistically by withholding information or opposing clients' wishes unnecessarily. We can avoid this too.

Specht and Specht (1986b) argue that contracting with clients for providing service is the final stage in establishing the definition of clienthood. Contracts are not necessarily formal written documents but may be no more than loose agreements between worker and client. Even after intake and designation as a client, the status of clients may change, as we pass them to different parts of a large agency for different forms of help, or as their own, community, family and other agencies' perceptions change as it becomes known that they are receiving services.

Becoming and being a client leads also to the process of ceasing to be one. This, again, involves recognising circumstances which lead to an impulsion – this time away from the agency. Understanding when it is appropriate to stop involvement with an agency is also an important factor. In any of these moves, clients are again affected by their own social understanding, information gained from the worker, legal pressures, and knowledge and attitudes derived from the client's social circle.

The context of social work

Social work characteristically takes place in an organisational context of agencies; that is, associations of people constructed to achieve particular purposes. This is true even of private practice or working with self-help groups, which form very simple, less structured agencies. Agencies are another set of social relations through which social constructions influence social work. They are formally controlled by management boards representing the communities served, by political election, with government agencies, or through another nominating process with private or voluntary agencies. As organisations, they are subject to influences, whether economic, political, organisational, bureaucratic or theoretical, different from those affecting workers and clients. I have explored these points more fully elsewhere (Payne, 1996a).

Agencies also exist in a political and social context which affects how they and workers operate and how they deal with clients. For example, a climate of approval or disapproval of social work or welfare expenditure affects social work. Agencies also have a history, context and structure which may affect how we perceive them. For example, workers in a mental hospital that was formerly a 'lunatic asylum' may carry stigma which older people associate with the history of such institutions. Also the building that they work in may not be appropriate for modern practice. Equally, the medical setting and the need to work with a multi-disciplinary team may affect how we undertake social work.

Social work construction and the construction of 'theory'

So far, we have seen that a socially and historically formed route brings clients and workers together within an organisational context in the process called 'social work'. Particular influences can affect any or all of these routes. For example, party political views might affect clients or workers individually, or agencies through their management committees. Therefore, philosophies or policies of agencies or local government or the social expectations of people surrounding worker, client and agency affect their behaviour. Equally, what happens between worker and client within the agency context affects wider social constructions of welfare, and the role of welfare in society more generally. This is an example of the spiral of influences, discussed above. For example, local people's perceptions that agencies and workers help people who are 'undeserving' might lead to welfare spending becoming less politically acceptable. Another example might be scandals in which workers sexually abuse children in residential care, or fail to protect young children from violence from their parents. These might lead either to greater spending but more severe controls on discretion in practice, or to a rejection of the value of social work in protecting children.

The social construction view that we are exploring presents the relationship between workers, clients and their context as *reflexive*; each affects the other. Many views of social work recognise this fact inadequately because they are based on a catalytic model in which the competent social worker helps to resolve or cure the problems of an inexpert client. This *medical model* is a traditional feature of social work. It has been criticised as leading to fragmented help being

offered according to specialisations which treat clients as problems
rather than as whole beings. Other consequences are poor communication with and involvement of clients in the helping process, and
reductions in clients' independence and personal power (Katz, 1983).
Weick (1983, 1986) argues that a health model should replace the
medical model. According to this, we see people as responsible for
healthy living. Workers facilitate healing processes which recognise
the interaction of personal and environmental factors and rebalance
them to provide a more healthy environment for everyone.

In a catalytic model of social work, workers' expertise comes from
understanding of 'theory', supported by empirical research. Agencies
and workers are relatively unchanging, and interpret information
according to their professional assumptions. Clients cannot present
themselves in a radically different way, because workers will reinterpret their presentation according to the workers' conventional
assumptions. The route to clienthood reinforces those assumptions, so
that clients learn what to expect and how to behave. New knowledge
and 'theory' are brought into social work through social pressures on
the political and community leaders who form the highest echelon of
management. It also enters social work through research which affects
the literature and training of workers. So new knowledge and 'theory'
are applied to social work by collective academic and social processes
rather than by response to actual social situations presented by clients.
Some social trends are likely to be absent from or under-represented
in agencies because of the process by which clients come to it.

I call such a view of social work 'catalytic' because catalysis is a
chemical reaction in which substances are put with a catalyst. A reaction takes place between the substances that would not occur if the
catalyst were not present. By a series of combinations with the other
substances, the catalyst helps the reaction to work, but it emerges
from the process having re-formed into its original state.

Is the picture as presented by this model accurate? Some evidence
for it is contained in the unresponsiveness of social work agencies to
radically different social trends. For example, social agencies were
slow to recognise failures in providing services to ethnic minorities in
Western countries, because of endemic racism in training, management, policy and practice (see Chapter 11). Black people distrusted
agencies and white people and there was failure to communicate
across racial and social boundaries because of different life styles and
cultures. A general social movement recognising these issues applied
political and intellectual influence to social work. Personal responses

to the world that workers saw around them did not seem to reflect the changes. We might make similar points about the failure to recognise serious inequities in the response to women's roles in caring within welfare and conventional social systems.

Such an inadequacy in response, however, probably derives more from the inflexibility of agency structures and socially formed attitudes among workers, rather than 'theory' and knowledge not taking account of social changes. Ellis (1977), for example, showed that European conceptions of children's needs differed from those held by West Africans, leading to inappropriate interventions in West African families. Many grass-roots agencies are acceptable to ethnic minorities and respond appropriately to women's roles and wishes. These seem to show that with workers and managements who have appropriate attitudes, outside large institutionalised agencies, ideas and 'theories' which are similar to conventional social work 'theories' are helpful to groups which social work agencies otherwise seem to reject. There is also evidence that workers do respond to social trends which appear in their work, but cannot always affect their agencies or attitudes within them to take this further. One particularly important example is increasing violence towards workers. Brown *et al.* (1986) argue that there is more violence because people who would have stayed in institutions are discharged to the community. Small (1987) similarly claims that violence to social workers reflects changing social patterns, and is incorrectly ascribed to breakdowns in relationships. Violence towards workers and the fact that they suffer from stress and possibly burnout (Gibson *et al.*, 1989; Davis-Sacks *et al.*, 1985; Jayaratne *et al.*, 1983; Fineman, 1985; Cherniss, 1980) draws attention to the fact that relationships with clients affect and change them. So the potential exists for clients to affect social work and its agencies directly.

The catalytic model, then, does not adequately describe some aspects of social work. A reflexive model sees workers and agencies not as catalysts, but as capable of change by their interaction with clients. Gitterman (1983) argues that many difficulties in getting clients to accept help are part of a struggle for dominance between the worker and professional prerogatives, the client's wish for control and the agency's attempts to manage what goes on within it. Since 'theory' describes and explains what workers do, it must also respond to the realities of its social constructions. Otherwise, we would reject or amend it.

A major feature of any acceptable model of social work 'theory', therefore, is the extent to which it can offer explanations of and guidance in dealing with the pressures put by clients on the perceptions of workers of their social circumstances. A 'theory' which is inadequate in representing the real needs of clients as presented to agencies is likely to be only partially accepted, or to become supplanted.

So far, I have argued that social work *itself* is reflexive because it responds to clients' demands on a service affecting workers. Theoretical development reflects this, because we reject or amend 'theories' which fail to meet demands actually made.

To take this further, 'theory' must also develop in response to demands made by clients on agencies and workers affecting the interpretation or acceptance of theoretical ideas. 'Theory' is a statement of what social work is and prescribes what social workers should do in various situations. It follows that we define the nature of social work and its 'theory' not by academic development and experimental testing but by what social workers actually do. And that is created by their reality, the demands made by clients in the context of the basic values and social structures established within the occupation of social work. A modern social work 'theory' must therefore respond to the modern social construction of reality both by clients and by workers and their social environments; if it fails to do so, it will be unsuccessful. The recognition of the need for 'theory' to be reflexive like this is a feature of more modern social work 'theories' such as ecological systems approaches, where the interaction with the environment is strongly recognised (see Chapter 6), and Marxist, radical and empowerment approaches (see Chapters 10 and 12).

According to this view of social work, its 'theory' must be constantly changing in response to practice constructions by its participants. Therefore, accounts of its nature cannot be universal. Instead, it is a variety of activities which have common features in most social constructions of it. In saying this, we must remember Berger and Luckmann's (1971) view that a social construction is an (at least partially) *agreed* view of the world which is accepted within a social group as a 'reality'. That is, it is agreed to be at least a reasonable representation of the world which helps us to deal with things external to us.

Conclusion

In summary, then, I have argued that social work is socially constructed through interactions with clients, because they themselves become defined as clients by social processes, through its formation as an occupation among a network of related occupations, and through the social forces which define it through its organisational, agency and social context.

Going on from these points, the social construction of social work suggests that its 'theory' at any time is constructed by the same social forces that construct the activity. 'Theory' for practice will inevitably respond to current social pressures, so that present interests and concerns colour it. Yet it also reflects the histories of theoretical, occupational and service context. The strength of influence of those histories in constructing present 'theory' varies from time to place to person, but they are always there, alongside present social forces.

The implication of a social construction view is that social work 'theory' should be seen as a representation of more or less agreed understandings within various social groupings within social work presented through the medium of language in text which contains accounts of those 'theories'. The struggle between competing understandings and constructions of social work is manifested in the differing theoretical constructions and languages which form the 'theories' discussed in this book. That struggle is a politics. That is, people and groups seek influence over social constructions of social work and thus over the actions of workers in their profession through seeking broader professional acceptance of particular 'theories' expressed as coherent, agreed forms of understanding. In turn, this may influence perceptions of social work within welfare services and within wider society, which will start the spiral of influence again as these perceptions will affect how social workers act within their work.

2

Using Social Work Theory in Practice

What this chapter is about

Chapter 1 presented a social construction approach to social work 'theory'. I argued that all social relations, with social work an example, are constructed by the interactions of their participants within a social context. In a circular process, those constructions affect conventions within which people act, which alters their actions. This creates a continuing spiral of change in action and social construction. This also happens with social work practice 'theory'. This book is about one aspect of this spiral: how different kinds of 'theories', once we construct them, may be used in practice.

The next step, therefore, is seeing what those 'theories' consist of and how we might use them in practice. This is the focus of the early parts of this chapter. Then in the later parts, as preparation for our review of different groups of theories in Chapters 3–12, I look at different ways of grouping the 'theories'.

What are social work practice 'theories'?

We return the problem, mentioned in Chapter 1, of there being no agreement about what 'theory' or social work practice 'theory' is. I have enclosed the word 'theory' in quotation marks for this reason. Indeed, it is dubious to think that we could define the shifting sands of ideas which affect actions in social construction spirals. This is because they change all the time. However, social construction suggests that there is shared acceptance of some ideas which, for practical purposes, people treat as reality. We can therefore explore practice 'theories' in the agreed, organised, formal, written statements of them. We can also research how they are used in practice. So I take it that the various groups of ideas considered in this book exist and are used as 'theories'. This is because we can see them being presented and debated within the formal social work literature. We use these presentations and debates about them to explore the 'theories'.

This section deals with debates about what social work practice 'theory' is. Arising from this discussion, I describe my view of the nature of 'theory' for the purposes of this book. We saw in Chapter 1 that there is a 'politics' of social work 'theory', and the same is true of all 'theory'. The politics involves people debating the kinds of 'theory' that are most valuable and seeking influence for their position. Since the 1970s, this debate has focused on two positions about social work epistemology; that is, the basis on which we know and argue about our understanding of the world. These positions have hardened around the postmodernist views of 'theory' and, alternatively, modernist, positivist or 'hard science' views of social work 'theory'. I look at these two views in the next two sub-sections.

Subsequently, I look briefly at their application and at the debate between them in social work. Since there are different views about explaining and understanding social work through 'theory', there must be similarly different views about how to find out about or research social work. Accounts of the positivist position, therefore, focus on how it sees both methods of enquiry and approaches to explanation.

Positivist views of theory

Applying the term 'positivist' to the second position is conventional, but it does not convey the full complexity of the various philosophies of logical positivism. Christopher Bryant (1985) identifies the logical positivism of the French school (for example, Saint-Simon, Durkheim), value debates in Germany and Austria (for instance, Weber, Habermas) and American 'instrumental positivism'. Kolakowski's account of it, cited by Bryant, is as a set of rules for judging the validity of knowledge. The rules are as follows:

- *Phenomenalism* proposes accepting as knowledge only things which we can see evidence for through our own experience or observation.

- *Nominalism* proposes that any general notion must refer to and summarise matters for which we can adduce evidence through experience or observation.
- *Values* are not knowledge, because we cannot discover evidence for them.
- *Belief in the unity of scientific method* means that positivists accept one approach to investigating the world to provide the evidence that they require to support knowledge.

These, except perhaps the last, may seem obvious, which shows how this modernist belief system has become a taken-for-granted part of our world. Modernism is a way of thinking which developed in the sixteenth and seventeenth centuries during the period of intellectual ferment in Europe called the 'Enlightenment'. The Enlightenment led to a change in ways of thinking about the world. A paradigm shift (in the sense used by Kuhn, 1970) changed our model of the world. Before this, people accepted religious and secular authority as the basis for knowledge. The Enlightenment led to acceptance of the view that knowledge comes from enquiry into natural phenomena through research. Such developments in thinking led to a flowering of scientific knowledge and the Industrial Revolution. In turn, economic development led to urban and industrial growth.

Hammersley and Atkinson (1995: 4), explain modernist or positivist methods of enquiry, and Katz (1995b) summarises them in relation to social work as follows:

- *Experimentation in physical science* is the model for all research. *Essentialism* promotes the idea that people, cultures and society have characteristics in reality, discoverable by such research. Research is not valid unless 'quantitatively measured variables are manipulated to identify the relationships among them'.
- *Universal laws* state consistent relationships among variables. This leads to *totalisation* (Katz) – that is, explaining everything according to one view of the world and emphasising sameness rather than difference. In social science, statistics are used to show where there is a high probability that something is always valid. Positivists therefore place high value on findings which we can generalise to similar situations.
- *Neutral observation* of things that we may actually observe is given priority. Standardised data collection which gives similar

results with all observers is emphasised. Intangible or singular information is dismissed.
- *Teleology* – Modernist and positivist methods of enquiry see societies or humanity as moving towards social or human goals (such as liberation, self-fulfilment).

Obviously, this thinking and methodology connect to the 'rules' for evaluating what knowledge is summarised above. Zimmerman (1989) regards these as 'protocols' in natural science, rather than essential characteristics. He argues that we should not reject using scientific methodology to assist developing and validating 'theory' where it can be appropriately used. Wakefield (1995) argues that positivist views elevate the requirements of proof in highly complex and individual human interactions to an unnecessarily high level for everyday practice. Scientific methods are better than other methods at identifying causation and enabling results to be generalised to other situations, but causation may be so complex that this is impossible.

The values of social work imply movement towards social goals. Many social work 'theories' present systems of thought and action which can guide workers' practice comprehensively. The fact that they do so led to 'the "theory wars" of the 1970s' (Epstein, 199: 322) or the 'gladiatorial paradigm' (Rojek, 1986) in which different 'theories' were set against one another and compared. However, the existence of competitive 'theories', none of which was wholly satisfactory or comprehensive, suggests that we need a more complex understanding of social work 'theories' and their relationships.

Postmodern views of theory

'Postmodernist' views of 'theory' offer this more complex understanding. These relate to ideas of the post-industrial society. That is, industrialised society, with its associated ideas and values, where many people work at specialised manual jobs in large factories, is disappearing. A more flexible but fragmented society is replacing it, where 'knowledge-based' work is more important, and we agree less about social structures and values.

Postmodernist thinking questions uncritical allegiance to modernist modes of thought. It points out that knowledge is a human *representation* of reality, using ideas and words in a language of symbols. Ideas symbolise – that is, stand in place of – reality; they are not reality itself.

Accepting this leads us to ask about the communication of those symbols. We know that humans can bias language they use. Language can reflect different social assumptions, and people often misinterpret communications. So ideas cannot be independent of the character, interests and social position of the human beings who use it to communicate with and understand one another. Of course, we can try to be as precise as possible in professional and scientific communication. Still, our ideas that we try to convey to others inevitably affect and are affected by social assumptions.

Knowledge, then, will reflect important social forces, and it is used in social relations. An important set of social relations, identified by Foucault (1972), is that of power relations. We use knowledge to gain power over others. Knowledge, we have said, is only our *representation* of reality. If we can get others to accept our representation, our view of knowledge, we gain power over them. For example, suppose we persuade others that criminal behaviour comes from offenders' alienation due to unemployment. We can then work for political acceptance of a policy of finding work for unemployed offenders, rather than sending them to prison. Particular power relations often produce ways of thinking which lead to knowledge that inevitably reflects the power relations. For example, professionalisation is often concerned with the control of knowledge. This is because the creation of a profession involves gaining acceptance that the occupational group which seeks professional status should control specialist areas of knowledge and practice. So, whereas specialised professional knowledge appears to benefit clients by being useful to helping them, it may, through the power relations involved in creating a profession, oppress them by confirming the dominance of educated people over them.

Postmodernist thinking, therefore, does not accept claims of knowledge and understanding at face value. It attempts to *deconstruct* such claims in order to see what ideas and social relations are represented by the surface symbols which claim and describe a piece of knowledge. Understanding is always ambiguous. We can see simultaneously what reality is said to be (that is, what the knowledge is), who says it is like that and their involvement in social relations which create their particular way of looking at it. Through looking at the social relations involved in creating this way of looking at the world, we can begin to see alternative views. This is because we can usually identify how an idea or piece of knowledge has developed through arguments with others. We never look at one side of the argument and say that it is the 'truth'. Instead, we seek to understand how the whole complex of arguments – or discourse – about a phenomenon show different sides and views of it. This presents a more complex but perhaps more representative view. An example of this process is my suggestion, above, that we can understand social work as the interaction of three different views on the activities and social structures that most people associate with social work. Social work is not 'something' in this way of thinking; it is a complex of views of what people understand it to be. A discourse is not only written or spoken arguments. It also consists of what people do and how they relate to one another. With many social phenomena, an outsider looking at what is going on disagrees with what the participants say is happening.

Postmodernism and social construction in social work

Postmodernist ideas have begun to have influence on social work in the 1990s (for example, Chambon and Irving, 1994; Howe, 1994; Pardeck *et al.*, 1994; Parton, 1994). Among other things, they interpret how post-industrial society affects the 'social' – that is, all aspects of the organisation and fragmentation of society which are concerned with constructions of relationships among people, and consequently the responses of social work to modern society (Parton, 1996). Obviously, these views of theory relate closely to the social construction view of social work 'theory' that I presented in Chapter 1. Indeed, postmodernism is not just one 'theory' of the world; how could it be, taking the view it does of the nature of knowledge? Social construction is part of the postmodernist complex of ideas.

Constructivist and social construction views argue that no one view of reality can comprehensively cover what a worker needs to know. Dean (1993: 57–8, emphasis original) distinguishes these views as follows: '*Constructivism* is the belief that we cannot know an objective reality apart from our views of it... *Social constructionism*... stresses the social aspects of knowing and the influence of cultural, historical, political and economic conditions.' Constructionist and postmodernist ideas do not argue that agreement about theories of action is impossible. Quite the contrary, they say that people understand things by conforming with socially agreed representations of the world which we accept as reality. The constructionist asks who makes the agreement and how it comes about. Many postmodernist and related sets of ideas further emphasise power relations expressed in language which cause ideas about the world to be more or less

powerful with particular groups or individuals. Such approaches have
been particularly important to feminist writers. This is because feminist epistemologies rely strongly on women sharing and developing
new meanings through social interaction in consciousness-raising
groups (Davis, 1993). However, Brown (1994) argues that seeing
feminism as a movement towards social goals is a modernist position,
treating all women as the same. Instead, we should recognise diversity
of experience and social position. Similarly, she argues that anti-racist
movements limit the possible diversity of black experiences and
reduce it to a claimed common experience. Katz (1995b) also argues
the importance of not universalising all black experience to claim it is
the same and needs the same response. These examples show how
postmodernist ideas value diversity and complexity, rather than
simple solutions. They are also reflexive, seeing the mutuality of
influence between ideas and social situations. Thus such ideas fit well
with social work because of its reflexive nature (see Chapter 1).

Positivist and postmodernist debates in social work

Positivism or modernism have influenced social work 'theory'. Mary
Richmond (1917), an important early writer, stressed the scientific
base of 'social diagnosis'. Germain (1970) presents the history of
social work 'theory' as a struggle to develop a more scientifically
defensible system of thought. Social work sought status and
respectability through having a scientific approach to understanding
human problems. Two factors led to changing perceptions of the
scientific status of social work in the 1960s. First, the scientific
validity of behavioural psychology led to increasing criticism of the
status of psychodynamic theory. This had impact on social work
because of its reliance then on psychodynamic theory. Second, empirical studies of social work intervention, both in the United States and
Britain, did not show that it was effective.

The American 'empirical' or 'empirical clinical' practice school of
thought developed in the 1970s. It is similar to what Everitt *et al.*
(1992) call 'research-minded practice'. That is, it looks to research
methodology to find what practice may be effective, to provide
analysis of social issues and problems and to criticise the 'taken-for-
granted'. 'Empirical practice' arose from psychology and behaviour
modification faculties mainly in the United States, which influenced a
new generation of doctoral students to use empirical research methods

(Reid, 1994). Criticism of traditional social work from a positivist perspective came from two important writers: Fischer (1973, 1976, 1981) in the United States and Sheldon (1978, 1982, 1984, 1986) in Britain. Their argument was that, since we could not show that traditional social work practice was effective, we should abandon it and replace it with empirically tested practice, which would be based on behavioural approaches.

A new debate grew up in the 1980s, with the increasing influence of constructionism, constructivism and postmodernism, and a series of papers, particularly by Witkin (1989, 1991) and colleagues (Witkin and Gottschalk 1988; Gottschalk and Witkin, 1991), Atherton (1993, 1994) and Heineman (1981) in the United States led to an explicit constructionist view in the literature. Positivist approaches are criticised as unable to question their own assumptions about the objectivity of empirical data and for lack of concern with meaning as opposed to number (Haworth, 1991; Wakefield, 1995). Qualitative or constructivist methodology provides a critical framework for evaluating the conceptual base as well as empirically supported outcomes of social work. Reid (1994) and Franklin (1995) argue that this, together with exploration of construction ideas, must be made more relevant to practitioners, since neither positivist ideas nor epistemological debate have had much impact on practice thinking. Atherton (1994) and Hawarth (1991) both argue that attaching moral value to positions in debates about different emphases in quantitative, qualitative and social construction research is an extreme reaction.

This trend is fervently resisted by Thyer (1993, 1994) and colleagues (Harrison *et al.*, 1992), Fischer and Sheldon (citations above). In the United Kingdom and Europe, influence from explicitly postmodern ideas is a feature of the 1990s. However, radical theory has been more influential than in the United States, with its questioning of professionalisation through scientific knowledge. Therefore, there is in Europe wider acceptance of the validity of more flexible views of knowledge and research. They coexist with hard scientific views, both being seen as relevant to understanding effectiveness and evaluating theoretical concepts.

The constructionist response to positivist views falls into four groups. First, recent studies have validated the effectiveness of social work by concentrating on more closely defined services and outcomes as compared with earlier broader studies. Also, earlier evidence of ineffectiveness does not have to be read so pessimistically (Smith, 1987). More focused techniques similar to or derived from behavioural approaches are more effective. Fischer (1981) has gone so far as to claim that this change constitutes a change in the basic 'paradigm' (in the Kuhnian sense – see Chapter 1) of social work. Gordon (1983) argues, correctly in my view, that Kuhn's model is not intended to apply to areas of professional knowledge or to debate appropriate methods for research in any given area. Also, in Gordon's view, Kuhn himself opposes 'rank empiricism', and Fischer wrongly equates 'quantifiable' with 'empirical'. This has a broader meaning and should include qualitative research and tested accumulation of experience.

Second, to follow on from the previous point, the positivist critique ignores, according to Smith (1987) and Heineman (1981), other philosophical and research traditions which are equally acceptable and useful in related fields. Smith argues that the positivist view has an unreasonable hold among lay people and within social work. Jordan (1978) and England (1986) argue for an artistic and imaginative approach to understanding social work, although Smith rejects this because it does not provide clear enough practice guidance.

Third, positivist views have difficulty in dealing with human activities because human behaviour is hard to define clearly, and outcomes tested may not connect with inputs examined. Human activity is subject to interpretation and differences of perception and is affected by the context in which it occurs (Smith, 1987; Ruckdeschel and Farris, 1982; Rein and White, 1981).

Fourth, and most important, on the positive side, constructionist and postmodern views acknowledge and celebrate the diversity of social and personal experience. They draw in marginalised groups and individuals with whom social workers work who are outside conventional theories and explanations (John, 1994). They provide useful ways of exploring the observable fragmentation and uncertainty of explanations of human and social life (Irving, 1994).

Social work and related theories

Positivist and postmodern views of social work 'theory'

In the previous section, we saw how general debates about the nature of 'theory' have echoes within social work. Inevitably, these debates mean that there is also disagreement about what a social work 'theory' is. Again, two positions exist, one broadly positivist, the other leaning towards postmodernism. This section explores these two views.

The positivist view is a strict application of scientific method. This argues that a 'theory' is a general statement about the real world whose essential truth can be supported by evidence obtained through scientific method. In relation to practical theories used in activities such as social work, Williams *et al.* (1989) suggest that the process of theory development in positivist views comes from showing that an approach to practice *can* work in particular cases, moving on to show that it *does* work in a series of cases, and then showing *how* it works.

In postmodernist views, the meaning of 'theory' is looser. It is a generalisation which takes in three different possibilities:

1 *Models* describe what happens during practice in a general way, applying to a wide range of situations, in a structured form, so that they extract certain principles and patterns of activity which give the practice consistency. Clark (1995) describes this as a system of classification that enables systematic and economic description and explanations about whether a practice conforms or not to the model.
2 Approaches to or *perspectives* on a complex human activity express values or views of the world which allow participants to order their minds sufficiently to be able to manage themselves while participating. Clark (1995) describes this as a framework or academic discipline.
3 Explanatory *'theory'* accounts for why an action results in particular consequences and the circumstances in which it does so. This is the positivist meaning of 'theory'. Clark (1995) describes this as concerned with whether something fits an established 'causal narrative'.

Views based on scientific method distinguish models and perspectives from 'theories'. They argue that 'theory' must explain in a provable way *why* something happens, not simply describe it in an organised way or provide a way of thinking about the world. Some 'theories' offer all three aspects of 'theory' in the postmodern sense. Others focus on providing a model for action. Some writers emphasise the degree to which a 'theory' is based on empirically tested principles.

Karger (1983) suggests that arguing for social work knowledge to be based on scientific method seeks to enhance the academic and professional status of the profession in general and particular groupings within it, without having much interest or value for many practitioners. Such arguments are about the 'politics' of 'theory'. Distinctions between levels of perspective, 'theory' and model, therefore, may derive from the politics of 'theory' rather than any valid differences in character. Writers about perspectives seek wide influence on practice, and focus on the interest and significance of their ideas. They are less concerned with detailed application or 'scientific' proof of the validity of their ideas, and may reject the worth of such proof anyway. Claims that an account of social work is a true 'theory' in this sense are attempts by other writers to strengthen the acceptance of their ideas by appealing to scientific validity. Models which focus on prescribing what to do are promoted because of their practical usability, as evidenced from experience or empirically tested effectiveness.

Many debates about distinctions between perspectives, 'theories' and models arise, then, from attempts to gain support in debate for the particular features of their account of social work. However, the distinctions are unhelpful in a practical activity like social work, since perspective, 'theory' and model are necessary in each case. Because social work is practical action in a complex world, an effective 'theory' or perspective must offer a model of explicit guidance. Failure to do so often renders an account subject to criticism (as with early radical 'theory') or leads to its rejection in daily practice (as with early cognitive 'theory'). Yet if action is not entirely pragmatic, it must be based on justifiable evidence about what is valid and effective, so a model should be backed by explanatory 'theory'. Model and explanatory 'theory' can' only gain consistency over a wide range of social work and offer general usefulness if they offer a comprehensible view of the world which allows us to transfer ideas between one situation and another and to order a pattern of work. Hardiker and Barker (1991) argue that the 'metaphorical and semantic' aspect of 'theory' contributes to understanding and interpreting clients' needs to a wider society, what Philp (1979) describes as the social role of social work in advocating for the oppressed to the powerful. This helps in their reintegration from the special status of client towards functioning where they do not need such a status.

I argue, then, that social work 'theory', in the sense of organised accounts of social work designed to offer guidance in practice, succeeds best when it contains all three elements of perspective, 'theory' and model. Where one of these is weak or absent, the 'theory's' value is vitiated. For example, radical theory was weakened by its focus on perspectives rather than explicit models for action, and this lack is being addressed by more recent accounts (for example, Fook, 1993). Often, one or the other is absent simply because it has not been fully set out, and we can identify its presence. For instance, task-centred work claims to be primarily a model, but drawing on learning and cognitive 'theories' validates its effectiveness. More broadly, it expresses a perspective about social work activity which implies the importance of human action and experience as a basis for learning about the world and being accepted within it. As 'theories' of social work develop, they become more successful by expanding their initial focus on perspective, 'theory' or model to include elements of the others.

We cannot say, neatly, that explanatory 'theories' derive from general perspectives, which provide the overview, enabling models and prescriptions to be built up from them. I shall argue later in this chapter that there are a variety of ways in which 'theories' influence one another and practice, and in which practice influences 'theory'. This is a logical corollary of taking a social construction view, since within such a view, the circular process of influence will be continuing. Each aspect of 'theory' influences the others. Evidence for effectiveness and ideas for the perspectives may come from many different places. Similarly, practices may grow up, perhaps responding to new problems or legislative and administrative changes, and become incorporated by relevant perspectives. Thus, ideas of networking grew up in different places and may be used in empowering or feminist work or from a systems 'theory' approach.

The title of this book takes the looser, postmodern view of what a 'theory' is. This is because, as we shall see, most social workers use 'theory' to mean ideas that influence them as opposed to things that they do in practice. Also, it is because my own perspective lies within a postmodern, rather than positivist, framework. I include, within the idea of 'theory', perspectives, 'theories' in the positivist sense and models. This is what I mean by 'theory' in the remainder of this book now that I intend to remove the quotation marks around the word. When I refer to theory in the positivist sense, I refer to 'explanatory theories'.

Levels and types of social work theory

Not all theories relating to social work are practice theories of the type we have been discussing. Rees (1991: 73–81) and Fook (1993: 39–40) distinguish three different levels of theory. Drawing on the work of Smid and van Krieken (1984), they express these ideas as follows:

- *Materialist social theory (Rees)/broad theory and knowledge base
  (Fook)* is mainly concerned with the political and economic
  structure of societies and the purpose of social institutions,
  particularly social work and welfare, within them.
- *Strategic theory (Rees)/theories of practice (Fook)* develops
  methods of intervention and accounts for how social workers act,
  or should act.
- *Practice ideologies (Rees)/specific practices (Fook)* are
  concerned with how they carry out all their experience and
  knowledge in practice.

Each of these is related to the others. The first two would influence
the others.

Sibeon (1990) distinguishes between formal and informal theory.
The first is written down and debated within the profession and academic work. Informal theory consists of wider theories and values
which exist in society and constructions from practical experience.
This may include ideas from formal theory. He then (p. 34) distinguishes between three different types of theory, shown in Table 2.1.
Theories of what social work is relate to the material considered
briefly in Chapter 1 and in Payne (1996a): that is, the three different
views of social work which construct its nature. Theories of how to do
social work are the focus of this book, which explores different ways
of formulating theories of casework, groupwork and community
work. Theories of the client world are those which help workers by
explaining the nature of the phenomena with which they are dealing.
These are sometimes referring to knowledge for social work (see
Barker and Hardiker, 1981; Sutton, 1994). Much of this material is
contested in its own domain. Attachment theory, for example (see
Aldgate, 1991; Howe, 1995), is frequently used. It contains helpful
analysis and knowledge about how relationships develop and may
become damaged. Much of it develops from psychodynamic perspectives, and so takes a particular viewpoint about human behaviour. It is
also controversial, since it implies a position in the nature–nurture
debate about the extent to which development is influenced by inborn
characteristics or interpersonal experiences.

Table 2.1   Types of theory

Types of theory	'Formal' theory	'Informal' theory
Theories of what social work *is*	Formal written accounts defining the nature and purposes of welfare (e.g. personal pathology, liberal reform, Marxist, feminist)	Moral, political, cultural values drawn upon by practitioners for defining 'functions' of social work
Theories of *how to do* social work	Formal written theories of practice (e.g. casework, family therapy, groupwork)	Inductively derived and unwritten practice theories constructed from experience
Theories of the *client world*	Formal written social science theories and empirical data (e.g. on personality, marriage, the family, race, class, gender)	Practitioners' use of experience and general cultural meanings (e.g. the family as an institution, normal behaviour, good parenting)

Source: Adapted from Sibeon (1990).

Social work and wider theories

Social work occasionally develops its own theoretical perspectives from their outset. Task-centred work is an example. More commonly, however, its theories select from, embroider and develop external ideas. These come from other occupational and professional groups, wider ideologies in society and theoretical perspectives from related academic fields of study. This is probably an inevitable characteristic, since social work must respond to social movements in society as we construct it through the political and social construction processes outlined in Chapter 1.

Accreting theory in this way means that social work ideas connect to and originally came from wider bodies of knowledge and theory. Social work adapts ideas to its use over time, within social work literature and debate. Much of this may be decoupled from developments in the main body of theory. Thus, social work's distinctive view of a theory has the same view of the world and may share some of the same original literature with the external body of literature. Some influence may continue in either direction. Usually, though, for workers in everyday practice, the connections are relatively sparse.

However, specialist agencies, which are often multi-disciplinary, using particular theories, also exist. Social workers there have more contact with the wider theoretical world of this perspective. They may borrow and adapt new ideas to their practice as social workers. Joint contributions both to social work and wider literature may be influenced by this experience. This is one way in which new ideas filter into social work. The broader the literature, generally speaking, the more influential it will be. Partly, this is because widely debated ideas will influence both clients' and workers' social contexts. So, clients may be more aware of sets of ideas in common currency, and colleagues in other agencies may be more able to interact with social workers about them. Thus, feminist or humanist ideas have a broad constituency within philosophy, literature and the social thought. Debates are part of the currency of everyday discourse. Cognitive theory, on the other hand, is a technical psychological theory which few outside psychology and medicine have heard of. The flow of ideas from the feminist and humanist thought into social work (or into anything) is likely, therefore, to be stronger.

We can, therefore, conceive of two situations in which social work theory transfers from wider bodies of theory. First, in the politics of social work theory, it may have become incorporated within a general approach to social work which most workers carry out or within one of the three views discussed in Chapter 1. Second, this general approach to social work may be applied in theoretically specialised settings. The particular perspective and its wider theory then becomes more important in what the worker does in that setting than it is in general social work. A worker in a women's refuge, for example, might be closely in touch with and committed to feminist theory. A worker in a therapeutic community for mentally ill people might be in touch with aspects of psychoanalytic theory on groups and institutions. Workers in an acute psychiatric unit might be actively involved in behavioural and cognitive treatment regimes.

Wider bodies of theory need to be considered, but they may have no direct or influential relationship with the usual use of the related social work theory. This book focuses on the social work theory used in non-specialist social work. Workers in specialist agencies or with particular theoretical interests will have greater knowledge of and commitment to that theory than the average worker. In general social work, theories which would be clearly distinct, and perhaps incompatible in some debates within wider theoretical bases, have become entwined or connected in various ways. Attempts to relate systems and psychodynamic theories of various kinds are an example. Debates and conflicts also exist within social work. The mutual criticism of traditional (psychodynamic) and radical (socialist-collectivist) theories is an example.

Figure 2.1 Relationships between general and social work perspectives, theories and models

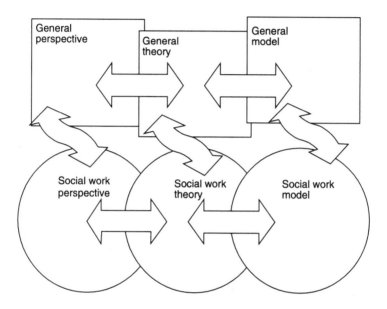

Figure 2.1 sets out in diagrammatic form many of these connections. In addition, each set of social work and wider theories has connections and disagreements with other social work theories. The focus of this book is, in each case, with the social work theory and its literature. Connections elsewhere are acknowledged rather than explored.

The politics of social work theory and application

I have argued so far that we must understand social work practice theory in the wider contexts of theory and knowledge with which it interacts. We can also see its interactions with different types and levels of theory and knowledge within social work. Practice theories are constructed by these interactions. Saleebey (1993) argues for the value in practice of generative theory, based on narratives and discussion of practice which gives workers flexible ideas which cast doubt on conventional views. This is more useful than formal modernist theory, which is hard to align with daily experience. In everyday practice, workers construct informal theories which guide their actions from their own wider value systems and personal experiences, which may include formal theory. Application, I have argued, can be seen as the process of gaining greater influence for the formal within the informal and of understanding the origins of the informal within the formal. Secker's (1993) study of the development of social work students in Edinburgh suggests that an everyday approach, using informal theory, was more typical of students before training. Social work training and professional development is one way in which workers learn how to achieve this application of the formal to the informal. However, Secker's study shows that most students found it difficult to apply formal theory. How social work theory is applied can be seen as the practical outcome of the politics of social work theory. On the other side of the circle, construction can be seen as the process of influencing the formal with informal constructions.

Debate about the application of theory to practice and practice to theory relates to debate about the nature of social work. To what extent is it a theory-based activity or generated primarily from practice? To what extent is its nature independent of what is practised? Answers to these questions bear on everyday practical issues about power and autonomy among interest groups within and having influence from outside on social work.

What are those interest groups? Clients, as in one sense participants and in another the objects, have an interest in the effectiveness and convenience of the formal and informal theory used. Because its fit with clients' own views of the world helps effectiveness, workers often construct the informal to interpret the formal in a way which helps clients to participate. If we acknowledge the importance of agency context as an aspect of social work, the agency's managers and its ultimate political masters have an interest in maintaining control over the nature of the activity which social workers undertake. Among the ways of dong so is to control the nature of the knowledge they use. Social work academics have an interest in the development and successful application of theory that they work on, in conveying it successfully to students and practitioners and gaining influence for their ideas and the institution that employs them. Always, these groups have an interest in the successful application of theory and in the contributions of different theories to the applicability of social work.

Workers are another important interest group. They have an interest in being able to undertake interesting, useful work in satisfying ways. The work comes through the agency, and a degree of safety and support can be gained from following the agency's prescriptions for practice. Theories present an alternative set of prescriptions for practice, which are autonomous of the agency and give the worker a degree of autonomous power over their practice. Social workers also use theory within the politics of their daily practice to offer *accountability* to managers, politicians, clients and the public. It does so by describing acceptable practice sufficiently to enable social work activities to be checked to see that they are appropriate. Theory may also offer *justification* for particular explanations of their activity. Using theory for accountability and justification may be questioned. Perspective theories are concerned with relating social work activities to broader categories of activity in society, rather than seeking to explain, describe or prescribe social work activities systematically. A particular system of social work activities is then justified because it meets some wider social aims. Many social work theories do this to some extent, especially where they claim to rely on particular human values: existential or humanist therapies are an example. Some theories are primarily intended for this purpose: Marxist and feminist therapies are an example. Other theories justify or explain social work theories by showing how they relate to general models or theories about human behaviour or society. The social work branch is then justified to some extent because it can be shown to fit into an accepted model of explanation or description. Systems or psychoanalytic theory are examples of this use of theory in social work.

Applying ideas in practice presents difficulties to workers. Gaining influence for practice within ideas is also problematic. Social work and other occupations frequently debate links between theory and practice. Carew (1979) identifies several different issues of concern. First, there is the concern that social work should be empirical or scientific. This is part of the politics of competition between models, and between modernist and constructionist views of the value of scientific method; see above. Thus, Sheldon (1978) describes the theory/practice link as 'tenuous' primarily because it does not follow the precepts of the empirical practice movement.

Second, there is a concern for the effective implementation of theory from specific sources, so that various authors wish to see more (or less) use of ideas and knowledge from, say, social sciences in general, psychology, psychoanalysis or Marxist theory. This is a concern that practice may be partial, or not take account of the range of available information. Another difficulty may be that social workers find it hard to integrate these many ideas into one system of thought which may be applied practically. The problem here is that there is so much to know that it is hard to use in an organised way. This problem was identified in Secker's (1993) study of social work students, mentioned above. Students in the middle and latter parts of training used theory extensively. Most had great difficulty in integrating it, kept finding conflicts between different theories and were unable to make connections between theory that they were taught and informal sources of theory. A few were fluent in integrating theory. These were students who had particular social skills. They listened well, and tried to tie ideas to what they heard when meeting with clients. They could develop ideas, drawing on a range of different courses and seeing connections, rather than seeing pieces of knowledge as separate. Also, they discussed their ideas effectively with the clients concerned, so that they could test out the validity of their application. It may be, then, that successful application requires social and interpersonal skills, and the self-confidence to discuss ideas actively as part of practice.

Third, there is a concern that social workers find it hard to put into operation knowledge and theories that they may possess and understand. The problem here is that we cannot turn the ideas into practical action. Various reasons have been suggested for these difficulties. One issue may be that social work knowledge is largely borrowed from other disciplines. Therefore it has been created for other purposes, and may be hard to convert to practical use. Pilalis (1986) proposes that there are two continua: from reflex action to purposeful action and from non-reflective thought to reflective thought. In integrated practice, action and thought interact with and influence each other. Such ideas relate to the work of Schön (1983). He argues that many professions do not operate through 'technical rationality', but have common techniques for improvising according to informally learned guidelines. They respond to new situations intuitively, following the guidelines. When the situation is too complex, they reflect on and adjust the guidelines. Thus, professional activity responds to a constant process of reflection and readjustment.

Another issue which often arises is the inadequacy of social work's education and training in helping social workers to transfer knowledge effectively. Hindmarsh (1992) studied 22 new graduates of social work in New Zealand, and summarised much of the world literature. She argues that many people are motivated to come into social work through a sense of opposition to the *status quo*. They seek through helping others and supporting social change to act on this feeling of opposition. Their training gives them confidence, self-awareness and a personal framework of practice and identity as a worker. They experience agencies as creating barriers through their formal management systems to putting that confidence and identity into practice. As a result, workers become alienated and isolated. Their experiences in agencies and training play out the oppositions they experience in their view of the world. This raises the issue of whether theory and knowledge are appropriate but the way we transfer it is wrong, whether it is inappropriate and should be replaced by a perspective drawn more from agencies or whether the agencies are inappropriately organised to offer social work. As Smid and van Krieken (1984) point out, we may reasonably see these arguments as a struggle between academic and practice institutions for influence over the nature of practice.

A further issue is about whether the theories available in social work are suitable for practice. They may, for example, be too generalised to enable workers to apply them to specific circumstances or too limited so that, although apparently useful, they never apply to the complex situations which social workers deal with.

How do social workers see the practice/theory relationship? Carew (1979) found in a study of 20 social workers in the North of England that few used theory explicitly in their work. Most thought it was important, but that its use was unconscious or as a framework rather than as an explicit guide to action. Mostly, they had acquired through practice a series of skills which allowed them to follow procedures for dealing with problems that clients raised. These were unrelated to specific knowledge, but were generally gained from casework literature. Barbour (1984) studied 20 English social work students and distinguished two approaches to using theory. Students who took a 'helping perspective' sought sets of principles that were directly applicable. Others took a 'healing perspective', and had a more generalised view of what a good social worker brought to interaction with clients. Sometimes respect for the dignity and worth of clients was seen as incompatible with the use of theory, which was seen as treating clients like guinea pigs. This approach is consistent with Pithouse's (1987) study of teams in Wales, where he found an informal consensus about ways of assessing what characterised a good social worker, which were unrelated to theoretical or agency expectations. Barbour found that there were three models by which the students understood the integration of theory with practice:

1 '*Seeping-in*', where students had acquired general ideas and methods, but were unable to say where these had come from.
2 *Amalgam*, where particular theories were used where they seemed relevant, and each student built up a stock of 'professional lore' to be used as required.
3 *Personal style*, where knowledge was integrated with students' personality to form a seamless whole.

Harrison (1991) studied how 25 social workers in Britain used theory. He argues that workers had three 'cognitive guides' (that is, ways of thinking about) to practice, which focused on seeking common ground with the client in understanding the clients' situation. These were as follows:

- *Comparison and classification.* The situation was compared with the agency's function, previous experience and social science understanding, and classified according to previously experienced cases. There was a focus on issues which suggested a response according to conventional or established methods of procedures.
- *Application of a generic theory of practice.* The situation was reframed to be concerned with networks or communities rather than individuals, so that contacts in a wider area of concern could be established. There was a concern with social rather than psychological processes.
- *Heuristic search.* The workers looked for divergent information and ways of looking at the situation, including political and moral dimensions. They avoided looking for similarities and generalisations.

Typically, according to Harrison, workers use one of these approaches consistently or two or more in a sequence. I would suggest that the first represents a worker who focuses on the issues presented and operates according to procedures. The second seeks a broader canvas for action and tries to avoid 'blaming the victim', positioning issues presented by clients in wider forms of explanation. The third approach is wholly humanist. I think these align with particular views of social work: the first is individualist-reformist, the second, socialist-collec-tivist and the third reflexive-therapeutic. Each of these perspectives gave workers a basis for testing out ideas about what to do, which were appraised according to their likely success. They did not experi-ence work as highly programmed or ordered, but as a 'seamless integration of thought and action' (Harrison, 1991: 155) following from their typical mode of thought.

In an important series of studies, Curnock and Hardiker (1979; Hardiker, 1981) showed that in several English settings workers used theoretical knowledge inexplicitly, although this may be subject to the criticism that such knowledge may have been gained from general rather than professional sources. Also, Carew (1979) argues that we cannot describe inexplicit knowledge as organised theoretical understanding. Cocozzelli and Constable (1985), in an American study, confirmed that general approaches to clients rather than explicit use of theory is the most common relationship between theory and practice. They found that a theoretical preference for technique (active versus reflective), emotional attitude to the client (task-orientated versus person-oriented) and for defining problems (as stemming from the individual or from society) correlated with practice actions. Olssen (1993), in a Swedish study, got 88 social workers to define eight 'naïve theories' and six 'naïve treatment theories' which they used. The explanatory theories were lack of love, deficient upbringing, trauma, stress, lack of inner resources, biological constitution, material shortcomings and a mixture of these factors. The naïve treatment models were: catharsis, re-education, advocacy, compensation (giving clients something previously missing in their lives), working through problems (getting clients to articulate ideas and supporting them in taking action themselves) and practical support.

Hearn (1982) notes that one difficulty is defining what 'theory' and 'practice' mean. Often, they are caricatured so that theory means what is learned on courses and practice is what is done in agencies, and Sibeon (1982) suggests that one model of the relationship is that of an academic division of labour between colleges and the field. Barbour (1984) confirms this problem and proposes three different meanings of theory:

1 grand theory providing a comprehensive conceptual scheme;
2 middle-range theory about specific aspects of society (for example, labelling theory) or of undertaking practice (for instance, task-centred casework);
3 anything learned in college rather than in placement.

These distinctions include some aspects of the different levels of theory discussed above.

Another difficulty identified by Hearn (1982) is confusion about the nature of the theory–practice relationship. Several relationships are possible, and often complaints about them come from a failure to recognise, or a rejection of, some of the possibilities. Thompson (1995) suggests several ways of 'narrowing the gap' between theory and practice. These involve learning cycles and reflective practitioner approaches (for example, Schön, 1983) in which theory and practice influence each other. Workers should also avoid extremes of claiming that all practice is divorced from theory or common sense, or that practice is possible with no theory. Instead, they should continually seek awareness of relevant research, analyse the 'critical incidents' in their practice, work in groups to develop ideas and critical thought, and seek continuous professional development in order to avoid getting cut off from the world of ideas. In arguing for practitioners to take an active role in testing and developing theory, for example, Brennan (1973) shows that the conventional conception is that such activity is outside normal practice.

At least six different models (derived partly from Carr, 1986) of the relationship between theory and practice may be identified. These are set out in Table 2.2, with objections to each of their approaches to dealing with theory–practice relationships. Obviously, none of the models described offers a full and indisputable analysis of theory–practice relationsips in social work. Table 2.2 makes clear that various disputed models of this relationship exist. Theories might derive from academic, practitioner or managerial sources, and recognise the primacy or balance of one or several of those sources. This suggests that we should be looking for a number of ways of joining theory and practice from different positions. We should avoid struggle between different elements of occupational control for influence concealed as a debate about the 'true' nature of social work theory. Hearn (1982) contends that we should avoid seeing theory and practice as two ends of a dumb-bell, but rather as always intertwined and relating to each other in a variety of ways.

Thinking theoretically in practice

Application of theory in practice is, therefore, difficult and should not be regarded as the meeting of two opposites, but rather as a series of complex relationships. How, then, can workers find a way through these complexities to think theoretically in practice? There are three approaches to this task: using theories to interrogate, clarify and criticise each other, using theories selectively, and using theories together to modify each other. This section deals with each of these in turn.

Table 2.2 Different types of relationship between theory and practice

Types	Objections	Arguments against the objections
1 General theories of behaviour or social life contributing to social work are used to originate practice theories and existing practice is tested to see if it accords with the theory; if not, it is adapted; if the theory still fails, practice experience discredits it or forces a change in the practice theory or the contributing social and psychological theories.	Theories persist because of academic support when practitioners find them hard to use (e.g. many social science concepts – Hardiker, 1981).	Theories can be used to stimulate debate and for teaching clarity, and do not need to be applicable; they may helpfully give ways of looking at things, rather than guidance in action; theories may not be universally useful, but may help some practitioners – the objectors may be non-users rather than justified in rejecting a theory.
2 General theories are designed to produce practice prescriptions which are testable according to scientific method; theories which will not produce testable prescriptions are rejected; those which fail in testing are rejected.	Many social workers (according to positivists) accept theories without empirical validity.	Empirical testing may be difficult with human beings, and action may be needed in which an untested theory gives useful guidance; people disagree about what kinds of evidence are acceptable – positivists may be too strict.
3 Theory is a process of enquiry and debate in which proposals for action are tested against accumulations of experience and ideas.	Leads to cycles of disagreement on ideological grounds rather than clarity; leads to acceptance of ideas in debate without any empirical validity.	Theory about practice is always unfinished, there is no final certainty, so a cycle of debate may be realistic; at least this approach allows practitioners to take part in theory development, rather than simply being given theory to use.
4 Theory is a series of generalisations based on the accumulation of practice, experience which it articulates and conceptualises.	Unlikely to have public credibility because it is not 'scientifically' tested.	Public may prefer theory tested by experience rather than experiment.
5 Theory comes from a variety of sources to offer models of practice, but action according to such models is altered or limited by organisational and political constraints.	Leads to a too ready acceptance of constraints which may be unjust impositions on clients; difficulty of deciding when constraints should apply and when they should be opposed.	Constraints are real and need to be included in theory if it is to be practically useful.
6 Theory develops from practice experience but is tested and altered by empirical research and intellectual debate.	Practice-derived theories may be hard to test; they may also be used without testing.	This approach allows practitioner involvement – even primacy – in theory development; ensures that academic work is developed on firm practice base.

Source: Adapted from Carr (1986).

Using theories against each other: critical analysis

I have devised elsewhere (Payne, 1996b) some ideas which may help
to make concrete some possibilities for critical practice; they are
as follows:

- *A dualities approach.* Many concepts, especially value concepts,
  include within them implicit references to their opposites. For
  example, when we have a problem with confidentiality, we can
  ask ourselves: 'What is the difficulty about openness which this
  confidentiality issue implies?' Again, with self-determination:
  'What rule-following is being required of the client that raises
  this problem with her self-determination?' Berlin (1990) argues
  that dichotomous thinking of this kind is a useful habit of mind,
  but highlights extremes and may be insufficiently complex to deal
  with real-world problems.
- *A critical contrastive approach.* Many concepts, especially
  theoretical concepts, benefit from being set against their contrasting
  perspective. Difference helps us to criticise what we are doing. The
  idea of resistance is an example. Caseworkers sometimes judge
  resistance as unhelpful, as something to be overcome. Workers at a
  more general social or community level, on the other hand,
  sometimes ally themselves with or support resistance to social
  ideas which oppress cultural or community ideals. However,
  psychologically, resistance is a defence against damage. At times it
  might usefully be supported to avoid damage, and community
  resistance can obstruct useful change and might need to be
  overcome. From a general psychodynamic perspective, for
  example, resistance is often seen as a sign that something important
  is being kept back by a client and needs to be revealed. However,
  an ego–psychological approach might propose the support of the
  defence, and a worker has to make a professional judgement of
  which approach to take. Marxist social workers would often see
  resistance on behalf of community ideas as appropriately supported
  against capitalist hegemony. From time to time, though, particular
  ideas might be seen as supporting the hegemony and are therefore
  rejected and not supported. In each of these cases a theoretical
  position is taken which informs a judgement taken as part of the
  work role. Each must decide whether to attack or support the
  resistance that they face. The perspective of the other might help
  them evaluate their choice. Marxists evaluate community and

cultural resistance as significant and supportable, depending on its emotional importance to individuals. Psychodynamic workers can decide to overcome emotional resistance if they see the powerlessness it creates in the client.

- *A power analysis approach.* The analysis of power relations in any situation enables us to consider the political issues present. It is useful to consider the pathways of client and worker and the development of the agency situation in which they meet as giving a history of the political factors which form their interaction (Payne, 1993).
- *A thinking–emotions approach.* We tend to think about clients on a rational level in theories such as task-centred casework or in cognitive-behavioural work. In psychodynamic and humanist approaches, on the other hand, we tend to concentrate on emotional motivations. We need to beware, in practice, of seeing clients' problems as solely concerned with their thought processes or perceptions or with their emotions or lack of self-control. Where we find this happening, we should ask ourselves, 'What are the emotions (or what ideas does this behaviour represent) here?' This is a special case of the critical contrastive approach.
- *The tri-perspective approach.* I introduced in Chapter 1 the idea that all social work is constructed from three different perspectives, and referred above to Harrison's (1991) proposition, which identifies three similar 'cognitive guides' to practice which social workers in his study had; he suggests they typically try only one, or alternatively two or more in succession. However, these perspectives are typically all present to some degree and we should explicitly seek them out so as to question our own approach to a situation. For instance, where we find ourselves implementing the agency's requirements and trying to get clients to fit in (individualist-reformist), we can ask how we can collaborate to change the situation (socialist-collectivist) and what personal power and development the client can be enabled to achieve (reflexive-therapeutic) to get other perspectives on our work.

Choosing one theory: selectivity

Some practice theories are written to be self-sufficient, covering all or most eventualities that workers might encounter. These imply loyalty to the use of one theory only. Typical theories of this type, such as psycho-dynamic theory, attempt to be comprehensive. This may be possible where a worker has studied all the complexities of a theory and is acting on it. It is easier in an agency that focuses on that theory. Other theories are written to specify the circumstances in or problems with which they should be used (such as crisis and task-centred theory, respectively). Here, they may be selected for use when such circumstances arise. Yet workers often retain in practice only a hazy set of ideas which, although we may recognise them (Curnock and Hardiker, 1979), do not form action according to a particular theory. Loewenberg (1984) argues that this is because less wide-ranging 'middle-range' theories are needed, fitted into an overall professional ideology. Some theories which workers sometimes find useful do not offer a complete solution for all social work situations. Therefore, sometimes, workers must put theories together. Also, as we shall see in relation to eclecticism, there are difficult problems in knowing enough about a range of theories to select among them appropriately.

However, selection as an approach simplifies the application of theory. It works if a theory may be used comprehensively or if it is clear enough to be grasped adequately to use in the circumstances to which it may be applied.

Putting theories together: eclecticism

Hartman (1971) argues that we must each make our own definition of 'theory' in order to practise. Research by O'Connor and Dalgleish (1986) on beginning social workers in Australia shows that they did create and retain their personal models of social work during their early experience of practice. However, they had difficulty adjusting it to the agency setting. Hugman (1987), in a similar British study, did not find so many difficulties. He argues that helping beginning workers construct personal models may help make therapeutic 'theories' appropriate for their social and service context.

Since our social construction view celebrates the diversity of the human experience with which social workers deal, the variety of possibilities about their work and the confusion of ideas that they might use in guidance of their work, it would press many workers to work eclectically. That is, they put aspects of different theories together. There are two focuses for eclecticism. One is where, as part of work on a caseload, different cases are dealt with according to different theories. This is a form of selectivity, except that the worker is making a commitment to using several theories rather than one within their overall workload. The second is where we bring aspects of different theories together to be used simultaneously in a particular case situation. Workers might do this differently with different members of a group of clients (for example, a family), by using different theories successively (such as, first, crisis intervention in an emergency, followed by psychodynamic work for the longer term) or by moving between different theories from moment to moment or day to day. It is this latter form which most people mean when they discuss eclecticism. Epstein (1992: 321–30) reviews five models of eclecticism:

1 *Systematic integration* – An integration model with guidelines about criteria for selection of theories and a consistent structure would enable different ideas to be used systematically. However, such a model would be very complex and difficult to construct.
2 *Constructed personal practice models* – Individuals or a group of colleagues working together would create their own collection of theoretical ideas, based on an assessment of their particular practice needs. One problem would be gaining approval from managers for using a specific system.
3 *Systematic treatment selection* – Select a model and slot other ideas into it in an organised way.
4 *Informal convenience approaches* – An informal process of picking up and including new ideas in a personal approach. Careful checking and discussion with others will help decide how best to incorporate it in a worker's repertoire.
5 *Casual applications* – These are accidental concurrences of something workers hear of which fits with a situation that arises.

Epstein is concerned that workers should incorporate ideas consistently, rather than on a casual basis, and develop them into a pattern of repeated practice, rather than picking up ideas and using them occasionally as they seem to fit.

Is there evidence that social workers are eclectic, or that eclectic theories exist? Three forms of evidence are relevant. First, there are research studies of social workers' attitudes. Second, some texts explicitly attempt an eclectic approach. Third, some texts approach social work in an eclectic way.

The evidence for a degree of eclecticism exists in research studies of social workers. Jayaratne (1978) surveyed 267 American social workers in the mid-1970s and found that there was a primary allegiance to psychodynamic approaches, but that 'eclecticism is the predominant mode of intervention' (p. 626). Research by Kolevson and Maykranz (1982), covering nearly 700 American practitioners and teachers, shows that they have very weak allegiances to specific theories; they speculate that this may be because of poor theoretical grounding in their training. British studies (such as DHSS, 1978: 134–6) comment on the pronounced lack of theory in the approach of many workers surveyed. However, there is also evidence (for example, Curnock and Hardiker, 1979) of inexplicit or naïve (Olssen, 1993) use of theory.

Fischer's (1978) behaviourist text is specifically eclectic. He argues for selecting techniques appropriate to particular needs of clients, chosen according to effectiveness demonstrated by research evidence. This, therefore, argues a modernist approach to using theory rather than one concerned with being eclectic.

Many other social work texts are eclectic in other ways. Some are theoretically eclectic in that they specifically include aspects of other theories. For example, Woods and Hollis (1990) on psychosocial theory include family therapy, role and communication theory. Systems theories (see Chapter 6) explicitly seek to be eclectic, since they try to offer an overarching theory which includes many or all other social work theories.

Many basic social work texts concentrate on presenting the processes, skills or techniques of social work rather than offering any particular theory to understand personal or social behaviour. Part of this derives from the broadly applicable social work processes within which most theories are practised. For example the traditional 'study–diagnosis–treatment' formulation has developed into the idea of process of intake, assessment, action, and evaluation or review. Approaches to these processes may be similar in many theories. For example, psychodynamic writers, behaviourists and radical writers – in the accounts given in this book (for example, Compton and Galaway, 1994; Hudson and MacDonald, 1986; Fook, 1993) – all comment on how assessment begins the process of treatment, because defining problems begins the response to them. These ideas or developments in service delivery such as community social work (in Britain) or case (care) management might be more relevant to practice prescription than theories which try to explain why particular social work actions result in worthwhile change in clients. Against this, ideas such as case (care) management do not seek to explain how social work works. They merely establish, in an individualist-reformist approach, administrative systems within which social work may be more effectively provided (see Payne, 1995 for a more extensive discussion of case/care management).

Moore (1976) argues that being eclectic means a reliance on workers' skill, knowledge and value bases, which offer a secure base for moving among theoretical ideas. Since there is evidence that eclecticism is widely apparent in social work, is it a satisfactory way of dealing with the problem that there is a multiplicity of theories to choose from in practice? To go further, should we take up an eclectic or inclusive theory instead of others, because it allows us to use several approaches within it? Further still, are the sorts of theories that we have been examining irrelevant to practice, and a technical or developmental theory which simply presents techniques or offers descriptions of stages of work all that is necessary? To answer these questions, we need to look at the arguments for and criticisms of eclecticism. These are set out in Table 2.3.

It is not clear in much of this research and commentary what kind of eclecticism is being discussed or to what extent it is practised (for example, between different cases, or at different times in the same case). The extent to which the difficulties or advantages of eclecticism are achieved depend on how much movement between theories there is and the extent to which this is organised or thought out. There are, obviously, arguments in favour of eclecticism in using theory, but there are difficulties, particularly if it is unplanned or leads to wild, momentary variations in approach which confuse clients. This suggests that eclecticism should be a cautious and planned act, rather than an assumption that 'anything goes'. A social construction approach suggests that a shared construction would often take place within groups of workers, responding to the particular needs of clients served, and involving them in its development. In doing so, it is, in my view, crucial to understand and consider the connections, oppositions and consistencies among theories, using the critical approach suggested above, and selecting appropriately too. So the different ways of using theory together discussed in this section may not be too far apart.

Table 2.3 Arguments for and against eclecticism

For	Against
Clients should be able to benefit from all available knowledge, so theoretical perspectives should not be limited.	Clients may not benefit, since workers acquire work styles early in their career and may miss theories which are devised later.
Empirical knowledge about skills or communication are valid irrespective of theory, and should be used as part of applying any theories.	Eclecticism avoids the professional responsibility to accumulate and integrate knowledge in social work.
There are many links between different ways of helping.	
Theories work at different levels (e.g. task-centred theory gives specific guidance about particular situations while psychodynamic theory offers very wide-ranging ideas about interpreting behaviour); theories at different levels can be used together.	There is no clear basis for deciding how to use one theory rather than another, or selecting one from a range; therefore, the decision to use one theory rather than another is purely arbitrary or based on personal feeling rather than rational decision.
Some theories do not pretend to cover all areas of work (e.g. Marxist theory does not provide psychological knowledge or skills guidance) and so must be used in conjunction with others, provided care is taken about how they match.	Workers would need to understand many theoretical approaches, some very complex and needing supervision and study; this is not possible for most workers much of the time; if something went wrong with a highly technical theory, they might not notice or be able to put it right.
Many aspects of social work are the same whatever theory is used (e.g. the sequence of beginning, middle and end phases; assessment, diagnosis and planning; use of tasks and contracts) so a broad approach to social work can be constructed from these without worrying about theory.	Practising so as to join many different theories together may cause a worker to lose a common core of practice.
Many of the distinctions drawn between theories are not relevant to practice which concerns itself with general and practical ideas like assessment, rather than ideas about human behaviour, social environment or the human condition, which are secondary to helping people.	Many theories use similar techniques but with different justifications, or within a completely different understanding of society or human beings; theories might inherently conflict without the worker being aware of or understanding the contradictions; this may be confusing for clients and workers.
Social work involves personal commitment and use of personality in a close relationship with clients, and sticking to one theory may be uncongenial for the worker or client in a particular case; human variety requires us to choose from the widest possible range of theories to make the personal element of social work possible.	

Cautious, coordinated and planned application should help to overcome the problems with eclecticism discussed in Table 2.3. We can thus use ideas where they effectively meet workers' and clients' needs, taking account of the range of possibilities, avoiding unhelpful options, and seeking to develop ideas from the basic theories. The purpose of this book is to provide the resource of a starting point with access to the literature on theories likely to be useful to facilitate thoughtful rather than casual eclecticism.

Analyses of social work theories

Practitioners criticising practice, selecting or incorporating theories in a personal construction are faced with a wide choice among apparently comparable and useful theories. The purpose of the remainder of this book is to offer information about some of those theories, to enable comparisons of their value and to see how they may be selected and combined. Some doubt whether this is a useful enterprise. Solomon (1976), for example, considers that theories and models of social work are not comparable because they often deal with different things (for example, the functions of practice, the process of change, the sequence of helping processes, the nature of problems to be dealt with). Some, she argues, are based on particular methods of change, while others extend into fields of therapeutic change beyond social work. This sort of criticism shows why it is so important to consider carefully how we select and group theories.

Various attempts have been made in the past to select and group theories in useful ways, and we now turn to discussion of how this might be done.

Casework

Several books exist whose writers and editors try to review and compare a range of social work theories. Table 2.4 summarises the coverage of some of these. This is not a complete analysis, since many of these works specifically deal only with casework or what in the United States would be called clinical social work (for instance, Roberts and Nee). Two companion books of Roberts and Nee (Roberts and Northen, 1976; Taylor and Roberts, 1985) review and compare group and community work theories; these are considered later. I include some discussion of group, residential and community work in chapters with related casework or general theories. Some of these works of review, while not defining their coverage as casework, concentrate on this field (for example, Howe, 1987). A recent British review (Hanvey and Philpot, 1994) contains a mixture of practical guidance by well-known writers and accounts of theoretical models. This is, therefore, not wholly comparable with other reviews but shows what areas of principled practice interest British social workers in the mid-1990s. To some extent a practical rather individualist-reformist book, it somewhat eschews ideas such as radical or empowerment theory in favour of the particular formulations of chosen writers, although it covers the conventional and managerially respectable, such as systems and behavioural theory. Croft and Beresford's (1994) 'participatory' approach, for example, has much in common with empowerment, and welfare rights is a limited but practical aspect of both radical and advocacy theory. Lishman (1991) distinguishes between 'models of understanding human development' and models of intervention. The first group includes what I have called 'perspectives', such as psychodynamic or structural approaches, as well as fairly restricted theories of development such as attachment theory and Erikson's (1965) life-cycle approach to development. Since her book is explicitly for practice teachers (fieldwork supervisors), it presumably reflects concepts she thinks will be unfamiliar to practice teachers. Whittaker and Tracy (1989) offer an analysis of a wide range of therapeutic approaches, and propose three major 'knowledge foundations': these are also what I have called 'perspectives' which might underlie more detailed models of practice. They give priority to the 'ecological paradigm', and also value psychodynamic ego psychology and social learning theory. An earlier edition (Whittaker, 1974) argued that there were four: psychodynamic, behavioural and systems theories, and the existential and humanist approaches. The ecological approach is often presented as a systems theory, and contains major elements of a psychosocial approach. It has in some respects replaced psychosocial work as the repository of basic social work concepts such as 'person-in-situation', now often rendered, as by Whittaker and Tracy, as 'person-in-environment'. Social learning and ego-psychological theory are also more recent emphases within Whittaker's earlier preferred behavioural and psychodynamic ideas. Here we can see the development and changes of emphasis within social work theories.

Some analyses of social work theories are empirical and so presumably reflect actual distinctions used in the field. Cocozelli and

Constable's (1985) study of clinical social work in the United States, for example, distinguishes between psychodynamic, behavioural, existential, family, gestalt and problem-solving therapies.

Frameworks for analysing theories

Some writers have attempted more than just description of social work theories. They have tried to group them to show connections, or underlying principles which different theories share. One possible way of doing this is to analyse the content of each theory according to a standard set of categories. An alternative and more sophisticated method has a conceptual scheme placing theories in relation to one another.

Table 2.5 gives four examples of the approach of evaluating or describing theories according to a common set of categories based on the work of Whittaker and Tracy's (1989) 'areas of enquiry' of approaches to practice, Turner (1983), Meyer (1983), Kettner (1975) and Roberts and Nee's (1970) instructions to authors of chapters on particular theories in their book. Meyer is primarily concerned with examining the internal consistency of theories, and their fitness for modern practice. Hence, her analysis requires less description and includes capacity for use with self-help groups and non-professional staff. Whittaker and Tracy's and Roberts and Nee's categories seek a largely descriptive analysis, whereas Kettner includes some measure of both elements. The categories used vary, therefore, but overlap.

The second method of grouping theories is by categorising them according to an organising concept. Whittington and Holland's (1985) classification of social work theories is particularly important. Howe's (1987) review of social work theory takes it up. It is based on Burrell and Morgan's (1979) sociological work. They propose that philosophical positions about the nature of society range from subjective (humanist, postmodernist, constructionist) to objective (modernist, postivistic, scientific). An alternative dimension ranges philosophical positions about the nature of order in society. It deals with whether they understand society as changing in a radical way or as a regulated set of social interactions. We can assess social work theories according to where they fit into these two continua. Figure 2.2 gives some examples of how this works. We may criticise such approaches to categorisation because they set arbitrary continua for analysis and because we may always question the placing of theories within the axes (Stenson and Gould, 1986). For example, theories are regarded as mutually

60

Table 2.4 Alternative reviews of social work theories

Categories of theory	Roberts and Nee (1970)	Turner (1986)	Howe (1987)	Lishman (1991)	Hanvey and Philpot (1994)
Psychodynamic	psychosocial functional problem-solving	psychosocial psycho-analytic functional problem-solving ego psychology	psycho-analytic	psychodynamic Erikson's life-cycle approach to development psychodynamic counselling	'casework'
Cognitive-behavioural	behavioural modification	behaviour therapy cognitive	behavioural social work	behavioural social work cognitive-behavioural	behavioural approach
Family treatment	family therapy	family treatment			family therapy
Crisis theories	crisis intervention	crisis		crisis intervention	crisis intervention
Task-centred	task-centred	task-centred	(allies with behavioural approaches)	task-centred practice written agreements	task-centred work
Systems theories		systems life model	not seen as a major category		systems approach

Social psychological/ role theories	socialisation	role theory communication theory neuro-linguistic programming	attachment theory bereavement/loss	community work alternatives to custody
Sociological/social development	(separate volume in series)		community social work	
Group theories		(casework only)	(casework only)	groupwork
Humanist/existential approaches		client-centred existential gestalt transactional analysis	client-centred (groups a number of existential ideas under the heading of 'seekers after the self')	
Radical theories		Marxist radical/radical structuralism consciousness-raising (includes feminist social work) feminist	structural approach	participatory approach welfare rights feminist approaches
Anti-racist/anti-discriminatory theories				anti-racist social work
Empowerment and advocacy				welfare rights participatory approach

Table 2.5 Frameworks for comparing social work theories

Whittaker and Tracy (1989)	Turner (1983)	Meyer (1983)	Kettner (1975)	Roberts and Nee (1970)
purpose	general attributes	ideological base values	writer's philosophy of social work basic values	general characteristics of approach
knowledge base	perception of person	underlying social and psychological theories	knowledge base from psychology and sociology	behavioural science foundations
composition (who is involved)		unit of attention <(i.e. individual, group or community)>	level of intervention	
	perception of functioning	problem definition (i.e. how sorts of issues dealt with are decided)		target group (includes definition of problems)
		are prescribed actions relevant to above and explicit?	how specifically are aims, procedures and outcomes stated?	
role of worker role of client	the therapist	use of professional relationship	roles and responsibilities of client and worker: − fully stated? − active or passive − importance of relationship	
		desired outcomes use of time (long- or short-term) differential use of staff (i.e. is it possible?) work with self-help groups (i.e. is it possible?)		

63

empirical validation

effectiveness research
(i.e. is it possible?)

research validation
(i.e. has it been done?)

target group

target groups of clients
input of worker and client
to decisions

initial phase
assessment of client
in situation

description of process:
beginning phase
assessment

therapeutic qualities

strategies and techniques
of interaction

how effectiveness is
evaluated

ending phase

treatment principles
and methods

strategies and techniques
of helping
indications
contraindications

implementation (e.g. training,
organisation support needed)
setting

exclusive and neatly set in a particular position, whereas often they overlap and share things in common. Equally, conflicts of ideology which do not relate to these axes may not be represented. Howe (1987) treats both psychodynamic theory and behavioural approaches to social work as both representative of functional ideas, whereas there are considerable differences between them.

Figure 2.2   Analysis of social work theories

Theories of radical change

	radical social work ('raisers of consciousness')	Marxist social work ('revolutionaries')	
Subjective			**Objective**
	interactionist ('seekers after meaning')	traditional social work ('fixers')	

Theories of regulation
(note: Howe's labels for each grouping are given in brackets)

Sources: Whittington and Holland (1985), D. Howe (1987).

Groupwork

Several attempts have been made to classify groupwork theories, and some of these are set out in Table 2.6. Roberts and Northen (1976) present an analysis which includes several forms of groupwork allied to casework theories, such as functional and problem-solving groupwork. Their book attempts to parallel the models of practice covered in their book on casework theories. More recent classifications rely on the ground-breaking article by Papell and Rothman (1966), and there is broad agreement about this perspective which is based in current groupwork ideology (see, for example, Bundey, 1976; Brown, 1992).

This offers three fundamental approaches. The remedial model, particularly associated with the work of Vinter, presents the group as a place in which individuals who have problems, very often of how they function in social roles, are brought together in a group to help them change their deviant patterns of behaviour. We might regard any therapeutic model of groupwork as remedial in approach. The mediating model, associated with the work of Schwartz, is humanistic in philosophy, using a terminology associated with systems theory. In this approach the group is a place for helping people examine and establish their social roles in a safe, supportive but challenging environment. Encounter groups are normally regarded as a separate humanist and gestalt form of groupwork concerned with personal growth (see Chapter 8) but might also be regarded as mediating in philosophy. Developmental approaches, associated with Bernstein, are concerned with group dynamics. They assume that groups have a life of their own, independent of the actions and thoughts of members, and the purpose of the group is understanding of self- and group-dynamics. Developmental approaches are broadly psychodynamic, based particularly on the work of Erikson (1965) and ego psychology, theories of group dynamics and social psychological ideas about conflict and group membership (Balgopal and Vassil, 1983). Although this is a typology from the United States, British group dynamics theory, associated with the work of Bion (1961), could also broadly be described as developmental. Glassman and Kates (1990) offer a humanist groupwork model which seeks to combine both mediating and developmental approaches. Brown's (1992) account of groupwork theories extends the range of ideas in a looser but more differentiated analysis.

Feldman and Wodarski (1975) carried out an empirical study of groupwork methods in the United States, and found traditional (broadly developmental) styles of work, remedial approaches and some behavioural approaches in which the group was used as a supporter and place of management of behavioural changes (see Chapter 5). They also designated a group-centred or non-treatment method, in which, while clients met as a group, the worker did not try to achieve change in any organised way, but assumed that the presence of people possibly with shared circumstances or problems would be beneficial and that clients could help one another. This may be typical of many pragmatic uses of groups in everyday practice, and with self-help groups which do not seek to promote therapeutic change.

Brown, for example, has with colleagues (Brown, 1994; Brown *et al.*, 1982) tried to develop a specifically British analysis of groupwork. This involves time-limited groups with aims of meeting agency objectives by achieving individual change in clients, using a sharing approach and co-leadership. Douglas (1993) has also offered a wide analysis of groupwork theory. There have been several attempts to develop groupwork approaches carrying out wider therapeutic ideas, such as feminist, humanist and task-centred groupwork. I deal with these in relevant chapters. Heap (1992) argues that in Europe, groupwork is becoming more multi-disciplinary (although I think this is a worldwide trend) and is less central to social work practice. He also points out the growing importance of self-help groups. Supporting and stimulating these has become a major focus of groupwork development, and begins to merge with community work. It is an important part of Mullender and Ward's (1991) self-directed groupwork (see Chapter 12).

Community work

Analyses of community work recognise the fluidity and range of activities in this field. York (1984) suggests that several conceptualisations of community work divide it into three types. He categorises these as concerned with organising community agencies, developing local competences and political action for change. He argues, however, that all community work involves facing a series of dichotomies:

- directive versus non-directive work (Batten, 1967);
- task or problem versus process approaches;
- initiating versus enabling roles for the worker;
- treatment versus reform.

Many of these issues are represented in distinctions made between different types of community work. I summarise two analyses in Table 2.7, with my description of the meaning of the categories identified.

Community work is not treated in this book, although many social workers practice it and a community orientation is important in many agencies. Community work, however, must be regarded as a distinct form of practice, which calls upon a theoretical and knowledge base which is more sociological and less psychological than casework and groupwork. However, the social development model of social work practice (Chapter 9) has significant elements of community work within it. Some views of social work give importance to using community approaches as part of social work, particularly radical, anti-racist, feminist and empowerment approaches (see Chapters 10–12).

Table 2.6 Classification of groupwork theory

Roberts and Northen (1976)	Feldman and Wodarski (1975)	Papell and Rothman (1966)	Douglas (1979)	Balgopal and Vassil (1983)	Brown (1992)
generic	traditional		eclectic		time-limited 'mainstream'
organisational					
psychosocial		remedial	remedial	remedial	
functional					
mediating		reciprocal	reciprocal/mediating	mediating	
developmental/humanist	group-centred		group-centred/process/developmental/maturational stage/personal growth	developmental	psychotherapeutic person-centred models/gestalt/psychodrama/transactional analysis
task-centred			task-centred		problem-solving/task-centred/social skills
socialisation					
crisis intervention					
problem-solving	behaviour modification		behavioural	behavioural	guided group interaction
		social goals	social goals		social goals/social interaction/self-directed
					self-help/mutual support
					empowerment
					intake/assessment/induction

Table 2.7   Models of community work

Taylor and Roberts (1985)	Popple (1995)	Explanation
Community development	Community development	Helping groups come together and participate in gaining skills and confidence to promote services and facilities in their locality
Political action	Community action	Direct action often at local level to change government or official policies and practices or attitudes of powerful groups; in Europe, often class-based
Programme development and coordination	Community care	Cultivating social networks, voluntary services to achieve better working of and coordination and participation in welfare services
Community liaison	Community organisation	
Planning	Social/community planning	Concerned with participation in better planning of services, analysis of social problems and policy goals; evaluating services and policies
	Community education	Concerned with participation in and developing opportunities for involvement in education for deprived groups
	Feminist community work	Improving women's welfare; challenging and changing gender inequalities and enabling women's participation in resolving policy and social issues of concern to them
	Black and anti-racist community work	Challenging racism; enabling black people's participation in resolving policy and social issues of concern to them

Other aspects of social work

Some writers include *family therapy* within social work theory (see
Table 2.4). This is a form of practice in which all or several members
of the family are treated together on the assumption that their prob-

lems arise from interactions among them all. These therapies are excluded from this volume, although their use in social work and connections with social work theories are considered in relevant places. One reason for this exclusion is that there are several schools of thought in family therapy, and exploring them would extend the length of the book (and the competence of the author). Also, family therapy is more a multi-disciplinary area of practice in which several occupational groups operate and to which several, including social work, have made contributions. It is reasonable to regard it as a form of practice from which some social workers borrow as part of social work, or an occupational grouping into which they move, rather than as an activity which has been adapted to social work (see Payne, 1996a). Many social workers see themselves as practising social work with special relevance to families, and taking into account the family context as part of the 'person-in-situation/environment'.

Residential care can be viewed as a setting in which other treatment theories are used (for example, Jones, 1979; Ward, 1980) in which case no separate theoretical perspectives are relevant, or as a distinct form of social work activity justifying theories of its own. Writers such as Ainsworth and Fulcher (1981; Fulcher and Ainsworth, 1985) regard residential care as a form of groupwork carried out in residence and call it *group care*, a term which they extend to day care, and to settings in health care, education and criminal justice systems outside the social services. They see group care as an occupational focus, a field of study and a domain of practice in each of these settings. Lennox (1982) also sees residential care as a setting for groupwork, but identifies different forms of groupwork particularly relevant to residential work which are more marginal in casework practice: behavioural approaches, encounter groups and transactional analysis. Whittaker (1981) distinguishes psychoanalytic approaches, the child guidance movement's influence, guided group interaction (for example, Polsky, 1965), educational and behavioural approaches as important theoretical influences on residential care.

Davis (1981: 9–21) proposes three ideological approaches to residential care:

1 *Optimists* claim that although many institutions are damaging to their inmates, this is not necessarily the case, and beneficial residential care is possible.
2 *Pessimists* claim that institutionalising features of residential care always damages inmates, so we should abandon it.

3 *Radicals* argue that residential care as at present offered may be
damaging, but that communal living should in principle offer
opportunities for unselfish self-actualisation that are not present
in ordinary capitalist society or in other therapies.

Sinclair (1988: 162–3) reviewed the evidence presented to the
British Wagner committee on residential care and detected three
ideologies within it:

1 *Christian love* proposes that care should be guided by a
recognition of the importance of every individual. This is similar
to the social work philosophy of respect for persons.
2 *Therapeutic value of communal* living espoused by therapeutic
communities who argued that 'living together' must be used as
part of therapy in order that removal from normal environments
can be appropriate. This is similar to the radical view outlined
above, except that supporters of therapeutic communities would
not necessarily agree that the purpose of communal living should
be to enhance people's experience of cooperative living in order
to combat the alienating effects of isolation in capitalist societies.
3 *Individual rights*, the normalisation approach, which suggests that
the aim of residential care should be to return people to life styles
which are valued by ordinary people in that culture.

Such ideologies have a bearing on possible theoretical perspectives
in residential care. Much of the literature is pragmatic and draws out
skills without a theoretical base (for example, Clough, 1982), but
some perspectives are identified by some writers. They are connected
to other theoretical approaches, and are dealt with in the relevant
chapters below. *Behavioural* approaches rely on behaviour modification techniques often using token economies (see Chapter 5) and
radical approaches implement the ideology identified above (see
Chapter 10). *Systems* theories have been applied to residential care
(see Chapter 6). *Empowerment* theories include self-directed groupwork which is also relevant to residential care. *Reality therapy* is a
form of cognitive therapy having residential care origins (see
Chapter 5). *Therapeutic environment* theory is psychodynamic in
origin and is dealt with in Chapter 3. The applicability of general
theories of social work to residential care is, then, possible. However,
the pragmatic nature of much residential care literature and variable
uses of theory suggest that there is as yet a very unclear theoretical

basis for residential work to be claimed as a completely separate form of theoretically supported social work activity.

Conclusion

This chapter completes the first part of the book, which examines the place of social work theory in social work. I argued that theory is practically useful, and that its variety and confusion can be organised and understood. The relationships and oppositions between theories provide a context in which their value can be assessed against one another, and against the modern social context in which they must be used. We can now move on to examining the selected groups of theories in Chapters 3–12 and assessing their value to social workers in the modern context in Chapter 13.

3

Psychodynamic Perspectives

Wider theoretical perspectives

Psychodynamic perspectives are based on the work of Freud and his followers, and on developments of their work. They are called 'psychodynamic' because the theory underlying them assumes that behaviour comes from movements and interactions in people's minds. Also, it emphasises the way in which the mind stimulates behaviour, and both mind and behaviour influence and are influenced by the person's social environment.

Psychoanalytic theory has three parts: it is a theory of human development, of personality and abnormal psychology, and of treatment. Two important basic ideas underpin the theory (Yelloly, 1980; Wood, 1971):

1 Psychic determinism – the principle that actions or behaviour arise from people's thought processes rather than just happening;
2 The unconscious – the idea that some thinking and mental activity are hidden from our knowledge.

These ideas are widely accepted. For example, both ideas include the assumption that slips of the tongue (colloquially, Freudian slips) and jokes reflect hidden or unknown confusions in people's thought processes. Commonsense meanings do not always fully represent the complexity of psychodynamic ideas. Yelloly (1980: 8–9) gives the example of the meaning of 'unconscious' to show how full psychodynamic ideas are. *Resistance* arises when some thoughts and feelings are not compatible with other beliefs that we hold strongly. Here, the mind does not allow the contested ideas into the conscious by a process called *repression*. Many repressed thoughts are dynamic in the sense that they cause us to act, even if we are unaware of them. The psychodynamic unconscious consists of these forcibly hidden ideas which are there whether or not we think about them, and which are often deeply concealed. *Aggression*, where people turn destructive impulses against others, is an important term.

In the *developmental theory* of psychoanalysis children are thought to go through a series of developmental stages. These occur as *drives* (originally translated as 'instincts') which are mental pressures to relieve physical needs such as hunger or thirst. Having such a need creates tension or *libido,* which gives us the energy to act in order to meet the need. Among physical needs sexual tension, even among young children, is very important in creating drives.

At each stage, particular behaviours are important, but as we progress through the stages we use the behaviours associated with previous stages. So, in an early stage, babies gain satisfaction from sucking (for example, at a mother's breast to satisfy the need for food). Later, sucking can also be satisfying – for example, in the use of cigarettes, sweets or in sexual activities. However, adults have a wider range of satisfying activities to choose from. Some people become unconsciously attached to behaviour associated with particular stages (*fixation*). They are driven to seek that form of satisfaction to an unreasonable degree. Consequently, they cannot use the full repertoire of behaviour available to them.

Children start in a stage of *primary narcissism* seeking only gratification of their own needs. They learn through social interaction, at first with parents, that they must compromise. In each stage the focus of attention is on a different need; oral (hunger), anal (excretion), phallic (identification with same-sex parent), Oedipal (attraction to opposite-sex parent), latency (drives are managed through resolution of Oedipal conflicts) and puberty (social learning). Erikson (1965) has expanded on the stages of development. He suggests that at each stage the rational mind deals with a maturational crisis presented by the social circumstances of our life. His work, which has influenced social work, especially crisis intervention, emphasises cultural and social pressures rather than inner drives (Yelloly, 1980: 12).

Associated with stages of development is the idea of *regression*. This occurs when people who have progressed through the later stages fall back to behaviour associated with earlier stages under some present stress. Regression is contrasted with fixation, when individuals are stuck in the behaviour of the early stage.

Psychoanalytic *personality theory* assumes that people are a complex of drives forming the *id* (literally 'it', an undifferentiated pressure from an unknown source – Wood, 1971). The id pushes us to act to resolve our needs but our actions do not always bring the desired results. Development of the *ego* follows from this. It is a set of pragmatic ideas about how we may understand and manipulate the environment. The ego controls the id. For example, children control the excretion of faeces as the ego learns that disapproval and discomfort follow inappropriate excretion. The ego manages relationships with people and things outside ourselves: *object relations*. The *superego* develops general moral principles which guide the ego.

Among important features of the personality is how the ego manages conflict. The need of the ego and superego to exert control over the id in the cause of social responsibility creates further conflicts. *Anxiety* results from such conflicts. The ego deals with anxiety by bringing into play various *defence mechanisms*, of which repression, already mentioned, is one. Other important ones are as follows:

- *Projection* – unwanted ideas associated with something the ego wants to protect become attached in our minds to another person or thing.
- *Splitting* – contradictory ideas and feelings are kept in separate mental compartments, and applied to different people or situations with inconsistent results.
- *Sublimation* – energy (from the id) which is directed towards unwanted activities (often sexual) is redirected towards more acceptable activities.
- *Rationalisation* – acceptable reasons for particular activities are devised, when the real ones are unacceptable and repressed.

Freud's later work concentrated on ego and object relations. This was picked up after his death (in classic works by Anna Freud and Hartman) and has been influential as the basis of much psychoanalytic thought today. Ego psychology and object relations theories consider that children have the capacity to deal with the outside world (object relations) from an early age. Development of the ego is the growth of our capacity to learn from experience. This especially uses rational parts of our minds through using thinking (cognition), perception and memory.

Certain psychodynamic theorists and practitioners have achieved widespread and sometimes criticised influence on social work, pre-eminently Melanie Klein (1959; Salzberger-Wittenberg, 1970); Winnicott (1964) and Bowlby (1951). Their influence comes from their focus on work with children. Klein discusses two emotional life 'positions' which emerge in early childhood. One is a persecutory position, which comes from fear of being alone and failing to survive; the other, depressive, position arises later from fear of destroying the mother. Experiencing these helps people to learn tolerance of ambivalence, and anxiety about being destructive. Winnicott's work is concerned with object relations. It is about how children learn to adapt from focusing on their inner world by developing capacity for dealing with the outside world. Bowlby directed the psychoanalytic interest in early mother–child relationships towards research and theory about maternal deprivation. This is the idea that if we deprive children of contact with their mothers, their personal development is impeded. In recent years, this has developed into a more extensive theory about the importance of attachment (Bowlby, 1969, 1973, 1980; Aldgate, 1991; Howe, 1995). Attachment is particularly to the mother but also elsewhere. Experience of it affects the development of other relationships subsequently. The effects of loss of attachment are especially important. Such loss extends from death to loss of a parent by divorce (Garber, 1992). Evidence suggests that deprivation and disadvantage have major damaging effects on children's develop-ment and later life. However, relationships between children and parents, and a variety of other factors, including the social environ-ment, is relevant, not just maternal deprivation. Many social and psychological factors help protect against the damaging effects of deprivation (Rutter, 1981).

The idea of loss has a wider importance in psychoanalysis. Mourning is regarded as a response to all kinds of loss, not just the death of someone close (Salzberger-Wittenberg, 1970). Parkes (1972) interprets bereavement in many situations as regression to childhood experiences of stress due to loss. Pincus (1976) argues that, in typical family reactions to death, hidden feelings about past relationships may be disclosed. The intensity of feeling when grief takes hold is particularly susceptible to psychoanalysis. However, Smith (1982) argues that much behaviour in bereavement and loss comes from social expectations of behaviour in such situations. She proposes that a phenomenological or existential interpretation of bereavement is more appropriate (see Chapters 7 and 8).

These more modern psychoanalytic developments link with sociological ideas, especially the idea that people are part of social systems
and play a social role. Recent work in the object relations tradition
particularly by Kohut (1978; see also Eisenhuth, 1981; Lane, 1984;
Lowenstein, 1985) emphasises that children develop a perception of
their 'self' and their difference from the surrounding world at a very
young age.

Treatment theory in classic psychoanalysis required therapists to be
'blank screens', making themselves as anonymous as possible so that
patients projected their fantasies onto the therapists. *Transference*
occurs when the patient transfers unconscious feelings about their
parents onto the therapist, and treats the therapist as though they were
that parent. This was a way of revealing unconscious ideas. By stimulating transference, conflicts arising from early relationship difficulties with parents and causing present behaviour difficulties are
revealed. Social work adapts this idea, referring more generally to
how emotional remains of past relationships and experiences affect
our present behaviour, especially in relationships (Irvine, 1956).
Counter-transference occurred when analysts irrationally reacted to
patients bringing in past experiences to the relationship. An example
is given later in this chapter.

Most psychoanalytic techniques are concerned with revealing
hidden thoughts and feelings. Undesirable behaviour is thought to be
caused by repressed conflicts leaking out in various ways, requiring
more than ordinary attempts to disclose its origins. Once revealed and
properly understood, the conflicts would no longer cause difficulties
in behaviour. Thus, traditional psychoanalytic therapy is concerned
with giving people *insight* into their repressed feelings. This is
another emphasis which has been altered in ego psychology. It often
concentrates on how people manage their relationships with the
outside world through extending rational control of their lives.

Connections

Understanding psychodynamic theory is a prerequisite to examining
other social work theories, since its influence is pervasive, as we shall
see. A variety of schools of thought and applications or developments
have grown up. Although most use psychodynamic ideas in general,
there is, mainly in the United States, interest in applying ideas from
psychodynamic theorists who are a long way from Freud and the

mainstream development of psychoanalysis (such as Borensweig on Jung, 1980; O'Connor on Adler, 1992). Modern psychoanalytic theory has moved away from the idea of drives as the basic influence on behaviour (Lowenstein, 1985). It is more concerned with how individuals interact with their social world; it has become more social than biological. Brearley (1991) usefully summarises these concerns as about three key relationships: between self and significant others, between past and present experience and between inner and outer reality. This has come about through the influence of ego psychology (E. Goldstein, 1984). Ego psychology has become closely linked with systems models, particularly in ecological systems theory (Germain, 1978; Siporin, 1980), and crisis intervention.

A recent appraisal of the role of psychoanalysis in social work (Pearson *et al.*, 1988) shows that there is a range of developments, and in different countries various streams of thought. Ego psychology, for example, has been much more strongly influential in the United States than elsewhere, whereas object relations theory has two differing streams of thought: one British, based around the work of psychoanalysts such as Fairbairn (1954; McCouat, 1969) and Guntrip (1968; Hazell, 1995); and a different approach in the United States (E. Goldstein, 1984). Lacan (1979) has developed a line of psychoanalytic thought which has enabled some writers to make links with Marxism (see Bocock, 1988: 76). This is because he reinterprets the unconscious as a structure of symbols like language, to which our conscious behaviour points. Our society and culture impose these symbols upon us (Dowrick, 1983). If this is so, we can make ideas from Marxist historical materialism fit with some interpretations of psychoanalysis. Such ideas are closely related to postmodern ideas, which stress how language interprets and structures our experience of the world. Another radical ideology, feminism, has also attempted an interpretation of psychoanalysis as an explanation of patriarchy (that is, male domination of social relations and oppression of women). Leonard (1984), in his attempt to construct a Marxist approach to individual psychology, is doubtful of the intellectual viability of these attempts to interpret psychoanalysis in a radical way.

The politics of psychodynamic theory

Psychoanalytic theory has influenced social work theory in three phases (Payne, 1992). Before the 1920s in the United States, and the late 1930s in Britain, it had little impact. Then there was a period in which it was dominant, until the end of the 1960s. During this period it formed so powerful an influence that it created approaches within social work which remain to this day. Since then, it has been one of many contested theories, used by specialists, but retaining influence because of the strength of its influence on basic social work practice. Therefore, its theories of development, personality and therapy are not explicitly practised in a widespread way. Its influence is more complex and indirect in the following ways:

- Freud has influence on Western culture. Many of his ideas are common currency, and appear in social work because of this rather than because the theory has been directly applied to social work.
- There are different aspects to his work, developed at different times. Ideas came into social work at intervals. Ego psychology, which is now important, arrived later than basic psychodynamic ideas.
- Freud inspired both followers and dissidents, so some related theories share ideas with Freud but sometimes disagree with his approach.
- Psychodynamic ideas were the first strong explanatory theory in social work, and so have created the environment to which later theories have naturalised. They thus influence a range of theoretically distinct ideas in practice.
- Its therapy has influenced social work's permissive, open, listening (Wallen, 1982) style of relationship (indeed, the emphasis on relationship at all; see Perlman, 1957b) rather than a directive and controlling style. It also encouraged seeking explanation and understanding of personality rather than action.
- Psychodynamic theory influenced social work's emphasis on feelings and unconscious factors in particular (Yelloly, 1980) rather than events and thought. Many ideas such as the unconscious, insight, aggression, conflict, anxiety, maternal relationships and transference come from psychodynamic theory. These are terms which are often used in watered-down strength as a common language in social work and in everyday life. Psychodynamic theory gains in importance by their continued availability to practitioners.
- The theoretical sophistication and complexity of its ideas make it attractive and interesting to explore, as compared with newer and less-developed theories (Fraiberg, 1978; Lowenstein, 1985).

- The continued influence of the specialised settings and groups of social workers who practise psychodynamic work explicitly has a wider impact – in Britain, for example, the Group for the Advancement of Psychodynamics and Psychotherapy in Social Work (GAPS) and its journal.
- The important focus in social work on childhood and early relationships and maternal deprivation comes from psychodynamic theory.
- The emphasis on mental illness and disturbed behaviour as a focus of much social work comes from the importance in the 1920s and 30s of social work's association with psychiatry and psychodynamic treatment.
- Insight as an important part of social work understanding and treatment comes originally from psychodynamic theory.
- We give less emphasis to social factors in social work than to psychological and emotional ones because of psychodynamic theory's influence (Weick, 1981).

Woods and Hollis: psychosocial therapy

Woods and Hollis (1990) offer a famous account of casework from a strong psychodynamic base. The 1990 edition is the fourth, and moves increasingly towards being a general social work text, incorporating other perspectives, particularly ecological systems theory – said (p. 9) to be inseparable from psychodynamic theory – and family therapy. The first two editions were by Hollis alone; she died after publication of the third. It is in the tradition of diagnostic theory, whose most important exponent was Hamilton (1950). The crucial elements are the idea of the *person-in-situation* (some writers, following ecological theory, now refer to the 'person-in-environment') and the *classification of casework treatment*. The term 'casework' is retained, although in the United States the term 'clinical social work' is often used as a substitute. However, the latter's meaning is unclear, since it may refer to a setting where medical treatment is the focus. The empirical base of the theory is accumulated practical experience, and quantitative research methods are considered inappropriate to individual responses to human difficulty. Also, social workers may have a role where measuring effectiveness by conventional indicators would be difficult.

Casework is about improving relationships among people within their life situation – the person-in-situation. Social work has always considered, and must consider, internal psychological processes, external social factors and how they affect one another. People are affected by *press* from the environment and by *stress* from conflicts within themselves. Social work aims to resolve problems which arise from a 'disequilibrium between people and their environments' (1990: 28). Clients may be affected by problems within various social systems, or between them. Press and stress interact with each other in a complex way. There is a strong emphasis on personality, described in psychodynamic structural terms (namely, id, ego, superego). The ego is the main focus for dealing with the outside world. Defence mechanisms are important for understanding how people interact with the environment. This emphasis gives the book a psychoanalytic and psychological bias, despite claimed concern for social issues. Workers may be able to act successfully by affecting the environment directly, but rarely do so alone: direct work with clients on their attitudes and reactions is usually required (p. 48). It is important to modify the *balance* of forces affecting a client. The most significant sociological concept used is role theory; communication problems are also relevant.

Sources of distress come from three interacting factors:

1 *Press from the environment in current life situations.* For example, Sandra, a young mother, was worried because she was getting angry and hitting her children. Her stress came from the need to manage an old damp house in a street where there was a great deal of stealing from houses. It meant she could not fulfil her wish and need to be a loving and successful parent.

2 *Immature ego or superego functioning from hereditary or developmental problems.* Strong childhood needs and drives retained into adulthood causing unreasonable demands on the situation. For example, Christine felt rejected by a rather cold mother and father who were busy with their careers. She continued to seek love and affection, making her husband feel unable to respond enough. George, a man with learning disabilities, had been overprotected by his mother, so that he had not learned socially acceptable methods of relating to women. In a day centre he was aggressive or over-affectionate. He had not learned to manage relationships very well with people and things outside himself.

3 *Defence mechanisms or superego functions which are too rigid.*
For example, John had parents who insisted on very high
standards of behaviour at the table, and sent him to bed when he
could not conform. Hungry, he later took food from the kitchen,
and was reported by the parents to the police for stealing. Their
rigid standards, derived from childhood, made relations with their
son very difficult.

Psychoanalysis involves releasing and dealing with the deeply hidden
feelings, and this is what is often meant by 'deep' casework or going
'deeply' into a problem. Social work is concerned with the balance of
forces and modifying how these affect one another by working on
current behaviour or memories. Even affecting one aspect of the situation will affect others as the balance changes (compare this with the
ideas of homoeostasis and reciprocity in systems theory – see
Chapter 6). This is done by achieving 'internalised modifications'
(p. 55) by various means:

- *Ventilation.* The client expresses feelings such as hostility or
  aggression which, while suppressed, are misdirecting their
  thinking and action. This treatment approach is related to
  catharsis and abreaction in traditional psychoanalytic theory.
- *Corrective relationship.* The client experiences with the worker a
  relationship like that of mother and daughter which compensates
  for a previous unsatisfactory relationship. This implies
  transference and counter-transference in worker–client
  relationships.
- *Examine current personal interactions.* The client is helped to
  understand how these are affected by past relationships and
  experience.

The treatment model emphasises '*reflective* procedures' as clients
are thinking about and trying to understand their person-in-situation
in a helpful *relationship* with the worker. 'Reflection' here means
thinking about and trying to understand. Workers also try direct
influence on the client and environmental situation. So in the cases
of Christine, Sandra and George (above), the worker would establish a relationship with each. In Christine's case, she could discuss
how she had experienced her parents' attitudes. The worker could
join with her in discussing her own experience. They could see
together how their experiences were leading them to act now in rela-

tion to others. In Sandra's case, alongside an understanding relationship concerned with exploring her feelings, the worker would help Sandra to say to herself that she would not hit her children, to identify times when and situations in which this happened and find ways of avoiding them. The authority of the agency would be used to try to get Sandra rehoused. With George, the authority would allow a worker in the day centre to work out with George a simple set of rules of appropriate behaviour, and, as he made mistakes in applying them, to stop him at the time and show him what sorts of behaviour might be more appropriate.

Hollis's *classification of casework methods* covers communications within interviews with clients and communications during environmental changes. It developed from several previous classifications. Some of these emphasised the difference between direct work with clients and indirect work in the environment. Others focused on the difference between supportive work and work seeking social or personal change. Hollis's classification is summarised in Table 3.1, and is particularly concerned with identifying appropriate approaches in interview situations of communication between client and worker.

From this brief summary table, it is obvious that the environmental work is much less fully realised than the individual work. It is seen in terms of the worker's relationships with individuals surrounding the client rather than intervention in agencies and communities or at a political level. Responsibilities for changing inappropriate agency services are acknowledged.

Moving on to other aspects of psychosocial casework, Woods and Hollis attach importance to integrating family therapy into social work, which has always focused on individuals within families. This is an example of the strong concern in social work for the family as a social institution.

Psychosocial study reflects the origins of psychosocial casework in diagnostic theory, one of whose principal tenets was the importance of distinguishing between the different categories of problems presented by clients so that casework could be directed appropriately. Giving importance to *differential diagnosis* is a mark of psychodynamic theory (see Turner, 1983). In Christine's case, for example, it is important to distinguish between the effects of her past relationships with her parents and other factors which might be possibilities in such a case. For example, women often become depressed because of lack of support from their husbands in their life. The demand for love and affection from the husband might easily have been a product of such feelings.

Table 3.1   Hollis's classification of casework methods

	Procedures in client–worker communications	
Procedure	*Purpose*	*Worker's actions*
Sustainment	Reduce anxiety, poor self-image, and low self-confidence. Set up relationship with worker.	Express *acceptance,* interest, shared concern with client. *Reassure* client that worker understands strong, irrational feelings. Express confidence. *Encourage* client in the relationship and planned activities. *Reach out* by showing a wish to help. *Non-verbal behaviour* such as eye-contact and touch may be sustaining.
Direct influence	Promote particular behaviours by force of worker's opinion.	Move through degrees of directiveness: state opinion, suggest, underline, urge, insist. Advice given by trusted worker is appreciated, but important decisions should come from client's reflection, not worker's imposition. Emphasise approved behaviours. In the end act (e.g. remove child from abusive parents). Avoid inadvertent influence by biased phrasing and language.
Exploration, description, ventilation	Understand clients' view of situation and selves. Bring out feelings.	Psychosocial study. Anger, hatred, grief, anxiety, guilt are brought out and reduced in strength by being expressed. Avoid ventilation if it becomes habitual. Limit ventilation in joint interview (e.g. with husband and wife) where it may offend the other and obstruct progress.
Person-situation reflection on 1 Others, outside world, client's health. 2 Effects of behaviour on self and others. 3 Own behaviour. 4 Causes which lie in interactions between self and others and outside effects. 5 Self-evaluation. 6 Worker and treatment process.	Improve clients' understanding.	'Extraflection' about knowledge and understanding of situation (e.g. health, other people, housing, money). Consider effects of clients' behaviour on others and selves. 'Intraflection' about clients' own responses to situation. These are rarely explained directly. The technique is to lead client to look at issues and achieve self-revelation. Clients examine how external stimuli affect internal responses and produce behaviour. Self-evaluation about values and self-image. Client should examine agency limitations, requirements, the worker and feelings about coming for help.
Pattern-dynamic understanding	Promote client's understanding of patterns of behaviour and thought.	Encourage reflection on patterns of behaviour, especially where these reveal ego defences (e.g. avoidance, hostility). Identify superego problems (e.g. being too hard on yourself; excessive reliance on religious books). Discuss strong needs (e.g. strong emotional needs, unreasonable fear) perhaps through client's reactions to worker. Identify personality disorders.
Developmental reflection	Clients' understanding of the effects of the past.	Unlike psychoanalysis, not a major feature. Should only be used when relevant; encourage re-evaluation. Avoid intellectualising as a defence. Transference sometimes explains unexpected behaviour towards worker, so focus on worker–client relationship.

Procedure	Purpose	Worker's Actions
Types of resources	Services for client.	Use own agency services efficiently, seek to improve them. Use resources of secondary setting (e.g. hospital, school, court) where worker works. Use workers in other agencies; use non-social work agencies. Use 'instrumental collaterals' (e.g. employers, landlord) in relationship with clients; where dealing with powerful people, wait for the right moment. Use 'expressive collaterals' in relationship involving feelings with clients. Worker should identify with client, not other workers or agencies.
Types of communication	Relationships with collaterals.	Same procedures used as in worker–client communications with other people who are relevant to the client (see first four procedures above). Confidentiality to client should be considered before discussing with others.
Types of roles	Acting on behalf of client.	Act as provider, locator or creator of resources; act as interpreter of the client to others. Act as mediator between clients and others. Act as aggressive intervenor between client and others (e.g. child protection).

Procedures in environmental work (table title)

The important first stage of social work is to establish a relationship. There has been a move towards more informal, less distant relationships, with both having skills and knowledge to contribute, and encouraging client participation. However, the worker should take responsibility for effective communication, restricting openness to where it is relevant to the client's needs, rather than meeting the worker's need to feel comfortable or liked. Social relationships, or the impression that this is the nature of the relationship, deny the reality and should be avoided.

Psychosocial study at the beginning of contact with clients gives an interim view of the problem and direction of work on it. After this, psychosocial study (gathering and ordering information), diagnostic understanding (thinking about the information) and treatment proceed together. *Study* involves observation, examination and deduction about existing and recent relationships, environment and events in the client's life. Does it fit with the *average expectable environment*? If not, we might expect environmental pressure to be a factor. *Clients' capacity* for functioning normally or well should be assessed, as well as actual behaviour. Detailed analysis of patterns or sequences of events helps to disentangle complex relationships. In families, communication and the extent to which relationships are complementary – that is, feeding on each other – should be explored. Early history should be explored if particularly relevant. *Diagnostic understanding* involves both worker and client in deciding what is the trouble, and what can be changed. Then, *dynamic understanding* is an attempt to explain why the problems exist. They are then classified into categories which help identify social consequences. *Health* problems show where social consequences need to be prepared for. For example, a cancer patient may need preparing for death. *Problem* categories – for example, parent–child, old age, unemployment – identify the focus and the major requirements for treatment. They also show where others may be involved and need to share in the work. *Clinical* diagnosis identifies major personality characteristics which will be relevant.

The next stage is to choose *treatment objectives*. Long-range aims will be an improvement in clients' personal and social lives. Motivation and clients' and others' social values are relevant in deciding a particular target. Intermediate aims come from the problems and dynamic understanding. Workers must consider whether change is realistically possible and select aims accordingly. Resistance must be assessed to particular options and directions. The needs, wishes and policies of other family members, agencies and important individuals will be factors in the decision. Some factors may be impossible to change, and workers should identify and work round these.

Treatment procedures must be chosen to accord with the aims. When clients are anxious in the early stages, workers must choose acceptable procedures, without sacrificing the need for movement. The client's personality and situational factors should affect the choice of procedures. For example, if the client is overwhelmed with practical problems such as poverty, these should be the focus. Ethnic factors, where present, may predominate. Pattern-dynamic and developmental reflection are only useful where behaviour and thought patterns are a serious factor, and clients are able to work on such issues. Major areas of concern will be anxiety (such as about being a good parent) and guilt (for instance, about failure to help an elderly relative).

Alternative psychodynamic formulations of social work

Functional theory arose in the United States during the 1930s, contesting pre-eminence with diagnostic theory, which became the forerunner of psychosocial casework. The latest extensive book expressing the view is Smalley's (1967). It is a significantly distinct form of practice found only in the United States. However, Dore (1990) argues that functional theory's lasting influences on social work include the idea of self-determination, the importance of structuring practice around time and the emphasis on process and growth. Functional theory is distinct from structural-functionalism (see Chapter 7). The term 'functional' is applied because it emphasises that the *function of social work agencies* gives practice in each setting its form and direction.

Another distinctive feature of functional social work is that its psychological base derives from the work of Rank, a disciple of Freud. Rather than work from diagnosing illnesses and treating problems, functional social workers emphasise helping their clients in personal *growth*. The casework relationship releases capacity for growth. Greater emphasis than in psychosocial casework is given to social and cultural issues in human development. Functional social work stresses that social work is a *process* of interaction between clients and workers rather than a series of acts or procedures as psychosocial casework has it. Hofstein (1964: 15) defines process as 'recurrent patterning of a sequence of changes over time and in a particular direction'.

Smalley also applies functional theory specifically to group and community work. Phillips (1957) and Ryder (1976) describe functional groupwork.

Five basic principles of functional social work (Smalley, 1970) are as follows:

1 involving the client in diagnosis and understanding of the issues worked on, which are constantly changing;
2 conscious understanding and use of *time phases* (beginning, middle and end) – this is a classic feature of functional social work;
3 use of *agency function* gives form to the work, offers accountability and a concrete role for clients to understand;
4 clear understanding of the structure or form of the *social work process* – again, a classic feature of functional social work;
5 social work uses relationships to engage clients in helping themselves.

Functional theory avoids taking a medical and problem-based model, and emphasises positive, forward-looking change instead. Social causation and issues are more important than in psychosocial case-work. It is less concerned also with internal feelings and more with interactions with the outside world.

Problem-solving casework is another analysis of casework practice made by Perlman (1957a). Her book was an important text for many years. It is psychodynamic in its approach because that was the accepted psychological base of social work at the time it was written (Perlman, 1986). Her work was distinct from the conventions of diagnostic social work because it emphasised dealing with the presenting problems of the client and current difficulties in the environment (Abrams, 1983). There is less emphasis on irrational and internal motivation. Perlman empha-sises the importance of looking at four aspects of the situation: the *person* with whom work is done, the *problem* presented, the *place* where work is done, and the work *process*. The model thus takes in these two latter aspects which are associated with functional social work; Perlman was influenced by several ideas from functional theory (Perlman, 1986). Clients are assumed to have failings in their capacity to solve problems, and need help in overcoming obstacles to improving their coping capacity. This approach is rooted in ego psychology (Perlman, 1970: 169; 1986: 261), with its emphasis on how the ego manages outside relationships. The book concentrates especially on study and diagnosis of the problems; treatment is ill-defined. Perlman (1986: 261) claims that this is intentional since 'the essential elements of the total helping process... are to be found... within the first few hours'.

Perlman's model is an important forerunner of task-centred case-work, which has developed the idea of problem analysis (see Chapter 4). It is still used as the conceptual basis of important texts, such as that of Compton and Galaway (1994), who expand it with a more detailed analysis of stages of practice, drawing on task-centred work and systems perpectives. The idea of 'problem' as a concrete defini-tion of the issues looked at by a social worker and client is widely used as a pragmatic basis for planning work, outside a formal problem-solving perspective (for example Bunston, 1985; Sucato, 1978). We should not necessarily see such uses of 'problem' as allied to Perlman's model.

Ego psychology and ego-oriented casework offer a more explicit formulation of the relationship of modern psychoanalytic theory to casework activities. Early influential works promoting this perspec-tive (Parad, 1958; Parad and Miller, 1963) laid foundations for it as a separate and identifiable stream of social work thought. E. Goldstein

(1984) provides a clear and practical introduction. She identifies two sets of contributing ideas:

1 classic Freudian theory, with its emphasis on the unconscious and the ego's role in defending the mind and mediating between different parts of the mind;
2 modern ego psychology, with its emphasis on the ego as the rational, problem-solving part of the mind, dealing with the outside world and minimising the aspect of managing unconscious drives.

She deals with ego-oriented practice in three aspects: assessment, intervention and the worker–client relationship.

Assessment involves looking at clients' present and past ways of *coping*, an important concept in ego psychology. This includes emotion and practical coping with things that happen to clients and things that they have to do, their inner capacity and external circumstances. The starting point is to share the problem, discuss the ways clients have already tried, and look for other possible ways of dealing with it. The plan of action then involves choosing between three major strategies:

1 improving clients' internal capacities;
2 changing outside circumstances affecting them;
3 improving how their internal and external worlds fit together.

This is similar to the person-in-situation formulation of psychosocial work.

Intervention may be either ego-supporting or ego-modifying, and applied either directly through psychological means or indirectly on clients' environments. These distinctions also informed Hollis's classification of practice. Goldstein's distinction of these two approaches makes useful differences in practice clear. *Ego-supporting* interventions focus on present behaviour, conscious thought and environmental change. They involve learning or mastering new skills, through experiencing a worthwhile relationship with the worker. They use directive and educational techniques and are more likely to be short- rather than long-term. *Ego-modifying* interventions, by contrast, concentrate on past and present unconscious feelings and drives, and avoid environmental changes. Efforts concentrate on giving insight into feelings and resolving emotional conflicts, understanding transference in the worker–client relationship, use non-directive and reflective techniques and are generally long-term.

Client–worker relationships are similar to but different from ordinary human relationships. Their special features are as follows:

- Client needs form the basic aim of the interactions, instead of both parties' needs being involved, as in most relationships.
- Workers involve themselves in the relationship in a disciplined and controlled way, rather than simply by inclination and emotional response.
- Important social work professional values are always involved, so whatever the client's personal characteristics or behaviour, the worker is always prepared to take part. This is not typical of ordinary relationships, where inclination, liking and the sort of responses made affect relationships.

Client–worker relationships have rational and irrational aspects. The former are about the tasks to be undertaken and work towards the agreed objectives. The latter come from the feelings involved in past relationships. So, for example, Howard was a social worker who in his teens had been homosexually assaulted, and was working with Joe. Joe had come for help because of his feelings of isolation and lack of self-worth arising from concealing his homosexual life style, which he had been unable to reveal to his parents, his brother and sisters. A plan for talking to his brother and then disclosing this important part of his person to his family was agreed. However, this relied on Howard's personal support and involvement through these proceedings. Joe came to experience Howard as cold and rejecting, and felt that he could not go on. In exploration with his supervisor, Howard identified his anger towards the person who had assaulted him as the past event with present feelings which was getting in the way of his relationship with Joe. Howard's feelings about this event were unresolved. That is, he had hidden his anger at this exploitation of his person, rather than expressing it fully and coming to a rational view that he had not been badly hurt. He could not avoid fearing that others, like Joe, might cause similar hurt elsewhere. He was entitled to his anger and fear, but hid it because he accepted that applying it to others like Joe was unreasonable. Nonetheless, his rational understanding of that did not overcome the expression of his hidden feelings, and this why Joe could sense his rejection. This case is an example of counter-transference; how irrational aspects of a past relationship brought forward to a present one can get in the way of using the special helping features of worker–client relationships. It also illustrates the importance and role of supervision, another important social work practice derived from psychoanalysis.

Therapeutic environments: an application to residential care

Psychodynamic theory has been applied to residential care work through a variety of theoretical developments. Righton (1975) shows the theoretical relationships between three different theoretical positions:

1 *Planned environment therapy* (Franklin, 1968; Wills, 1973) was based on work with maladjusted adolescents originally in the Second World War. It has its roots in psychoanalytic theory, and radical education, including the work of Homer Lane (Wills, 1964), Neill (1964) and Lyward (Burn, 1956).
2 *Milieu therapy* is a mainly American concept, used in the work of writers such as Polsky (1968), applying psychodynamic groupwork with maladjusted young people. It also includes ego psychology and the ideas of Lewin (1951) on field theory and life space (that is, the total physical, social, cultural and psychological environment surrounding a resident) as a way of understanding interactions between individuals and within groups, particularly in residential care with adolescent offenders (Redl, 1959). Keenan (1991) shows how life-space work focuses on the purpose for clients being in residential care.
3 *Therapeutic communities,* which derive from the work of Maxwell Jones (1968) and Clark (1974) in psychiatric hospitals. This has also been applied in community settings including day hospitals (Whiteley, 1979), and in hostels and housing schemes of various kinds through the worldwide work of the Richmond Fellowship (Jansen, 1980; Manning, 1989).

The psychodynamic groupwork of Bion (1961) influenced some of this work. A related area of influence is the work of psychodynamic organisation consultants, particularly those from the Tavistock Clinic and Institute (Brearley, 1991). Well-known contributions include Menzies-Lyth's (1988) work, particularly showing how staff facing difficult emotional situations in hospital settings used psychological defences to maintain their emotional equilibrium. Bettelheim's (1950) influential and atmospheric accounts of psychoanalytic residential care practice with disturbed children calls on his war-time concentration camp experience.

Perhaps the most widely influential of these models of residential care practice is the therapeutic community. Kennard's (1983) account of its main principles offers a useful summary of the practice of all three forms of work:

- Informal and communal atmosphere.
- Group meetings are a central aspect of therapy.
- All participants share in the work of running the community.
- Residents are auxiliary therapists.
- Authority is shared between staff and residents.
- Basic psychodynamic principles are accepted.
- Basic equality of all members.
- The community is a 'closed order' whose basic values cannot be disputed – a strong moral and ideological component.

Commentary

The brief account, above, of Woods and Hollis's analysis of psychosocial casework shows how its roots lie in psychoanalytic theory. However, it is an adapted theory, relying particularly on later ideas, and focusing on functioning in the present rather than exploration of the past. There is a concentration on feelings, on personal reactions to social situations rather than the situations themselves, exploratory reflection rather than action. Personality structure, defences and anxiety make significant appearances.

It is a caricature to say that there is no concern for social change. This is considered and approved, although with caution about its deviating from work on clients' personal needs (1990: 170); social workers' responsibility for leadership in policy change (p. 487) and priority for ethnic and practical problems is acknowledged (*passim*). Even so, the focus of this modern account of casework is on internal feelings about the outside world and on person and family rather than social factors.

The reliance on psychoanalytic systems and role theories is evidence of a theory which accepts social order. It is social and personal *disorder* which we must understand and deal with. Although things may be wrong with clients' present environment, the burden of this perspective is to help them accept it. The worker seeks social reform as a separate activity. The view is medical. Health is a frequently mentioned issue; diagnosis and treatment are uncritically accepted as the model. Controversial interpretations of internal dynamics are accepted as accurate representations to guide treatment. Study is about finding facts, and those holding postmodern and constructionist views and humanists would quarrel with the assumption that there is one understanding of any social situation to be identified. Woods and Hollis would accept a conflict perspective, and it is true that feelings are facts to be worked with. However, they do not press the possibility that the nature of the phenomena worked with may be ambivalent, unreconcilable with clients' interests or unresolvable, although they emphasise how difficult they are.

The existential critique of psychoanalysis goes further. In this view, the personality structures of psychoanalysis are illusions, and the adjustment achieved always inadequate or provisional. The only true understanding of humanity is an appreciation of the wholeness of internal and external experience and the paradoxes of existing but the inability to understand the meaning of existence (Krill, 1978: 40). Insight techniques may encourage self-preoccupation rather than change.

The behaviourist and cognitive critique also doubts the value of inferring personality structures. However, the main thrust of criticism from this perspective is that the approach is not easily testable empirically, since it relies on such inferences. Behaviourists argue that dependence on careful observation and description of definable behaviour is better. The emphasis on feelings and emotions rather than rational thought is also a failing, according to this view; it leads to lack of clarity and means that people may be disabled from acting if they believe that unchangeable things in the past are causing their present behaviour. A cognitive theorist would argue that people can manage their behaviour from their own rational minds and need training to do so. It is important not to caricature psychodynamic theory from this perspective. Modern psychoanalysis too largely concentrates on how people can manage their world rationally through the ego and object relations.

More broadly, features of psychodynamic social work that arouse critical comment are as follows:

● It has a *scientific*, and originally biological, approach to
  explanation, in a theory which cannot be easily tested in

conventional scientific ways. Many argue that these do not reflect respect for human self-determination (Strean, 1979).

- Its account of female development and personality is weak to the extent that it is seen as reinforcing *stereotypes of women* as domestic, child-bearing, socially, intellectually and perhaps morally inferior, although some use has been made of the account in developing feminist perspectives on psychology. Mitchell (1975), for example, argues that psychoanalysis is a useful means of understanding how men achieve and maintain supremacy in a patriarchal society. Sayers (1986, 1988) contends that not enough attention has been given to explaining women's resistance to subordination in a patriarchal society and that psychoanalytic theory can also be helpful here.
- Related to its scientific approach, psychoanalysis operates on a *medical model* which assumes the patient's sickness, which an expert therapist cures, rather than a more equal model of relationships between client and worker.
- Originating in middle-class, Jewish Vienna, it is very limited in its *cultural assumptions*, so that it assumes that deviations from a limited, white, middle-class norm are abnormal behaviour to be cured. In recent years this has been controversial in that psychoanalysts may see variations due to ethnic difference as abnormalities needing treatment. Similarly, its attitude to homosexuality as requiring treatment and as associated with maternal relationships has been regarded as objectionable (Strean, 1979: 56).
- The use of *insight* as a major therapeutic technique may lead psychodynamic workers to stop at the point where clients have understood what is happening to them emotionally. This does not help them to take practical action to do something about it. Since psychoanalysis is non-directive, this tends to make workers' help insubstantial.
- Its use of concepts sometimes induces workers to *blame the victim* for social problems of agency inadequacies, by interpreting the client's behaviour as maladjusted if it conflicts with the assumptions of the worker or agency. Gitterman's (1983) example is the use of psychological 'resistance' to avoid responsibility when clients are unhappy with aspects of the agency's service.
- It is a theory for a talking therapy, preferring verbally able clients with psychological problems, who can take part in discussion and self-examination. This plays down the importance of less

articulate, working-class clients with more practical problems
(Strean, 1979).
- Environmental factors are given less prominence than internal
  psychological ones. This limits the possible range of
  interventions, and narrows the assumptions from which workers
  start (Strean, 1979).
- Psychodynamic ideas have limited concern for social reform,
  which excludes a major element of social work (Strean, 1979).

On the positive side, understanding psychodynamic perspectives
helps us understand many of the origins of important ideas in social
work: 'conflict', 'aggression', 'concern for mother–child relationships', 'ego', 'sublimation', 'repression' and 'resistance' are all terms
we use, often without a thought for their technical meanings in the
theories from which their use originates. These perspectives have
proved a rich source of ideas and understanding. Many people value
them because, with all their limitations, they give a sense of the
complexity of human lives and developments and of how our minds
and bodies interact with each other and the social environment.

4

Crisis Intervention and Task-centred Models

Wider theoretical perspectives

The classic formulation of crisis intervention as a technique is that of Caplan on preventive psychiatry (1965). The method's origins, therefore, are in mental health work, and on prevention rather than treatment of illness. Parad and Parad describe the development process (1990b: 12–16). Lindemann's (1944) paper dealt with grief reactions in various groups of patients, showing how people coped with bereavement crises. They managed better if they had coped with previous crises in their lives, less well if they had not resolved past problems. A group of mental health workers around Lindemann and Caplan constructed the ideas of crisis intervention while working with several community mental health problems. Their work continues concerning preventive networks, and has led to a variety of developments influencing networking ideas (see Chapter 6). Theoretically, crisis intervention uses elements of ego psychology from a psychodynamic perspective. So it focuses on emotional responses to external events and how to control them rationally. Young (1983) analyses crisis intervention concepts alongside parallels in Chinese philosophy, suggesting that we might transplant the theory to Chinese culture. She points to the 'doctrine of the mean', that is, maintaining our system in balance leading to a state of harmony and the Chinese assumption that people naturally gravitate towards fulfilment. The idea of *wu wei* proposes that life is constant change, which people should study and with which they should harmonise.

Task-centred work originated wholly within social work, from a famous series of studies by Reid and Shyne (1969), Reid and Epstein (1972a, b) and Reid (1985). See Marsh (1991) for an account of them. In these it was discovered, first, contrary to expectations, that truncated long-term treatment was as effective as long-term treatment which ran its full course, second that 'planned short-term treatment' was effective and, third, that the task-centred model of practice devised as a result was effective. In its focus on problems, it had links with Perlman's problem-solving approach to casework (see Chapter 3), which it has largely displaced.

Both models and cognitive-behavioural methods are probably the most widely used examples within social work of a range of 'brief treatment' approaches in social work which have become more important in recent years. Epstein (1992: 41–2) compares ten different models. She contends that among them criteria for selection of clients, the organisation of treatment procedures and the approach to terminating contact vary considerably. Compared with longer-term and particularly psychodynamic models, however, she argues that generally the focus is on 'up-front' problems. Also, advice and guidance are given, contrary to convention in more psychotherapeutic approaches.

Connections

These two models of social work have some common features, so presenting them together offers comparison and contrast. Both stress brief interventions, though they may string these together in a series. Epstein (1992: 102) treats both as examples of a range of brief treatment methods, all the others being described as psychotherapy or therapy. Reid (1992: 12) acknowledges the influence of crisis intervention on the development of task-centred work. Golan (1986: 309), viewing the relationship in the opposite direction, holds that research on task-centred work supports practice interventions in crisis intervention. Roberts and Dziegielewski (1995) treat crisis intervention as a form of brief cognitive therapy. Gray (1987) describes task-centred work within a crisis intervention psychiatric team. Both crisis and task-centred work are structured, so action is planned and fits a pre-ordained pattern. 'Contracts' or other explicit agreements between worker and client are used. Circumstances in which each may be used are specified.

Task-centred work also links with behavioural approaches (Howe, 1987). Some suggested links include the use of contracts, but in fact these are widely used outside behavioural work (Corden and Preston-Shoot, 1987a; Hutten, 1977). Neither approach is formally connected with behavioural approaches. Crisis intervention is explicitly based on psychodynamic ego psychology. Task-centred casework rejects any specific psychological or sociological base for its methods and seeks to be 'eclectic and integrative' (Reid, 1992: 13; see also Reid, 1990; Epstein, 1992: 327–39). This then led to an attempt to replace it with a behavioural 'planned short-term therapy' (Wells, 1982). Many basic behavioural ideas, such as conditioning, play no part in task-centred work, and it deals with broader classes of behaviour than behavioural work normally covers. However, Gambrill (1994) argues that, as it has developed, it has increasingly used behavioural methods, and that its reformulation of these confuses the development of theory by denying its origins.

Both the circumstances in which crisis and task-centred work should be used and the focus of work differ. Crisis intervention is, classically, action to interrupt a series of events which lead to a disruption in people's normal functioning. Task-centred work focuses on defined categories of problems. Both try to improve people's capacity to deal with their problems in living. Crisis intervention uses practical tasks to help people readjust, but an important focus is their emotional response to crises and long-term changes in their capacity to manage everyday problems. Task-centred work focuses on performance in practical tasks which will resolve particular problems. Success in achieving tasks helps emotional problems. Crisis intervention has a theory of the origin of life difficulties. Task-centred work takes problems as given, to be resolved pragmatically.

Task-centred work rejects long-term involvement between worker and client assumed by insight-giving and supportive therapies, and concentrates on exposed problems rather than their underlying causes. Reid and Epstein (1972a: 26) specifically distinguish the approach from crisis intervention. They say task-centred work deals with a wider range of problems, and emphasises clear definitions of target problems, tasks and time limits. They stress links with functional casework with their emphasis on time limits, client self-direction and having a clear structure and focus in the process of work. They use Hollis's classification of casework procedures (see Table 3.1).

The main writers on crisis intervention are represented in the book which introduced the subject to the social work literature (Parad, 1965a), and later updated (Parad and Parad, 1990a). We can usefully combine crisis intervention with support systems work and networking (Mor-Barak, 1988; O'Hagan, 1991: 144–5).

The politics of crisis and task-centred theory

The success of these two approaches to social work comes from the attractiveness and practical usability of the basic ideas of 'crisis' and 'task'. The theoretical models were developed at the time of social work's translation from a small-scale, undeveloped profession into being a servant of extensive welfare states. Parad and Parad (1990b: 4–5) reject 'theory' as a description of crisis intervention, reserving this term for 'scientific' theory – see Chapter 2. The focus and brevity of these treatments offered an economic approach in this expansion, compared with longer-term methods, which would have stretched costs and the size of the workforce to an impossible extent. Moreover, involvement in the front line of public services put social workers in touch with crises in the lives of clients, in a way that trying to deal with longer-term problems or offering care in the workhouses of the Poor Law and their successors did not involve. Task-centred work offered clearer accountability and a focus on outcomes, too, for an influx of less experienced, less well-qualified and less supervised workers employed in settings requiring public scrutiny. It is also generic, and can be applied in any setting with any client (Doel and Marsh, 1992: 6). The research-demonstrated effectiveness of task-centred work also strengthened its political acceptability to agency managers and funders, and supported a profession which was at times embattled about its effectiveness. Some research support for crisis intervention also exists (Parad and Parad, 1990b: 16–18). Task-centred work has also been popular with clients because of its clarity and sense of direction, and because it involves clients actively in a sense of partnership (Gibbons *et al.*, 1979). However, its simple concepts belie its complexity, and it is hard to train people to use it well (Marsh, 1991: 167).

Neither model focuses on social change, and this makes them attractive to public agencies and supporters of individualist-reformist views of social work, compared with those favouring the explicit political critique of radical theories which also had a currency as these models arose. Crisis and task-centred theory have had greater staying power. The partnership approach and clarity of task-centred work and the emphasis on looking at environment pressures have led to claims that they are both effective in use with anti-discriminatory work, in offering empowerment and dealing with structural oppression (Ahmad, 1990: 51; O'Hagan, 1994).

Although crisis intervention seems specific in focus, it is a general technique for dealing with clients' problems. Parad (1965b), for example, argues that people approaching agencies do so when they experience crises in their capacity to manage their lives. The crisis is what motivates them to come, or leads other agencies to refer or require them to seek help. Thus, all clients can be seen as 'in crisis', so that crisis intervention is relevant to all social work. The use of Erikson's (1965) analysis of life crises through which we all pass makes clear the concept's relevance to many personal difficulties.

Crisis intervention has been used in mental health services. It became associated with the idea of using multi-disciplinary teams of doctors, nurses and social workers to visit clients at home in an attempt to avoid damaging and unnecessary admissions to psychiatric hospital (Fisher *et al.,* 1990; Chiu and Primeau, 1991). Helping people to deal with severe reactions to loss and bereavement on death, for example, or when divorce or child-care problems lead to the break-up of families are other common uses of the techniques. They are also relevant in many medical and other situations where loss or traumatic changes arise. Examples are Gilbar's (1991) account of work with women with breast cancer and rape crisis work (Edlis, 1993).

In the United Kingdom, the term 'crisis intervention' is sometimes misused to refer to 'a crisis for the worker or the agency' (Browne, 1978: 115). O'Hagan (1986) treats 'crisis intervention' as an overall term referring to work in emergency and night-duty teams and some intake teams in the local authority social services. He regards it as particularly relevant to child protection work and mental health emergencies (O'Hagan, 1991). The classical usage of the term is retained in several services designed to respond to mental health emergencies (Davis *et al.,* 1985; Parad and Parad, 1990a; Roberts, 1995) and the emotional aftermath of major public disasters (Sefansky, 1990).

Crisis intervention: Naomi Golan

Golan (1978) offers a well-articulated account of crisis intervention theory. The following summary is based largely on her book. She outlines the main points of the theory as follows:

- Every person, group and organisation has crises.
- *Hazardous events* are major problems or a series of difficulties which start crises off.

- Hazardous events may be *anticipated* (like adolescence, marriage, moving house) or *unanticipated* (such as death, divorce, redundancy, environmental disasters like fires).
- *Vulnerable states* exist when hazardous events cause people to lose their *equilibrium*, which is their capacity to deal with things that happen to them.
- When equilibrium is disturbed, we try out our usual ways of dealing with problems. If these fail we try new problem-solving methods.
- *Tension and stress* arise with each failure.
- A *precipitating factor* on top of unresolved problems adds to the tension and causes a disorganised state of *active crisis*. This account presents crisis as a sequence, but Parad and Parad (1990b: 5–7) describe it as a configuration or matrix, seeing many events as interlocking.
- Precipitating factors may be presented to the worker as the client's main problem, but these are *not* the crisis, only a point in the sequence. The clue to this is often immense emotion associated with apparently minor events.
- Stressful events may be seen in one of three ways, each with its own typical response, as shown in Table 4.1. Holmes and Masuda (1973) produced a scale-of-life events allocating points to indicate their degrees of stressfulness – for example, retirement, 45 points; death of a spouse, 100 points. People experiencing events generating more than 300 points in a year were more liable to depression, heart attack and serious illness.

Table 4.1   Stressful events and responses in crisis intervention

Stressful events	Response
threats	anxiety
loss	depression
challenges	mild anxiety, hope, expectation and more attempts at problem-solving

Source: Golan (1978).

- The more successfully past problems were dealt with, the more problem-solving strategies will be available, so states of active crisis are less likely. Unsuccessful problem-solving in the past leads to people falling into active crisis often and finding it hard to escape.

- All crises reach resolution in 6–8 weeks.
- People in crisis are more open to being helped than those who are not. Intervention in crisis is more successful than at other times.
- In 'reintegration' after active crisis, people become set in their newly learned ways of solving problems, so learning effective problem-solving during the crisis improves coping capacity in the future.

Roberts (1991) describes seven stages of working through a crisis. These are as follows:

1 Assess risk and safety of clients and others.
2 Establish rapport and appropriate communication with clients.
3 Identify major problems.
4 Deal with feelings and provide support.
5 Explore possible alternatives.
6 Formulate an action plan.
7 Provide follow-up support.

Presented with clients, workers consider whether crisis intervention is relevant and the point reached within the crisis process. The whole situation in which the client exists and its interaction with psychological issues in the client's life should be considered. Lukton (1982) calls this, adapting the conventional term from psychosocial case-work, the 'person-in-crisis' situation. Charles, for example, saw a worker two weeks after his father had died, feeling very distressed. It is tempting to see the death as the crisis, but in fact it was the precipitating event, since when looking into his story, the worker found that he had recently moved away from his father for the first time to another town to take up a new job. Such life changes can be very stressful. This formed a hazardous event. He had already lost his equilibrium and was in a vulnerable state because he felt lonely and without support in the new town. He had tried to deal with this by going out with some new friends and joining a social club, but he did not feel part of the group in either situation. On occasions he had drunk too much and this had been embarrassing. He had thus tried to deal with his problems, but failed, and was suffering from increasing stress and tension as a result. He had been returning to his father's home at weekends, and his father's sudden death, once he had dealt with the immediate practical and emotional consequences, had emphasised his loneliness even further. Too strong a focus on the death as a crisis would fail to deal with the underlying problems that had created the state of active crisis from an event that he might have coped with if he had not already been facing this series of problems.

It follows from this set of ideas that people who suffer a lifetime of stresses will be more quickly incapacitated by problems. They find it harder to cope with them than others who have the chance to deal steadily with their problems. Also, people who can be helped to deal with problems effectively now will learn strategies which will prevent states of active crisis arising so easily in the future.

The steps in *reintegration*, in Golan's view, are:

- *Correcting cognitive perception* as clients gain a more accurate and complete view of the events which have affected them.
- *Managing feelings* involves getting the client to release extreme emotion and the worker accepting it (for example, it is acceptable to grieve for a dead relative).
- *Developing new coping behaviours.*

With Charles, the worker's exploration of the sequence of events helped to disclose to him that he was not assailed by a series of unconnected disasters. All these painful experiences fitted into a pattern which he could deal with as a whole. Aside from releasing a good deal of emotion around his grief for his father, which he was doing anyway, he was also able to release, for the first time, anxiety about his job responsibilities, his fear of failure and mental illness due to loneliness and depression. He was also able to study some elementary ways of building up social relationships, and went to a class on making friends and social contacts.

Golan thinks tasks are important in crisis treatment (1978: 73–6), but she does not use 'task' in the same way as task-centred theory does. Here, it is an emotionally or socially necessary role or series of actions in the client's life – something that must be gone through to achieve reintegration. Parad and Parad (1990b: 7) focus on 'affective, cognitive and behavioural' tasks. However, Golan proposes a similar process to Reid's task-centred work:

- explore the various options;
- help select a solution;
- apply for a service;
- test the service;
- get used to and gain skill in using the service.

Workers offer support and help throughout this process.

Golan also distinguishes these *instrumental or material-arrangement* processes from dealing with psychosocial tasks which involve:

- coping with feelings of loss and threats to security, self-esteem;
- trying new coping mechanisms for managing anxiety;
- offering support during the stressful period of seeking new services;
- helping the adjustment to use the service;
- helping clients realise what they have achieved, or to feel all right about loss.

Golan then presents a model for treatment, which is described in truncated form in Table 4.2. Treatment strategies are analysed following Hollis (see Chapter 3), and families and groups are seen as effective places for treatment. Different kinds of crisis are categorised. The work of Erikson (also mentioned in Chapter 3) is important because he defined personal development as a series of crises, and it is argued that crisis intervention can be used preventively to avoid some emotional consequences of such life crises. Using humour is one way of breaking an impasse (Pollio, 1995), reframing the context, humanising the situation, and freeing a client who is stuck in one means of problem-solving. However, it should not be used where it might be demeaning or confusing to the client.

Table 4.2 Golan's model of crisis intervention

Beginning phase: *formulation* *(1st interview)*	*Middle phase:* *implementation* *(1st–6th interview)*	*Ending phase:* *termination* *(7th and 8th, if necessary, interviews)*
A: focus on crisis state	*A: data collection*	*A: termination decision*
concentrate on 'here and now' get client to express emotional responses as emotions reduce, explore hazardous event discover type and effects of vulnerable state assess disturbance caused by crisis state	get missing data check inconsistencies select main themes (loss, anxiety, challenge)	check period since referral and remind client propose spacing of contacts and finishing deal with resistance to termination

Beginning phase: formulation (1st interview)	Middle phase: implementation (1st–6th interview)	Ending phase: termination (7th and 8th, if necessary, interviews)
B: evaluation decision statement – account of circumstances and priority problems check client's priorities decide main problem	B: behaviour change check client's coping mechanisms in problem area set realistic short-term goals set overall tasks jointly work out practical tasks jointly work out 'thinking' tasks	B: review progress summarise progress review main themes reminder of tasks covered, goals reached, changes, incomplete work
C: contract define goals, tasks, for client and worker		C: plan future discuss present problems discuss client's plans help client feel that process is ended help client feel OK about returning with other problems

Source: Golan (1978).

Task-centred casework: Reid and Epstein

The definitive statement of task-centred casework is in Reid's books (1978, 1992) and in Epstein (1992). The pioneer statement is in their joint *Task-Centered Casework* (Reid and Epstein, 1972). It has been explicitly applied to groupwork and family work (Reid, 1985; Fortune, 1985). A recent British interpretation (Doel and Marsh, 1992; Marsh, 1991; Doel, 1994) offers a less technicist terminology and a full bibliography.

In task-centred work, workers resolve problems presented by clients. Any social work theory should, therefore, show how problems arise, what they are and how we may deal with them. Brief work with explicit time limits is an essential feature of the approach.

Task-centred work is concerned with problems that

- clients acknowledge or accept;
- can be resolved through actions taken outside contacts with workers;

- can be defined clearly;
- come from things that clients want to change in their lives;
- come from 'unsatisfied wants' of the client rather than being defined by outsiders. For Reid (1992: 18–19) only acknowledged problems offer the necessary degree of partnership. Doel and Marsh (1992: 23) also include problems imposed by formal processes, such as courts.

Clients share some problems with others in their lives, who may acknowledge and define the problem in the same way. Agreement does not always exist about shared problems; people other than the client may see them differently. For example, with Joan, a young woman, the worker discovered that her inability to find a job was worrying her most, and began to work out a plan for undertaking a series of tasks to share the task of finding one. Before completing this, however, she visited the home to find that Joan's mother preferred her to remain at home to help domestically with the elderly grandparent who was also living with her. Also, Joan's father felt that working in a shop, which she preferred, was not socially acceptable. He wanted her to learn office skills at college. The worker had first to resolve different perceptions of Joan's family duties before being able to continue with job-finding.

Reid classifies the types of problems with which task-centred work is effective into eight categories, shown in Table 4.3.

Table 4.3   Problems with which task-centred work is effective

Interpersonal conflict
Dissatisfaction in social relationships
Problems with formal organisations
Difficulty in role performance
Decision problems
Reactive emotional stress
Inadequate resources
Psychological and behavioural problems not otherwise categorised, but meeting the general definition of problems in the model

Source: Reid (1978).

Workers should try to understand clients' problem-solving behaviour, especially where explanatory theories account both for how problems are caused and resolved. We should assess the *direction and strength of clients' wants.* Some wants support one another, while others are in opposition. Wants start action off, but clients' *belief systems* shape the wants and acceptable ways of fulfilling them. In Joan's case, for example, the desire for a job was enough to start her seeking the worker's help. However, the type of job that she believed was possible – shop work – and her lack of desire to spend time in college to gain qualifications for office work meant that the direction of job-seeking had to be changed from the father's preference. Alternatively, her socially conditioned expectations might be raised, so that she would look for more interesting and demanding jobs.

Beliefs guide action and are changed by interactions between the worker, client and others. Such beliefs are *points of leverage* which can help change beliefs, as in cognitive therapies. Points of leverage are as follows:

- *Accuracy*, where workers help clients understand how accurate their beliefs are.
- *Scope*, where workers help clients see the implications or range of beliefs which clients think are more limited.
- *Consistency*, where distortions due to dissonance between one belief and another can be removed by the worker.

Again in Joan's case, the worker found it useful to explore whether her assessment of her capacity to get better qualifications was accurate, by discussing the different perceptions of father and daughter. She also explored with Joan how she might limit the scope for moving on to more interesting jobs in the future if she failed to take qualifications now, since she might get used to having a wage coming in and be loath to return to college. Joan and the worker also explored the mismatch between Joan's desire to do something interesting (as shown by her wish to find a job more interesting than her domestic responsibilities and her wish for the independence deriving from having a job and a wage) and the likelihood that a low-grade job would prove boring very quickly.

Emotions arise from the interaction between beliefs and wants. Fear or anxiety arise because clients believe that a want is lost or threatened. Unconscious motivation may affect beliefs or wants but not (directly) behaviour. Joan, for example, was afraid of getting stuck at home and was reacting too quickly and to her disadvantage as a result.

Action is behaviour carried out with intent, so understanding actions involves understanding intentions. *Plans* are descriptions of intentions formed by the interaction of beliefs, wants and emotions. Planning means assessing alternative options, preferably away from the situation in which action is needed. When a plan is acted upon, the outcome gives feedback to the actor. Actions often occur in *sequences* and the problem may lie early in the sequence. For example, if my son misbehaves, I might slap him, and then feel guilty because I believe that slapping a child is wrong. Is slapping appropriate to stop the misbehaviour? This may be so if he is over-active today and needs a warning and reminder to think about and moderate his behaviour. But suppose the problem is that I ignored him, causing him to misbehave to gain attention. Deciding not to slap him would not be effective as a resolution of the problem of inappropriate slapping, because this plan mistakes the problem, and he would probably misbehave more to get attention, which the early misbehaviour did not achieve. A better way to solve the problem of inappropriate slapping would be to play with him and show him that I have more time for him.

Clients may not have *skills* to perform actions needed in particular circumstances. Skills may be learned directly or generalised from other situations. Going through a series of small steps may help such learning.

Some *social systems* generate or affect clients' beliefs, or respond to actions providing feedback in ways that distort further actions, whether for good or ill. The environment surrounding clients may therefore be important. Action sequences may in this way become *interaction sequences*, so that actions affect one another in circles or spirals. This idea comes from communication theory. *Organisations* may form a context for actions, labelling or categorising people or generating 'collective beliefs' about certain sorts of people. For example, staff in a school may come to believe that children from a particular housing estate are disruptive. This may in turn affect what the children believe about themselves, and what their parents and other agencies think about them. Going further, this may then affect how people involved act towards one another.

The *intervention strategy* has two aims:

1 helping clients to resolve problems of concern to them;
2 giving a good experience of problem-solving so that clients improve future capacity to deal with difficulties and are more willing to accept help.

Worker and client identify *target problems*, carry out *tasks* outside the agency setting and *rehearse and review* achievements.

This account of general principles shows how the model's ideas come from a variety of psychological and sociological sources. Social learning theory influences the mode of action, identifying targets and tasks and rehearsal. Communication theory is present in the concern for sequences and interactions of behaviour. The emphasis on belief shows a cognitive element. The identification of influence from the environment, and particularly organisations within it, suggests ideas borrowed from systems theory.

The aim of *assessment* is not, as in psychodynamic theory, to study clients' emotional responses or life history, but to identify

- action requirements;
- obstacles to action;
- unchangeable constraints.

Clients wanting less formal, more friendly or more personally involving relationships should seek alternative forms of therapy. Where clients cannot maintain a focus on a limited range of problems, less structured or more exploratory methods such as crisis intervention should be used. Task-centred work helps in protective work (for instance, with the parents of abused children) but should not be used where authoritarian protection or social control are the main priorities. Client actions will not change some physical and mental illnesses, so task-centred work can only be part of interventions here. However, it may help deal with social consequences of illness or disability.

Problem specification is the first step, taken early on through agreement with clients to undertake a short period of assessment. Doel and Marsh (1992) use a newspaper metaphor. We look first at the front page for the main news, then scan for headlines, identify the storylines (details of the problems) and client quotations (putting the whole issue in the client's words). The social context of the problem and others' responses to it are important. The process presented by Reid (1978) is as follows:

- *Identify potential problems* by helping clients describe difficulties in their own way. Summarise and test out workers' perceptions of problems.

- Reach *tentative agreements* on how clients see the main problems.
- *Challenge unresolvable or undesirable* problem definitions (for example, where the client unreasonably wants a deserted spouse to return).
- Raise *additional problems*, having first accepted the client's definition of priorities, where the client does not understand or accept additional problems.
- Seek *others' involvement* if necessary.
- Jointly *assess the reason for referral* if someone else compels the client to attend.
- Get *precise details* of when and where problems arise.
- *Specify* the problem, usually in writing.
- Identify clear *baselines* of the level of present problems (see Chapter 5 for further discussion of baselines).
- Decide *desired changes*.

In the phase of *contract creation* – Doel and Marsh (1992) call this making an agreement – worker and client reach specific agreements on action. The process is as follows:

- Agree to work on and specify one or more client-defined problems (Doel and Marsh – the selected problem).
- Rank the problems in order of priority.
- Define the desired outcome of treatment (Doel and Marsh – goal; Epstein, 1992, limits goals to specifiable outcomes).
- Design the first set of tasks.
- Agree the amount of contact and time limits.

Reid prefers oral contracts to written ones because they are less frightening, unless several people are involved or the problems are complex. Doel and Marsh (1992) prefer written agreements in order to make goals less fuzzy and invoke the client's commitment.

Task planning takes place in regular sessions with clients. Tasks are explicitly planned, practicable for clients to do outside the sessions and agreed between worker and client. They may involve mental or physical action (for example, to decide this or do that). *General tasks* set a policy for the treatment process, and *operational tasks* define what the client will do. Tasks may be *unitary*, involving just one action or a series of actions, or *complex*, involving two different actions (for example, to seek a new flat and take part in occupational therapy). They may be *individual*, undertaken only by the client; *reciprocal*, so that if the client does this, the worker or a relative will do that; or *shared*, so that the client and another important person will do it together.

The *task planning process* is as follows:

- possible alternative tasks are identified, through generating *task possibilities* (Reid 1992: 57–8);
- an agreement is made, and explicitly secured with the client (Reid, 1992: 60);
- implementation is planned;
- the task is summarised.

Task implementation then takes over the sessions between worker and client. This involves the following:

- A recording system is set up, especially where a sequence of or repeated actions are required.
- Strategies are identified (for example, a series of increments, setting limits, setting precise targets, mental tasks, use of paradox, tasks to be done by client and worker concurrently, involving other people).
- Incentives for finishing a task are agreed if these are not built in.
- The client's understanding of the value of the task and how it helps to meet the goal is checked. This helps establish motivation (Reid, 1990: 58–60).
- Relevant skills are practised, by simulation (for instance, the worker acts out an employment interview) or by guided practice (such as helping a person with disabilities try out a new adaptation to her home in a day centre). Reid (1992: 50–3) calls these *session tasks*. That is, they are work undertaken among clients or between client and worker in the session. They include planning and expressing and dealing with anxiety and other feelings.
- Obstacles are analysed and removed. These may relate to motivation, understanding, beliefs and emotions such as anxiety or anger and lack of skill (Reid, 1992: 73–94).
- The worker's contribution is planned.

The *worker's tasks* may involve the following:

- working with people other than the client to help the client to complete their tasks (such as preparing the way with another agency);
- arranging for rewards and incentives for success;
- sharing tasks with clients where they have insufficient skills or resources to do them alone.

Worker and client review achievements jointly in each session.

Mr and Mrs Knowles were an example of some of these processes. They were referred to a mental health advice service, with the problem that Mrs Knowles had become slightly agoraphobic, and now was unable to go out, except with her husband in the car. She was, for example, unable to do the shopping or go out on her own to see friends. She felt a little embarrassed by this. There were no resources to carry out a behaviour modification programme involving the worker. Instead, he explained the basic principles of doing things in stages, having Mr Knowles alongside for support, and with the idea of getting relaxed before moving on to the next stage. They then discussed a series of events in which they would go out in the car and Mrs Knowles would get out of the car, then later would go part of the way to a small shop, all the way, later still buy some things, and then progress in stages to going to the supermarket. The contract included the worker being available on the phone if any difficulties arose. This programme worked effectively without further interventions.

The *ending phase* involves client and worker in the following actions:

- describing the target problem as it was and as it is now, including checking whether it was the most important problem (Doel and Marsh, 1992: 81–2);
- assessments by the worker, client and others involved of any changes and achievements;
- planning for the future (for example, how the client will use any skills learned or changed circumstances) and helping clients manage evident future problems;
- additional contracts, to extend the process to finish off properly, or to establish new problem and task definitions;
- an explicit end where (as in residential care or continuing supervision of a client subject to legal requirements) contact with the worker or agency continues;

- movement to a long-term treatment process, or arranging for follow-up to check that progress is maintained;
- referral to another agency for additional or alternative help.

Commentary

The general success of both these models of practice should not blind us to areas where they are not effective. In both cases, they are not effective where constant debilitating crises and long-term psychological problems are the main issue. They may be used in child protective work or in a long-term case to achieve results with a specified problem or a particular crisis. Often in such cases, however, supportive work, provision of services and longer-term efforts at change or supervision to prevent deterioration or risk will be required. Neither model works well with clients who do not accept the right of the worker or agency to be involved.

Both theories represent a trend in social work to clearer, more focused activity than the long-term, non-directive, insight-giving methods of psychodynamic work. However, they are in the traditional lineage of social work problem-solving, using a conventional social work individualising relationship with clients who are treated on a medical model with the aim of getting better. Crisis intervention, with its more psychodynamic roots, offers a greater emphasis on emotional responses and irrational or unconscious behaviour than task-centred work, which assumes greater rationality on the part of clients.

The idea of contract has been criticised. Rojek and Collins (1987, 1988), using concepts from discourse analysis, argue that it offers a false sense of equality between workers and clients; false because it neglects the radical analysis of the position of social workers who have all the power and authority of the state, profession and class to impose their will upon clients. They propose that in using terms like 'contract', workers imply to clients an equality which in a sense enables them to take greater power in the relationship. The fact that this power imbalance exists makes it difficult to use contracts in the way proposed by activities such as task-centred work; it prevents the mutual cooperation which the model assumes and which is the origin of its success. Replying to this, Corden and Preston-Shoot (1987b, 1988) argue that the contract can benefit client–worker relationships by helping to make these explicit, and at least more specific so that each knows more clearly what is going on. In fact, also, contract work does achieve results in allowing clients to attain desired ends.

More broadly, Gambrill (1994) argues that task-centred work – and by extension many forms of brief therapy – provides a minimal response to severe social problems. It thus conceals resource inadequacy and the failure of political will to respond realistically to deep-seated problems of poverty and social inequality. Its effectiveness in dealing with presenting problems may result in society's avoiding longer-term and more deeply seated responses to social oppressions.

5

Cognitive-behavioural Theories

Wider theoretical perspectives

Cognitive and behavioural ideas come from two related streams of psychological writing. Historically, learning theory came first, and developed into clinical psychology using a behaviour therapy based on psychological research. Sheldon (1995) expresses the essence of the theory nicely as a separation of mind and behaviour. The psychodynamic and perhaps conventional view is that behaviour comes from a process which goes on in our minds. This has connections with philosophical ideas about what the mind is, and whether it is the seat of our humanity, what Christians call a soul. A related question is whether environmental influences limit people's freedom or whether they are free to act according to their will – that is, what their mind wishes. Learning theory does not deny that this may be so, but argues that we cannot know what is happening in someone else's mind. Therefore, we can only study and influence the behaviour which emerges. We learn most behaviour, except some inborn reflexes; that is, it originates from influences outside ourselves. Therefore, we can learn new behaviour to meet our needs or replace existing behaviour if it is causing us problems. The therapy, therefore, focuses on doing things which consistently lead to changes in behaviour. It does not concern itself with what changes may take place in our mind during this process.

Social learning theory (Bandura, 1977) extends these ideas by arguing that most learning is gained by people's perceptions and thinking about what they experience. They learn by copying the example of others around them. Helping this process can enhance therapy.

Cognitive theory is in part a development of behaviour theory and therapy, recently building particularly on social learning theory. It also grew out of therapeutic developments of a pragmatic kind, devised by writers such as Beck (1989) and Ellis (1962), who were concerned with psychiatric conditions such as anxiety neurosis and depression. In social work, Glasser's (1965) reality therapy, which originates from residential work with young women, has been important. Because the originators of this work were dealing with disorders of the mind, they moved towards trying to incorporate thinking within their model of therapy. Cognitive theory argues that behaviour is affected by perception or interpretation of the environment during the process of learning. Apparently inappropriate behaviour must therefore arise from *mis*perception and *mis*interpretation. Therapy tries to correct the misunderstanding, so that our behaviour reacts appropriately to the environment. According to Scott (1989), different approaches include Beck's concern with distorted thinking about ourselves, our lives and our future leading to depression or anxiety, Ellis's focus on irrational beliefs about the world and Meichenbaum's (1977) emphasis on threats we experience. This latter idea, particularly, relates to some ideas in crisis intervention.

Gambrill (1995) identifies the main features of behavioural work as follows:

- It focuses on specific behaviours worrying clients and others around them. If behaviour is changed, we remove the concern.
- It relies on behavioural principles and learning theory.
- Workers make a clear analysis and description of problems, based on direct observation. Assessment, intervention and evaluation methods are explicitly defined.
- Factors influencing behaviour are identified by changing factors in the situation and looking for resulting changes.
- Clients' assets are discovered and put to use.
- Important people in clients' environments are involved.
- Intervention is based on research evidence of effectiveness.
- Progress is monitored using subjective and objective measures, comparing data about the present with data about the situation before intervention.
- Workers are concerned to achieve outcomes valued by clients.
- Workers help clients use changed behaviours in many situations (generalisation) and maintain improvements after intervention has ceased.

Gambrill (1995) reviews a range of different behavioural approaches. The basic form of behavioural work is concerned with changing contingencies and behaviours. *Radical behaviourism* includes thoughts and feelings as behaviours, treating them as the cause of other behaviours. This prevents seeing thoughts and feelings as emerging from unknown areas of the mind. Thoughts and feelings are, therefore, caused, and we can change them like any other behaviour. *Cognitive-behavioural* methods are therapeutic procedures which focus on changing thoughts and feelings alongside, instead of or as a precursor to changing behaviours. *Social learning theory* is one form of cognitive-behavioural theory which focuses on how we learn from social situations by learning how others act successfully (vicarious learning). *Neo-behaviourism* is behavioural treatment particularly concerned with stress and anxiety disorders. Cognitive and behavioural ideas have much in common with models such as task-centred work, and there is a degree of mutual influence. Humanist and phenomenological ideas also have relevance because of the concern with ideas of mind and with cognitive attempts to link thinking with doing.

Some basic ideas from learning theory and behavioural treatment are necessary to understand the approach. This account starts from that of Fischer and Gochros (1975), because of its clear and comprehensive organisation of the theory.

We can identify four types of behaviour therapy:

1 respondent or classical conditioning (the stimulus–response approach – Jackson and King, 1982);
2 operant conditioning;
3 social learning;
4 cognitive therapy.

All are directly applicable in social work.

Respondent conditioning is concerned with behaviour (anything we do) which responds to (is produced by) a stimulus (a person, situation, event, or thing usually in the environment). *Conditioning* is the process by which behaviour is learned; that is, connected more or less permanently with the stimulus. When we have learned a response to a stimulus, we have modified our behaviour. Respondent conditioning is also known as *classical conditioning* because it derives from the first experiments in the field by Pavlov.

Many behaviours are *unconditioned*. They happen naturally. An unconditioned stimulus produces an unconditioned response. For example, people's eyes water in a high wind, they salivate when given food, they withdraw their hands sharply when burned, they are sick when they eat a noxious substance.

Behaviours are *conditioned* when responses become *associated* or paired with a stimulus that does not naturally produce the response. An example would be if our eyes were trained to water when we were given food. We call these conditioned stimuli and conditioned responses.

Extinction occurs if the association between conditioned responses and stimuli is not kept up. The conditioned response fades away and loses its connection with the stimulus.

Some kinds of behaviour are incompatible with other behaviour. For example, a completely relaxed person cannot be anxious or violent. *Counter-conditioning* seeks to associate desirable responses with particular stimuli, in competition with undesirable responses.

The most commonly used counter-conditioning technique is *systematic desensitisation*. Clients are taught the practical techniques of relaxation or are offered other means of personal support. Then they are slowly introduced to the unwanted stimulus, using the relaxation or support to fight against their anxiety. This is often used with agoraphobic or school-phobic people. We saw a simple example of this in the case of the Knowles in Chapter 4. Here, relaxation and Mr Knowles's presence counter-conditioned against Mrs Knowles's agoraphobic anxiety. *Assertiveness training* is another technique used where people lack confidence. Workers help them practise appropriate forms of behaviour in a supportive environment, and they are enabled to use these in, ideally, increasingly difficult real life situations.

Counter-conditioning is used in sexual therapy. Pleasant sexual responses are learned in supportive surroundings and are gradually introduced into more ordinary sexual situations which had previously caused anxiety. For example, a man who ejaculates prematurely learns to control ejaculation when stimulated by his partner when full sexual intercourse is not permitted until he feels confident of control. Transfer to sexual intercourse follows later.

One example of these techniques is in conditioning children who are enuretic; that is, they wet the bed when they should have learned to avoid this behaviour. A loud buzzer or bell is connected to an electrical contact placed within soft mats under the child. The buzzer sounds when some urine reaches the mats, and the child wakes and can complete urination in a toilet. This process has two effects. First, the child is conditioned to wake when the bladder is full, so avoiding bed-wetting. Second, the tone of the bladder muscle is improved, strengthening the capacity to get through the night without wetting. These responses are set up as a form of counter-conditioning to the natural process of reflex urination when the bladder is full (Morgan and Young, 1972).

Most behaviour does not develop from unconditioned stimuli, and *operant conditioning*, the second major form of behavioural work, deals with a wider range of behaviours. It is concerned with behaviour with operates on the environment, and can be used with complex and thought-out behaviour. In contrast, respondent conditioning is mainly concerned with learned automatic responses.

Operant conditioning focuses on the consequences of behaviour. Something happens (an *antecedent* event – A) which produces a behaviour – B – which tries to deal with the event, and because of that behaviour, consequences – C – arise.

Workers manage *contingencies* which affect the relationships between behaviour and consequences which strengthen or weaken behaviour by *reinforcement* and *punishment*. Reinforcement, whether positive or negative, strengthens behaviour. Punishment, whether positive or negative, reduces behaviour. Positive always means doing something; negative always means taking something away. Both can be used together. More information is given below, in discussing Sheldon's (1995) account of cognitive-behavioural work.

Extinction is also an operant learning technique. It differs in principle from extinction in respondent conditioning. It means removing the relationship between behaviour and its consequence. In negative punishment, we may remove a consequence which has nothing to do with the behaviour, as in the example given above. Extinction might be used where avoiding homework led to arguments between child and parents. The arguments positively reinforce not doing homework, because they take up time and emotional energy which can then not be applied to the homework. Instead of arguing, parents put child and homework in a room, thus withdrawing the reinforcing behaviour. Unlike extinction in respondent conditioning, this is not solely avoiding making a response. It is positively removing the relationship between a consequence and the behaviour which led to it.

Positive reinforcement is usually preferable to or should be used with other techniques. For example, extinction gives no control over the behaviour which might replace the undesirable behaviour; it might be equally undesirable. Positive reinforcement allows the encouragement of favoured behaviour alongside extinction. Also, unwanted behaviour may increase temporarily to test out the new response and this is hard to cope with, so encouraging useful behaviour makes the process easier.

The main process in *social learning* is *modelling*. Hudson and MacDonald (1986) describe it as follows:

- A person sees someone else performing an action and pays attention to it.
- The observer 'forms an idea' or codes in their mind how the behaviour is done, including some rehearsals in practice or in their mind.
- The observer identifies circumstances in which the behaviour occurs and has its consequences.
- When an appropriate situation arises the observer repeats the behaviour according to the 'idea' of it which they have formed.

Seeing a feared behaviour performed by a role model helps many clients to appreciate that there are no adverse consequences.

Scott and Dryden (1996) classify *cognitive-behaviour therapies* into four categories:

1 *Coping skills* contain two elements, a 'self-verbalisation' – that is, an instruction to ourselves – and the behaviour that results. Difficulty in coping with situations may come from inability either to work out what to do to self-verbalise or to act on our instructions. Meichenbaum's (1985) Stress Inoculation Training (SIT) aims to reduce and prevent stress by teaching clients what to say or do in difficult situations. Also, we make changes to reduce stress in the client's environment.

2 *Problem-solving* is different from Perlman's (1957) psychodynamic social work theory (see Chapter 3). That is concerned with seeing human life as a process of resolving life issues. Here problem-solving is more like task-centred work: clients are encouraged to 'lock on' to and define a problem, generate solutions to it, choose the best, plan ways of acting on it and reviewing progress.

3 *Cognitive restructuring* is perhaps the best-known form of cognitive therapy and includes Beck's cognitive therapy (CT) and Ellis's rational-emotive behaviour therapy (REBT, formerly RET). In CT, clients collect information about how they interpret situations, and the worker questions and tests out how these

work. In REBT, irrational beliefs dominate clients' thinking which leads to 'awfulising' – that is, seeing things as unreasonably negative; low frustration tolerance – that is, feeling that bearing uncomfortable situations is impossible; and 'damnation' – that is, feeling that you are in essence bad because you have failed at something. Workers question and attack the irrational beliefs which underlie these reactions.

4 *Structural cognitive therapy* is concerned with three 'structures' of belief in clients' minds: core beliefs are assumptions about ourselves; intermediate beliefs are explicit descriptions clients make of the world; peripheral beliefs are plans of action and problem-solving strategies used daily. Workers focus on beliefs at the periphery which cause problems, but use the process of change to explore the origins of these beliefs in deeper ideas.

Connections

The main aims of behavioural social work are increasing desired behaviours and reducing undesired behaviours, so that people respond to social events appropriately. This increases their capacity for leading a full and happy life. Insight into the client's problems often helps because it speeds learning, but there is no evidence that it is necessary or that it is enough to get people to change. Warm personal relationships between worker and client help in behavioural work as in other forms of social work. Behavioural social work can be used in many social work situations. Gambrill (1981), for instance, explains its use in working with child abuse situations with both children and parents; it is helpful for its clarity in setting goals for behavioural achievements. Herbert (1987) describes the use of behavioural techniques in a practical way with a wide range of children's problems.

Thyer and Hudson (1987: 1) usefully describe the relationship between general behavioural work and behavioural social work as follows:

> Behavioral social work is the informed use, by professional social workers, of interventive techniques based upon empirically-derived learning theories that include but are not limited to, operant conditioning, respondent conditioning, and observational learning. Behavioral social workers may or may not subscribe to the philosophy of behaviorism.

The implication of this view is that workers do not have to import the model whole into all their work. They may use aspects of the model where it is useful. However, this approach suggests that there is nothing of other aspects of social work contributing to the model as it is used in social work. It is, in this formulation, the use of borrowed techniques. This suggests that behavioural approaches may not serve well some wider social purposes and issues within social work.

Hanson (1983: 142–3) maintains that, although therapeutic uses were being made of the basic psychological theories in the 1950s, it was not used in social work until the 1960s when traditional social work came under radical attack.

Thomas (1968, 1971) in the United States and Jehu (1967, 1972) in the United Kingdom were the first significant interpreters of the psychological literature within social work. Significant recent writers are Hudson (Hudson and MacDonald, 1986) and Sheldon (1995) in Britain, and Fischer (1978; Fischer and Gochros, 1975), Gambrill (1977, 1995) and Thyer (1987, 1989) in the United States.

Cognitive theories have established a position in social work theory during the 1980s primarily through the work of Goldstein (1981, 1984), who sought to incorporate more humanistic ideas in them. This possibility is suggested by the concern of basic behavioural ideas with the nature of mind. Humanist ideas (see Chapter 8) claim that perceptions and their processing legitimately vary and that the only reality is what is perceived and understood. Allied to cognitive ideas, this allows an acceptance of the accuracy of the client's understanding of the world. There is, therefore, no need to see clients' perceptions as wrong and to attack them. This element of acceptance renders cognitive and behaviourist therapies in ways which seem more natural to the conventions of social work. Including the humanistic element is, then, the crucial aspect of Goldstein's work and the later writings of Werner (1982, 1986). However, writers such as Scott (1989) have more directly incorporated the ideas of cognitive theorists in social work formulations. Writers such as Sheldon (1995) restrict material on cognitive therapies to limited interpolations into a mainly traditional behavioural perspective. Hudson and MacDonald (1986) are dubious about the incorporation of cognitive approaches into behavioural models of therapy.

The politics of cognitive-behavioural theory

Controversy surrounds cognitive and behavioural models of treatment, because they have been at the centre of the positivist debate (see Chapter 2). Behaviourists mounted a trenchant attack on psychodynamic models of social work. They criticise its ill-defined outcomes based on assumptions about psychological structures within the mind which we cannot examine empirically. The strong argument for behavioural and cognitive methods, which is pressed continually in writing about them, is their empirically tested success in attaining results. Accepting this argument requires acceptance of the scientific method and modernist ideas about knowledge. One advantage of doing so is the acceptability of scientifically proven methods when working with other professions, particularly medicine, whose knowledge base is scientific. In this way, behavioural and cognitive methods contribute to arguments for the professional standing of social work in comparison. Again, accepting this argument means accepting the assumption that this is a desirable attainment.

Cognitive-behavioural methods have attained a limited use in specialised settings with particular client groups. They are often used for school phobia, childhood problems and in psychiatric settings, particularly, in the case of cognitive methods, with mild anxiety and depression. One reason for this is that clinical psychologists, and to a lesser extent other medical and nursing staff in such settings, can offer supervision and provide a sympathetic environment and a patient-centred setting for therapeutic methods. Such advantages are rarely available in conventional social work agencies.

Incorporating cognitive methods is disputed. Some writers (such as Sheldon, 1995) treat these as a development in basic behavioural methods, much as social learning theory has been. Others consider them a major new and different set of techniques, which have to some extent developed independently. Because they introduce a concern for internal mental processes, some think they damage the scientific credibility of behavioural methods, although in practical terms they have achieved their own research validation (Scott and Dryden, 1996).

A major difficulty with cognitive-behavioural methods is their technical character, with many jargon terms and formal procedures, apparently worked out in set systems. To some workers this seems non-human. However, such an approach may suit some clients or workers who like to see an ordered, explicit approach to problems which can be clearly explained and justified.

There are also objections on ethical grounds, since the worker manipulates behaviour rather than it being under the control of the client. This could lead to behaviourist techniques imposing workers' wishes on unwilling clients, in pursuit of social or political policies which could, at the extreme, be used for authoritarian political control. Behaviourists argue that clients' consents are ethically required and practically necessary to success. Also, the most ethical treatment is one that works best, and behaviourist approaches are well-validated as effective. All techniques can be abused in the wrong hands. Many other techniques are manipulative in a way which is hidden from clients; an example might be the use of paradox. Watson (1980: 105–15) argues that this is not a sufficient answer to the ethical problem. Behaviourism inherently assumes that all behaviour is caused. If clients decide that they want changes which might be achieved by behavioural methods, then they are acting using their own reasoning freely in the sense of deciding without constraint on their decisions. However, what happens if the client's behaviour is considered socially undesirable, by a court, or by people able to put social or other pressures on a client? They might be persuaded that their behaviour is right, good or adaptive to social conditions. In such cases, we are moving from unconstrained reasoning to decisions being made in pursuit of social goals. The only ethical position, which maintains clients' rights to self-determination, is to use the technique only where the client's own purpose is to free themselves from behaviour; for example, where it is compulsive, and clients cannot, but wish to, control themselves.

Sheldon (1995: 232–4) argues that any social work methods, including behavioural methods, are not so powerful that they can overcome resistance, and that other kinds of work also involve control and limitation of freedom. However, this seems a weak protestation when behavioural methods particularly claim that they are successful beyond other social work or therapeutic techniques. Moreover, we should not put clients in the position of having to resist, but should protect them from this. Sheldon further argues that we should measure any disadvantages alongside the model's advantages.

Behavioural models have sometimes been misused. Residential care homes, for example, have used the reward and punishment aspect of behavioural methods in oppressive or abusive ways. One instance is the 'pin-down' scandal in residential homes for children in Britain (Levy and Kahan, 1991). Here, certain behavioural ideas justified locking children up for long periods without day clothes. Sheldon

(1995: 237–41) argues that in this sort of situation some methods are used where the people concerned are already motivated to oppress clients. Any method could be misused to do so.

Behavioural social work has had considerable influence, particularly in the United States, but it has not succeeded in gaining widespread usage, except in specialist settings or for particularly relevant problems.

Sheldon: cognitive-behavioural therapy

Sheldon's recent account of behavioural therapy takes some account of cognitive contributions. Additional material is included here from Scott (1989) and from other writers. Most behavioural writers cover similar ground.

The basic principles and methods of behavioural work were described above. These are applied in the therapeutic situation. A crucial element is choosing reinforcers. These are chosen according to whether they have an observed effect on behaviour. Generalised reinforcers are often chosen which have an effect in several different situations. Large changes of behaviour should be divided into small steps. A schedule of reinforcement should be worked out, as follows:

- *Continuous reinforcement* of every instance of the desired behaviour will work quickly.
- *Shaping* means reinforcing small steps towards the desired behaviour. For example, Joe is a mentally ill man who often speaks loudly and threateningly to people in his household. We start by reinforcing slightly less loud behaviour. When this is more commonplace, we only reinforce much less loud behaviour, then keeping quiet for longer periods, then being less threatening, then being more friendly and so on. Eventually, we can achieve quite complex changes of behaviour.
- *Fading* means steadily reducing the amount or type of reinforcement once the desired behaviour is achieved, so that behaviour can be transferred to a new setting. For example, Joe might be reinforced at first by a cigarette, then by verbal encouragement. Eventually, we want him to respond just to people showing how uncomfortable they are by a piece of his behaviour. Unless we do this, we are 'training and hoping' and we are likely to get a shift back into past behaviour patterns when we

stop reinforcing. This is why people in residential care often seem to do well, but fail when discharged.
- *Intermittent reinforcement* is used when a behaviour is not always reinforced.
- *Ratio* schedules of intermittent reinforcement reinforce after a set number of occurrences of the desired behaviour.
- *Interval* schedules reinforce after a set period of desired behaviour.

Ratio or interval schedules may be fixed (completely regular) or may vary around a typical period or number of behaviours. Variable schedules are most resistant to extinction (particularly variable interval schedules) and more practical, since very consistent reinforcement may not be possible.

Modelling or vicarious learning (described above) both reinforces existing responses and creates the possibility of using new or unused responses by observing how others behave and how successful or otherwise the behaviour is. We do this generally, and at certain stages of our lives; for example, in teenage years or when there are many changes, we pick particular people as models. We then combine and edit observations from different sources to create our own identity. Workers can have an input at each stage of modelling (see above). Bandura (1977) emphasises the importance of *perceived self-efficacy* – that is, our own view of how good we are at things like this. These are made up of two aspects: the outcomes we expect from certain sorts of behaviour, and the efficacy that we think we have in doing tasks like that. For example, someone who abuses drugs and is part of a subculture of people who share the habit may not see many beneficial outcomes from giving up (outcome expectations). However, even if they would like to be back in the 'straight' world, they may feel they do not have enough strength of purpose to give up (efficacy expectations). There are criticisms of Bandura's theories. They are less parsimonious than operant and respondent theories, which explain all these things much more simply. However, they do offer a way of understanding more complex aspects of behaviour that social workers are likely to be dealing with.

Sheldon (1995) moves on to point out that much learning through modelling is cognitive; that is, we think ourselves into the situation we are observing, work out how we would act and so on. In practice, stimulating such thinking in a client is useful. Feeling what it would be like to act as the model does through *empathetic learning* can be an important part of this. *Cognitive-mediational theories* concern how performances we observe are coded into a series of images and words, and then retrieved. This works better if people 'speak-along' with what they are doing as they reproduce the performance.

Assessment is a crucial aspect of cognitive-behavioural work, because it depends on detailed understanding of sequences of behaviour. Also, different reinforcers will affect different clients, so each case must be carefully individualised. Therefore, assessment and definition of the antecedent events, the specific behaviours and detailed consequences are all important.

Sheldon's analysis of the distinguishing features of cognitive-behavioural assessment is set out in Table 5.1. Cognitive interviews use techniques based on the psychology of memory to help stimulate accurate recall in situations where evidence of child abuse or similar traumatic circumstances is required (Westcott, 1992).

A suitable assessment sequence is as follows:

- Gain descriptions of the problems from different viewpoints.
- Get examples of who is affected and how.
- Trace beginnings of problems, how they changed and what affected them.
- Identify different parts of problems and how they fit together.
- Assess motivation for change.
- Identify thought-patterns and feelings which come before, during and after incidents of the problem behaviour.
- Identify strengths in and around the client.

Throughout any work, it is important to continue monitoring what is happening. This is particularly so where there may be damage to clients or others. Workers constantly need to examine factors which may have changed levels of risk. Being involved in a complex sequence of changing behaviours can blind us to changes in social factors which create risk.

Problems must then be reduced to their component parts. A chart covering antecedents, behaviour and consequences for specific events can be useful in doing this. Workers should focus on precise descriptions of behaviour, rather than judgements about it. For example, 'he banged his fist on the table' is a better description of behaviour than 'he became frustrated', because it is precise, observable, changeable and not arguable (he might have been angry, not frustrated).

Table 5.1 Sheldon's distinguishing features of cognitive-behavioural assessment

Focus	*What to assess*
Emphasis on visible behaviour causing problems, or the absence of expected or adaptive behaviour	Who, what, when, how, how often, with whom. What is done, what is not done, what is done too much, what too little, what is at the wrong place or the wrong time.
Attributions by people of meaning to stimuli	Doubts, worries, fears, frustrations, depressions explained by people involved and revealed by behaviour or absence of expected behaviour.
Present behaviour and thoughts and feelings that go with it	Looking for past causes distracts work: try to control the size of the problem to limit action. Explore what maintains the behaviour in present repertoire. Learning history (e.g. inappropriate responses, inability to learn, inability to discriminate between crucial aspects of situations).
Target sequences of behaviour	What behaviour needs to be increased or decreased? What new skills or reduction in emotions are needed to perform alternative behaviours?
Identify controlling conditions	Where do the problems occur? What are the antecedents? What happens during the sequences? What happens afterwards?
Identify people's labels, but avoid prejudiced attributions	How do people involved describe or explain the problem? How far is that prejudiced or name-calling, rather than explanatory?
Flexibility in listening leading to a clear hypothesis about behaviour.	Do not be so task- or behaviour-centred as to squeeze out the complexities of the people's stories. Explore things that they might not see as relevant or have excluded. Come to a clear statement about a piece of behaviour that can be changed, and how it will be changed.

Source: Sheldon (1995: 111–18).

Problems need then to be put in hierarchies. In doing so, we need to consider agency priorities, clients' views, their capacity and motivation to make one change rather than another, the availability of mediators (people in the environment who can record behaviour and administer reinforcement) and whether goals are fair, feasible and non-discriminatory.

The next stage is to find a basis for evaluating change. This is often based on 'single case' experimental designs (Gingerich, 1990; Nelsen, 1990). Careful definition of target behaviours is followed by measuring in a planned way how often it occurs in a 'baseline' period. The intervention follows. Occurrences of the behaviour during and after intervention are also measured. Sometimes after one period of intervention, there is a 'reversal period' in which the worker returns to their own baseline behaviour and the target behaviour is again measured. Intervention then starts again. In this way, we can test whether the intervention is indeed affecting the behaviour. Follow-up visits are also important, to check that changes are maintained, and provide a motivation for maintenance. If a probation officer has limited aggressive behaviour in a client through behavioural work in a day centre, and discovered that this is also maintained at home, a visit every month and then every two months for a while to check up may be an important motivational factor for the client.

Following this, workers use various techniques for working behaviourally. These fall into two groups, response control and contingency management. Response control techniques involve activities such as modelling, social skills training, assertion training, various cognitive approaches discussed above and techniques such as systematic desensitisation. These have already been discussed as examples explaining the wider theoretical perspective of behavioural therapy.

In contingency management the following possibilities might be achieved:

- Identify and reinforce to amplify the frequency or force with which a client uses an existing piece of behaviour.
- Shape existing behaviour towards desired ends.
- Where there is an excess of unwanted behaviour, use one of the following techniques:
  - reinforce incompatible preferred behaviour;
  - negatively reinforce the unwanted behaviour (as by withdrawing an aversive stimulus when the client does something preferred);
  - reduce the frequency by extinction (that is, withdraw reinforcement of the unwanted behaviour);
  - punish unwanted behaviour.
- Change the stimuli that elicit the behaviour.

Choosing reinforcers is a crucial part of deciding what to do. Ideally, reinforcers should arise naturally from the situation, help clients understand the reasoning behind reinforcers, especially if they are a bit artificial, and focus on non-material generalised reinforcers such as praise, affection and attention. I said above that reinforcers must be seen to work. We can find them by seeing clients in their day-to-day life and seeing what reinforces them and asking them and people around them. Premack's principle means using behaviour that the client likes and carries out frequently as a reward for less common behaviour that we want to encourage. For example, if a youngster enjoys chatting with friends on the street corner and we want to encourage homework, we can make agreeing to going out conditional on doing an hour's homework first. Then the amount of homework can be increased and the amount of chatting allowed decreased. Sometimes we can consult a checklist of possible reinforcers. Reinforcers have to be strong enough to compete with the unwanted behaviour, they must be practical to present, using mediators – that is, the therapist's agent in the everyday situation.

Scott's (1989) account of cognitive-behavioural work contrasts with Sheldon's by focusing on cognitive interventions. His argument (Scott and Dryden, 1996) for using cognitive therapies is that they are brief, widely applicable, highly structured, easily learned and effective. This makes them understandable to client and worker and usable in a hard-pressed agency. He examines four areas. These are child behaviour problems, emotional disorders, such as anxiety and depression where cognitive therapy has had most influence (Scott and Stradling, 1991), interpersonal problems, such as marital problems or lack of social skills and self-regulation disorders, such as controlling drug abuse.

In child behaviour problems, Scott describes groups for working with parents. These focused first on consistency and used a social skills approach to building up parents' capacity to deal with their children. Parents role-played dealing with difficulties, so that both parents in a household learned the same approach. This was then practised at home. Praise (reinforcement) was given for success. Parents then learned about time out, fines and penalties when dealing with their children. Again, there was practice and homework. Later sessions reviewed these experiences, then rehearsed parents in thinking through future problems. Although the focus here is on helping parents think out their problems, we can see many aspects of Sheldon's accounts of behavioural work used in these sessions to reinforce parents' successful behaviour and avoid unsuccessful behaviour. Work on anger control is also described. Ronen (1994) argues that cognitive-behavioural work can be effective in direct work with children in enabling them to exert stronger self-control over behaviour.

With emotional disorders, Scott expounds the practicalities of using Beck's cognitive therapy for dealing with depression. Careful assessment of the precise aspects and degree of depression experienced by clients is carefully assessed, and there is a well-tested instrument for doing so. Early work with clients is behavioural, trying to develop and shape more appropriate behaviour. This gives immediate progress. Later sessions focus on cognitive therapy. Clients keep a record of 'automatic' thoughts in particular situations which lead to depression. These are thoughts which come into their head as they experience emotions. Each of these is 'tested in a laboratory' of questions. These are: 'How realistic is it?', 'Who gives the authority to hold that view?' and 'Does the assumption help achieve a goal?'. Workers and clients together look for self-defeating thought patterns. With anxiety, clients may be demoralised; over-vigilant to see problems and failures; avoid situations where they are anxious, which obstructs normal living; and have physical consequences, such as muscle tension, or emotional problems such as procrastination, so that they can never make a decision.

In marital therapy, Scott proposes a programme with three elements: behavioural exchange; cognitive restructuring; and communication and problem-solving training. Assessment is by interview, exploring the problem behaviours, much as Sheldon (1995) proposes – see above. Also, a variety of scales and questionnaires is used. These structured forms of assessment are much more common in cognitive-behavioural work than in other forms of social work. Early parts of the programme are designed to change specific, clearly defined behaviours which are easily changed. This helps couples realise that it is possible to derive satisfactions from their partner. Each partner makes a behaviour exchange. Each gets something they want, and is helped by the other to achieve it. There is a written contract, with a penalty if it is not achieved and a reward if it is. The rewards are not at first made contingent on one another, because if one fails, the whole contract collapses. Eventually, the behaviours can be made to connect. For example, Sally and Peter disagree, among many other things, about his spending all his time in the garden and her spending too much money buying clothes. His redundancy has caused him to spend more time in the garden. However, because they rely on her part-time wage, they have less to spend, but she resents this because it means she cannot spend so much on her clothes. The contract is that she will help for an afternoon in the garden to plant vegetables to aid the household finances and he will come with her to buy something cheap but nice: a silk scarf. Both agree to limit their complaints about the other around these activities. The rewards are the tasks themselves. The penalties, if they fail to control their behaviours, are his doing all the housework alone for a week, or her spending all her non-work time at home for a week. A regular review and exploration of difficulties can lead to better understanding of what each wants from the other and how to communicate effectively.

Cognitive restructuring can take place around trouble-shooting when behaviour exchanges go wrong or other relationship difficulties arise. This involves the worker pointing up and debating issues, using the 'laboratory' questions discussed above. Communication training involves a sequence of treatment in which first the worker provides feedback, using specific examples, of communication patterns which do not work. Then, the worker offers alternative communication patterns. Finally, the couple rehearse the different communication patterns before trying them out as homework.

An influential application of cognitive therapy is the 'reasoning and rehabilitation' programme used in the Probation Service and other criminal justice settings. Devised by Ross *et al.* (1985, 1988, 1989) in Canada, it has been applied in the Welsh STOP (Straight Thinking on Probation) (Raynor and Vanstone, 1994; Raynor, *et al.*, 1994) programme and elsewhere in the United Kingdom. It is prescriptive, following a detailed manual of action, using an explicit teaching programme. This covers self-control techniques, thinking skills, social skills, teaching about thinking of others, victim awareness, creative thinking, critical reasoning, thinking about others' perspectives, about our effects on others, emotional management and giving the offender experience of being a helper of others themselves. This gets offenders out of stereotyped thinking about their own needs and position, and allows them to see situations more broadly and from different perspectives. They are also able to think out their problems more rationally and find alternative ways to deal with them. Although successful, the approach has been criticised for its racism and lack of flexibility, since it forces workers to comply with strict procedures, treats people as machines, does not respond to the real causes of much offending which lies in poverty and the deficiencies of capitalism (Neary, 1992; Pitts, 1992). This approach fits well with an increasing emphasis on 'offence-focused' work with offenders. Such work concentrates on offenders reviewing their offences and patterns of behaviour which lead to them. Another example is Fishbein and Adzen's (1975) theory of reasoned action.

Group and community behavioural techniques

While Sheldon's account is almost entirely about individual work, both Fischer and Gochros (1975: 115–19) and Hudson and MacDonald (1986: 165–6) quote a variety of studies to show that behavioural approaches can be effectively used in groupwork. This may be by using a conventional group as a supporter and reinforcer to individuals undertaking behavioural programmes or by undertaking interventions with several people at once in the group. Such arrangements may help people with similar problems – for example, alcoholics, or those who come from the same background, such as a local group of teenagers with offending problems, or people who are within the same family or social group. Typically, according to Hudson and MacDonald, the group works together on problem assessment, goal-setting, discussing and deciding on strategies and in modelling and rehearsal. Social skills training is particularly useful. Rose (1981) discusses behavioural groupwork with a cognitive approach using social learning about 'self-defeating' and coping cognitions. However, Hollin (1990), discussing work with offenders, points out that social skills may only be a part of the reasons for clients' problems, so effective training should be part of multiple approaches to clients' problems. Wright (1995), discussing residential work with young boys with behaviour problems, showed consistent improvements with a cognitive-behavioural skills training programme. However, she emphasises the importance of recognising and dealing with other problems and developing a clear shared treatment philosophy involving a range of staff.

Burgess *et al.* (1980) describe the use of social skills training with a group of sex offenders in prison, which gives a good example of the range of techniques that may be applied. Three techniques in varying combinations were used. Micro-teaching of small elements of skills in interactions with others was one element, such as use of voice, eye contact, posture. Assertiveness training to help prisoners express their opinions and seek their interests without interfering with others was another aspect. Role-playing of increasingly complex events which might occur in the prison developed this aspect of the group. It then moved on to situations which might arise outside the prison. Workers' modelling of skills was important, and prisoners were given homework to practise with. At the end of each group meeting, a winding-down session of social conversation was arranged. A similar group for adult psychiatric patients is described by McAuley *et al.* (1988). Here, quite damaged clients learned to understand their own behaviour through explicit interventions in time-limited groups.

Although most community work is not orientated towards individuals, Mattaini (1993) shows behavioural analysis used to support community work practice. He proposes techniques for changing antecedents of behaviour in community settings, changing consequences and reducing behaviours which do not help the community achieve desired objectives.

Residential work

Behavioural approaches are an important grouping of theories of residential work (Hudson, 1982; Ryan, 1979). The most common approach is the use of *token economies*. These are systems for managing the total programme of a residential establishment, in the same way that therapeutic environments, discussed in Chapter 3, manage the total experience of residence. Thus, they are not treatment programmes for individuals which happen to be carried out in residence, but represent an approach to residential work in the round. Token economies have been used in schools and residential homes for adolescents with behaviour problems and for offenders. It has also been used with people with mental illness and learning disabilities (Birchwood *et al.*, 1988).

Token economies are an operant conditioning system using interval (or sometimes intermittent ratio) reinforcement. Staff in the establishment agree (according to Sheldon, 1995) a list of behaviours to be strengthened. Tokens are given for continuing these behaviours for a certain period or for performing behaviours a set number of times. Clients collect the tokens and exchange them for desired goods and for privileges. There is, in effect, a price list of rewards, each reward requiring a specified number of tokens. Unskilled staff can be used to maintain the system (Fischer and Gochros, 1975: 288–9).

Token economies are useful for *discrimination training* (Sheldon, 1995; Fischer and Gochros, 1975: 287). This helps people learn what sorts of behaviour are appropriate to particular social circumstances.

Pizzat (1973) gives an extended account of a residential programme using a variety of reinforcers. He shows that in the early stages, or when clients are first admitted with extreme behaviour difficulties, they need a phase of immediate reinforcement to gain quick improvement. This can then be backed up by a system giving tokens at specified times of day. Later still, the establishment offered a weekly allowance unconnected with specific behaviours for good conduct. Otherwise, social and self-reinforcement were adequate at this stage. This is a helpful account of a range of behavioural techniques used in a residential setting, and shows the importance of developing the various forms of reinforcement carefully.

Sheldon (1995) notes that, although token economies are successful in changing behaviour, there are problems in maintaining them over a period. In most residential establishments, clients are not carefully selected, and most are not large enough to offer several separate stages, as Pizzat's was. As a result, staff have too wide a range of problems to deal with. It may also be hard to ensure that staff and others impose the system uniformly, and not all may believe in it sufficiently. Supporting staff adequately is important. Outside pressures such as courts, health or local authorities may limit the degree of control necessary to impose a consistent system. Birchwood *et al.* (1988), in a recent review of the research, support these comments, and claim that social modelling may be an equally effective form of treatment.

The sum of these difficulties may lead to excessive rigidity or rewarding residents for acquiescence rather than progress in appropriate behaviour. Behaviourial systems can be used for part of an establishment or during a phase of particular difficulty, to get quick results. Goldapple and Montgomery (1993) describe a programme which used cognitive and behavioural methods with serious drug abusers in residential care. This improved the drop-out rate, so that no residents left, although long-term treatment goals were not always achieved. Possibly this is because residents were rewarded by the practical attention to everyday activity, while longer-term work was needed for substantial improvement in behaviour. Davis and Broster (1993) describe successful cognitive-behavioural-expressive interventions in residential care with aggressive young people. These used a log-book of perceptions in individual sessions, stress management techniques and behavioural learning of coping skills. They warn that workers should avoid allowing expression of violent ideas, if this seems to lead to strengthening them, and that workers and regimes may stimulate violence through their actions. De Lange *et al.* (1981)

describe a group in a residential care setting for young offenders using cognitive-behavioural methods through role-playing solutions to common problems on video.

Commentary

Both behavioural and cognitive approaches are clearly valid and widely applicable forms of treatment, whose effectiveness is supported by research (Sheldon, 1995; Scott *et al.*,1989; Stern and Drummond, 1991), but whether good results can be maintained over time is more uncertain. It depends how careful workers are to generalise behavioural and cognitive learning to ordinary social situations. Much practice and research into it is by psychologists and the social work contribution to the general literature is marginal even in the United States. It is questionable whether the almost wholly individualistic therapy presented by some writers, such as Sheldon (1995), easily transfers to general social work settings, although it could clearly do so. One difficulty is that it requires skill and experience to construct behavioural programmes, and this requires supervision by someone already expert in the procedures. Where there is no existing group of practitioners, this is difficult to provide. Thus, behavioural work is used in pockets, and particularly in clinical settings where psychologists and other professional groups with training in the techniques are available for training and support. See Wong *et al.* (1987) for a discussion of this point in relation to chronic psychiatric patients in hospital.

Among the advantages of cognitive work is the explicit, structured guidance on practice offered, and the assessment instruments often employed. This gives stronger guidance to workers lacking in confidence in trying a new technique. On the other hand, it may become constricting and limiting to flexible responses by workers to clients' problems. One advantage is that looking at particular behaviours means that we do not label the whole person as abnormal, as psychodynamic theory might do. Different behaviours may be adaptive in different environments and cultures. So, behaviour which is appropriate to and comes from different genders and ethnic cultures is not assumed to need change in learning theory. In psychodynamic theory, behaviours are considered acceptable according to that theory's ideas of the origins of that behaviour, so behaviour which does not fit in with the dominant culture but might be acceptable in a minority ethnic culture or an oppressed gender comes to be disapproved of. While

Fischer and Gochros (1975) note this point about learning theory, they do not note that the idea of adaptive behaviour still requires a minority or oppressed culture to align itself with the majority culture. There is still a risk that a therapy which seeks to change behaviour so that it adapts to an environment undervalues minority forms of behaviour and less dominant aspects of the culture.

Social learning methods, especially social skills training, are more widely used than conventional behavioural methods. The reasons for the lack of impact of these techniques might be threefold. First, the explicit attack on the conventional psychodynamic form of social work and the alliance of behaviourists with the positivist critique of the effectiveness of social work seems to have led to a degree of defensiveness. Second, the specific techniques are distant from the standard non-directive approach of social workers, and have a mechanistic terminology and procedure which they may feel uncomfortable with. Third, there have been some ethical criticisms which, while not wholly valid, might have reinforced the reserve of social workers and the feeling that this is not in the style of social work. However, an alternative critique came from a sociological perspective, systems perspectives, and it is to this that we devote the next chapter.

6

Systems and Ecological Perspectives

Wider theoretical perspectives

Systems ideas in social work originate in the general systems theory of von Bertalanffy (1971). This is a biological theory which proposes that all organisms are systems, composed of subsystems, and are in turn part of super-systems. Thus, a human being is part of a society and is made up of, for example, circulation systems, cells, and these are in turn made up of atoms which are made up of smaller particles. The theory is applied to social systems, such as groups, families and societies, as well as biological systems, although the social systems aspect of the theory is less well-developed than biological or technical systems (C. Payne, 1994). Hanson (1995) argues that the value of systems theory is that it deals with 'wholes' rather than with parts of human or social behaviour as other theories do.

Mancoske (1981) shows that important origins of systems theory in sociology lie in the social Darwinism of Herbert Spencer. Siporin (1980) argues that the social survey research of the late nineteenth century in England (for example, the work of Booth and Rowntree), information theory and the ecological school of Chicago sociologists in the 1930s were also antecedents.

The main concepts are as follows:

- *Systems* entities with *boundaries* within which physical and mental energy is exchanged more than it is across the boundary.
- *Closed systems* have no interchange across the boundary, as in a closed vacuum flask.

137

- *Open systems* occur where energy crosses the boundary which is permeable, like a tea-bag in a cup of hot water which lets water in and tea out but keeps the tea leaves inside.

Another set of concepts focuses on the way systems work and how we may change them (Greif and Lynch, 1983):

- *Input* – Energy being fed into the system across the boundary.
- *Throughput* – How the energy is used within the system.
- *Output* – Effects on the environment of energy passed out through the boundary of a system.
- *Feedback loops* – Information and energy passed to the system caused by its outputs affecting the environment which tell it the results of its output.
- *Entropy* – Systems use their own energy to keep going, which means that unless they receive inputs from outside the boundary, they run down and die.

A simple example of these processes is if you tell me something (input into my system). This affects how I behave (throughput in my system), my behaviour changes (output) and you observe this change. So you receive feedback that I have heard and understood what you said (a feedback loop).

The state of a system is defined by five characteristics:

1 Its *steady state*, how it maintains itself by receiving input and using it.
2 Its *homoeostasis* or *equilibrium*. This is the ability to maintain our fundamental nature, even though input changes us. So, I may eat cabbage, but I do not become cabbage-like. I remain me, while the cabbage is digested and gives me energy and nourishment. Part of it becomes output, through heat, activity and defecation.
3 *Differentiation*, the idea that systems grow more complex with more different kinds of components over time.
4 *Non-summativity*, the idea that the whole is more than the sum of its parts.
5 *Reciprocity*, the idea that if one part of a system changes, that change interacts with all the other parts. They therefore also change.

As a result of reciprocity, systems exhibit both *equifinality* (reaching the same result in several different ways) and *multi-finality* (similar circumstances can lead to different results) because the parts of the system interact in different ways. Social systems may possess *synergy*, which means that they can create their own energy to maintain themselves. So, human beings interacting in a marriage or in a group often stimulate each other to maintain or strengthen relationships, which build up bonds within the group and make it stronger. This is an example of non-summativity, because these bonds could not be achieved without the interaction within the system. Without creating synergy, the group or marriage would have to be fed by outside energy or entropy would occur. Thus, synergy negates entropy, and is sometimes called *negentropy*.

Connections

Systems theory had a major impact on social work in the 1970s and has been a subject of controversy for almost as long. Two forms of systems theory are distinguished in social work:

1 general systems theory;
2 ecological systems theory.

Hearn (1958, 1969) made one of the earliest contributions, applying systems theory to social work. The greatest impact came with two simultaneously published interpretations of the application of systems ideas to practice (Goldstein, 1973; Pincus and Minahan, 1973). These gained considerable influence in the United Kingdom through interpreters such as Vickery (1974; Specht and Vickery, 1977) and Olsen (1978). The later development by Siporin (1975) and Germain and Gitterman (1980; Germain, 1979a) of ecological systems theory had considerable impact in the United States. Brown (1993) shows the application of the idea of 'boundary' and environment to groupwork. Elliott (1993) argues that systems theory can be integrated with social development ideas (see Chapter 9) to apply the latter to social work in industrialised countries. Kabadaki (1995) shows how the possibility of intervening at different levels in society is particularly relevant for social development work.

The politics of systems theory

Systems theory was one of several strands of theoretical development responding to dissatisfaction with psychodynamic theory. Its sociological focus seemed to counter the failure of psychodynamic theory to deal adequately with the 'social' in social work. It also became influential at the time when separate social work specialisms were being perceived as aspects of social work as a generic activity. In the United States and United Kingdom, separate social work professional organisations had been merged (in the 1950s and 60s respectively). In the United Kingdom, separate local government agencies had been merged in the Seebohm reorganisation. Its focus on 'wholes' (Hanson, 1995) was thus an attractive contribution to social work. Roberts (1990) sees it as one of several integrating conceptual frameworks developing in social work then. Indeed, two influential writers, Pincus and Minahan (1974) and Goldstein (1973) described their theories as 'integrated' and 'unitary' respectively. Another source of influence was its importance in family therapy, which also began to develop and influence social work in the mid-1970s. Here, systems theory is a major perspective, since it provides a way of understanding how all members of a family can affect and influence one another. This capacity to deal with analysis of relations among people in groups was also important in gaining usefulness in residential care (C. Payne, 1977; Atherton, 1989).

Compared with radical theory, the other critique of traditional social work theory which was influential at this period, systems theory did not propose critical ideas which rejected many aspects of current social organisation and social policy. One reason for its success is that it accepts and analyses existing social orders rather than, as with radical theory, analysing and rejecting them. It thus fits well with a profession and agency structure which is part of the state and has authority and power. It grew to influence when social work was expanding and taking up roles in state agencies in many countries. Unlike radical theory, it relates successfully to psychological theories, since it does not reject theories at this level of human behaviour, but permits their incorporation in its wider framework.

Its broad focus allowed it to incorporate many aspects of other theories. Leonard (1975: 48) writing from a Marxist perspective, argued that systems theory can help in understanding institutions, their interaction with one another, and how change might be brought about in a radical way, provided that the theory is not used simply to suggest that systems maintain themselves wholly stable. More traditional writers, such as Woods and Hollis (1990) incorporated it into their accounts of psychodynamic practice. Preston-Shoot and Agass (1990) attempt such a combination. They argue that psychodynamic theory (but this might apply to any psychologically based theory) offers useful understanding of human emotions, interactions and internal responses to the outside world. Systems theories offer a context for such understanding, showing how public and private interact, how various change agents might be involved and that workers and their agencies might themselves be targets for change. Together, these sets of ideas enable workers to manage the stress of emotional pressure from their interpersonal work by seeing it in a wider social context. They also highlight the fact that we cannot maintain awareness of complex social or interpersonal situations continually. Maintaining two related but separate ways of understanding enables us to switch between an interpersonal and social focus. The connections between the two theories are their emphasis on patterns of behaviour and social relations, which connect with each other and connect us to each other.

Applying systems theory to social work practice: Pincus and Minahan

Pincus and Minahan's widely used book (1973) explicitly applies systems ideas to social work. The principle of their approach is that people depend on systems in their immediate social environment for a satisfactory life, so social work must focus on such systems. Three kinds of system may help people:

1 *informal or natural systems* (such as family, friends, the postman, fellow workers);
2 *formal systems* (like community groups, trade unions);
3 *societal systems* (for example, hospitals, schools).

People with problems may not be able to use helping systems because:

- Such systems may not exist in their lives, or have the necessary resources or be appropriate to their problem (for instance, elderly people may not have relatives or friendly neighbours, so they are without that kind of informal system in their lives).

- People may not know about or wish to use them (for instance, a child abused by parents may not know where to go for help, or may fear to go to the police or social services in case they are taken away from their parents, whom they love in spite of the abuse).
- The system's policies may create new problems for users (such as dependence, conflicting interests).
- The systems may conflict with one another.

Social work tries to see where elements in the interactions between clients and their environment are causing problems. Neither client nor environment is necessarily seen as having problems. The interaction between them may be the difficulty. The aim is to help people perform life tasks, alleviate distress and achieve aims and value positions which are important to clients. 'Life task' here means activities in our lives which have meaning and importance for us, as it was in crisis theory (see Chapter 4).

Social workers are concerned with the relationship of 'private troubles' to 'public issues'. They work on general consequences of personal problems and effects on individuals of more general issues. Social work tasks are:

- helping people use and improve their own capacities to solve problems (such as learning new child-care skills in order to improve relationships in the family);
- building new connections between people and resource systems (like helping a newly disabled man to feel happy about going to a local social centre, by introducing him carefully, and making sure he is welcomed and not rejected because of his disability);
- helping or modifying interactions between people and resource systems (for example, helping a social security claimant present their case so it has a greater chance of success);
- improving interaction between people within resource systems (such as families, other agencies);
- helping develop and change social policy;
- giving practical help;
- acting as agents of social control.

Pincus and Minahan define four basic systems in social work, which are set out in Table 6.1. Social work gains in clarity if workers analyse which system the people with whom they are dealing fall into.

Table 6.1   Pincus and Minahan's basic social work systems

System	Description	Further information
Change agent system	social workers and the organisations that they work in	
Client system	people, groups, families, communities who seek help and engage in working with the change agent system	*actual* clients have agreed to receive help and have engaged themselves; *potential* clients are those whom the worker is trying to engage (e.g. people on probation or being investigated for child abuse)
Target system	people whom the change agent system is trying to change to achieve its aims	client and target systems may or may not be the same
Action system	people with whom the change agent system works to achieve its aims	client, target and action systems may or may not be the same

Source: Pincus and Minahan (1973).

Relationships between workers and others may be:

- *collaborative,* where there is a shared purpose;
- *bargaining,* where agreement needs to be reached;
- *conflictual,* where their purposes are in opposition.

Again, clarity is facilitated in analysing the nature of the relationships with each system, and engaging in relationships appropriately and honestly.

The social work process is seen as a series of phases with associated skills, summarised in Table 6.2.

Ecological systems theory: the life model

Germain and Gitterman's (1980) 'life model' of social work practice is the major formulation of ecological systems theory; Germain edited a collection of articles demonstrating its application across a range of social work (1979a). She argues that there are close parallels with ego psychology in the importance given to the environment, action, self-management and identity (Germain, 1978). However, both sets of ideas are conceptually distinct and can be used without each other.

Table 6.2 Phases and associated skills in social work practice

Phase	Activities	Skills and methods
Assessing problems	stating the problem	each problem has three parts, which should all be stated: social circumstances, people deciding that the circumstances are a problem and the reasons for their decision
	analysing the systems	consider how they affect the social situation
	set goals	include steps leading to the main goal; decide on feasibility and priorities among goals
	set strategy	who is to be involved from each of the four basic systems? points of entry to those systems and resources, relationships needed and difficulties expected
	stabilise the change effort	check on problems for client arising from changes and try to prevent them
Collecting data	questioning	verbally, in writing or using projective tests
	observation	watching client at home, in simulations, or using stimulating techniques (e.g. playing with anatomically correct dolls in child abuse cases)
	check records	written, other formats, verbal
Making initial contacts	availability	to people in the client system
	contacting	get in touch with other parts of a system having met one
	overcome ambivalence	remove resistances to being helped
	promoting	demonstrate the value of the agency's work to the client system's aims
Negotiating contracts	primary	between worker and client
	secondary	between worker and other systems
	define content	important aims of each party, tasks each will perform, describe change process
	set up good relationship	explain purposes of contract, make its terms clear, work out disagreements
	deal with resistance	involve other members of system or other systems (e.g. to remove fears about their reactions or prove that they will help), accept and acknowledge resistance, offer new information, encourage hope, set trial goals, use groups for collective influence
Forming action systems	decide size and composition	e.g. client + worker only, client + family + worker, worker + other agency, client + worker + other agency

Phase	Activities	Skills and methods
	operating procedures	length of contacts, time of meetings, frequency, place, rules of behaviour (e.g. permissive or controlled)
Maintaining and coordinating action systems	avoid entropy of system	build up relationships well; make roles, communications, power, loyalties, attitudes, values and aims consistent; avoid changing or be explicit about changes in roles, operating procedures, system activities, system changes
Influencing action systems	affecting any parts of systems affects all other parts – multi-finality	use knowledge and experience, material rewards and services, legitimate authority established relationships, status, charisma and personal authority, control over information
Terminating the change effort	concluding evaluation	draw together evaluations of progress made during above activities
	separate from relationships	
	stabilise change effort	

Source: Pincus and Minahan (1973).

The life model sees people as constantly adapting in an interchange with many different aspects of their environment. They both change and are changed by the environment. Where we can develop through change and are supported in this by the environment, *reciprocal adaptation* exists. Social problems (such as poverty, discrimination or stigma) pollute the social environment, reducing the possibility of reciprocal adaptation. Living systems (people individually and in groups) must try to maintain a good fit with their environment. We all need appropriate inputs (like information, food and resources) to maintain ourselves and develop.

Where transactions upset the adaptive balance stress results, and this produces problems in the *fit* between our needs and capacities and the environment. Stress arises from:

- *life transitions* (for example, developmental changes, changes in status and role, restructuring of life space);
- *environmental pressures* (such as unequal opportunities, harsh and unresponsive organisations);
- *interpersonal processes* (for example, exploitation, inconsistent expectations).

As in crisis theory, not all stressful events lead to actual stress. Whether they do so depends on personal and environmental circumstances and especially perceptions of the events. In this sense the life model stresses the importance of cognition and capacity to control the outside world.

The main aim of social work is 'to strengthen the adaptive capacities of people and to influence their environments so that transactions are more adaptive' (Germain amd Gitterman, 1980: 10) While this does include environmental change, the emphasis on adaptiveness illustrates the way ecological theories assume a fundamental social order, and play down possible radical social change.

Problems arise from transactions in people's life space being maladaptive. The client's view of the problem and the transactions should be considered. Empathy is important in entering the client's world. We may deal with each of the three areas of life problems simultaneously, but one may gain priority. The worker–client relationship is a transaction to which each brings other transactions (for example, the worker–agency relationship; client relationships in the family). Three areas of transactional problems often arise in worker–client relationships:

1 social definitions of role and status (such as clients' fears of workers' class or official status);
2 agency structure and functions (like policies);
3 professional perspectives (for instance, ethics).

The three phases of practice are initial, ongoing and ending. Assessment involves identifying objective and subjective facts, making hypotheses to be tested while remaining open to further information and responsive to the client's wishes. A variety of methods is used, directed towards improving adaptive capacity in people and the environment and improving interactions. The client's own capacity, self-direction and action are emphasised.

In the *initial phase* the worker prepares by thinking over and researching theoretical understanding of the problem and by gaining emotional contact with the client's feelings and responses. Role-playing incidents leading to problems can help in empathic understanding, so that workers can identify with and incorporate the client's view into their understanding. Reverberation (remembering similar experiences in the worker's life) and awareness of personal feelings and reactions to the client are important. These emotional responses must be integrated with objective assessment.

For example, Harriet came to a social work agency complaining about her husband's violence towards her. An interview was fixed with a specialist worker, with experience of these difficulties. This delayed the initial response to her difficulties, but ensured that the first response would be well informed and understanding. Harriet described in general terms her fear of her husband, but the worker could not get an idea of how these events arose, and acted out with her two or three events, to see if a pattern of interaction was apparent. This also gave her a clear picture of Harriet's distress. Details of the family and its children's needs were collected, and information about income and possible help from Harriet's family and friends.

Different interactions may arise, depending on whether the service is sought, offered or imposed. Where it is the latter, some degree of acceptance by the client is needed, and the early stages involve finding common ground. Clienthood only begins when the service is accepted and the agency agrees to give it. Where clients seek the services, workers provide a welcoming, courteous, supportive environment and encourage clients to 'tell their story.' Where the service is offered, it should be clearly explained and confusions or questions dealt with, before moving on to how the agency may help.

Worker and client then agree about the problem and what each is to do. Both contribute; reciprocal accountability should be defined. Concerns should be divided into:

- problems;
- priorities;
- commitments.

Children may need a more responsive approach 'tuned' to their rhythm and enthusiasms. Adults often require more structured, cognitive work. The time-scale and time structure of the process should be explored; people experience time differently – for example, in attitudes to punctuality (Germain, 1976).

The *on-going phase* concentrates on change in one or more of the three areas of focus. Life transitions are experienced by everyone, corresponding with biological changes, and affected by social and cultural expectations, constraints and opportunities. Transitions are often a source of stress but offer opportunities to stimulate *innate* adaptive mechanisms or learn *acquired* ones.

Cognitive development occurs in stages, and stress can arise from damage to or deprivation of cognitive development or from conflict in cognitive styles (for instance, between the worker's and client's ways of thinking). Status changes and role demands also cause stress arising from different expectations among friends, family, organisations and institutions. Crisis events also cause stress because normal coping mechanisms cannot manage.

The worker's aim in working with *transitions* is to help people progress through them with undamaged or improved adaptive mechanisms. The worker's three roles are:

1   enabling (for example, strengthening the client's motivation, validating and supporting the client, helping to manage feelings);
2   teaching (like helping clients learn problem-solving skills, clarifying perceptions, offering appropriate information, modelling behaviour);
3   facilitating (such as maintaining clients' freedom of action from unreasonable constraints, defining the task, mobilising environmental supports).

In Harriet's case, for example, the worker discussed with her the various options and explored what each of them would be like; this disclosed Harriet's fear of confronting her violent husband, but also her anxiety about leaving and coping with the children on her own. The worker helped Harriet to work out precisely what she would do, and this enabling approach made Harriet more confident about taking on either option. Before deciding whether she would confront her husband, Harriet accepted some teaching through role-play of ways in which she could do so appropriately, and the worker also acted to facilitate Harriet's decision by making tentative arrangements for her to retreat if need be to the local women's refuge.

In working with *environmental problems and needs*, the field of concern is the social and physical environments, including political and economic structures. The power of bureaucratic organisations, their system of status definition, structures and their socialisation of people into unhelpful attitudes can all obstruct clients' adaptation to their environment. Social networks are also important aspects of their environment. The physical environment includes the *natural* and the *built* worlds, which affect opportunities and obstacles in our lives. For example, one elderly client of mine lived in a rural area some miles from the nearest shops in a small group of cottages with very uneven access roads. Although she was not particularly immobile, this isolation prevented her from managing as well as she would have been able to do closer to town. Fortunately, there were several empty houses near her daughter, and we were able to arrange for her to rent one. Although the move was difficult, she could manage again, being nearer the shops and her daughter's help.

Life experiences can often make clients feel that the world is unresponsive to their needs. In one case, two elderly clients discharged themselves from hospital in spite of considerable and life-threatening disabilities. On investigation, we discovered that they were in different wards of the hospital which was divided into male and female wards, and they had not troubled staff to arrange for them to visit each other and they wanted to be together. We guaranteed a daily period together, and they agreed to be readmitted. The worker must concentrate on the interface between clients and organisations and social networks and on aspects of the physical environment which cause stress. In this area of work the worker's roles are:

- *mediating* (for example, helping the client and the system meet and deal with each other in rational and reciprocal ways, as in the hospital example above);
- *advocating* (for instance, pressurising other agencies or individuals to intervene, including taking up social action);
- *organising* (such as putting the client in contact with or creating new social networks).

In dealing with *maladaptive patterns of interpersonal relationships and communications*, the worker is dealing mainly with families, which organise a network of statuses and roles, and are also the place where basic survival needs are met (such as shelter, food, sex). Families have to develop communication mechanisms internally and with the outside world. The nuclear family and the structure and role of families in our lives apply many stresses. Similar issues arise in *formed groups*, where clients come together in the agency to share work on a life task which they have in common.

In the *ending phase*, client and worker may be affected by a painful separation, and need preparation and careful work to end successfully. The process is affected by time factors (for example, if a client of a hospital worker is discharged suddenly), type of services (as often, when individual casework leads to more intense relationships), and relationship factors (as where the worker has played a parental role). Separation may also be affected by workers' and clients' experiences of relationships and losses.

The worker should prepare by reviewing the client's previous experience of loss. They may need to work through stages of denial, negative feelings, sadness and a feeling of release and having made progress. An evaluation of progress by client and worker, sometimes as part of an agency review system, should be part of the ending phase.

Social workers should take responsibility for using information from their casework to take up social issues that arise from their cases with their agencies and more widely.

An alternative formulation of ecological theory is Meyer's (1983) *ecosystems* perspective. It claims to be more flexible than the life model, because it explicitly uses other explanatory theories, rather than creating its own. It is particularly useful for assessment (Greif, 1986), and focuses assessing networks of family and environmental support, using genograms and ecomaps as visual devices (Gilgun, 1994). Wakefield (1996) identifies four arguments for its combination of general and ecological systems: its ability to analyse circular connections in transactions between worker and client, its value in assessment, its integration of other social work theories and its inclusion of social factors to balance individual casework. He concludes that all these arguments are flawed, for the reasons discussed below.

Networking and social support systems

An important development of systems theories of all kinds is the analysis of networking in social support systems. This focuses both on planned formal support groups and on enabling 'informal' or 'natural' carers to help friends, neighbours and family members who are in need (Garbarino, 1983; Walton, 1986). A network, according to Seed (1990: 19) 'is a system or pattern of links between points... which have particular meanings' for those involved. Social workers focus on clients' networks and agency links which form a pattern in clients' daily lives. The aim is to identify formal and informal social networks, extend them and make them usable in helping the client. Networks may be more or less dense or of varying quality, depending on, respectively, the amount of contact between particular parts of the network and the value placed upon it. They may also have a variety of features (such as being concerned with home, work, leisure, care).

Networking, according to Garbarino, can be either *personal* or *social*. Personal work uses the psychological strength and skills of clients, aiming to improve their competence by enabling self-help and empowerment. In this direction, networking has connections with social skills training and radical empowerment approaches (see Chapters 5 and 11). Social helping uses nurturing and feedback to stimulate clients' support systems. Both personal and social help seek to invest in clients who are enabled to become involved with a network and thus offer resources to others while being helped themselves. In conventional social work, clients are helped, and then move out of the helping system; in this approach they stay in the helping system to help others. The worker's role is as an intermediary between people, rather than concentrating on a relationship with the client and a few others. The aim is interdependence between the client and others rather than the independence of the client. The worker acts as a consultant rather than as a clinician and is empowering rather than being a simple provider of services.

Caplan's work (1974; Caplan and Killilea, 1976) in the mental health field used support systems for people coming out of institutions and is an important source for these ideas. It led to an influential study by Collins and Pancoast (1976) of attempts to support informal helpers of former mental patients. Several studies use general systems theory in relation to volunteer projects in local schools (Davies, 1977), ecological systems theory in several different projects (Whittaker and Garbarino, 1983) and competence in dealing with the environment (Maluccio, 1981). Considerable effort has been made to understand and build up informal networks of neighbours to support people at risk (Abrams *et al.*, 1989; Bulmer, 1986; Wenger, 1984, 1994; Willmott, 1986, 1989). Work with elderly people in their local community suggests that the nature and type of networks will be affected by how nearby close relatives live, the proportion of family, friends and neighbours involved and the amount of interaction in networks (Wenger, 1994). Relatives and especially spouses are relied upon for most personal care, although social support may come from neighbours and friends. Friendship networks can be very important where people are socially isolated or stigmatised (Richardson and Ritchie, 1989). Maguire (1991) divides work in support networks into 'clinical' interventions in the network, case management and system development, that is improving and increasing links.

Specht (1986) shows that social support applies to a wide range of social relationships and organisations, whereas social networks refer to a specific set of interrelated people. He argues that there is little evidence that there are untapped resources available in the community to support people with problems in the United States, and there is empirical support for this view in the United Kingdom (Abrams, 1984; Bulmer, 1987). Timms (1983) and Allan (1983) suggest that a supportive service to existing social networks is appropriate, but attempting to replace formal provision with informal care or to change the existing patterns of informal care is likely to be unsuccessful. This is confirmed by Cecil *et al.* (1987) in a study in Northern Ireland.

Atherton: systems in residential care

Atherton (1989) interestingly applies systems thinking to residential care. He focuses on the fact that systems thinking is concerned with the way people relate to one another within social situations, rather than as individuals. Because, in residential care, people are part of a group of staff and residents and all have contacts with an outside world as well as interrelationships within the residential unit, it is difficult to deal with the complex understanding needed to work effectively in this setting. The systems idea of *boundary* helps to limit the complexity to particular issues or relationships within the residence or within the network of the client. Similarly, the idea of *feedback loops* helps to identify the interaction of different factors in creating a situation which workers must deal with. Systems theory also helps to create a focus on present *communication* among people in residence, both as a way of explaining how problems are maintained in the situation and as a way of intervening. This avoids the complexity of trying to work on complex past causes of problems. His ideas thus make direct use of communications theory ideas (see Chapter 7).

Residences are bounded by the fact that everyone lives together. This means that residences are *self-regulating systems*. This has advantages of security, but can lead to prescriptive rather than descriptive thinking, which is a disadvantage of residential care. Thus, rather than exploring and trying to understand what is going on to develop people's skills and capacities to live their lives more effectively, staff and residents often focus on controlling events. They do this by establishing norms for how things *ought* to be done and attempt to minimise risk by reducing unexpected events adversely affecting the smooth running of the residence. In this way, residential units try to establish homoeostasis or a balance, which enables them to manage external events and other factors which may upset their smooth running, rather than a steady state which allows them to incorporate change.

Atherton distinguishes between residential regimes which operate as skeletons and those which operate as shells. The analogy, as with much systems theory, is biological. Skeletons provide a framework on which life can be built which is flexible and allows growth. Shells protect a vulnerable system, but do not allow much growth or flexibility within the carapace. Skeleton systems are more open and permit more effective interaction across boundaries; shells limit interaction with the outside world.

This analysis helps Atherton to describe different ways in which residents manage relationships with others in the residence and elsewhere, and ways of developing practice so that it helps residents and the residential unit become more open and flexible in dealing with the outside world. It is a useful example of how systems theory can be applied to understanding complex interactions and provide guidance on worthwhile directions for social work intervention.

Commentary

Systems and ecological theories, with their attempts at structuring and technical terminology, form a very different style of theory from traditional social work practice, which emphasises individualisation and psychology. They are among the few comprehensive sociologically based theories of social work. Advantages of the systems approach are:

- More emphasis on changing environments than psychological approaches.
- It is interactive, concentrating on the effects of one person on another, rather than on internal thoughts and feelings.
- It alerts social workers to the possibility of alternative ways of achieving the same object (equi- and multi-finality). This reduces the stigma arising from diversity of behaviour and social organisation which some psychological theories that concentrate on normality and deviance tend to create (Leighninger, 1978).
- It is unitary (Goldstein, 1973), integrated (Pincus and Minahan, 1973) or holistic (Hearn, 1969; Leighninger, 1978), including work with individuals, groups and communities, and does not emphasise any particular method of intervention. Instead, it provides an overall way of describing things at any level, so that we can understand all interventions as affecting systems.

Particular explanatory theories form part of this overarching universe. Workers choose theories appropriate to levels of intervention with which they are involved. They thus avoid sterile debates about whether they are concerned with individual change or social reform. However, this raises the problems associated with eclecticism (see Chapter 2), that selecting theories to use on any organised basis may be difficult.

● It avoids linear, deterministic cause–effect explanations of behaviour or social phenomena, because equi- and multi-finality show how lots of energy flows can affect systems in many different ways. Patterns of relationships and how boundaries are shared or *interface* with one another are important ideas.

There are, however, problems with such claims:

● Because it is expository rather than explanatory (Forder, 1976), it sets out ideas in a novel way which makes them easier to grasp and makes connections between different levels of society and individual behaviour. However, it does not explain why things happen and why those connections exist. It is therefore hard to test empirically.

● It is not prescriptive (Germain, 1979b: 6), so it does not tell us what to do, where or how to affect systems (Mancoske, 1981). Also it does not allow us to control the effects of interventions in a system, because we do not know how each part of it will interact with the others. It assumes that affecting one part of a system will affect other parts, but in practice this does not seem to happen (Siporin, 1980).

● It is over-inclusive. Not everything is relevant and it does not help to decide what is. Many things may not fit into a general schema, deciding on boundaries may be complex or impossible, and it may be assumed that things are related in a system without checking to see if they actually are (Leighninger, 1978). In encouraging social workers to concentrate on the wide-scale issues, it may lead to the neglect of the small-scale and the personal (Siporin, 1980).

● Systems (particularly ecological) theory may overstate the importance of integrating parts of the system and assume that all the parts of a system are needed to maintain it, and are or should be interrelated. It thus tends to assume that systems are or should be conserved, and should maintain equilibrium rather than change or be changed. Also, systems theory tends to assume that conflict is less desirable than maintenance and integration, which may not be true in practice (Leighninger, 1978).

- The idea of feedback implies slow and manageable change, but what if radical change is needed? Systems theory makes little provision for this and does not deal with the problem that feedback sometimes amplifies deviance rather than reducing it (Leighninger, 1978).

- The ideas of entropy and survival as aspects of systems are analogies with the behaviour of physical systems, and like many of the biological and physical analogies in systems theory, may not have a general application to all social systems (Leighninger, 1978). Should all systems (for example, families torn by strife) seek to survive? Do they? Should entropy be exported to the environment, or cause a system to leach energy from what may already be an environment poor in energy? For example, should a poor family make demands on the resources of a poor neighbourhood, or should resources be redistributed from richer neighbourhoods? Such questions raise political issues that the model does not deal with, and it seems to assume a local, non-political resolution when applied to the daily round of social work.

- It has a complex and technical language which does not fit well with a human activity like social work (Germain, 1979b: 6) and often alienates workers as a result. This is a common criticism of borrowed technologies which systems theory shares with behaviour modification. By contrast, the ideas of conflict, need and drive in psychodynamic theory, or genuineness and alienation of humanist theory seem much more attractive.

- Because it is a very generalised theory it is hard to apply to any specific situations (Germain, 1979b: 7; Leighninger, 1978) and, on the other hand, applications might be very variable. One worker might interpret a situation in one way, another worker in another and it would be hard to judge which is right.

As well as these practical criticisms, there are also ideological doubts about systems theory. Many of these stem from criticisms of social systems theory in sociology because of its structural-functional perspective on society, and particularly that of Parsons (Evans, 1976). Mancoske (1981: 714–15) summarises these criticisms as follows:

> Critics claim that Parsons' action theory is less a systems theory than a statics theory, it is not empirically verifiable as developed, and is so abstract and vague that concepts are undefinable. The emphasis of action theory is on function, not process of interaction, and this negates the meaning of systems.

Mancoske argues that in its social work formulations, the criticisms of systems theory as static are weak, because usually considerable attention is given to change, both individual and social. Evans (1976) suggests that there is no logical connection between *social* integration, which is about whether there is social harmony or conflict in society, and *system* integration, which is about causal links between different social structures, which may be conflictual or change-orientated. In social work interpretations of systems theory, however, and particularly that of Pincus and Minahan, he argues that there is a hidden assumption that all systems are interdependent. This is only true of closed systems; open systems are much more flexible, and it is important to make the distinction clear. Siporin (1980) points to Marxist criticisms of systems theory which claim that it does not take account of the incompatibilities of class interest in capitalist societies and how these prevent any integration in such a society. Devore (1983) argues that the life model is better at dealing with social class, ethnic and cultural differences and life style than many other theories, but still lacks specificity in dealing with issues affecting black people.

Radical, anti-discriminatory, advocacy and empowerment theories are the other major sociological theories of social work, but social psychological, role and communications theory offer a more social psychological approach to social work activity, and the next chapter is concerned with these.

7

Social Psychological and Communication Models

Wider theoretical perspectives

The subject matter of social psychology (Hogg and Abrams, 1988) is the effect of relations within and between groups on creating and maintaining social identities. This includes ideas about how people behave in relation to, and therefore influence, others and the effects of social factors such as stigma, stereotyping and ideology on behaviour in groups. Following from this, social psychology considers the effects of communication and therefore language and speech upon social interactions. A substantial area of 'communication studies' has grown up concerned with language and other symbols of communication between human beings as individuals, within groups and more widely in organisations and social collectivities (Burgoon *et al.*, 1994; Corner and Hawthorn, 1989).

This area of study has direct relationships with social construction and postmodernist views of knowledge. Communications research involves understanding how human beings use language individually and in social situations to give meaning to particular views of the world. Power relations derive from the use of language to construct a view of the world which, if socially accepted, influences others. People such as social workers use language in this way to influence clients, which means that the processes through which they do so give power over clients. Equally, as Lyon (1993) argues in relation to the study of roles, creating roles is a process of constructing a place in social relations for ourselves.

Concepts from role theory, the idea of labelling and the whole area of social psychological research into human interactions have been important in social work. Breakwell and Rowett (1982) propose a social psychological approach to social work. It emphasises in particular how relationships are formed and managed by people in social situations, issues of identity related to matters such as stigma, group behaviour, the effects of environments, territory, and the need for personal space, and material on social and personal change. Kelly's *personal construct theory* proposes that people manage their behaviour according to 'constructs' in their mind about how to behave, which have been developed from past experience. We construct events differently from one another. Therefore, looking at and changing people's constructs may help to change behaviour, in the same way that cognitive theory (Chapter 5) proposes. This approach may also be a useful way of understanding social interactions (Tully, 1976). It has relationships with phenomenological and existential ideas, considered in the next chapter, which proclaim the variety of interpretations of the personal and social world that are possible.

Important ideas have also come from the micro-teaching of personal and social skills (Kurtz and Marshall, 1982), which we have already encountered in relation to social skills training in behavioural approaches to social work. Similar ideas have also grown up around the development of counselling through the work of Rogers and Carkhuff (see Chapter 8) using experiential techniques. These enable clients to learn practically skills that counsellors are helping them acquire. Micro-training grew up to offer a practical basis for using such techniques among helping professions. It includes the use of video for viewing actual behaviours, and detailed attention to feedback on specific behaviours (Kurtz and Marshall, 1982).

Groupwork and residential care have used many aspects of social psychological research into group and inter-group behaviour, and have constructed it from theories relevant to social work. Community work has also used this research to provide some basis for constructing work methods (Sutton, 1994).

Connections

Because of their psychological base, and experimental, research-based epistemology, social psychological approaches to social work have close links with cognitive approaches to social work. However, the focus on interpersonal and inter-group behaviour and therefore on language and communication have led towards a more social learning and cognitive approach and away from traditional behavioural views. As these forms of psychology have developed a more constructionist approach, the focus on language as a social creation and as a process for forming social structures and understanding have enabled the inclusion of ideas such as roles as 'performances' and communication as a form of social construction. This, in its turn, brings connnections to the humanist and existential models of social work, discussed in the next chapter.

The politics of social psychological and communication models

It is perhaps surprising, in view of its social rather than individual focus, that no consistent development of a social psychological theory occurred within social work. The main reasons for this are threefold. First, its focus on inter-group and interpersonal understanding and its experimental epistemology were not easily converted to individual casework. Second, partly because of its epistemology, there is no coherent theoretical model offering a set of principles of action for transfer into social work, as there was in psychoanalysis or behavioural and cognitive theories. These were devised for therapeutic purposes and could therefore be quickly adapted. Third, and as a result of this, specific knowledge has been acquired from social psychological work, especially for groupwork, without a model of action being created.

However, because of the importance of family therapy during the 1970s and 80s, the communication theory base of family therapy became more widely understood within social work. It provides a fairly comprehensive theory of action well supported by research and experience. It expresses many important values in social work, especially listening to clients and focusing on their behaviour and experience. However, it does not provide a coherent account of social work with wider social purposes. Therefore its use has been limited to mainly therapeutic or clinical situations, or to explaining and understanding particular patterns of behaviour in general social agencies, rather than providing a general theory of action. This is how it has been used – for example, in Lishman's (1994) book on communication in social work. However, Nelsen's (1980) account attempts a comprehensive model for action. The question whether it succeeds in meeting more than aspects of a social work theory is considered more fully in the commentary below.

Role theory

Writers such as Strean (1971) and Davis (1986) stress the contribution of sociological and social psychological insights of role theory for social work, while Perlman (1968) considers that 'social role' is useful for understanding relationships and personality. Because role theory is about our interactions with others and how their expectations and reactions cause us to respond in characteristic ways, she argues that it offers *social* explanations complementing psychological under- standing of personality. Perlman emphasises work, family and parental roles as determinants of personality and behaviour, showing how traditional social work theory emphasises these social institu- tions. Biddle and Thomas (1979) offer a collection of useful articles on role theory and research.

Role theory is related to structural-functional theory in sociology. It assumes that people occupy positions in social structures. Each posi- tion has a role associated with it. Roles are sets of expectations or behaviours associated with positions in social structures. The idea implies that roles are always to be considered in the context of rela- tionships, since it is only in relationships that roles can be identified (Munson and Balgopal, 1978). Roles create our identity as others see it. Because of the way others react to us, roles as others see them build up our own concept of our identity (Ruddock, 1969). Roles may come from our own expectations or those of others. They may be *ascribed* to us as a result of some circumstance (such as being a woman or black or disabled), or *attained* by us through something that we have done (like being a writer or Member of Parliament). A *role-set* is a collection of roles which go with a particular social position; by occu- pying that position you gain some or most of those roles. So, if you are a father, you are often expected also to be the main wage-earner in a family, the disciplinarian of your children, and you are usually also a husband, son-in-law, and you may well be a brother-in-law and grandfather as well. How we see our roles affects how well we manage change. Howard and Johnson (1985) give the example of single-parent families. American research found that people with traditional assumptions about the proper role to play in marriage find it harder to adjust to being a lone parent than people who experienced role flexibility in their marriage.

Role *complementarity* exists when roles, behaviour and expectations all fit together well with the expectations of surrounding people. Role *conflict* exists when one role is incompatible with another role. *Inter-role* conflict occurs when different roles held by one person are incompatible. *Intra-role* conflict occurs when expectations from different people of the same role disagree. Role *ambiguity* arises when we are uncertain about what a role entails. One difficulty in social work is that in order to maintain the special features of the professional relationship, workers separate to some extent their own personal attitudes and behaviour from the behaviour expected in their professional role. This separation may be difficult to balance with greater equality and openness in relationships with clients (Munson and Balgopal, 1978). One reason is that this form of *role distance*, even if professionally appropriate, may be mistaken by clients or others, for a distaste for occupying the role, because that is a more common reason for people having role distance (Ruddock, 1969: 14).

The value of these ideas is that some behaviour can be understood as role conflicts and uncertainties. This is easy for clients to understand, it does not criticise them in a personal way, and so it is easy to intervene and create change. Moreover, role theory takes in a social perspective on behaviour, so it is a useful link between behaviour problems and social environment.

For example, Clare, a middle-aged woman, was working as a secretary, having been divorced by her husband. She had brought up her children successfully alone. Her elderly mother, also alone, suffered from failing sight, was registered as blind and later had a fall in her home. The doctor to both families suggested that they should live together, and Clare would provide greater security for her mother. This arrangement became difficult and a social worker was asked to help. Using ideas from role theory helped to explain that there was role conflict here between Clare's working role, which was important for her self-esteem (this is often the case with work), and her role as a caring daughter. This was both inter-role conflict, because work and daughter roles conflicted, and intra-role conflict, because it appeared that the mother's expectations about the role of a caring daughter conflicted with Clare's and, indeed, those of the doctor and Clare's daughter who still lived at home. Looking more deeply into the situation, Clare was suffering from role ambiguity, because she understood and appreciated all these views of her role as daughter, so she was herself uncertain about how she should behave.

In this example, role theory clarifies what is happening, without blaming individuals or criticising their behaviour or thoughts. However, proponents of more psychological ideas would criticise this approach for neglecting the strong feelings which might arise, and prevent people from changing their behaviour or resolving the conflicts revealed. Ruddock (1969) argues that role theory is insufficient to explain particular behaviour on its own. Other forms of explanation are required alongside it. Nonetheless, it is a useful concept, in his view, for linking explanations of behaviour with social factors.

This approach can also be criticised from a radical perspective, because it fails to emphasise wider social pressures leading to the oppression of women as carers, when social provision to help them accept their responsibilities is not available. Also, women's roles as carers, in a Marxist perspective, relate to their position as a reserve pool of labour in society, to be made available if there is not enough male labour, and as the centre of families reproducing oppressive capitalist social relations in which unsupported, exploitative expectations upon daughters exist.

So, while role theory helps to explain how social patterns affect individual clients, its structural-functional approach may lead to our assuming that roles exist and are a necessary part of the pattern of society. If so, we may fail to question whether those patterns are appropriate and might usefully be changed. Moreover, role theory does not provide techniques for behaviour change and dealing with emotional and personal responses to role conflicts. It merely makes them apparent.

Another way of looking at roles exists, typified by Goffman's (1968b) work. In social interaction, people need to find out about others, and they do so by picking up signs from others' behaviour. This makes it possible for us to influence others' views of us by managing the information they receive from us. We give 'performances' designed to give an appropriate impression. Roles, in this view, are 'enactments' of the social expectations attached to a social status. We may have a number of parts (the dramatic analogy is intentional) in the performance of a role, and we may act different parts in different situations. Our performance is usually 'idealised' so that it includes common social expectations. Some aspects of the role are emphasised, others concealed. So, in another famous book, Goffman (1968a) is concerned with how stigmatised people manage the impressions other people get of that aspect of them which is socially disapproved, so that they can 'pass' as relatively normal. People often work together in 'teams' to share the responsibility, particularly in organisations, of enacting socially approved roles, and they can share behaviour which is not in role 'backstage' as a relief when they do not have to put up a front. In a series of books, Goffman (1972a, b, c) extends these ideas into a comprehensive analysis of how socially expected roles can explain many different forms of behaviour.

These ideas relate to symbolic interactionism (see Chapter 8). They emphasise how roles are formed by social expectations and *labelling*. Labelling originates from the work of Lemert (1972) and Becker (1963). According to Lemert, most people occasionally act in a deviant way, and the crucial issue is the response of the surrounding social environment to that act. Sometimes, people are put through a social system which labels them as deviant or criminal. Once labelled, they are likely to live up to the social expectations of their label, and to be encouraged to act in more deviant ways. This leads to an even stronger labelling process. Becker shows how social groups create deviance by making rules and deciding whom they are applied to, labelling them as 'outsiders' to normal social life. 'Moral panics' (Cohen, 1972) about particular forms of deviance, such as hooliganism or rowdy behaviour at sports events, mean that social concern about that form of deviance rises. This strengthens the labelling process. In turn, people are caught by the expectation that they will be deviant and this encourages deviant behaviour.

For example, John was an adolescent boy from an inner-city area, who as a keen supporter of the local football team, went with a group of friends to a game, and was arrested for rowdy behaviour in the town centre. With a minor criminal record, he was encouraged by social pressures to show off in other ways, to live up to his 'criminal' standing in the eyes of his friends. This led to a number of other daring exploits, which came to the notice of the police, particularly because, being black, he was easily identifiable. Having gained a local reputation for being 'bad', he was excluded from the local youth club, and spent more time on the street, with others who had been similarly excluded. This led to further offending. Eventually, court proceedings led to social work involvement. By exploring this history, the worker could see the process by which he had become separated and alienated from a more conventional social background, and steps could be taken to reintegrate him into less deviant social settings, such as another youth club, and help him find acceptable and status-enhancing activities – membership of a rock band.

This approach acknowledges better than role theory the alienating effect of oppressive interventions by authoritative agents of the state, such as teachers, youth leaders and the police. However, its weakness is that it does not help to change attitudes and patterns of behaviour which may be well established. Also, it tends to accept conventional social responses to the behaviour, at the same time assuming that behaviour is in essence socially created, which, if it were true, would mean that conventions would have little force. These ideas thus fail to question the social circumstances which lead to deviance and alienation in the first place, and how the power of agencies such as the police and courts is crucial in creating deviance among some social groups (mainly working-class groups) and not among others.

Their value as ideas, however, is that they draw attention to how official agencies, such as those employing social workers, may play a part in the social creation of problems they are set up to deal with. We need to take care, therefore, in assessing and providing services to avoid stigmatising systems and behaviour (Levy, 1981). There is research evidence suggesting that social workers often label clients negatively (Case and Lingerfelt, 1974; Gingerich *et al.*, 1982).

Communication theory in social work

Communication theory helps develop some of the social psychological ideas discussed above and decide on appropriate direct interventions with clients. It brings together a number of psychological studies, particularly of a group of psychologists and therapists in Palo Alto, California, of whom the best known is possibly Satir (1964, 1972), whose work is about the complexities of human interaction particularly through speech and in attempts to change patterns of behaviour. Anthropologists and social psychologists such as Birdwhistell (1973), Scheflen (1972; Scheflen and Ashcraft, 1976) and Hall (1966) are also relevant. They are concerned with the micro-level of detailed physical movements associated with communication, and broader cultural issues, such as territoriality, personal space and proxemics, which is about how closeness and related factors affect relationships. Related to this work is neuro-linguistic programming (MacLean, 1986), which originates from the detailed study of the language interactions of therapists.

Nelsen (1980, 1986) argues that communication theory can offer a useful connection between many theories of social work. Much of the energy which maintains the equilibrium of a system (see Chapter 6), such as an individual, family or social group, consists of information and reactions to it. Many theories of personality which are used in social work, such as ego psychology, are concerned with how the individual processes reality, and this too relies on communication. Behavioural theories, similarly, rely on people's capacity to understand the patterns of their behaviour; cognitive theorists are concerned with how reality is perceived and interpreted. Communication is, therefore, an essential part of any worker's understanding. Communication theory and research have established knowledge and a framework for such understanding.

Nelsen's (1980) book applies communication theory which has been developed elsewhere to social work in general, rather than, as with some family therapy texts, to a particular form of therapy. It is, therefore, used as the basis of the account given here. Lishman (1994) selects from the same material to explore more pragmatically useful ideas for practice. This illustrates the political problem of social psychological research in social work theory. That is, it is often used piecemeal to provide evidence for practice, rather than as a coherent theoretical model.

The starting point of communication theory, according to Nelsen, is that when we take some action, we always do so in response to some information that we have received. Information might be facts, or other things that may be learned, such as emotion, memories, bodily sensations, or an idea about how someone feels about you. We perceive the information, and then we evaluate it; this is information processing. As we evaluate communications, we give *feedback* to the communicator, who thus gains some idea of how we have perceived and evaluated the communication. We came across this idea when discussing systems theory. We all have our own internal rules for processing information, which mean that we think some things are important and not others. This leads to *selective perception.*

So, for example, a young mother with two toddlers had found the younger child difficult to manage as a baby – he had cried a lot and disturbed her. She gained a perception of him as difficult. Therefore, she interpreted behaviour from him as disturbed when it was aimed at getting her attention and love. She accepted similar behaviour from her elder daughter. The boy responded to her rejection of his attention-seeking behaviour by becoming more demanding, thus reinforcing her perception of him. So, she came to see all his behaviour as difficult, selecting out from his repertoire of behaviour the bad or difficult things and not noticing behaviour which would ordinarily have been acceptable. So, selective perception and the feedback from it reinforced a cycle in which his behaviour became more demanding, causing her in turn to become more rejecting. While such understanding can be useful in practice by showing what is happening and how it might be possible to intervene, from a psychodynamic perspective, it might be argued that it fails to take into account what emotional or unconscious pressures caused her to have her initial selective perception. Therefore, from this viewpoint, action to interrupt the cycle of behaviour might not help because the psychological forces causing the inappropriate perceptions are not dealt with. This approach might also ignore important factors in the situation. A women-centred approach, for example (see Chapter 11), would look at social expectations of motherhood, and the factor of the different sexes of the children.

Many people have problems with communication, because they perceive information badly or what they select is hard for others to understand. This may be because their evaluation is poor, because they do not give feedback which others understand well or because they do not perceive the feedback that others give them very well. These problems, called an *information processing block*, often lead to difficulties in relationships.

Some communication is *verbal*. Feedback that we are listening to verbal communication can be comforting to speakers. *Non-verbal* communication, such as how we hold our bodies or move or how close we sit, also gives information to others. *Metacommunication* is discussion about the nature of the relationship between people.

We are all always communicating. Even silence or absence is communication, because others interpret it. Relevant communication may be symbolic and non-verbal as well as verbal (Lishman, 1994). All communication must be evaluated within its context. Behaviour which is strange in one place at one time would be perfectly normal at another. For example, I was once asked to see a client who was behaving in a disturbed manner by a doctor who had seen her in an emergency. He thought she was mentally ill. When I enquired, I discovered that her husband had declared his homosexuality and left her to live with a man, and she was understandably distressed. Her distress mimicked the symptoms of mania. By failing to explore the context, the doctor had misunderstood the communication.

Most communication forms *patterns*. People become accustomed to balanced and predictable ways of communicating between those with whom they regularly have contact. This forms the basis of their relationship. We saw this in the case of the mother and her 'difficult' son. Furlong (1990) argues that social workers fall into a pattern of using words such as 'help', 'support' and 'encourage' which imply positive relationships with clients. This implies cooperative endeavour of a therapeutic kind. He argues that on occasions more directive words would form a more effective pattern for getting clients to complete tasks. Pugh (1996) analyses the use of patterns of language within comunication to show how they give evidence of attitudes, create identity and are used to express power in relationships and social structures. Communication always has *content*, which is its surface material, but in a relationship, the metacommunication may give added or different meanings to the apparent content. The way content is presented offers a proposal of a certain sort of relationship. So, how workers behave towards clients says something about how relationships between them are expected to be. We saw in discussing role theory how apparent distance due to professional roles might be misinterpreted. Patterns of communication often express power, domination or subordination. Communication theory may, therefore, help us to identify oppression and inequality. Social psychology generally has a lot to say about oppression and discrimination between groups (Hogg and Abrams, 1988).

Communication theory is especially about control in relationships. *Symmetrical* relationships are equal, and the people concerned behave similarly towards one another. *Complementary* relationships are unequal, but each contributes a particular role within the interaction; as in an employer–employee relationship. Most relationships contain elements of both these types, but lean towards one or the other. Successful relationships vary between the two tendencies; this includes worker–client relationships, since a worker should never be always in control. *Metacomplementary* relationships exist where one person lets go of power or forces the other to take it. This happens, for instance, when a social worker tries to get a client to make decisions in the process of their work together. *Symmetrical escalation* occurs when both sides of the relationship (all or several sides in a group or a family) keep trying to cap one another in an effort to gain or give up power. Understanding such behaviour helps workers to identify gender, ethnic and other power inequalities.

All communication involves giving *messages* to which a *response* is given. Both messages and responses contain content and relationship communications, usually at the same time. Responses may be *accepting, rejecting* of the content or relationship material in the message, or may be *selective*. Workers need to be aware of clients' responses to their communications. Such responses may be verbal or non-verbal, and sometimes the messages given by one may conflict with those given by the other. Lishman (1994) identifies features of relationships which research shows to be helpful in building relationships. This includes genuineness, warmth and acceptance: these concepts derive from the work of Rogers (see Chapter 8). Encouragement and approval, empathy, responsivity and sensitivity are also important. Workers must attend and listen carefully to what their clients say. Careful communication is also required when sharing information, to make sure it is communicated properly, and in making a contract.

Some social work uses the communication theory idea of *paradox*. The idea of this is that some forms of difficult behaviour occur as people try to gain power in a relationship. If the power is given freely, the person giving the power gains the ascendency, so there is no point in using the difficult behaviour, which should then go away. So, if a client is aggressive, and the worker sits back and allows the aggression to be poured out in the worker–client relationship, the worker gains the power. Aggression does not work for this client any longer. This can be taken further by setting clients tasks using paradoxes. For instance, a man who constantly ignores his wife can be set the task of doing so every evening for an hour. This is incredibly difficult to do, and helps him learn what is confirming and ignoring behaviour both for her and for him.

Similar points may be made about communication in small social systems such as groups and families. Patterns of communication give evidence of *operating rules* within the group. When some sort of upset in the equilibrium of the group arises, the rules (reflected in communication patterns) are brought into play. People newly in a group have to work out operating rules between themselves, and these then become patterns of behaviour and communication. So, one member may be the one who shows the anger, or takes the lead in making decisions. Workers dealing with established groups can affect how they work by trying to change the operating rules. In a system, giving information introduces energy which will affect the whole system, so persuading one group member to behave and communicate in a different way, or getting all or some members to agree about how they will act, should produce wider change as all the elements of the system become affected. Operating rules are often about sexuality, power, dependence, assertiveness and separateness. As with all systems theory, however, this approach can be criticised because it does not help us to be precise about what change will bring the desired result. We can see that some change will result from affecting the system, but with all the complex interactions, some unintended results may occur.

People often bring operating rules into groups and families that they have learned in relationships elsewhere. So, past relationships affect those in the present. Group environment, culture and communication affect relationships, which then affect other relationships, which go on to create a culture about appropriate behaviour in relationships. There is a cycle in which communication connects present, past, relationships and environment in a complex way.

Communication theory is particularly useful in *initial interviews*, where new relationship patterns are becoming established, and so communication is at a premium. Context is very important. As we saw in Chapter 1, clients often come with perceptions of what is appropriate in a social work agency gained from the social context outside. In particular, they often arrive assuming that they are inferior in a power relationship. Social contexts, such as a low status office or scruffy waiting room, may make them feel more inferior. The content of initial communications will be about gaining useful information, but there will also be proposals about suitable relationship patterns. Much of this will be about the power of the parties and it is up to the worker to establish the appropriate pattern. In group and family work, these initial establishing proposals will be made among group members as well as with the worker.

In *assessment*, workers should consider the information that clients are using to decide on their behaviour, its sources, its communication and what blocks may have got in the way of processing that information appropriately. Clients are at risk when blocks exist. The blocks may be internal – such as immense emotions or external, such as poverty leading to hunger – or social in the present or the past. In these areas, communication theory helps us make connections to empowerment theory, which is concerned with removing disempowering blocks: some such blocks may be learned communication patterns. Likely patterns of relationship and communication in the client's environment must be examined, and the operating rules of their family or other systems may be relevant. The possible need for second-order change must be examined. One way of doing this is to look for the typical pattern of behaviour in operating rules when the worker proposes some change.

Discussing constructivist assessment, Neimeyer and Neimeyer (1993) argue that people 'make meaning' from narrative structures ('telling stories'). Neimeyer (1993) suggests 'laddering', whereby an interviewer helps someone to delve into the more complex implications of simple statements about themselves, taking a step at a time into more complex ideas. For example, someone who feels the need to keep her emotions controlled comes to see first the implication that she is therefore not relaxed in social situations, then that she can be uncomfortable, and that this leads her to be lonely. He identifies a number of similar devices, many of a cognitive nature, and some based on Kelly's personal construct theory to enable people to tell their stories in a structured way. Similarly, particularly with people from different cultures, organised exploration of people's family and life histories through 'oral history' can allow people to examine in a structured way the meanings and constructions they give to their own experiences (Martin, 1995).

During the process of *intervention*, the worker operates at the content level in four ways:

1 gaining information, using questions, an encouraging manner, and reframing clients' comments to show understanding of them;
2 giving feedback, showing how the worker evaluates what the client says, accepting, rejecting, neutral or selective;
3 giving information, including material which explains the worker's actions, so that waiting until the worker hears the full story is not seen as rejecting.
4 changing information coming to clients from elsewhere, to affect information which conflicts, or which is likely to be overwhelming or inaccurate.

Most communications which are close to clients' expectations are more acceptable and therefore likely to be more effective. Therefore, work should proceed in small steps. This also applies to relationship proposals and negotiation. The style of relationship should proceed in stages from what the client finds acceptable. The relationship will be complementary with children, less so with adolescents and tend towards symmetry with adults. So, working with very young children in trouble with the police, I often treated them fairly directively, and, while consulting them, made active suggestions about things that they should do, or specific arrangements for activities which would avoid patterns of delinquent behaviour. With older adolescents, my approach was rather more to offer a series of acceptable options for intervention, and discuss the pros and cons of the alternatives. With adult offenders, I would help them construct their alternatives for themselves.

Sometimes blocks occur between worker and client, when either content or relationship information proposed by one is rejected by the other, and the first misses the response which shows that this has happened. This can be prevented by paying careful attention to both content and relationship information and verbal and non-verbal communications. When it happens, both the missed response and the rejected information must be made apparent. Clients should be encouraged to be explicit when they disagree with or dislike a communication, thus learning to make appropriate feedback. Often, however, clients may not be clear about blocks, and workers must look out for uncertain or unclear responses. Over a period of working together, relationship operating rules should become (explicitly) more flexible and symmetrical. On several occasions, for example, I have found it useful to discuss with clients how we have gone about dealing with problems, how I have behaved towards them and why I think it is appropriate. When asked to describe the typical way I work, many clients have a fairly good idea from experience how I help interviews to progress, and what my reactions will be to certain things that they will say. This is typical of many social relationships, and, as we have seen, these expectations of patterns will condition how people respond. This may be unhelpful. Clients can conceal information which will not be acceptable, for example. But it also sets a model of behaviour which, if it is useful, clients can follow.

Communication theory can also be useful in *inter-professional practice*. Positive feedback, clear communication of content, and through metacommunication about what relationships will be effective, may, for instance, make contacts with colleagues more useful to clients.

Commentary

The advantages of these models are that we can understand them easily, at least in general principle and apply them widely; communication theory, in particular, is based on a long, rigorous research tradition. They fit with other theories of practice. Workers who use other explanatory theories also use social psychological concepts. They may be applied either to assist in clarifying interactions in practice, or as a form of explanation for the minutiae of human problems. In the first case, the theories and the research which lie behind them give practical help in controlling and understanding relationships and interactions with clients and learning a technology of interviewing and interpersonal skills. Role theory, about expectations around social positions, gives an understanding of social relationships which, allied to better understanding of how communication patterns create such social expectations, creates a useful model for understanding both social and interpersonal aspects of social life. Communication theory also gives practical ways of intervening using such understanding. Social psychological theory encourages workers to pay attention to important aspects of behaviour which they otherwise might ignore or play down. It also offers fairly specific research backing for its information about communication behaviour, to set against more imaginative constructions about behaviour available in some psychological or sociological theories about behaviour. Role theory, also, is fairly specific and practical in its analysis of human interactions.

In the second case, workers who generally rely on broad-ranging theories of explanation appreciate having the fairly small-scale explanations of problems in interpersonal relationships to add to wider range theories. Communications theory is relatively neutral in major ideological debates between, for example, behaviourists and psychoanalysts or Marxists and functionalists, for this reason. Role theory, however, is generally functional in character. Both accept a role for environment, and also for internal thinking and emotions. However, they may not always emphasise sufficiently and permit intervention in the emotional and social origins of behaviour.

Role theory which sees roles as presentations of the self, and developments of communications theory which are concerned with how language constructs meaning in social situations present unthreatening ways of helping clients understand behaviour. These ideas connect social psychological theory to wider social aspects of situations. This permits, at least notionally, the possibility of using social psychological concepts in the understanding of the creation of social identity, rather than relying, as social work tends to, on developmental psychology as the basis for understanding human development. Such an approach might be useful since it would allow similar social construction concepts to be used at all ages, whereas developmental psychology tends to stop with teenagers.

Nelsen's (1980) account of communication theory creates a comprehensive theory of action at least in therapeutic situations but it has not succeeded in introducing communication and other social psychological concepts to wider use. This may be partly because her work was produced before more complex theories about communication, social identity and social meaning began to develop. As social construction views of social life are applied to practical social work more fully, we might see further contributions from social psychology than the piecemeal importations so far used. White *et al.* (1994) demonstrate that it is also crucial to participatory work in social development and more generally.

Other problems with communication theory lie in its concentration on the style and nature of the interactions rather than the content. Although content is said to be important, how to assess it is not well articulated. We noted criticisms of psychoanalysis that it encourages workers to look for inferred thoughts and problems behind difficulties that clients expressly present. Social psychology presents similar problems. The worker is seen as relatively competent, compared with the client, and may even be a manipulative and devious figure. One feature of the model, the use of paradox, particularly gives rise to this criticism. Compared with psychoanalysis, however, interaction with clients is relatively open in a communication model.

With the practical problems which many clients face, role and communication ideas have little to offer. Contacts with other agencies, and competence in everyday life may be enhanced for the client, but different techniques are presumably needed to gain social security entitlements.

8

Humanist and Existential Perspectives

Wider theoretical perspectives

Humanism and existentialism are ways of looking at life, based on well-established philosophies. Humanism believes in the capacity of conscious human beings to reason, make choices and act freely. This is different from being humane; that is, the practice of treating people with kindness because we value their humanity. Because of its focus on the human capacity to reason, humanism is often associated with atheism or agnosticism – that is, disbelief in gods or religion. This is because such belief requires faith rather than reason. It is also associated with democracy, because of its belief in the capacity of human beings to value and participate with one another in controlling their destiny. An example of such an association is Glassman and Kates's (1990) book on humanist groupwork, discussed below. They see groups as supporting democratic and humanist principles because they allow people's participation in working together on an equal basis.

Existential philosophy is concerned with the meaning for human beings of the fact of their existence. It focuses on the capacity of people to gain the personal power to control their lives and change ideas governing how they live. People are accepted as both 'subjects' and 'objects'; that is, they both act on and are affected by the environment. It is accepted that the environment contains absurd and alienating experiences and suffering. Major streams of thought are based around the work of Büber, Kierkegaard and Sartre. Sartre's work has had most impact on social work theory (Blom, 1994). Thompson's (1992) book, discussed below, applies Sartre's ideas to social work.

Many Eastern philosophies are considered to have relationships with humanism and existentialism, especially Zen Buddhism, but also Hinduism and aspects of Islam. This is because they emphasise the process whereby human beings realise their capacity to enhance their own well-being through spiritual self-development. The high value given to religious faith is an important distinction of such philosophies from humanism and existentialism. Such religious philosophies have had direct impact on the thinking of many therapists (see, for example, Claxton, 1986).

Some relationships exist between these ideas and 'green' political and social philosophies (George and Wilding, 1994). These emphasise the importance of human beings controlling their destructive capacities and living in harmony with their environments. These ideas have had some impact on residential care through communes focusing on shared living (Pepper, 1991). However, many might consider these views to be marginal in their social importance and in their influence on social work.

Similarly, we can see relationships with feminist theories. This is because they focus on women's shared experience in developing consciousness of their oppressed social position (see Chapter 11). Also the control of male capacities such as violence, which might be destructive of equal and harmonious social relations, is an important feature of feminist ideas. Here again, we can see importance given to humanist participative self-development, while recognising the need to control the destruction implicit in existing social relationships.

Connections

While they have specific philosophical meanings, in social work theory models of practice with certain features are grouped together as humanist. These models have in common ideas that human beings are trying to make sense of the world that they experience. Also, social workers are trying to help people gain the skills to explore themselves and the personal meaning that they attach to the world they perceive and which affects them. Humanist models propose that people's interpretations of their own selves are valid and worthwhile.

Such concepts are closely related to constructivist and constructionist views of the world. We saw in Chapters 1 and 2 that this precludes a focus on objective, neutral views of behaviour and social interaction (Allen, 1993). Workers generate multiple ideas through working with clients on constructing a variety of meanings to their experiences (Dean, 1993) and creating a new idea of their 'self' (Fisher, 1991). One approach may be to identify contrasts and dualities in experiences, eliciting and reconstructing accounts which involve experiences of power, choice and change (Fisher, 1991). Discourse analysis, related to postmodernist and post-structuralist ideas (Rojek *et al.*, 1989), similarly seeks to incorporate the reality of diversity and ambiguity into the way we represent clients, their social world and the role of social workers through language. Rodger (1991), for example, shows how using the language of 'contracts' in negotiations with clients about who is to do what within a social work relationship introduces uncertainty and conflict into the negotiation because of differences between professional and everyday understandings of the meaning of 'contract' (see Chapter 4 for another area of this debate).

Well-known systems of practice and writers in social work and related fields are regarded as humanist or existentialist. Their ideas have filtered into more general use. Examples are Laing's views of mental health, Rogers' client- (more recently person-) centred therapy; and a variety of writers such as Brandon and Keefe on thought systems such as Zen and meditation, the gestalt therapy of Perls *et al.* (1973), and occasional enthusiasts such as Bradford (1969), Krill (1978, 1990) and Thompson (1992) have provided a literature applying these ideas to social work. Goldstein (1981, 1984) has attempted to adapt cognitive theory and make it more social work-friendly by adding an explicitly humanist element. Berne's (1961) transactional analysis, although its origins lie in psychodynamic theory, is also often regarded as humanist in approach, because of its focus on self-understanding through analysis of patterns of communication and behaviour.

The politics of humanist and existential theory

Humanism is both basic and peripheral to social work theory. It is basic because many take it for granted as the fundamental attitude of social workers. It is peripheral in that it is not even treated as a perspective, since it is seen as more a general philosophical position informing practice than a way of defining a specific approach to practice. Existentialism and Eastern philosophies are even more a fringe interest, taken up by a few.

However, some writers have presented a critique of many social work theories and perspectives for being too technical and medical (individualist-reformist). In doing so, they are reasserting the importance of belief in the capacity of humanity to improve itself, which we often see as central to social work. They often also rail against the tendency to make social work, especially in large state agencies, too technical and bureaucratic. Emphasising the humanity of the objectives and ideals of social work is a counter-position (for example, Hugman, 1977). It seeks to re-establish the focus of social work as reflexive-therapeutic in character, and therefore in some respects opposed to socialist-collectivist and individualist-reformist. Nonetheless, existentialism particularly relates to radical concerns about alienation although the explanation and approach to alienation are different, and the valuation of democratic processes and human participation also speaks to radical and feminist approaches to social work. We have already seen that Goldstein's (1981, 1984) attempts to humanise cognitive approaches to social work create some alliances with technical and individual-reformist approaches to social work. Again, therefore, we can see the tensions between and connections among these different perspectives on social work.

Franklin (1995) and Laird (1995) argue that social construction and constructivist views may constitute an important shift in the way social work theories are considered. They argue that practice implications need to be developed. Saleeby's (1992) strengths perspective, personal construct theory, narrative psychology (White and Epston, 1990) including oral history (Martin, 1995) and various aspects of family therapy have been relevant. Crucial in many areas of work is the idea of working on clients' self-esteem, and self-understanding towards empowerment objectives (see Chapter 13). This can be important where clients experience oppression due to ethnic difference (Greene *et al.*, 1996). Family therapy, and through this activity social work ideas, have taken on social construction and constructivist aspects which are regarded as replacements or developments of systems ideas (Kelley, 1994). Particularly influential work has come from de Shazer (1985, 1988, 1991) and colleagues. Their solution-focused work (Walter and Peller, 1992), like strengths-focused work (see Chapter 6) has a positive, rather than problem-solving, emphasis. Behaviours which are not typical of problems that the clients identify as their reason for seeking help are used as exceptions to the 'problem', and as evidence for the possibility and a basis for building solutions. Change is assumed to be continual, with small changes building up to large ones. Clients' resources and existing cooperation with others are used to work towards solutions, with the client treated as the expert in their situation. We impose meaning on outside events, which we then influence by the meanings we have constructed. This circular process is interrrupted with meanings attached to the new solutions, which then form part of the reconstruction of the world.

Humanism, and such views of social work, are often taken as part of the cause of public criticism of social work for being vague and idealistic.

Some humanist influences on social work

Person-centred ideas

Carl Rogers (1951, 1961; Rogers and Strauss, 1967) is probably the most important humanist writer on therapy to have an influence on social work. His impact is, however, indirect, since his greatest significance is in the related field of counselling. Social workers' involvement in counselling work and training has moved his ideas into social work. Another significant influence is his formulation of the conditions necessary (and he would say sufficient but evidence does not support this, according to Patterson, 1986) to successful therapy. These are that *clients should perceive* that workers act as follows:

- They are *genuine and congruent* in their therapeutic relationship (that is, what they say and do reflects their personality and real attitudes and is not put on to influence clients).
- They have *unconditional positive regard* for clients.
- They *empathise* with clients' views of the world.

Carkhuff and his associates (Truax and Carkhuff, 1967; Carkhuff and Berenson, 1977) have adapted these ideas into a more general concept. These are first, honesty and genuineness; second, (sometimes non-possessive) warmth, respect, acceptance; and third, empathic understanding. Carkhuff's work proposes scales by which we may assess the extent of these in a therapeutic relationship. Empirical work has confirmed that these are the effective elements in therapeutic relationships. Rogers' development of understanding of the relationship and effective elements within it has been his major influence on social work.

The worker's approach, according to Rogers, should be non-directive, non-judgemental and, in later formulations should involve 'active listening', 'accurate empathy' and 'authentic friendship'. Rogers' early work is broadly psychodynamic (Rowe, 1986, quoting Hart) but developed a humanist perspective, concentrating on the importance of the 'self' seeking personal growth. There is an emphasis on the 'here-and-now' rather than on the history of clients' problems. Because of the belief in clients' uniqueness, diagnosis and classification of conditions is not accepted. Everyone must be treated as an individual.

Rogers' later ideas extended into taking up these humanist ideas in community work, in organisations and in political change. He proposes that we should enable people to take up their 'personal power' which we all possess to achieve their objectives (Rogers, 1977).

Besides Rogers' work, there are several humanist psychologies and therapies which were influential in the 1960s and 70s. Carkhuff and Berenson (1977) suggest that five ideas characterise them all as follows:

1 We can only understand ourselves in relation to others.
2 Our main anxiety in life is losing others and being alone.
3 We are guilty because we cannot achieve a creative life.
4 We alone have responsibility to act on our own decisions.
5 Therapy aims to help us act and accept freedom and
   responsibility in doing so.

Many ideas in humanistic psychology derive from Maslow's concern for 'self-actualisation' and the attainment of 'human potential.' (Maslow, 1970). Maslow's basic theory, like psychoanalysis, supposes that the motivation to act for such purposes comes from a need which derives from something that we are lacking. Frankl's logotherapy is typical in emphasising that we each must find our own meaning in life (Arnold and Gasson, 1979). A development of Frankl's work in family therapy proposes that the human search for meaning is best achieved within a family context (Lantz, 1987). Some writers (for example, Keefe, 1986) promote meditation for exploring oneself and one's potential, and in increasing workers' capability to be empathetic with and conscious of clients' needs.

Eastern, humanist and symbolic ideas

Brandon (1976) offers Zen ideas as a useful contribution to social work. His is an intense and personal vision in which workers should use all the elements of their personality to arrive at an authentic inter-relationship with people in distress. Unlike many humanistic approaches to therapy, which have been criticised as therapies only for the mildly disturbed, seeking greater personal fulfilment, he seeks to approach people in extreme difficulties. Work is directed towards self-understanding, enlightenment (the Zen concept is *satori*, a leap towards intuitive understanding) and self-growth for both worker and client. An important idea is 'hindering' the client's movement towards self-development, and enabling clients to avoid the many features of their environments which do so. Brandon's is an attractive approach, relying on personal charisma and genuine sharing between clients and workers.

Several writers, of whom England (1986) is recently pre-eminent, argue that we should see social work as an artistic endeavour rather than as an application of social science. Many writers use art and liter-ature to aid understanding of the world and to assist in helping (Rose, 1992; Sanders, 1993). Black and Enos (1981) claim that phenomeno-logical ideas validate this approach. This is because phenomenology argues that we can only understand human behaviour from the view-point of the people involved. Methods are required to explore and understand individual viewpoints. England extends this into a humanist theory of social work, based around the ideas of 'coping' (a concept important in ego psychology) and 'meaning'. As in personal construct theory (see Chapter 7), how social workers, clients and others around them attach meaning to events crucially affects how workers will deal with them. The idea of making sense is a way of humanising and inter-preting clients as worthwhile parts of society. Lantz and Greenlee (1990) show in a discussion of working with war veterans the impor-tance of seeing a sense of meaning in distressing past situations.

Laing (1965, 1971) explicitly uses existential ideas as well as psychoanalysis in his early work on theories of mental illness. These have had some influence in social work, particularly in the United Kingdom. In later work he became more radical and mystical (Sedg-wick, 1972). His important work is on schizophrenia, and argues that we can understand this major psychotic mental illness as a person's reaction to a bewildering or possibly damaging social environment. He gives great importance to the 'self' in his discussion of the 'false-self system' and self-consciousness. Later, he picked up the ideas of communication theories in the family, in particular the *double-bind* of Bateson *et al.* (1956). He proposes that disturbances in family communications lead to one family member being caught between conflicting demands from others, leading to disturbed reactions diagnosed as schizophrenia. Particularly in psychiatric settings, Laing's work has taught social workers to be cautious about medical diagnoses which fail to consider social and family factors as possible elements in the cause of problems. More widely, symbolic interactional and phenomenological sociology has influenced work in settings where other people who are often regarded as deviant (such as offenders) are dealt with.

Symbolic interactionism is a sociological and social psychological perspective deriving from the work of George Herbert Mead (1934) and Blumer (1969). The basic idea is that people act according to symbols (ideas that stand in place) of the outside world, which they hold in their minds. They create their symbols through interpreting interactions between themselves and the outside world, using language. Their self is similarly created because, to have interactions with the outside world, they must have an idea also of the being which is undertaking the interaction. To think about the world, therefore, people have to have interactions with themselves. Such ideas have links with personal construct theory (see Chapter 7), in which people's behaviour is seen as organised according to the internal constructs they hold about the external world. Ramon (1990) argues that symbolic interactionist ideas help workers and clients understand the process of leaving psychiatric hospital. This experience can be interpreted as a rite of passage in anthropological terms, as a transition crisis and as a process which threatens and requires the reinterpretation of self-identity.

Chaiklin (1979) argues that symbolic interactionism offers an alternative for social workers to a purely psychological mode of understanding human behaviour. Focusing on interactions and symbols may be less demanding emotionally for both client and worker than the traditional close relationship. Moreover, these ideas assume the basic normality and competence of most people, rather than assuming illness or maladaption and an inability to control their own destiny. One of the most important of these is the idea of labelling, which we met in Chapter 7.

Many of these ideas relate to role and social psychological theories explored in Chapter 7, for two reasons. First, symbolic interaction and related sociological ideas are concerned with social expectations and interpretations which are the meat of role theory, and accepting and interpreting roles are important aspects of the use of symbols in interaction. Second, as we noted in Chapter 7, Goffman's ideas of role, in which people are seen as presenting themselves in different ways according to the social circumstances of the moment, are a significant variant of role theory, which stems from symbolic and phenomenological ideas.

Although broadly sociological, such ideas also offer important explanations for intense emotion. Smith (1975), for example, shows how the feelings associated with bereavement may be fully explained not by conventional explanations from psychoanalysis which rely on 'biological, instinctual and internal psychic processes' (p. 79), but by phenomenological explanations. On this basis, grief arises from the unique place allocated to certain relationships (such as marriage) within social expectations, and from the reorganisation of our social constructions of our world according to such expectations. When the relationship is lost, a social reconstruction must take place. Moreover, at the personal level, we construct ourselves including the lost person, and that internal reconstruction must also take place.

Wilkes (1981) argues, from a broadly humanist standpoint, that many 'undervalued groups' of clients whose disability or problem we cannot cure immediately would benefit from social work which was concerned with exploring meaning within their lives. The worker would share experiences in a liberating way, rather than make a fetish of method and achieving specific therapeutic aims, which is inappropriate with many clients.

Krill's work, formulated in articles in the 1960s (for example, Krill, 1969) reached full expression in his book (1978). It is an eclectic model, taking insights from Rogers, gestalt psychology, Zen and similar philosophies, but its starting point is existential philosophy. Existentialism is presented as about how we cope with the fact that our existence faces us with wanting to live a life which nonetheless has many unsatisfactory aspects. In later work (Krill, 1990), he focuses on the importance of finding meaning within subjective understanding of the world. In finding subjective meaning, people should not be seen as the categories of their problems. Rather, they have personal freedom to be creative in dealing with the 'spirals of desire' that affect them. He argues that mere wishes become more intense as we experience them continually. This might lead to addiction, for example. To change, people need to broaden the range of their interests, but focus on particular interests. As a result, they can move from simply thinking about something, to seeing it as possible and then to being committed to it.

Transactional analysis

Transactional analysis (TA) derives from the work of Eric Berne (1961, 1964) and has some obvious links with psychoanalytic personality structures, and some aspects of its terminology. It is, however, usually regarded as a form of humanistic therapy since its basic principles rely, unlike the more deterministic psychoanalytic theory, on the assumption that people are responsible, autonomous agents who have the energy and capacity to control their own lives and solve their own problems – they are prevented from doing so only by left-over failings of early childhood behaviour patterns (Pitman, 1982). TA developed completely independently of psychoanalysis, with its own literature and training schemes. Pitman (1983) provides an introduction applying it to social work, Coburn (1986) a briefer account, but it has not been widely integrated into social work with other techniques. It is, rather, a system of therapy which specially and separately trained people sometimes undertake within social work agencies. Some of the jargon, especially 'games' and 'strokes', is used without calling on the full system of thought.

There are four elements of TA: structural, transactional, games and script analyses. *Structural* analysis proposes that our personality has three 'ego states', ways of thinking about the world. These are associated with typical behaviour patterns. The parent state is a collection of attitudes typical of the sort of injunctions that a parent figure might give to a child, and the sort of perceptions that a child might have of such a figure. The child state contains feelings and attitudes left over from childhood, typically rather self-centred, but also uncontrolled and potentially creative. The adult state manages, mostly rationally, the relationships between the ego states and with the outside world. These concepts are like the psychoanalytic structures of superego, id and ego, but TA is less concerned with internal interactions among parts of the mind and with drives and irrational responses. *Transactional* analysis is about how ego states in one person interact with those in another. Transactions are exchanges between people's ego states, which may be open or hidden. When open and hidden messages involve different ego states or transactions, problems arise.

There are three kinds of transaction: 'complementary', where only two ego states are in play; 'crossed', where several are involved but verbal and non-verbal messages are consistent; and 'ulterior', where again several ego states are involved, but the open messages are different from the hidden ones. In practice, workers use transactional analysis to find out which ego states are involved in transactions, and help clients use communication more constructively.

Games analysis is concerned with patterns of interaction and behaviour. People have three groups of emotional needs:

1 stimulation, which they fulfil by artistic, leisure and work activities;
2 recognition, which is met by receiving 'strokes' either non-verbal or verbal, positive or negative from others (for example, respectively a smile and a thank-you; or a scowl and a criticism);
3 structure in life, particularly of time.

The pattern of strokes and life experiences that we get used to in childhood sets up our life position, which is about how we feel about ourselves and others, and our general attitude to the world. There are four life positions (Harris, 1973), set out in Table 8.1.

Table 8.1   The four life positions in transactional analysis

Life position	Meaning
I'm OK – you're OK	you feel good about yourself and others
I'm OK – you're not OK	you feel good about yourself but not about others, so you tend to blame others for your own problems, and criticise them (rather like projection in psychoanalysis)
I'm not OK – you're OK	you feel bad about yourself and see others as more powerful and capable than yourself, so you tend to feel inferior and incompetent all the time
I'm not OK – you're not OK	you are critical of both yourself and others

Source: Harris (1973).

Games are typical patterns of ulterior transactions which recur, reflect and promote damaging life positions. Workers analyse games with clients, who can then understand and avoid them in favour of more satisfying interactions. *Script* analysis is concerned with seeing how transactions in the past have led to present life positions and games.

From this brief account, it will be seen that TA is an attractive formulation of behaviour, emphasising communication patterns, which relates closely to more conventional communication theory (see Chapter 7). Its evident links with psychoanalysis should not be overemphasised, since it has travelled a long way from instinctual drives and determinism. There are clear relationships with ego psychology and psychodynamic structures of the personality. As a method, it may be criticised in the same way as psychodynamic theory for relying on insight. Other criticisms are that the technique is largely psychotherapeutic and does not have much to say about clients' practical problems of poverty and oppression. At least, however, supporters of TA would say that they can be helped to avoid oppressing themselves. Finally, it can be argued that it is a shallow technique, giving superficial accounts of behaviour in a jargon which might make some people feel that they are not being treated with respect, rather than permitting a thoughtful analysis of behaviour. For some people, on the other hand, its entertaining and unportentous terms can help them look at their behaviour in a new, easily grasped way. This is enhanced by a diagrammatic technique, shown in Figure 8.1, which shows each personality in a transaction in terms of their parent–adult–child ego states and how these are interacting with one another.

Figure 8.1   Diagrammatic representation of ego states in transactional analysis

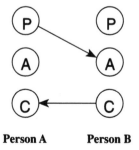

Person A   **Person B**

Explanatory note: In this case, person A's parent is communicating with person B's adult, while person B's child is communicating with person A's child.

Glassman and Kates: humanistic groupwork

Groups have process, which here is 'democratic mutual aid' among group members, and purpose, which is the changes we want the process to bring about. This account of groupwork derives from democratic and humanistic values:

- people's inherent worth and capacity;
- people's responsibility for and to one another in social life;
- people's rights to belong and to be included;
- people's rights to participate and be heard;
- people's rights to freedom of speech and self-expression;
- differences among group members enrich all;
- people's rights to freedom of choice;
- people's rights to question and challenge professionals;

Groups develop in a series of stages. People's behaviour and the themes of group interaction are consistent within stages. Humanist theory allows members to use groups' development actively in pursuing their personal development. More authoritarian group theories mystify and limit behaviour to certain stages and stimulate particular behaviours in particular stages. The stages are as follows:

- *We're not in charge*. Group members approach the group with caution, uncertain about group norms. The worker helps them explore possible ways of behaving in the group, and prevents any member imposing external assumptions.
- *We are in charge*. Some members attempt to impose their agenda or direction on the group. There is resistance to this and conflict. The worker helps them explore the various consequences of proposals, and so the group begins to agree norms.
- *We're taking you on*. Group members struggle with how to use the worker or whether to reject their involvement. The worker helps them explore various ways of using their contribution. This involves accepting and exploring the reasons for the occurrence and viability of attitudes of hostility and rejection, or acquiescence and subjection.
- *Sanctuary*. Members feel that the group is more satisfying and less complicated than real life, and see it as an escape from their problems. The worker helps them use the security they have created to work on real problems.

- *This isn't good any more.* Group members do not want to take the risk of struggling with their problems, but having had their security upset feel disenchanted with the group. The worker helps them retain the valuable experience of the support of the group while seeing that they can work on their problems.
- *We're okay and able.* By working through their ambivalence about whether the group can help them, group members learn that they can work out difficult problems. This gives them confidence to work on their purpose. They choose from the various options available to them from the skills in the group. The worker helps them make decisions and confronts attempts to jump into action thoughtlessly or avoid action on difficult issues.
- *Just a little longer.* Group members want to keep on with the security of the group, since it has been successful in helping them with their problems. However, they can now use the experience to manage more effectively on their own. The worker helps them separate from the group, valuing and confirming the helpful progress made.

The objective of groupwork is to develop the democratic mutual aid system and simultaneously help group members express and carry out ('actualise') their purpose. These two main functions use various interactions, set out in Table 8.2. In this table, the columns for developing democratic mutual aid and actualising purpose are not necessarily aligned. I have presented them so as to make reasonable connections between the two purposes. In addition, workers use several techniques to achieve both purposes. These are as follows:

- *Demanding work, directing, lending vision and support,* where workers use their own commitment to move members forward when they are stuck, by focusing their attention on acting and helping them to do so. All these techniques require workers to be active and positive, rather than being reflective and neutral.
- *Staying with feelings,* where workers act as a model for expressing feelings positively, but also help members with expressing feelings when they are uncomfortable.
- *Silence* conveys respect and support for members who are struggling with difficulties.
- *Exploration* helps involve members in free-flowing activity. Open-ended questions, curiosity and interest stimulate involvement.

Table 8.2 Techniques and activities for achieving dual objectives in humanist groupwork

Actualising purpose		Developing the process	
Techniques	Activities	Techniques	Activities
Enable group members to use democratic norms, including rights to belong and be heard	Aid collective participation Scanning (pay attention to each group member in turn)	Identify themes for group's work Give experience of planning, role-playing and organising	Programming: plan and participate in a group programme: initiation, options, tasks and tools, experience, evaluation
Make decisions and develop rules of behaviour in the group	Engage group as a whole Check for opinions, weave consensus, compromise		Role rehearsal, plan future activities, try out useful behaviours Confrontation: challenge and require instant change in behaviour
Develop leading/following skills	Process 'here-and-now', point out important events and reaction patterns, get group to observe itself		Dealing with unknown: discuss ideas about future changes
Respect members' differences		Share feelings about each other's behaviour	Group mending: start discussion on hurtful issues
Express feelings about the worker, especially around their power	Encourage expression; ask for reactions; point out avoidance; address expression of feeling	Help members to identify and express obstructive or helpful feelings	Self-disclosure: conveys humanness and fallibility

			Feedback
Develop and carry out goals together	Discuss how statements express changing needs; explore different needs and interests	Create activities for outside the group	Conflict resolution: define conflict, clarify themes, feelings, stakes, offer new perspectives
Express feelings to others helpfully	Control strong feelings; non-threatening atmosphere; limit personal details	Identify unhelpful thinking which interferes with group relationships	Group reflective discussion on details of particular events; sequences, feelings, interactions, choices
		Explain group process to help members be more self-aware	Data and facts: help study to avoid prejudice/bias
Develop emotional ties and better cohesion	Review the good and bad things about meeting and how people feel	Reinforce successful change, so members repeat it	Interpretation; 'reading between the lines' helps individuals
			Taking stock: make achievements clear

Source: Glassman and Kates (1990).

- *Identification* involves pointing to repetitive patterns of behaviour and thinking in the group.

The humanist aspect of Glassman and Kates's (1990) account of groupwork lies in its two specific purposes and its personal development objectives, achieved through group experience.

Thompson: existentialism and social work

Thompson (1992) provides a comprehensive assessment of the value of existentialist thought to social work practice, based on Sartre's ideas. Because it is at the centre of existentialism, he focuses on ontology, the study of being. This means the way in which we think of what it is like to be human. However, he also examines the implications for practice of social work's epistemology; that is, its view of knowledge. Also important is its view of the nature of society.

A central notion is *'being'*. 'Being-in-itself' is mere existence. 'Being-for-itself' is existence in which we are conscious, and can therefore have potential; for example, by making plans and decisions about how we want to be.

Existentialism rejects any prior expectations about how humans or society should live. People have *intentionality*; that is, they have the capacity to act bearing in mind goals about how they wish the future to be. This is different from the view of behaviourism or psychodynamic theory which claims that the past is an important influence on the present. Existentialism emphasises that it is our interpretation of the past which is important. Therefore, how we interpret it and act towards the future gives meaning to our lives. Consequently, humans are able through their personal freedom to create or define themselves. Personality and social structures are the products of choices made by free human beings. However, others apply labels to our behaviour, and this gives us something to hang on to. So, we begin to accept the limitations of the social expectations which are applied to what we do and what we are. This is one way in which we cope with the feeling that life is 'absurd'. This feeling arises because existentialists accept that there is no purpose to life imposed by, for example, a belief in God as an ultimate director of personal and social development. There is a 'theatre of the absurd' demonstrating human attempts to come to terms with absurdity. An example is Ionesco's *Rhinoceros*, where humankind slowly turns into the eponymous creatures.

People are therefore completely responsible for their own actions. This is an important aspect of existential ethics. We are free *to* act, but not free *from* responsibility to respond to our environment and pressures upon us; these are the facts of existence. *Facticity*, the reality of external things, is different from *contingency*, the possibility of acting on and changing those conditions. Realising this can be empowering but also disturbing and frightening. This is because 'being-for-itself' implies *nothingness*, because it means that conscious decisions may create negative outcomes. That negativity can have no purpose, again because there is no assumed overall direction of existence. Therefore, we feel 'dread' or anguish about the unknown and uncertain contingencies that may affect us. Failing to accept or running away from our freedom is 'bad faith', and leads to a false stability from accepting rigid social boundaries. Equally, 'being-for-itself' implies constantly changing and developing, but human beings often want to arrive at some stable destination, to be certain who they are. This is also bad faith, since it also seeks stability and certainty. In one sense, it is a wish to 'be God' by having this unrealistic sense of certainty about the world. This may be an important motivator for many people. The absence of this possibility often leads to 'despair'. However, the motivation for certainty and stability leads people to seek ways of creating or defining themselves, and may lead to their empowerment and liberation. Thompson (1992: 47) connects the idea of absence of bad faith with 'authenticity', the idea that our behaviour does not conflict with our conception of ourselves as we present it to the world.

This approach has many connections with cognitive ideas where 'irrational' thoughts are considered to mislead us in our judgement of situations and therefore in our ability to respond appropriately. If we can accept and use our freedom, though, we can look forward optimistically to 'self-definition' or 'self-creation', as we generate or contribute to our constantly changing personality and social situation. Within freedom is responsibility for creating ourselves, and the anguish which comes from knowing that we have created the negative as well as the positives in our creation.

However, while this is possible at the personal level, we must see the ideas which limit individual freedom as ideologies; that is, shared conceptions of the world which have their own social power on behalf of particular social interests. This requires action at the political level for liberation. Otherwise, political and social constraints prevent people from using their personal freedom. These ideas have connections to Marxist dialectical materialism. There, however, economic forces are often seen as in control of the sweep of history, limiting human capacity to make history freely. Similarly, Marxian alienation is about cutting workers off from the tools they employ to do their work, which are owned and manipulated by capitalists. While this explains much human misery, existential ideas go further and argue that alienation comes from all kinds of oppression (for example, because of race or gender). Existentialism seeks a complete social reorganisation, 'resocialisation', so that people can be free to take part in a process of continual reconstruction according to their needs and wishes. Such freedom would allow people to overcome alienation. Unlike some Marxist thought, there is no final ideal set of social relations – participants constantly reconstruct these. Such a view relates closely to postmodernist thought.

The 'other' plays an important part in these ideas. 'Being-for-itself' can only exist in relation to others. We can only experience many feelings (shame is the famous example) through the reaction of others to us.

The group is also important. Most groups are a 'series'. Here, people are individualised and competitive, even though a social situation links them. For example, several people may be neighbours and have a shared interest in sorting out arrangements not to interfere with one another's houses. Nevertheless, they do not have continual and complex social relations and would not necessarily help one another in difficulties. Some groups have solidarity, in which people are linked in multiple ways and share interests and activities in many different ways. They use their freedom to act in the interests of the group. Serial group relations is the most common state, and so we should nurture solidarity. Neighbours need to be encouraged and supported to help one another in difficulty and engage in a wide range of social activities. This would make the group stronger and more satisfying. Such ideas are related to ideas of network and community, where more links are seen as creating a 'better' set of social relations. Another important aspect of existential ethics is the value of 'commitment' to solidarity with others. In this way, existential thought emphasises the humanist value of 'holism', treating individuals and social systems as wholes. 'Totalisation' implies trying to create a synthesis of our understanding of social situations and their histories. Such a synthesis appreciates that we form understanding from interplay and conflict among many different points of view. 'Dialectical reason' is the process by which through constant internal and existential debate we try to develop our totalised concepts of the world. This interplay or (in Foucault's terms) discourse leads to constantly changing conceptions of the world.

Thompson argues that the strength of existentialism lies in its focus on ontology, the understanding of the fundamentals of human existence. This focus comes about through its ideas on being, nothingness and contingency. Most social work theories, he argues, are weak in considering these aspects of humanity, and this makes understanding social and personal relations unsatisfactory. He gives several examples relevant to commonplace social work practice.

For example, he examines several child-care situations. Many problems in parent–child relationships stem from problems for children about managing their own freedom without bad faith. Thus, John has temper tantrums when he is told he cannot do something. He is seeking the freedom to act, without accepting the responsibility to take into account social conditions in which he may exercise that freedom. A more appropriate response might be to negotiate opportunities to do what he wants. To achieve such a response, however, he needs to have experience of working within a family group with solidarity where people behave in the interests of the group rather than in their own interests. A father who is distant might not give John the chance to learn to negotiate. A father who is overbearing might induce bad faith; that is, John can accept the constraints on him as given, instead of seeing them as a responsibility to be taken on and negotiated about. Thompson distinguishes this sort of situation from the common-sense assumption that consistency, discipline and love are needed from parents. Consistency might also lead to bad faith, because the environment seems rigid and certain instead of offering freedom for change. Love is an attempt to 'possess' the other person by controlling their freedom. It seeks to impose a concern for and solidarity with the person who loves above other possible concerns and solidarities. Discipline is an attempt to create excessive certainty through conformity. Psychodynamic theory assumes that we achieve self-discipline by internalising or embedding parental views about appropriate behaviour into a child's self. Behaviourism assumes that we learn and reinforce behaviour by social expectations of disciplined behaviour. To existentialism, self-discipline (which behaviourism would reject) is an essential idea, because it implies accepting responsibility for the social character of the situation in which we act. It also assumes, however, that our discipline comes from the acceptance of those responsibilities within our freedom to choose. Psychodynamic theory, on the other hand, assumes a choice determined by parental controls, which in their turn mediated and interpreted social expectations.

Existential thinking suggests that the different projects of members of a family need to interact within a group with solidarity. Social workers might seek to improve solidarity; that is, commitment to group interests. This would help mutual support in pursuing all individuals' projects; that is, the ways in which different people in the family see their interests as developing. Children and family relations are not best understood by general principles of behaviour. Instead, we should consider their specific 'projects' and the constraints which restrict their freedom to carry them out with responsibility for reacting socially within their environment. General principles lead to bad faith because they lead to the expectation of an unreal consistency. Parents vary, and the important aspect of a successful relationship between parents and children is communication about the particular circumstances of a parental reaction to a child. For example, if the parent is worried and distracted, the child can understand a distant or tense reaction to a request if they know the parent's position. However, they will be confused if they do not understand. They can only accept their responsibilities for acting freely if they do understand and therefore if communication is effective.

In very young children, parents see themselves in the child, because of the strength of their influence. The child similarly gains a sense of self-worth from the positive feelings experienced from the parents. This gives parents and child a view of themselves and their value in life and is the origin of parental or filial feelings and the 'maternal instinct'. This is a powerful motivator, and encourages group solidarity in a family and can promote it elsewhere, as people seek it in other relationships and social situations. However, it can also stifle independence and distort perceptions so that it reduces the capacity to accept freedom and responsibility.

In exploring existential work with older people, Thompson points out that social workers are involved with the social consequences of ageing, rather than a physical condition. He also distinguishes between services for older people and social work with them. Existential views of ageing point to the significance of contingency; that is, the freedom to act and to change, and the fear of the uncertainty which arises from that freedom. Older people experience significant uncertainty: the ultimate uncertainty of approaching death, changes in life style through retirement, loss of companions and loss of community networks and familiar life styles on admission to residential care. Bad faith often leads to rigidity and sticking to unnecessary and conservative social rules. It is an avoidance of responsibility and therefore is bad faith to ignore the reality of approaching death and the social task of preparing for it. To existentialism, the problem may be that approaching death may cause people to accept restrictions on their freedom to choose various options in their lives: they may feel more restricted than they are. My mother, for example, decided that she was housebound after a fall, and thus restricted herself from a wider social life. However, in fact she could have gone out if she had not so readily accepted the restrictions on her. Existentialists would regard this as bad faith in accepting unrealistic restrictions on freedom to choose. Social work would seek to remove that feeling of restriction to allow us to make more choices. Another issue may be the need to attribute 'meaning' to life. To the existentialist, this can only come from making and having made choices. Present problems can prevent people from making a realistic assessment of the value of the choices they have made and might still make. The sense of self which has been built up can be destroyed by the experiences of ageing, and, consistent with existentialist assumptions, may need reconstruction. It is important that work contributes to the maintenance and building up of clients' sense of self. Otherwise workers will contribute further to the sense of destruction coming from unwanted retirement, from feeling devalued because older people are 'useless' in the labour market and from being unvalued in the family.

Workers should be politically informed in their work, by being aware of the general social and political issues which affect their clients. However, this is different from political work; that is, action to achieve political change. Thompson summarises his existential approach to social work in the practice principles set out in Table 8.3.

Commentary

The importance of considering humanist and existential contributions does not lie in their formal impact on social work theory in use within most agencies, which is slight. They are important in two ways. First, social work values are essentially humanist. Thus, ideas of treating people as wholes, and as being in interaction with their environment, of respecting their understanding and interpretation of their experience, and seeing clients at the centre of what workers are doing, all fit well with the central principles of social work.

Table 8.3   Thompson's practice principles of existential work

Principle	Practice implications
Freedom and responsibility are the main building blocks of human experience.	Avoid thinking that clients' behaviour is determined or unchangeable. Seek areas of life where clients can make choices and help them to do so. Aim to recognise elements of clients' situations which constrain their choice and remove these.
Freedom is a liberation and a burden.	Convert negative aspects of freedom such as anxiety, fear, 'bad faith' into positive ones such as self-control, confidence, self-esteem, authenticity.
Authenticity is the key to liberation; 'bad faith' is a common unsuccessful strategy for dealing with problems.	Workers must aim for authenticity; that is, accepting and using their own capacity to 'make a difference' to their lives and those of others. Clients must establish authenticity before other work can be done, otherwise they will rely on others or the straitjackets of rules and regulations to manage their lives.
Existence is experienced as powerlessness; responsibility must be accepted by everyone.	Clients struggle with immense problems. Workers must help them start to take responsibility in whatever limited areas are possible. As this is achieved, further progress in taking more collective responsibility (e.g. for solidarity in a family, or eventually for political action) can be achieved.
Existentialism requires a shared subjective journey and a partnership approach.	The starting point is accepting and recognising clients' feelings about their experiences and sharing a process of taking responsibility for acting.
Recognise and manage the tension between authority/control/legal duty and creative, non-directive work.	Understanding and seeing complex conflicts between these two aspects of social work is integral to recognising the conflicts which create the totalised view of the client's freedom and responsibility.
Existence is movement.	Natural stability is impossible. Social work seeks development and progress rather than disintegration.
Existential freedom and the process of self-creation is the basis of political liberation.	The first has to be obtained before there is a possiblity of achieving the latter.

Source: Thompson (1992).

The failure to import these potentially sympathetic ideas lies in the framework of social work in agencies which perform social control and bureaucratic functions. Also, many fundamental philosophies of humanism already exist in social work and do not need explicit importation. Agency function and social control imply that a range of external objectives and targets have to be imposed on social work activities. These are inimical to the extremely free approach of humanist therapies, where clients are in control of the exploration and are facilitated, not directed, by workers.

Symbolic interaction and phenomenological ideas form the second area of great importance in present ideas in social work of the material discussed in this chapter. These provide a basis for understanding human beings which is more flexible, less deterministic and less judgemental than many psychological ideas which social work uses. The interaction of clients' perceptions and interpretations of the world and the reaction of the world to clients shows how situations arise in which clients' apparently bizarre or bad behaviour is established or amplified by social processes. These ideas can be a useful way of explaining clients' behaviour and problems without blaming clients who are victims of these social processes.

The problem with these ideas and approaches to therapy is, however, their lack of clarity and the difficulty of forming clear targets and agreed explanations about the behaviour. This means that, although these ideas have potential explanatory power in advocacy for clients, they may not be widely accepted among powerful groups in society that workers seek to influence on behalf of clients. Also, they may be criticised for their vagueness and lack of rigour by positivists, and for the lack of any evidence of effectiveness of the techniques proposed. Answering this, the work on the effectiveness of therapeutic relationships shows the importance of empathic, valuing and genuine relationships, and attempts were made to measure these elements. Although such relationships are not sufficient for therapy to be effective, they are necessary to therapeutic success. So, while they must be present, for these techniques to be useful, they have to be part of other activities which intervene effectively in clients' behaviour or social circumstances. This material does not tell us, however, what we should do to intervene effectively in the client's situation within the relationship once we have achieved it.

A reasonable judgement may be, therefore, that ideas of respect for whole persons are an essential part of effective practice and of the value base of social work. These are fundamentally humanist ideas, and a reading of humanist therapies gives comprehensive access to ways of implementing these basic values comprehensively. In a sense they are a benchmark for social work, at least with voluntary, self-motivated clients, which helps to understand the values and tasks of more directed therapies which are more relevant to social and agency functions.

9

Social and Community Development

Wider theoretical perspectives

Social and community development is an aspect of the wider development of localities, areas, regions and countries. It is related to economic and industrial development. Ideas about development have a long history. European countries developed from the eighteenth century onwards, and many other countries in the nineteenth and twentieth centuries. Weber (1930) famously argued that non-European countries developed slowly because their cultural inheritance did not include the Protestant work ethic of northern European countries. Sinha and Kao (1988b) criticise this ethnocentric view, and argue that other Western concepts, such as individualism and achievement motivation, support it.

Economic and social development is now associated in many people's minds with former colonial countries, particularly in the Southern hemisphere. It also refers to areas or regions where economic development is sought in countries which are successful economically; for example, northern Britain, southern Italy and Greece in the European Union. The need for development refers to widespread poverty among populations (Jones, 1990). Associated issues are health and disability, education, women's roles, industrialisation, and urbanisation with its related problems such as crime and family break-up. Governments seek to increase the amount of economic activity in a region or country to combat poverty and this has other economic, social and political consequences (Alexander, 1994). Sometimes, social or community development is a strategy for dealing with those consequences. Governments may also seek to reduce the economic and social demands on the wealth and income of a region or country.

They might do this by, for example, trying to control population increase or social and health costs of the population.

In countries which are economically well developed, issues of social and economic development have been concerned with inner cities, declining industrial regions and planning of the environment. Dealing with the social consequences of these problems or of the development process has sometimes led to a call for *community development* or *organisation* practice. Many ideas for such work originate from work undertaken in the colonies of the main European colonial powers of the nineteenth and twentieth centuries.

The focus after the 1939–45 war was Eurocentric. The aim was to build nation states in former colonies, copying European models of statehood and welfare. This was emphasised by a political division (proposed by Horowitz, 1972) into the first world (the West), the second world (the Soviet bloc) and the third world (mainly economically underdeveloped nations, non-aligned in the political dispute between the first two 'worlds') (Spybey, 1992). The understanding of what a country was came from the European model of a centralised government, managing priorities for a country with defined boundaries. The understanding of development was also Eurocentric. The assumption was that, to be successful, states would need to create a developed market economy like those in Western countries. This led to the *modernisation* theory of development (see Hulme and Turner, 1990: 34–43). Traditional countries would be developed rapidly until they equated with Western countries. By the 1960s this approach was clearly not working, although particularly on the Pacific rim, the 'tiger' economies of Japan, Korea, Taiwan and their successors achieved this kind of development.

Marxist critical theory did not provide a satisfactory alternative to modernisation theory, because it assumed a single line of development to capitalist industrialised states. However, a neo-Marxist *dependency* theory developed in Latin America. This argued that a 'peripheral' group of underdeveloped nations was dependent for trade and investment on a 'core' of industrialised states. The core maintained terms of trade to their advantage. Integration into an increasingly globalised capitalist economy limited the possibilities for developing ways of life which were suited to the structure and culture of underdeveloped nations. Indian people, for example, are well integrated into a well-established culture. Economic and social problems arise from attempting to convert the largely rural, socially interdependent Hindu culture into one which can operate in an economic system which rewards industrialisation and individualist Western values. Focus moved from the nation state to changing the way the world economy worked to the disadvantage of underdeveloped or developing economies. Several countries sought to confront the issue of loan repayment.

By the 1980s, all these approaches were regarded as unsatisfactory (Midgley, 1984). An alternative response to the dependency theorists is termed *neo-populism* by Hulme and Turner (1990). This derives partly from the 'small is beautiful' philosophy of Schumacher and from politicians such as Nyerere. Small-scale development could be created from cooperatives working as rural villages, using labour-intensive appropriate technologies, rather than seeking urban development through Western exploitation. These were often unsuccessful, due to inappropriate government interference, poor management and conflicts with other forms of production (Tenaw, 1995).

Related to these ideas are the theories of *ecodevelopment* and *ethnodevelopment* (Hettne, 1990). Ecodevelopment seeks 'sustainable' development which does not encroach upon natural resources (Estes, 1993; Jackson, 1994). Development should, in this view, be more people-centred and concerned with local needs (Else *et al.*, 1986; Eziakor, 1989). Ethnodevelopment acknowledges that the focus of development cannot be the nation state or small groups. Ethnic groups within nation states often conflict over the use of resources and power in the nation. These factors must be acknowledged and worked with. An important related concept is the Latin American Catholic idea of 'liberation theology' (Gutiérrez, 1973, 1992; Evans, 1992; Skeith, 1992). This focuses on movement from oppression to liberation within concrete issues in daily life, rather than accepting oppression as preparation for an afterlife. Both personal and 'social' sin (namely, structural oppression by social institutions) must be overcome by non-violent social change through personal empathy with others and their social situation, in the same way that Jesus Christ acted. This provides a religious basis for seeking social change.

The place of social development in these theoretical movements is uncertain, since the major focus of development work is at the policy and economic level. During the period when modernisation theory was influential, development of welfare and other social provision continued, building on colonial progress, such as it was. Neo-populist policies place much of the concern for social provision within village and traditional social structures. This offers a role for social development in developing cooperatives or village structures (Burkey, 1993), but reduces the role of formal welfare. More recently, the focus on macro-economic issues has sometimes excluded concern for social issues and disempowered local communities (Friedmann, 1992). For example, the World Bank's 'structural adjustment policies' in Africa involved ignoring the social consequences of creating economic recessions in order to create the economic conditions assumed to be necessary for the development of free market economies (Adepoju, 1993; Hall, 1993b; Messkoub, 1992). Some countries attempted to develop welfare provision which reduced the impact of these economic rigours on the population.

Some of these more recent socially orientated approaches suggest a stronger role for social development. Also, movements for more indigenous and locally based development activities focused on local communities led to an emphasis on local development through education (Jones and Yogo, 1994). A strong focus on the role of voluntary or non-governmental organisations (NGOs) as leaders in this work (Thomas, 1992) led to an independence of external development efforts from centralised government control, overt political action (Booth, 1994a) and professional involvement (Chambers, 1993). However, many NGOs work with government, link with grassroots organisations, advocating and lobbying for poor communities (Edwards and Hulme, 1992). Local NGOs might be sought as useful partners in development (Salole, 1991a). However, effective management of their participation is needed, with a focus on ensuring consistency among cooperating organisations of values, ideology, practice approach and official or democratic mandates (Mwansa, 1995). NGOs create a diversity of activity and theoretical approaches. An example is indigenous community cultural theories in Thailand which focus on the idea of development of community as opposing the state (Nartsupha, 1991). Many of these have focused on women, partly because of their importance in local and family economies in many developing countries and also in response to worldwide feminist movements aiming to achieve greater justice, independence and self-control for women and to publicise issues of concern to them, especially child care (Fisher, 1993; Harcourt, 1994; Johnson, 1992; Wilson and Whitmore, 1994; Yasas and Mehta, 1990). Health and disability have also been important issues (Coleridge, 1993; Phillips and Verhasselt, 1994). Finally, important social movements responding to local ethnic and cultural needs in different countries also contest the significance of the centralised state (Wignaraja, 1993). Fisher and Kling (1994) argue that social movement theory connects community development ideas with wider forms of resistance among communities, by shifting the focus of socialist action from class-based to community-based action.

Connections

The distinction made above between community development as a phenomenon of Western countries and social development as a method in developing countries is not universally agreed. Neither method is clearly associated only with social work. They might equally well be regarded as separate professional activities, as part of wider development work, as part of other professional responsibilities or, with social development, as a separate professional career for Western workers in international NGOs.

However, social development is related to participatory approaches in all kinds of social concern and requires skills in interpersonal and group communication which relate closely to social work skills (White *et al.*, 1994; Craig and Mayo, 1995). Self-help organisations can also be important mechanisms for social development through generating increased interpersonal skills (Abatena, 1995). In participating, individuals can be involved through local grassroots organisations, enabling education to take place, and avoiding general political influences or social assumptions such as gender oppression dominating local wishes, which create social injustice (Agere, 1986; David, 1993; Mararike, 1995; Mulwa, 1988; Ukpong, 1990). Effective participation requires partnership which offers ownership of activities and outcomes for local participants rather than simply imposing inconvenient consultative arrangements on them (Salole, 1991b). Midgley (1987) argues that views that participation is important do not deal adequately with the role of the state in modern life, relying on individualist, populist and anarchist views of the world. Nkunika (1987) argues that appropriate organisational bases for facilitating participation are needed.

Historically, community work thrived in the same American and British settings from which casework and groupwork emerged in the nineteenth and early twentieth centuries (Lappin, 1985). Settlements allowing middle-class university students to work in working-class areas were particularly important. General improvement to poor localities naturally went along with welfare work. In many countries, community work is regarded as a third aspect of social work, although even in the United States where this convention is well established, it is generally less strong than casework. Elsewhere, as in Britain, its role as part of social work is well accepted, although it is much less strong. There are also separate occupational groups deriving from the role of community work as part of informal education and sometimes leisure services and as part of public participation arrangements in official decision-making (Rothman and Zald, 1985). In the United States and Britain, various government projects designed to deal with inner-city problems were a community work base in the 1960s and 70s (Brager and Purcell, 1967; Loney, 1983). Inner-city development is now primarily economic, and there is little official sponsorship of community work. However, recent British projects require local participation strategies.

Western concern with the problems of inner cities is relevant to the Third World concern about urbanisation, migration from rural to urban settings (Patel, 1988) and developing rural areas to reduce migration as well as for its intrinsic benefits (Muzaale, 1988). In some countries in mainland Europe, social pedagogy, *animation* and agology form separate occupations whose focus varies in different countries. The Netherlands has introduced a policy of social renewal, using community development to integrate action in deprived localities on employment, environment, welfare and education (Winkels, 1994). In some Nordic countries social pedagogy has a strong role in education and social welfare in informal group and community settings. *Animation* in France also has an informal education role through artistic work, concerned with social development and education through leisure activities (Lorenz, 1994: 99–103). A substantial literature on community work exists which overlaps these different aspects, although social pedagogy is not well established in the English-language literature. It developed from the work of German philosophers Diesterweg and Mager (Hämäläinen, 1989; Lorenz, 1994: 91–7), aiming at those social aspects of education which particularly focus on poor people in societies.

Two aspects of the social work role lead to an emphasis on community work. First, social work in hospitals and other institutions works on the boundary of the institution and the wider community. This involves concern for issues in the community which lead to admission and arranging for discharge. Social workers are inevitably concerned for community factors or inadequacy in services which increase clients' problems and which prevent or might enable discharge (Taylor, 1985; Taylor and Roberts, 1985). Second, many countries decentralise welfare provision in local communities and may promote informal, or non-state-organised welfare provision. This is as true in China (Chan and Chow, 1992; Chan, 1993) as it is in Britain (Payne, 1995). Social workers therefore may become involved in stimulating or relating to local provision. Popple (1995) describes this as 'community care work', following the British terminology. One important model of action in Britain is 'community social work' (Hadley and McGrath, 1980, 1984; Hadley *et al.*, 1987). This grew up in the 1970s and 80s in Britain as part of a philosophy of decentralising and debureaucratising social work provision (Hadley and Hatch, 1981). Social workers work in a decentralised team including ancillary and indigenous staff. They are supposed to maintain close links with community organisations and stimulate welfare provision in the locality. Many such activities have links with networking (see Chapter 6).

Another important related area is community or social action. This involves local action by oppressed groups, traditionally working-class groups, in identifying local or sectional interests which are not adequately provided for and campaigning or negotiating, often from a conflict position, with powerful groups or institutions for change which makes appropriate provision (Popple, 1995; Grosser and Mondros, 1985). Often, the action seeks for such provision to be managed within the community. Professional work in this area involves stimulating the creation of such groups and assisting and supporting them in engaging with institutions (Alinsky, 1969, 1971; Piven and Cloward, 1977; Jones and Mayo, 1974, 1975; Craig *et al.*, 1979, 1982; Smith and Jones, 1981). This is usually the province of specialist professionals. However, particularly in the United States, it is a social work specialism or involves social work agencies (Brager *et al.*, 1987). Also, work aimed at changing social policy from social work agencies is related to this. In the United States, systems theorists regard this as macro-level social work, and there is related literature (for example, Jansson, 1994). Social workers occasionally become involved with self-help groups in social action roles, but these are generally less conflictual in their approach. This form of community work is an important aspect of radical social work and, particularly in relation to self-help, empowerment (see Chapters 10 and 12). Important areas of community action focus on the needs of women and ethnic minority groups (Dominelli, 1990; Ohri *et al.*, 1982; Solomon, 1985), and it is an important aspect of anti-oppressive work (see Chapter 11).

The politics of social and community development

Social and community development is often peripheral to the main areas of social work practice in Western countries. In non-Western countries, however, if we exclude health and social security provision, it is often the main form of social intervention, although welfare provision is also sometimes needed and provided, especially in urban areas (Hardiman and Midgley, 1989: 237–57). It grew out of community development work in the later colonial period. The experience was reimported to Britain and the United States in the 1950s and 60s and formed the basis of an explosion of radical community action in the 1960s and 70s. Attempts were made to develop Western social work throughout the world, which has led to welfare services and social work education in casework and groupwork in many countries (Brigham, 1984). Walton and el Nasr (1988) call this the 'transmission' phase of interaction between Western and Third World social work. This was widely seen as inappropriate to indigenous cultures and social needs (see Midgley, 1981; also the discussion in Chapter 1).

During the 1980s, social development therefore became the model of work considered most appropriate to most developing countries (for example, Hall, 1993a; Midgley, 1989), and has been most strongly extended there. Schools of social work shifted from teaching Western social work models to a stronger focus on social development, but seeing social work's human focus as valuable to counteract economic approaches to development (Osei-Hwedie, 1990). This is at least partly to maintain their credibility in a period when ethnic and cultural interests have achieved importance in many countries. However, a good deal of theoretical development has come from Western writers, also in schools of social work, with experience of, and calling on work from within, developing countries. Following recent general development theories, sustainability in social development proposes forms of economic and physical development which nurture human welfare through decentralisation and democratisation (Lusk and Hoff, 1994).

Elliott (1993), among others, argues that the experience of social development in developing countries is relevant for Western countries. This is because Western countries face wide disparities in poverty and economic development within their borders, making a social development approach relevant to them. Because of its emphasis on participation and self-construction of problems and issues, it may also be helpful where countries seek to deal with the needs of isolated or marginalised communities; for example, where native populations have been oppressed by incomers (O'Brien and Pace, 1988). Social development theory is also a useful counterbalance to Western influence on global social work ideas, enabling a primarily non-Western model to gain wide relevance for practice.

Social development ideas

Social development has been variously defined, and the definitions are controversial. An important, often-quoted definition by Paiva (1977: 332) is: 'the development of the capacity of people to work continuously for their own and society's welfare'. This focuses on improving individual capacity. However, Paiva (1993) argues that this does not exclude four other important aspects of social development, structural change, socio-economic integration, institutional development and renewal. Jones and Pandey (1981: v) focus on the element of institutional development – that is, making social institutions meet the needs of people more appropriately – when they say: 'Social development refers to the process of planned institutional change to bring about a better fit between human needs and aspirations on the one hand and social policies and programs on the other.'

An early official view is contained in the Preamble of the International Development Strategy for the Second United Nations Development Decade, quoted by Jones (1981: 2):

> As the ultimate purpose of development is to provide increasing opportunities to all people for a better life, it is essential to bring about a more equitable distribution of income and wealth for promoting both social justice and efficiency of production... Thus qualitative and structural changes in society must go hand-in-hand with rapid economic growth and existing disparities... should be substantially reduced.

This movement in view from an official concentration on economic planning led to an emphasis on social planning. As a result, institutions could be organised to support economic progress (Hardiman and Midgley, 1980).

A more recent official view, influenced by ecodevelopmentalism (UNDP, 1994: 4), 'puts people at the centre of development, regards economic growth as a means and not an end, protects the life opportunities of future generations as well as the present generations and respects the natural systems on which all life depends'. This approach leads to emphasis on the importance of 'sustainable' human development, which

> enables all individuals to enlarge their human capabilities to the full and to put those capabilities to best use in all fields – economic, social, cultural and political. It also protects the options of unborn generations. It does not run down the natural resource base for sustaining development in the future. (UNDP, 1994: 4)

Asian writers (for example, Khandwalla, 1988; Sinha and Kao, 1988a) focus on understanding and aligning values represented in a society and in the development process. Booth (1994b), taking an ethno-developmental view, argues the importance of an increasing concern with *diversity*. By this he means exploring social differences which lie beneath geographical location and stage of development. At the national level, we should explore different historical and cultural bases for development, instead of looking just at economic indicators. Culturally, we should examine ethnic and gender differences, which affect how societies respond to social needs. At a local level, we need to respond to the particular needs and wishes of communities. The United Nations Centre for Regional Development local social development model (Jones and Yogo, 1994: 11–20) proposes a focus on people within their households, with the major interaction being between them and government and non-government development agencies. Each household has production, consumption and management activities. These refer, respectively, to facilities, labour and money for achieving things; housing, food, warmth, education and caring for living satisfactorily and the distribution of tasks, resources and welfare among members of the family.

We can thus identify moves in understanding social development which mirror ideas in wider development theory, discussed above. We have seen a shift from reactions to economic development alone, to seeing the need to balance economic and social objectives. This has progressed to a view that responding to detailed analysis of needs at the level of smallest living units is a crucial part of development which is empowering to people and self-sustaining.

Midgley (1993) divides social development ideologies into three types, as follows:

1 *Individualist strategies* focus on self-actualisation, self-determination and self-improvement.
2 *Collectivist strategies* emphasise building organisations as the basis for developing new approaches to action – institutional approaches.
3 *Populist strategies* focus on small-scale activities based in local communities.

Pandey (1981) identifies three basic strategies, defined in terms of their purposes rather than, as with Midgley, as types of activity:

1 *Distributive strategies* aim for improved social equity between groups nationally.
2 *Participative strategies* aim to make structural and institutional reforms to involve people in development and social change.
3 *Human development strategies* aim to increase the skills and capacity for people to act on their own behalf in improving the economy and institutional development of their area.

These distinctions may be compared with the models of community work reviewed in Table 2.7. Political, community action or planning strategies are not a focus of social development ideas, as presented here, but they might offer a methodology for distributive (Pandey) and collectivist (Midgley) strategies. Community development is aligned with participative and populist strategies. Feminist and anti-racist community work reflects the same ideological considerations as ethnodevelopmentalism and Booth's (1994b) diversities approach. Community work programme development, organisation, liaison and education all relate to individualist and human development strategies.

Midgley: social development

Midgley's (1995) book offers a coherent account of modern social development ideas. Social development is 'a process of planned social change designed to promote the well-being of the population as a whole in conjunction with a dynamic process of economic development' (p. 25). It seeks to create resources for the community by linking social with economic developments, rather than seeing welfare as dependent on economic growth. Social development must be compatible with society's economic objectives. It transcends residualist approaches which target welfare on the most needy groups in a society and institutional approaches which seek wide state involvement in welfare. Development is *distorted* when social progress is not aligned with economic development. This may happen where one group, often a white or colonialist minority, achieves wealth at the expense of an impoverished majority, or where military expenditure diverts expenditure from promoting welfare towards other objectives.

Social development aims to promote people's well-being, through creating social changes so that social problems are managed, needs are met and opportunities for advancement are provided. In setting these objectives, Midgley sidesteps potential debate about how and by whom well-being, problems, needs and opportunities are defined. Social philanthropy, whereby individuals take social responsibility through ideals of charity in Christianity, or *zakat* in Islam, for helping other individuals, is one organised form of welfare. Social work, where educated professionals provide personal help, and the provision of social welfare services are institutional structures through which social well-being is promoted.

Social development is unlike these forms of welfare in that it does not deal with individuals by treating or rehabilitating them to existing structures. Rather, it aims to affect wider groups, such as communities or societies and the social relations which take place in those societies. It is universalistic rather than selective and seeks growth, rather than simply returning people to an existing level of well-being. It seeks to follow a process of social change through deliberate human action. A long history of ideals suggests that such change in various ideologically preferred directions can be achieved by social interventions. An important context for such ideas in the twentieth century is the creation of the welfare state and the development of social planning. These provided, respectively, for extensive social intervention for the general benefit of populations in industrialised societies and for organising the environment and social provision in support of those interventions. Latterly, attempts were made to apply this in underdeveloped countries, especially through the agency of the United Nations and similar international organisations.

Social development is a *process*. The meaning of process is not as in psychodynamic theory, where it concerns the interaction of communications, actions, perceptions of them and responses to them. In social development, it is more concerned with the idea that interventions in a connected and coherently planned series are required. *Pre-conditions* for social development mean removing obstacles. Modernisation views proposed that education and literacy work would overcome traditional attitudes. Also, population control would reduce the pressures on family and community resources of large families. Migration from rural to urban areas should be reduced so as to prevent pressure on urban infrastructure leading to squalid conditions. However, these controls on freedom of action are oppressive, and efforts to impose them have often not been successful. An alternative view about obstacles to social development suggests that government interventions and unrestrained capitalism (for example, land or housing tenure; control of financial resources) have been just as significant as obstacles to development as modernisers' social factors.

Other writers, particularly Marxists, have suggested the importance of apocalyptic events to get development moving.

Several elements are required for an adequate social development theory. These are as follows:

- Development implies an ideological commitment to *progress*. However, this concept implies accepting modernist ideas that knowledge and social institutions move forward to a social ideal. Critics of such ideas see the economically developed countries of the West as being part of a process of social, economic and moral decline. Midgley argues that social development theorists do not adequately respond to critics of the idea of progress.
- Development is also taken to require *intervention*. This concept, however, may also be criticised. Intervention can lead to distortions which harm social relations. New Right perspectives oppose intervention because it interferes with the market and freedom of choice. Marxist, neo-populist perspectives argue that planners cannot know and be all things. Small-scale developments responding to local wishes are likely to be more responsive and about real issues faced by disadvantaged groups.
- *Economic* factors must also be considered. Social intervention in the cause of well-being has a value in its own right, not merely as a promoter of economic efficiency. It should not be subsumed in economic objectives, nor made dependent on their achievement. It is difficult to see how to promote economic and social development as part of the same activity. This is needed, however. Many individuals, families and small communities that social workers and social development workers deal with need to find effective ways of promoting their economic well-being while also dealing with personal problems.
- *Ideological* strategies which inform social development need to be considered. These are the individualist, collectivist and populist strategies mentioned above.
- The *goals* of social development may be to seek complete reorganisation of society according to some overall plan, or more modest steady improvements through smaller-scale changes. Some goals also focus on material improvements, while others focus on personal and group self-fulfilment.

Strategies for social development categorised by Midgley under the three headings mentioned above, operate at three levels in societies, as follows:

1 Individualistic strategies focus on helping people to become self-reliant and independent, although not necessarily self-interested. At the national and regional level, a creative *enterprise culture* does not put obstacles in people's way. Education and training, personal, financial and advisory support and transitional help from dependence on social security or relatives may all help people achieve economic self-reliance. This may lead to greater personal independence and emotional security. We might take similar approaches with mentally ill people or people with learning disabilities in achieving independence from institutional care. It might also be used for young people leaving care. Social workers have often been too concerned with traditional welfare concerns and failed to ensure that needs for education and opportunities for work and housing have been met. Helping groups of young people share skills and work together can also benefit them. In small communities, cooperative work or small enterprises using available skills, unpaid work exchange schemes with their own currency or a credit union can be participative ways of encouraging social development.

2 Collectivist strategies are communitarian in focus. They assume that people in existing social groups can organise themselves to meet their needs and gain control over resources and issue which face them. This is the basis of community work and community development. The number of links between individuals in a locality are increased, and opportunities for coming together around issues of concern are created. For those who share a problem, such as mental illness, or a human condition, such as being a woman and suffering gender oppression, this can lead to personal support, but more importantly may also lead to efforts to gain control of their situation. In other cases, shared responsibility for caring for elderly mentally frail relatives or a shared wish for improvement to local facilities may lead to cooperative work. This kind of work has a long history in community work. Work with community groups may focus on education, through studying local or industrial history, literature or writing skills or artistic work, such as music, community photography, painting murals or graffiti, or acting.

3 Government also undertakes development work. Statist approaches argue that this should be so because the state embodies the interests and social aspirations of its people. Only the state can develop through large-scale social planning and mobilise considerable resources. At a more individual or group level, the statist approach would be to campaign for service improvements and effective and coherent plans. Movements for equality, social justice and countering oppression often rely on achieving legislative change. For example, attempts have been made to change the law to avoid discrimination against disabled people or to promote the availability of services or protection for particular groups.

Midgley proposes an *institutional* perspective on social development pluralistically including elements of all three levels of work. This seeks to mobilise social institutions, including the market, the state and community organisations to promote people's well-being. Workers should accept and facilitate the involvement of diverse organisations in social development, through *managed pluralism*, working within the state, in local organisations and in commercial and market enterprises. A degree of training and clearly identified professional roles are required to distinguish workers with different interests from activists and community members. Social development effort should be located at every level of social organisation, not merely locally, but also regionally and nationally, so that these efforts may be mutually supportive.

Three approaches are needed to align economic and social development. Formal organisations and social structures are needed to coordinate economic with social development efforts. This might be done by social planning forums. We should plan to ensure that economic development has a direct benefit for social well-being. This might include encouraging landscaping around new industrial developments benefiting householders, social facilities such as day nurseries associated with new factories, and mutual activities, such as charitable donations and programmes. Also, social development activities should be devised which have a benefit for economic development. The community centre should encourage work training in an area with high unemployment, for example. Efforts to reduce crime on housing estates or encourage community businesses with social and economic objectives are another possibility. This also serves to avoid those concerned with unemployment or dereliction in their area seeing social help as irrelevant or as of low priority

Commentary

Midgley's attempt to create a theory of social development may be regarded as preliminary. So also is an attempt to import social development theory into wider social work usage. This is because Midgley's work contains very little development of models of action, and remains more a perspective promoting a particular form of action for incorporation more widely in social work. However, its relevance is shown by the examples of possible activities given in this chapter, and its links with community social work and community work.

The community social work connection also demonstrates that this perspective on social work can contribute to delivering service as part of the social work role. Such a perspective sees the organisation and development of services as relevant to social development of a more general kind.

However, the weakness of both Midgley's approach to social development and community social work is their acceptance of working within existing social structures. While they acknowledge critical perspectives, the response is even so to seek development within the accepted social order. Midgley makes much of the progressive, developmental approach of social development, as compared with the treatment perspective of much social work, but accepts formal institutional structures as a major part of social development work. Similarly, Hadley's community social work seeks to reform rather than transform the bureaucratic social work agency. His work also focuses community work onto welfare issues, rather than the priorities which people in the community might seek.

Social and community development perspectives, then, provide a wide social focus for workers' interventions to help oppressed people, much more so than systems theory, which focuses on the interpersonal. However, social and community development in this perspective confirms and promotes the existing social order, while the perspectives considered in the next three chapters incorporate it into a more critical perspective of the adequacy of the present social order to meet the needs of oppressed groups within society.

10

Radical and Marxist Perspectives

Wider theoretical perspectives

This and the two following chapters explore currently exploding developments in radical perspectives on social work. There are connections among these aspects of social work theory. 'Radical' can mean anything which involves major changes, but is usually associated with politically radical ideas which are socialist or 'left-wing'. Such ideas derive from Marxist political philosophy and sociology, incorporated in a range of political movements since the nineteenth century. There are many competing ideas within this tradition of thought which have been developing over more than a century. However, some typical ways of viewing the world arising from socialist thought affect social work:

- Problems are defined as social and structural rather than individual. That is, individual relationships are seen as the product of the social relations in a capitalist society. Not all accounts of social work called 'structural' have this implication: Wood and Middleman's (1989) 'structural approach', for example, is a systems approach.
- Inequality and injustice to particular groups in society come from their working-class position. Removal of inequality and injustice is a prime motivating factor for social action. Acceptance that inequality and injustice are a necessary part of society (for example, to provide incentives to improve ourselves) is inconsistent with being socialist. Analysing injustices affecting various groups is a significant part of socialist concern. This has led to the development of perspectives which have modified the

214

significance given to social class in traditional radical thought. Most important among these have been feminist thought and anti-discriminatory or anti-oppressive theory, which focus on the oppression affecting particular groups in society. These views broaden the range of factors which traditional socialist theory claims leads to inequality and injustice.

- Cooperative and sharing approaches to organisation in society through structures of equality rather than inequality are an important objective and motivating factor.
- The focus of change in socialist thought is political action and broad social change. Since inequality and injustice is a product of the structure of society, a final resolution of problems cannot be achieved in a capitalist society. Only significant social change will resolve the problems arising from capitalism. This requires a revolution in at least social and political thought.
- The idea of *praxis* means that we must implement theories in practice, so that practice reflects on and alters the theory. As we act, the ideas used in acting find meaning in and are therefore expressed by what we do, and change our view of ourselves as we experience the idea in practice (Ronnby, 1992). Theory must come partly from ideas outside daily practice, otherwise it would only be a simple reflection of that practice, but it must not be totally outside recognisable practice.

This account is designed to pull out of socialist theory some aspects which show where the social work interpretations of radical theory have come from. An example of such principles in action is Swartz's (1995) account of an urban job-training programme. The work promotes political education, tries to demystify services, partly by involving participants in making choices about the planning of service, and focuses on understanding how resources are inadequate to meet needs, and ways of dealing with this in a political context.

Connections

Rojek (1986) distinguishes three Marxist views of social work:

1 The *progressive* position. Social work is a positive agent of change. It connects more general bourgeois society (that is, a society in which capitalism has created a system which exploits

the working class) with representatives of the working class. Social workers are significant in promoting collective action and consciousness raising, so helping to achieve change.

2   The *reproductive* position. Social workers are agents of class control enhancing the oppression by capitalist societies of the working class.

3   The *contradictory* position. Social workers are both agents of capitalist control and undermine (at least potentially) class society. Although acting as agents of social control they also increase working-class capacities to function, and offer some of the knowledge and power of the state to clients in the working class. The existence of this contradiction in their role leads to other contradictions which eventually contribute to the overthrow of capitalist society.

The progressive position is that taken by writers usually described as radical, such as Galper (1980), and books edited by Bailey and Brake (1975a, 1980). A typical account of the reproductive position is that of Skenridge and Lennie (1971). The contradictory position is represented by the work of Corrigan and Leonard (1978). The reproductive position has not survived, and recent writings in the radical tradition (for example, Langan and Lee, 1989) reflect a progressive position modified by acceptance of the more sophisticated contradictory view and the inclusion especially of feminist theory but also of many aspects of anti-discrimination.

Radical social work criticises 'traditional' (psychodynamic) social work, and other theories relying on psychological explanations of social problems, and functionalist theories which tend to take for granted the present social order. McIntyre (1982) usefully summarises the radical critique of traditional social work:

● Explanations in traditional social work reduce complex social problems to individual psychological ones. They 'blame the victim', making clients responsible for problems which have social origins. In doing so, they deflect attention from social circumstances.

● It 'privatises' people with social problems. This cuts them off from others who would share that experience and possibly deal jointly with it.

● It strengthens and follows the oppressive social order of capitalism.

In spite of this critique, there are links between many radical theories and traditional social work. Webb (1981) identifies four main ones:

1 Both accept that society contributes to generating personal problems. However, traditional social work accounts of the process by which this happens and interventions within it are inadequate, as we saw in the case of psychosocial and systems theory.

2 In both, the relationship between people and society is transactional, reflexive or interactive, so that we can affect our social circumstances as they affect us.

3 Both seek client autonomy. Traditional social work criticises radical social work for ignoring it in pursuit of general social objectives which may conflict with individual needs and autonomy. Radicalism criticises traditional social work for ignoring the social constraints to conform.

4 Both value insight so that clients can understand their circumstances in order to act on them. However, the purposes and means of action are different, and each perspective would deny the value of each other's forms of action.

Allied to the radical critique of social work methods, there is criticism of social work's system of service. Because agencies are part of the social system which supports capitalism, they have inherent failings in helping the working class (Ryant, 1969). From these brief summaries of radical views on social work, it is possible to identify a number of issues which are the central concern:

- *Social control* and the extent to which social work exercises it through the state on behalf of ruling classes. The radical response is to be cautious of controlling activities.
- *Professionalisation* and the extent to which it is promoted by social work education to the disadvantage of the interests of oppressed communities and individual clients. Radical workers seek alliances with working-class and community organisations rather than professional groups.
- Is radical *practice* possible in view of social and agency constraints on radical workers and the individual focus of much social work? The focus on collective and political work has led to the suggestion that radical practice is not possible in agencies, which are politically controlled on behalf of ruling elites.

However, various methods of practice have grown up, associated with radical work. These are exemplified in the works by Mullaly and Fook, discussed below.

The politics of radical social work

Radical views of social work gained significance in the 1970s. Their influence waned for a while in the 1980s (de Maria, 1993). One reason for this may be that general political developments in many countries moved against them and they seemed defeated. Within social work, they were subjected to critical attack, and as a general approach it seemed impossible to sustain in practice. Their resurgence in the late 1980s and 1990s may reflect a number of factors. The failure of the Communist regimes of the Soviet Union and Eastern Europe seems to remove the source of attack that developing radical ideas was inimical to the political regime of the West. Increasing criticism of the failings of and inequalities generated by the conservative governments in power in many Western countries during the 1980s led to a re-examination and recasting of radical ideas. Simpkin (1989) argues that the need to respond to marginalisation of many social groups served by social workers remains, but more diverse radical responses could replace attempts to create a coherent radical theory. Such recasting also took place within social work, particularly with the influence of feminist thought. Some radical ideas remain embedded in social work thought from their period of influence in the 1970s. An element of social criticism deriving from radical thought is now more essential to social work theory than it was before this period of influence. These approaches also created a theoretical environment in which the development of forms of social work such as empowerment, advocacy and consciousness-raising grew up and became acceptable.

There would probably be wide agreement that social work has a social control function, in that one of its tasks is to promote conformity with what Pearson (1975: 129) calls 'the binding obligations of civil society'. However, if we accept that such functions are always legitimate, we fail to question whether that control is always exercised for the benefit of clients, or of the social groups to which clients belong. Satyamurti (1979) argues that care and control are mixed together as part of public policy in British social work agencies, and their functions are hard to separate. This is probably true for many of those countries in which social work is primarily managed by state agencies. Goroff (1974) suggests that the activities of many agencies in the United States reflect coercive social control. Radicals argue that this is often on behalf of the state, representing the dominant interests of capitalist society.

Radical social work has been concerned how the professionalisation of social work disadvantage clients' interests, and leads social workers to become part of the state and social interests which oppress clients, and seek their profession's development even where this is contrary to clients' interests. The work of Illich *et al.* (1977), proposing that professions are often established to act in their own interests rather than (as they would themselves suggest) that of those they serve, has generated a great deal of interest. The role of social work education is an example of this process. Radicals argue that it trains students for 'traditional' social work, reinforcing social control, individual explanations of clients' problems, and conventional rather than radical interpretations of society (Cannan, 1972). According to Statham (1978: 92), radicals should study traditional forms of theory and practice to see where it is oppressive.

Radical practice is presented by Bailey and Brake (1975b, 1980) as 'essentially understanding the position of the oppressed in the context of the social and economic structure they live in'. Casework is not rejected, only that which supports 'ruling-class hegemony'. 'Hegemony' means the use of ideology by the ruling class to maintain control of the working class.

De Maria (1992) sets out radical practice methods. These are as follows:

- social work action should be sensitive to relevant social causes;
- practice must be constantly tailored to the situation in which workers practise;
- workers should be alert to contradictions between claimed low-level gains (such as client empowerment) and concomitant high-level losses (such as service disempowerment);
- social work is concerned with inherent humanity, and no single political or theoretical position has a monopoly of values which support such objectives;
- critical thinking should lead to action;
- it is important to preserve narratives about real life which explain and point up injustices;

- we should focus on things which are marginalised by conventional thinking.

Radical social work also, significantly, argues that social work emphasises traditional conceptions of the family, which led to the oppression of women. Women were often clients of social work when many of the problems should involve and may have been caused by men. Such approaches became allied with the developing women's movement of the 1960s and 70s. A distinctively feminist form of social work practice grew up (see Chapter 11).

A particularly important radical perspective, based on the work of Freire (1972; Brigham, 1977), grew up in Latin America during the 1960s and 70s. Rather than a form of social action stemming from reform which maintains society in a steady state, liberation from the struggle to subsist requires revolutionary change (Lusk, 1981). A related set of ideas came from 'liberation theology' (see Chapter 9). These views led to a 'reconceptualisation' of social work in Latin America. Costa (1987) reviews a range of writing on these developments, emphasising the social worker as a wage earner in alliance with the working class, and political practice as part of social work. Among the techniques used is to seek the democratisation of social institutions so that clients may have influence within them, to create space and services especially appropriate for working-class people (such as welfare and civil rights), to become engaged with social movements, and to use professional associations and trade unions to seek change. Costa quotes Faleiros' four strategic alternatives:

1 *conservative* – social work works professionally without political engagement;
2 *denial* – workers become involved in popular political work, but do not try to change social institutions for clients' benefit;
3 *counter-institutional* – workers seek de-professionalisation, remove professional control and ask clients to make decisions (for example, anti-psychiatry, which rejects medical and social help for mental illness in favour of self-help);
4 *transformation* – workers seek the transformation of social institutions through support of clients, professional activity and political action. This concept is increasingly a focus of radical writing and teaching – see, for example, Coates and McKay (1995), and Mullaly, discussed below.

By implication, work in one sphere without accepting responsibility for other types of activity is likely to be ineffective.

Freire's approach focuses on education with people whose communities are oppressed by poverty and powerlessness. Such people are 'objects' who are acted upon, rather than having the freedom to act that people who are 'subjects' have. However, there is a 'fear of freedom', which must be disposed of. People develop an awareness of themselves within their environment, particularly their own culture (Poertner, 1994). This is done by education through involvement in critical 'dialogue' in which pure activism (trying to act without reflection and analysis) and pure verbalism (constantly talking about what to do without action) are merged together in praxis. This involves acting on analyses of social situations, and influencing the analysis by the experience and effects of the action.

One of the important aspects of this is *conscientisation*, which requires the consciousness of oppressed people to be raised. They become aware by this process of their oppression, rather than accepting it as inevitable. Through participation in dialogue and praxis, they can take action to lose their fear of freedom and some of their powerlessness. A Zimbabwean application of Freire (Moyana, 1989) shows how, by using education in creative work, it is possible to develop such consciousness without explicit participation in political action. Conscientisation has been connected to ideas of *animation* and agology (see Chapter 9) which have their influence on the continent of Europe (Resnick, 1976). These are concerned with promoting collective activity, particularly artistic and leisure, as an expression of community experience and as a medium of education. Agology is a service in which the worker guides and enables intentional planning of social and personal change. The same radical roots have given rise also to the idea of consciousness-raising as part of the woman's movement, and it has many of the same objectives in freeing women's perceptions, understanding of their oppressed state and taking collaborative action.

Mullaly: structural social work

As with Corrigan and Leonard, nearly two decades before, Mullaly (1993) starts from the position that the welfare state and social work are in crisis. Mullaly argues that this is because social work has failed to clarify its ideology so that it has a clear paradigm to underlie all forms of practice. He uses 'paradigm' as Kuhn sometimes does to

Modern Social Work Theory

imply a set of taken-for-granted contexts for theory which provide the basis for understanding and and giving practical meaning to concepts (p. 27). He contrasts a conventional view of social work, which accepts, participates in and seeks to reform the present social order with a progressive view which should be the basis of radical social work.

Progressive views include the following:

- a commitment to humanitarianism, community and equality;
- economic beliefs favouring government intervention, giving priority to social over economic goals and seeking equitable distribution of society's resources;
- political belief in participatory democracy;
- seeing social welfare as an instrument to promote equality, solidarity and community;
- seeking a social welfare state or structural model of practice;
- seeking social work that treats people with respect, enhances dignity and integrity, enables clients to be self-determining, accepts difference and promotes social justice.

Mullaly compares these with four paradigms of political social thought which might underlie social work:

1 *neo-conservatism* sees welfare as having a residual role in the current social order;
2 *liberalism* has an individualistic view of welfare;
3 *social democracy* seeks a participative and humanitarian social system;
4 *Marxism* has a class analysis which seeks a planned economy based on the collective effort of everyone.

He argues (p. 114) that a progressive view of social work has much in common with Marxism and social democracy. They seek many of the same objecives. This is particularly true of what he calls the 'evolutionary' (as opposed to revolutionary) Marxists. I described such a position, following Rojek (1986), as 'contradictory', above.

One difficulty with Mullaly's account is that he starts off from seeing his analysis of progressive social work as one possible point of view. However, when comparing it with political social paradigms, he treats it as the only social work ideal. This favours his analysis of socialist views as particularly relevant to social work. People who took a different view on relevant perspectives on social work might take a different view on relevant social work theory.

Mullaly calls the model of social work which emerges from this analysis 'structural social work' (based on Moreau's 1979, 1990, terminology). It derives from the view that social problems arise from liberal-conservative capitalism and not from individuals' failings. The specifically relevant failing is that inequality is inherent in capitalist societies. That is, it is a necessary part of their structure in order to provide incentives to people to compete and accumulate wealth, which is the only way of gaining control of your life in such a society. The inequalities are expressed through a social order in which differences in class, gender, race, sexual orientation, age, disability and geographical region allow people with economic and social power to define one aspect of these features of society as valid and to oppress those who do not possess this feature. Oppression occurs through excluding groups from opportunities, participation and a good quality of life. This structure is self-perpetuating because it gives people incentives to become powerful.

Self-perpetuation also occurs because capitalist society has established systems of life such as the family to reproduce unequal relationships. Women learn in families to accept less power in relationships, ethnic minority groups learn to accept exclusion from participation in many political and social situations, gay and lesbian people learn that their sexuality is unacceptable to others and so on. Traditional radical social work would concentrate on class and economic and income inequalities as the fundamental focus. Their consequences for family and community organisation might also be tackled. More recent developments would focus on other forms of inequality, including gender and race inequality.

The goal of structural social work is *transformation*. That is, it seeks to change the society in which this occurs, rather than simply dealing with the consequences of it. It will move from social relations based on inequality and supported by important social institutions towards social relations based on equality with a collective, participatory ideology. Analysis of society must move from an order perspective, which sees society as ordered and stable. This must be replaced by a conflict perspective which sees the interests of different groups as in conflict, and they are held together by some controlling others through control of resources. Change intends to alleviate negative effects of exploitation and change conditions of life and social structures that cause these effects.

In achieving changes, structural social work uses a dialectic. The aim is to increase the aspect in a contradictory society which achieves liberation and reduces that which tends towards oppression. In particular, the aim (using Freire's terms) is to create people who are subjects (they can create and control their own social structures) rather than objects (who are pushed around in others' constructions). Since social structures, according to a postmodernist perspective, are the product of people's constructions rather than existing in their own right, creating people as subjects helps to reduce the effect of oppression in social structures. This idea is the origin of empowerment theory and advocacy methods (see Chapter 13). However, the contradictory position also recognises that social structures form the extent to which empowerment and advocacy strategies can be successful. We must see the forces of empowerment as in conflict with the power of the social structure.

Mullaly identifies two settings in which structural social work is carried out: within and against the system, and outside the system. The main purpose in each case is transformational. This may be achieved or frustrated at any level, so that both casework and community work can be liberating and empowering, whereas both may also be oppressive.

In working with service users, Mullaly proposes that workers should have a particular approach to practice. Workers must see the political and structural implications of actions that they take to avoid oppressive actions and promote empowering ones. This understanding must be conveyed to clients to help them and the worker avoid the guilt and anxiety which arise from difficult social situations. Workers must also acquire a firm concept of oppression. This is not any limiting, frustrating or hurtful situation. Rather, it is one where a whole life situation constantly throws up barriers to desired actions in a way which is systematically related to oppressive social relationships. These arise because having more power, wealth and opportunity systematically advantage some and disadvantage others. Workers must develop methods which assist in empowerment, but it is the antithesis of empowerment that it is done for or to a client. Workers are instead engaged in a mutual learning process with clients, rather than providing expertise for them. They must also avoid behaving in ways which are themselves oppressive, perhaps to compensate for the lack of power in their own relations with society or with their agency.

Consciousness-raising or conscientisation involves the processes of reflecting on oppressive social structures to try to understand them and them exploring ways of acting on the understanding. Normalisation is another radical technique which is concerned with helping clients to understand that their situation is not unique but is shared with many others. They can get in touch with the others and work with them. Coates and McKay (1995) emphasise the importance of process connecting together theory, practice, ideology and experience. Feminist social work especially focuses on such commonalities between women, including the worker and the client. This meaning of normalisation should be distinguished from the theory of normalisation concerned with more effective and empowering institutional care; this is considered below.

Collectivisation is another technique which involves, after dealing with immediately stressful situations, referring clients to existing groups working on issues relating to the problems that they present or forming groups of people with similar social statuses or issues to confront. Coates and McKay (1995) refer to 'connectedness', a sense of shared reality and commonality which lies at the root of social awareness and collective action. Collectivisation helps people develop their self-concept. It also helps them to move away from individualised conceptions of their problems and themselves.

Redefining is another important technique. It involves helping clients to understand the social oppressive structures which lie behind their personal problems. It presents an alternative social reality or definition of the problem. *Validating* alternative views to oppressive ideas also empowers the client to see situations in new ways. Techniques include critical questioning, humour, metaphor and storytelling, cognitive dissonance (making people aware that how they understand things conflicts with how the world is), checking inferences drawn from clients' assumptions to show up inconsistencies, persuasion and the use of silence. The worker must develop a dialogical relationship with clients where there is equality and a mutual exploration of territory which they need to understand. It may be helped by techniques such as sharing case recording, reducing social distance by using self-disclosure, or providing information about the agency. Such acts enable the client to understand for themselves how things work. Many of these practice ideas are found in Moreau's (1990) work (Carniol, 1992).

In addition to working in these ways within the agency, structural workers must survive in and change the agency where they work. This is because, according to the contradictory position, it is both a vehicle for empowering clients while it also acts to frustrate their empowerment. Workers should seek to radicalise the agency by confronting and challenging oppressive acts, including colleagues' behaviour, such as jokes, which demean clients. Other areas for challenge are social situations which obstruct work and assumptions which pathologise individual clients rather than identifying structural oppression. Efforts should be made to use agency processes in ways which benefit clients most in need and avoid oppressing them. Agencies can also be induced to set up collectivising activities such as appropriate groupwork, and allow or encourage some of the radical techniques considered above. All these kinds of activities may place radical workers at risk of losing their jobs. However, promoting and pointing to empowering objectives within the agency's aims or policies and the freedom of control of their own workload can help workers maintain the autonomy to practise radically. Being competent and efficient is also important, both for the benefit of clients and to protect workers against victimisation because of incompetence. Mutual support and establishing systems for this are also important.

Working outside the agency, structural social work implies a range of activities such as the following:

- workers support and develop alternative services and organisations;
- workers take part in and promote empowering social movements;
- workers help to build coalitions among people with shared interests and goals;
- progressive trade unionism and work in professional associations help in both cases to support empowerment rather than further oppression by enhancing workers' interests;
- workers take part, and helping clients take part, in electoral politics.

Mullaly's book presents a full account of radical social work from a contradictory position. However, it focuses strongly on analysis and political and general social action. Discussion of work at the interpersonal level is less specific. Davis (1991) argues that structural social work is an essential aspect of practice, since it addresses major inequalities which all social workers face and must be an important part of the analysis they make of clients' problems. Workers need to understand how structural problems such as inequality are expressed in organisational arrangements and clients' life experiences.

Fook: radical casework

Fook's (1993) book attempts to present an interpretation of radical theory in a practical way, which can be carried out in work with individual clients. It thus complements work like Mullaly's, and answers criticisms of radical social work that say it cannot be implemented at an interpersonal level. She defines radical casework (p. 41) as 'individually oriented help which focuses on structural causes of personal problems, more specifically on the interaction between the individual and the socio-economic structure which causes problems'. Five main themes in radical social work are as follows:

1 *Structural* analysis traces personal problems to causes within the social and economic structure of societies.
2 *Social control functions* of social work and welfare services are constantly identified and expressed in everyday work.
3 *Critique of the status quo* in social economic and political arrangements is continual.
4 *Protection of individuals against oppression* is a major focus of work.
5 *Personal liberation and social change* are important goals.

Social work has tried to respond to its difficulties with technical solutions improving competence and efficiency or eclecticism, allowing workers to choose from different theories of social work. However, such developments can produce complacent or uncritical application of ideas. Everything appears to converge and be consistent. However, this is achieved only by generalising specific concepts within theories until they are meaningless. A variety of ideas have been useful to radical work. *Anti-psychiatry* attacked medical models of treatment and understanding, especially of deviance and mental illness. It valued personal experience of reality as part of understanding the whole picture and how the social environment can be 'the problem' even when individual behaviour appears difficult. *Labelling theory* stresses the need to avoid stigmatising and punishing people for behaviour that has at least in part social origins. *Unitary or integrated methods (systems theory)* emphasise the need to work on several different levels other than the personal, although it is weak in class and conflict analysis. *Ecological theory* is valued for its focus on the interaction between people and their surroundings. *Marxist and radical approaches* are central to a radical perspective containing the above five elements but fail to offer approaches to practice at an individual level. *Feminist perspectives* make the five elements drawn from radical theory more applicable at a personal level. *Structural social work* emphasises the structural aspect of radical analysis and is therefore central, but has not gained widespread commitment. *Discourse and postmodernist theories* offer a potentially useful technique for critical analysis but ignore the need to make structural analyses of people's interaction with the world. *Empowerment theory* and ideas about social change and social equality appear to fit with radical approaches but do not always draw on a structural analysis.

Table 10.1   Radical and non-radical analyses of elements of social work

Element	Non-radical – milieu emphasis	Radical – structural emphasis
Social factors	social milieu is relevant as background information; used for analysis	social structure is major factor in explanations of problems; used in analysis and practice
Individual and environment	individual adjusts and conforms with environment	work seeks changes between individuals and environments
Psychological and social factors	used and explored in work	work seeks to link them
Individual	'blames' or victimises the individual	focuses on individual help; respects individual, blames social structure
Social control functions of social work	accepted	critical analysis leads to care in implementation
View of society	accepts *status quo* or piecemeal reform	critical analysis of society
Autonomy and rights	protected within the system	defended against the system
Social change	limited or inhibited	seeks and contributes
Casework	only form of practice or isolated from other practice	undertaken as part of wider forms of practice

Source: Adapted from Fook (1993, Table 2.1).

Fook distinguishes between radical and non-radical work, as shown in Table 10.1. She argues that social work must develop an integrated practice focusing on the interplay between individual problems and social causes. It must acknowledge and constantly debate and criticise (but not reject) aspects of its work which contribute to social control. Casework with individuals must be allied with broader social work methods. She identifies four main aspects of social work and distinguishes radical and non-radical approaches to each, as in Table 10.2.

Table 10.2 Differences between radical and non-radical practice

Component of social work	Non-radical – milieu emphasis	Radical – structural emphasis
Social factors	**social milieu relevant to problems**	**socio-economic structure causes problems**
Examples	communication patterns	power imbalances and inequalities
	role expectations	dominant social practices
	group/family norms	dominant social beliefs
	past social experiences	historical and social change
	relationships/networks	labelling processes
	material resources	socio-economic structures
Assessment	**individuals cannot cope with their environment**	**socio-economic structure is inadequate for individuals' needs**
Examples	poor communication	lack of power
	role conflicts	ideological social restrictions
	conflict between group/family norms	conflict between interest groups; hidden social agendas
	negative learning from past	inability to change or manage social change
	poor social relationships, lack of social support, isolation	effects of labelling
	lack of material resources	prohibitive social economic structures
Goals	**help individuals adjust and cope with social situation**	**help individuals change and control structures affecting them**
Examples	improve communication	increase exploited people's power
	relieve stress, modify expectations	decrease ideological restrictions
	resolve conflicts	decrease exploitation; expose hidden oppressive social agendas; equalise power imbalances
	unlearn negative associations; separate present from past	increase capacity to change and control life; raise awareness of influence of historical and social change
	provide material resources	provide material resources by changing prohibitive social structures
Methods	**enable personal adjustment and coping**	**enable personal change and control**
Examples	skills training; practical help	social education
	passive use of resources	active use of resources
	emotional empathy	social empathy
	emotional support	social support
	develop self-awareness	critical awareness; empowerment
	family therapy; relationship work	advocacy

Source: Adapted from Fook (1993, Tables 3.3–6).

The radical approaches extend rather than oppose the non-radical approaches. In essence, she argues that non-radical approaches to social work do not go far enough. In the same way Barber (1991, 1995) argues that social work must develop a psychology of empowerment, based, he suggests, on learned helplessness theory (see Chapter 12). This develops individual empowerment, which can then contribute to community development and subsequently to political action.

In each of the four aspects of practice, she examines ways of implementing radical ideas in practice. Social factors require ideological analysis. Workers must explore how individuals reinforce dominant social beliefs, how those beliefs originate socially, how they are significant in the way other individuals deal with clients and how social institutions affect the client. One way in which this occurs is through social control. The worker must look at control by groups or institutions outside clients and their social circle and within their social group. Anti-oppression requires identifying through conscientisation what social restrictions limit people's freedom to act. In particular, workers should look critically at social labels affecting clients and seek to diminish their effects. The social critique that workers undertake should examine the following aspects of social situations in which clients are placed. These often allow workers to identify aspects of the social structure which oppress clients in favour of others' interests.

- beneficiaries;
- social functions of clients' social situations;
- conflicting interests;
- behaviour which demonstrates where interests lie.

Workers should also seek to examine the constraints on social and personal change affecting clients. Often, this arises from *alienation*, where the socio-economic structure forces people to feel estranged from control of their own lives, particularly in employment or in interaction with the powerful state. Understanding such issues requires an understanding of social changes in society over history and how they are affecting clients and people around them.

Assessment helps to begin the process of resolving a problem, but how we assess may limit or guide action in ways which are not radical. Radical approaches to assessment focus on differentiating the personal and the structural, and explore how each affects and is affected by the other. Structural factors may make personal problems worse, cause them directly or socialise people into expectations which prevent them from acting. Definitions of problems and deviance are structurally and politically created, and are therefore socially defined. Structural factors also determine economic conditions and directly affect how people can respond to problems which affect them. Assessment must also review *ideological restrictions*. These involve behaviour which restricts clients' freedom to act, such as stereotyping of clients and their roles in society, role conflicts and role socialisation. Restrictive beliefs are also important. Clients may be affected by unchangeable false beliefs about themselves or the world, conflicts in their beliefs, or values and socialised beliefs which are inappropriate to a new situation or damaging to their personal functioning. These issues, and see below under goals, are similar to the sort of objectives that cognitive treatments would seek to achieve. Institutional arrangements may restrict clients through restrictions in material resources, lack of power or opportunity or through conflicts between competing interest groups. Many problems come from social control processes; that is, attempts to oppress or exploit less powerful groups in society. Social labelling and stressful social change may also contribute to clients' problems. By exploring all these issues, the worker can focus on structural rather than personal issues contributing to clients' problems.

Fook identifies four radical casework goals:

1 *Decreasing ideological restrictions.* Behavioural restrictions can be cut down by broadening role possibilities, resolving role conflict, helping clients develop alternative roles, changing roles and increasing awareness of how we are socialised into roles. Belief restriction can be reduced by challenging false beliefs, helping clients find ways of resolving or tolerating conflicts in beliefs or values and modifying self-defeating beliefs. Structural restrictions may be affected by helping to redistribute or provide additional material resources, increasing power over and access to resources and equalising power between competing interest groups.

2 *Decreasing oppression and exploitation.* This might be achieved by modifying behaviour and beliefs, developing greater personal power and helping to link clients with alternative support systems.

3 *Decreasing the effects of labelling.* First, workers should help clients to understand how labelling affects them, thus shifting

feeling of self-blame and increasing self-worth. Workers might also increase clients' choices and opportunities to take up alternative roles.

4   *Enabling personal change.* This goal is concerned with helping people gain power and control over their own lives. Awareness of historical and social contexts can help clients understand and accept historical and social influences, and may help to reduce alienation.

A variety of strategies and techniques round off Fook's practice guidance. She starts with strategies for dealing with the agency's restrictions. These include careful documentation and research, together with analysis of agency policy and procedures which may allow experiences in individual cases to be used as part of changing agency processes. Tactics may be used such as raising discussion of alternative ways of understanding clients at case conferences and rejecting the use of inappropriate bureaucratic restrictions on what workers can do. Workers should accept 'the unfinished'. That is, small steps in progress are satisfactory, provided the issue is left open for further progress. Political and negotiating tactics include direct confrontation, posing an issue in polarised terms to draw attention to the conflict which exists within it. Workers can press a case by continually raising the issue and arranging for it to be brought up in a variety of ways. Presenting an extreme demand and accepting a lesser position may also help to make progress. Workers need to develop techniques for occupational survival, including mutual support.

Another group of techniques is concerned with developing critical awareness among clients. This does not necessarily mean politicising them or issues that they face. It involves sharing with them a process of exploring and understanding their situation. Clients' own perceptions and objectives should dominate. Workers may help by separating the internal from external factors affecting clients, so that they do not feel bad about their own contribution, when external effects are much more important. Critical questioning, challenging false myths and restricted behaviour and creating experience of alternative ways of thinking and living can contribute strongly to this process.

Advocacy on behalf of and involving clients is an important radical form of practice. So, too, is empowerment, which involves sharing with and giving clients experience of using power. The casework relationship may also be developed in a radical way. It should stress client autonomy and the reduction of oppression and exploitation.

Equality and sharing in the way that interviews are conducted can give clients important experiences. Careful collection of appropriate information, as suggested above in assessment, is also necessary. Educative processes in social work must focus on both action and awareness and understanding.

Resources must be used actively in radical casework. Information should be offered to increase the client's autonomy. Referral to other services should be used to extend clients' opportunities. Group, community and material resources can be used creatively to increase clients' equality and control of their lives. Empathy is important, because it allows clients to share their experiences and information more accurately, and therefore make better use of the process of education involved in social work. Support is also important but should not be limited to emotional sustenance. Alternative support networks can strengthen clients' control over their lives. Using techniques drawn from social network ideas (see Chapter 6) can help here. Wider social experiences can enhance personal validation. Workers should also support people in taking risks. Evaluation is also important to learning from and strengthening the client's perceptions of what has taken place and the worker's capacity to work effectively in the future.

Radical residential work

Lee and Pithers (1980) claim that radical social work has had little impact on residential work. They propose that residential care could be a significant alternative model for living in a collective community environment, which provides a counterbalance to family socialisation. Residential care practice could combat, in their view, deleterious effects of socialisation into dominant ideologies.

Commentary

Radical social work has been a controversial development, and the debate has stimulated a variety of criticisms of it:

- It tends to neglect the immediate personal needs of clients. Instead, it promotes their consciousness of some form of collective action. This is unethical, uncaring or impractical

because it is not what the social services are set up to do, or
provides only a partial explanation for the behaviour and events
which are met by social workers. Leonard's (1984) Marxist
individual psychology tries to connect broad general explanations
from the social theory with understanding of individual responses.

- Radical theory is weak in dealing with emotional problems. This
  is because its concentration on material and social issues and
  promotion of services like welfare rights advice ignores clients'
  humanity and emotional and personal problems. Instead, radical
  prescriptions come from the theory rather than being a response
  to the problems which at least some clients present. So, it risks
  failing in the opposite way to traditional social work.

- It does not prescribe what to do, but merely offers an approach to
  understanding the situation in which clients and social workers
  operate. It relies on insight which is criticised in relation to
  psychodynamic theories, but we saw with behavioural theories
  can speed people's responses to problems; but it does not say that
  insight brings immediate results since class struggle must follow
  class consciousness. Failure to offer prescriptions is true of other
  social work theories (for example, systems theories). It is likely
  that having a theory which offers an overall perspective on the
  situation is useful and radical theory can be accepted as one such.
  We have seen that recent developments such as Fook's (1993)
  work has put practical flesh on the theoretical bones.

- Its accumulation of information critical of the treatment of many
  different groups identifies many problems. However, it fails to
  provide a coherent statement of what this means and a
  coordinated view of appropriate action (Rojek *et al.*, 1989).

- It has a limited view of power and equates it with control. This
  allies social workers excessively with oppression, and does not
  fully identify the complexity of power relations among people at
  the personal level. As existentialists would argue, even victimised
  clients have a good deal of power (Rojek *et al.*, 1989).

- Although it claims to seek social change, it is impossible to
  ally all the interests of the groups involved, which often conflict,
  and in practice seems to move towards achieving only more
  from existing services for those claimed to be oppressed
  (Rojek *et al.*, 1989).

- Radical social work theory does not focus on religious oppression
  and human rights abuses, including torture and lack of political
  freedoms to express views and vote accordingly. This may be

because the texts come from Western countries where such rights are well established and their lack does not need to be strongly challenged. However, this cannot be assumed in many countries. Also, many Western countries suffer from some degree of abuses of this kind. Radical theory can thus be criticised for a lack of sense of priority. In one way, however, traditional radical theory has the advantage over more modern concern for inequalities, in that it focuses on structural inequality in particular of class and wealth. More modern concern with gender, race and other 'isms' can be criticised for focusing on what are to many people less fundamental issues.

- Conscientisation is claimed to avoid the problems of conventional insight therapies, because the aim is not just understanding but action. However, failure to act on insight represents poor social work practice in psychological models, and similar poor practice might affect the link between insight and action in structural social work theory. The criticism here may be of bad practice in conventional social work replacing it with good practice in radical work, whereas bad practice in any perspective might be just as ineffective. Radical theorists argue that much insight in psychological models of practice is concerned with encouraging action to change attitudes and achieve alignment with social expectations in the accepted social order. In radical theory, insight is concerned with achieving outward-going action to change the social order. The latter might be more successful because there can be alliances and mutual support. On the other hand, psychological change in desired directions through insight is inherently supported by the social system.

- It is an ideology, rather than a theory: that is, it does not offer an explanation which can be tested empirically. Marxists would answer that their method of investigation through historical analysis and debate is a legitimate form of study. Also, positivist science maintains the ruling hegemony by accepting and promoting the present social order, and is an inappropriate form of investigation for a radical theory. All theory represents ideological positions, often in support of the ruling class.

- Like many ideologies, radical theories define objections in their own terms and explain them away (objections are often taken to be representations of ruling ideologies). The same is said of other theories (for instance, in psychodynamic theory, objections or inability to accept the theory are sometimes claimed to arise from unconscious fears or conflicts in the objector).

- Some radical theories emphasise inadequate and oppressive environments and services as a better basis for explanation of clients' problems than individual psychology. At its worst, this can substitute blame for local environments and their occupants in general rather than blame for the individual victim as an explanation (Galper, 1975; Webb, 1981). This might lead social workers' support for clients to be seen in opposition to the needs and interests of others in the same environment, since the needs and wishes of the poorest cannot always be aligned with those of all the working class. Clarke (1976) gives an example of this in a conflict over facilities on a public housing scheme where workers in supporting one working-class group raised opposition from others.

To make an overall assessment of these criticisms, some practice prescriptions of radical social work concern collective action rather than individual help, or helping people to radical understandings of their personal circumstances. From such positions, their options are acceptance or long-term resistance. It is hard to see how this is widely helpful. Workers might have difficulties in official agencies which represent the ruling ideology in trying to promote radical approaches, and are likely either to be excluded or to become frustrated in their inability to take action.

It is important not to go too far with this criticism. Many agencies and clients in fact welcome radical and community-orientated approaches, and opposition does not mean that a perspective should be ignored. It may offer a useful view to contribute to work using other theories or to organise social workers' ideas, while not conflicting unreasonably with their function in the agency. In this regard, it is important to read carefully the more sophisticated analyses of the contradictory position, rather than assuming that all radical social work will necessarily require a conflictual approach to practice. More modern accounts of radical social work also contain much more sophisticated practice prescriptions which are easier to operationalise. It is also important to accept working in stages and not trying to achieve major social changes in every piece of work.

Among the advantages of the radical perspective which negate these general criticisms is that it highlights certain aspects of life, including the importance of power, ideological hegemony, class and status, professionalisation, gender and oppression. Marxism makes these ideas available to social work in understandable form, and has led to a substantial development of practice in relation to these ideas. Its emphasis on power in particular draws into social work theory perspectives which have direct relevance to sexism and racism in ways which few other theories adequately achieve. We can see such developments more clearly in the following chapter in anti-discriminatory and anti-oppresssive approaches.

11

Anti-discriminatory and Anti-oppressive Perspectives

Wider theoretical perspectives

Much of the wider theory and research related to this area of social work theory lie in sociological and, to a lesser extent, psychological writing.

There is a literature on ideas of 'race' and ethnicity as factors in social relations and social structure. Reviewing the history of such ideas, Banton (1987) shows how 'race' in Europe was at one time associated with lineage. In colonial times, attempts were made to distinguish between different racial types, often associated with skin colour. Types became connected in the nineteenth century with the development of evolutionary ideas in biology, so that the different types were seen as related to different evolutionary lines of development. Thus they came to be associated with social status, the more successful and dominant societies claiming superiority over others. As 'races' came in contact with one another, superiority and inferiority became associated with class positions in societies where there were different 'races' in contact. There was a movement from assumptions that biological differences between 'races' (which do not in fact exist, hence 'race' is often enclosed in inverted commas to indicate its lack of validity as a descriptive and analytical term) justified superiority to concern about cultural and social differences.

Among modern theories of race (Rex and Mason, 1986), many sociological, psychological and biological perspectives are represented. Some theories of relations between races are pluralist in character; that is, they presume the possibility of equal and valid relations between races and ethnic groups. An alternative position is Marxist or class-based. It assumes that relations are likely to be conflictual and concerned with the superiority of one which oppresses others. Therefore, concerns about conflictual social relations have driven a literature on conflict among races and the phenomenon of racism. Sociological analysis of race relations focused on class and status distinctions, these being the major factors in Marxist and more conventional analyses of social relations. *Racism* is a range of ideologies and social processes by which ascribed membership of assumed racial groups is taken to justify discrimination against other groups (Solomos, 1993: 9, adapted). It implies acceptance that one supposed race's superiority over others justifies its greater power over physical and economic resources and cultural values (Dominelli, 1988: 6–12, adapted). This is a worldwide phenomenon throughout history (Bowser, 1995), and affects different societies differently.

Another important strand in thinking about anti-discriminatory work comes from the influence of feminist thinking. This also has a history stretching back for more than a hundred years. Since the 1960s it has, according to Reynolds (1993) and Rojek *et al.* (1989), developed three perspectives which seek to explain inequalities between men and women:

1 *Liberal feminism* (Reynolds, 1993) or *gradualism* (Rojek *et al.*, 1989) focuses on how sex differences between women and men are translated by cultural assumptions into gender differences which then affect social relations. The answer to inequalities is to reduce inequality and promote equal opportunities through legislation, through changing social conventions and through altering the socialisation process so that children do not grow up accepting gender inequalities. Rojek *et al.* (1989) describe this as 'liberal gradualism'.

2 *Radical feminism* (Reynolds, 1993) or *separatism* (Rojek *et al.*, 1989) focuses concern on *patriarchy*, a social system characterised by men's power and privilege. This view values and celebrates the differences between men and women. It seeks to promote separate women's structures within existing organisations and women's own social structures. Rojek *et al.* (1989) describe this as 'radical separatism'.

3 *Socialist feminism* (Reynolds, 1993) or *activism* (Rojek *et al.*, 1989) emphasises women's oppression as part of structured inequality within a class-based social system. Women's oppression interacts with other forms of oppression (such as race, disability).

Oppressive social relations should be analysed and understood, so that diverse interests can be met in various different ways.

Liberal feminism is criticised for ignoring real differences in interest and experience between men and women, and for promoting equal *opportunities* which do not necessarily lead to fair *outcomes*. Radical feminism is criticised for focusing on gender differences and common experiences of women, since this leads them to ignore the diversity of interests among different groups of women. Emphasising gender difference may play down women's capacity to achieve social change and trap them in a 'victimised' role. Socialist feminism is criticised by radical feminists for its limited view of the different forms of power relations between men and women (for example, violence, sexuality). Focusing on class and economic oppression offers inadequate explanations of patriarchy.

The oppression of black women whose problems may combine racism and sexism has led to a distinctive approach from black feminist perspectives. An important wider debate which has relevance to social work is the issue of the role of psychoanalysis and its approach to women (see Chapter 3).

Other influences on anti-discriminatory thought have been lesbian and gay rights work and ideas on disability, mental illness and learning disabilities and the political economy of ageing (Phillipson, 1982; Laczko and Phillipson, 1991; Bytheway, 1995). Many of these factors interrelate (for example, age and ethnicity, Blakemore and Boneham, 1994; age and gender, Arber and Ginn, 1991), so that problems where two or more aspects of identity lead to social oppression may be magnified, or may lead to conflicts in response and attitude.

Connections

Concerns about social conflict led to attempts to frame an approach to combat racism within social work and to a lesser extent other related occupational groups. Radical social work texts in the 1970s often included items on what would now be called oppressed groups – for example, Milligan (1975) on 'homosexuality'; Hart (1980) on gay and lesbian issues; Husband (1980) on racism. Feminism also made its appearance in the early 1980s (for instance, Wilson, 1980; McCleod and Dominelli, 1982; Burden and Gottleib, 1987). These were only a minor feature of a traditionally radical class-based analysis, however. Major texts on work with minority ethnic groups appeared in the United States throughout the 1980s – for example, the first edition of Devore and Schlesinger (1991) appeared in 1981; Jacobs and Bowles, 1988; Pinder-hughes, 1989 – and in Britain in the mid-to late 1980s (for instance, Coombe and Little, 1986; Ely and Denney, 1987; Dominelli, 1988).

Feminist approaches also achieved major texts in the late 1980s (for example, Brook and Davis, 1985; Burden and Gottlieb, 1987; Hanmer and Statham, 1988; Dominelli and McCleod, 1989). They were also included in major reviews of theory, although race issues did not appear (Turner, 1986; Howe, 1987). In the 1990s, a stream of publications has appeared – for instance, Langan and Day (1992); Taylor and Daly (1995); both on feminism; Herberg (1993), on race – and there are also many journal articles and chapters, some of which are referred to below. Recent publications reflect more detailed and specific analysis – for example, Bricker-Jenkins *et al.* (1991), on feminist practice in clinical (that is, casework) settings; Langan and Day (1992), on a variety of feminist practice issues; Denney (1992) and Dominelli *et al.* (1995) on anti-racist work in probation; Schlesinger (1995), on work with minority and ethnic groups generally; Cavanagh and Cree (1996), on feminist work with men. The focus is often on situations where women suffered domestic violence, or are part of social categories where women are strongly represented as a result of gender difference, such as care-givers and older people.

Impetus was given to many of these developments by curriculum development activities of the UK and US education authorities for social work (for example, Norton, 1978; CD Project Steering Group, 1991; CCETSW, 1991; Patel, 1994 – all on race). Accounts of practice include material on anti-racism or black perspectives (for instance, Hanvey and Philpot, 1994) and virtually all American texts include it as a major area of knowledge and practice expertise. However, a recent text on practice does so, but refers only to feminism as a specific theoretical approach (Whittaker and Tracy, 1989). Some reviews of theory refer to neither (such as Lishman, 1991). This may reflect uncertainty about whether anti-discrimination is a separable theory of practice, since it does not refer to many social problems faced by social workers, and might be better regarded as a value principle which should 'permeate' all approaches to social work.

Social work in India interprets conflict between existing social groups as a problem of *communalism*. Chandra (1987) defines this as the belief that people following a particular religion consequently have common social, political and economic interests. This belief leads to conflict between different language, religious and caste communities (Miri, 1993; Kumar, 1994). Five conflict strategies have been identified (by Oomen, quoted by Kumar, 1994: 65–6):

1 *assimilationist communalism*, where particular interests try to recruit others to their cause;
2 *welfarist communalism*, where social services and benefits are limited to one community;
3 *retreatist communalism*, where groups withdraw from interaction with others;
4 *retaliatory communalism*, where communities act violently against others when they perceive threats or acts against them;
5 *separatist communalism*, where language or culture is used to create enclaves away from others.

Here, the issue is constructed to define the issue as excessive separation or conflict. The social work role might be conflict reduction and achieving fair distribution of resources. Applying this to some Western countries might raise a concern for anti-discriminatory strategies which focus on extreme separatism, and suggest that it is important to understand and respond to the specific perspectives and needs of minority groups.

A creation of the 1990s is an approach which includes all forms of oppression in a generic anti-discriminatory (Thompson, 1993) or anti-oppressive (Dalrymple and Burke, 1995) approach. Both make an analysis of discrimination – in Dalrymple and Burke's case drawing on the earlier work of Norton (1978) – which takes a concentric view of the relevant social forces. Figure 11.1 compares the terminology and approach of each. Norton's position sees the individual and their family and immediate community as 'embedded' (1978: 4) in a wider social system. The individual's primary identification is to the nurturing or immediate system. The wider or sustaining system is seen as 'taking on the attitude of the wider society in regard to oneself' (1978: 4). Thompson's (1993) anti-discriminatory theory links the personal, cultural and structural levels of analysis of social issues. His view has presumably been developed without reference to Norton (whom he does not cite), but is broadly similar. Here, the personal (P) level is about interpersonal relationships, and personal or psychological feelings, attitudes and actions between people, including social work practice, which is mainly carried out at this level. This takes place within a cultural context (C), which influences and forms individual thought and action.

That is, the C level refers to shared ways of thinking, feeling and acting. Thus, it is about commonalities between people within different groups, an assumed consensus about normality and the assumption that people conform to social norms created within particular cultures. We internalise these cultural norms. These levels are in turn embedded in a structural level, which is an established social order and a set of accepted social divisions. This established social order and its structures, and the cultural norms and assumptions and personal behaviour that results, come from acceptance of the social order and its divisions. Workers have a good deal of influence over the personal level, but decreasing influence over matters at the cultural and then structural levels.

Figure 11.1 Three concentric formulations of anti-oppressive practice

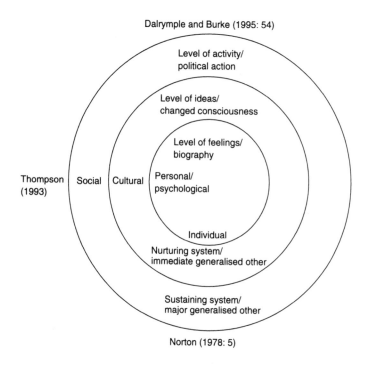

Dalrymple and Burke's (1995) analysis, reflecting an awareness of both their predecessors, develops a practice model involving the worker and client in a partnership committed to change in order to achieve greater equality in society. This operates at the level of feelings, reflecting the client's and worker's biographies, at the level of ideas, working to achieve a changed consciousness of both feelings and society and at the level of political action in wider society.

There are problems with a concentric view, because it may be taken to assume that wider social ideas and structures are always mediated by a more immediate culture in their effect on the ideas and feelings of an individual. Against this, the immediate culture may be in conflict with the wider society, and support an individual against wider ideas and structures. Alternatively, the individual may be in conflct with their culture and more in touch with wider ideas. Culture is in any case a difficult concept. It implies a relatively unchanging, dominating collection of social values, and assumes that members of an identified group will always accept all of these. In fact, the source of influences on an individual may be various and influences on a social or ethnic group may also be variable.

Thompson's (1993) analysis of anti-discriminatory practice is important as the first account to attempt to provide a theoretical rationale for practice across of range of discriminatory behaviour. He includes gender, ethnicity, ageing, disability and, less comprehensively, sexual orientation, religion, language, nation, region, and mental illness and impairment. This avoids separating different forms of discrimination into a hierarchy in which one was more important than another. All forms of discrimination were seen as important. They have a potentiating effect on one another so that suffering from more than one form of discrimination becomes increasingly affected. Being female, elderly and from an ethnic minority, for example, has been described as triple jeopardy (Norman, 1985).

This view makes the conventional radical criticism of the failings of traditional social work theory, which we met in Chapter 10. Since structure and commonalities arising from cultural assumptions are such an important part of personal behaviour, discrimination does not wholly or even mainly arise from personal prejudice, although in a particular instance this may be so. It arises first from the fact that powerful groups in society maintain discrimination in society as a way of preserving their power. They do so using their hegemony; that is, through their social control of beliefs about the nature of society which creates an ideology. Thus discrimination is created and maintained by personal beliefs and behaviour reinforced by ideologies which develop from the power exerted by groups in order to sustain and strengthen their dominant position within social structures.

One of the ways in which this is done is by the use of language and social assumptions to support conventions which are discriminatory.

Denney (1992) argues that post-structuralist theory provides a method for exploring through the analysis of court or agency reports how people have moved from assumptions to making discriminatory decisions. Another example is using use the words 'spastic' and 'idiot' as terms of abuse, when originally they were technical terms referring to a particular form or severity (respectively) of physical and mental (respectively) handicap. Again, I am white and grew up without meeting any black people until my late teens. I find it hard not to think of being white as normal and of being black as out of the ordinary. We tend just to take for granted such assumptions about ourselves and others. As a result, Owusu-Bempah (1994) shows, workers assume that self-identity in black children will be problematic, when they do not make the same assumptions about white children. This suggests that we need to be open and flexible in our views about all ethnic groups and listen carefully to their own perspective, rather than taking any issue for granted in relation to ethnic identity.

Discrimination means identifying individuals and groups with certain characteristics and treating them less well than people or groups with conventionally valued characteristics. An important aspect of much anti-discriminatory theory is analysis of the origins of discrimination. A well-developed feminist social work analysis exists. For example, Taylor and Daly's (1995) collection considers the historical development of women's role as subservient to men, in general social convention, in law, and in medical practice and religion, which have had a considerable influence on the development of social work. There has been concern about the way in which women's socialisation is inconsistent with male definitions of management, so that they do not attain senior roles in agencies consistent with their representation among social workers generally, and are sometimes unhappy about the way in which authority and power are exercised within social work (Hallett, 1989; Grimwood and Popplestone, 1993; Taylor, 1995).

Feminists seek to understand the lives and experience of women from their own perspectives and values, which are different from men's, and thus avoid being looked at from the point of view of men (androcentrism) (Hudson, 1985). In social work, it is argued that goal and task-orientated practice, and positivist demands for scientific practice, are male-defined priorities, using a male language and way of thinking (B. Collins, 1986). Walker (1994), however, points out the gains achieved by scientific method and argues that the criticism should be of the uses to which it has been put. Gilligan's work (1982) has been influential. She shows that women and men have different modes of reasoning about moral questions (Rhodes, 1985), and Davis (1985) argues that female 'voices' have been suppressed in favour of a male positivist perspective. Gilligan (1986) argues that this means that men and women have different ways of understanding and valuing the self and defining what is moral. Alternative ways of defining social work, and particularly of ensuring that agencies are not managed so as to exclude women and their perspectives, are required.

Pro-feminist ideas on working with men have developed aimed at reducing violence and sexual exploitation and, particularly in social work education, combating sexual stereotypes (Cavanagh and Cree, 1996). Work with men and boys seeks to remove damaging effects of their socialisation into conventional male behaviour, and to enable them to manage personal relationships more successfully. In particular, this should reduce their tendency to be isolated because of the expectation that men do not need help or support and their tendency towards aggression and violence (van Elst, 1994). Men should take part in combating the problems of gender stereotyping, which they, as well as women, suffer from (Thompson, 1995). Conflict over masculinity exists. For example, young men are the main clients of the prisons and the care system, there is often conflict over fathers' involvements in families when they break up, and men and women play different roles in family or informal caring (Pringle, 1995). Such social conflicts justify special attention to working with men so as to resolve issues of masculinity which cause problems for the men involved, or more widely. However, such work may be criticised if it leads to working with men for reasons other than their own needs. An example is Cavanagh and Cree's (1996: 183) statement: 'Remember that women are our first priority and that work with men is done in order to improve the quality of life for women.' Women may benefit generally or in particular from work with men, but statements of this kind may be criticised in the same way as radical social work where they subordinate the needs of the primary client to wider social objectives.

The politics of anti-oppressive theory

Anti-discriminatory and anti-oppressive approaches to social work take in a variety of perspectives and models of work which have developed in the late 1980s and 90s. There have been policy concerns in Western democratic states, particularly the English-speaking countries. These have partly arisen from examples of serious social conflict, such as inner-city riots in the United Kingdom in the early 1980s, which was largely ascribed to alienation of young black people, similar events and a high level of crime among black people in the United States and conflict in Germany over refugees from the East. Official responses to this were largely liberal. That is, they focused on reducing inequalities and marginalisation. Anti-discriminatory practice also springs from concerns within radical thought for groups of people within societies who suffer from inequality and injustice. Since radical theory questions the existing social order, it sees the problem as one of social order and structures rather than one of individual or group problems or disadvantages.

Many countries face problems of conflict between different ethnic and cultural groups in their own way. In some, there are 'indigenous' peoples, such as native Americans in the United States, Inuit people in Canada, Saami people in Nordic countries, gypsies or Romanies in southern Europe and Aborigines and Maoris in Australia and New Zealand (Dixon and Scheurell, 1995).

Since the attempts at an overall theoretical model seek to subsume feminist and anti-racist and other special concerns, this chapter presents all these approaches to practice together. However, this is a current area of theoretical development and it is unclear whether the generic anti-discriminatory/oppressive approaches will prevail, in spite of the strong ideological and theoretical roots of feminism in wider political, social and cultural ideology. Also, while generic approaches emphasise continuities and similarities among the theories considered here, this derives from a particular and basically structural analysis like that of radical and Marxist approaches. This analysis remains controversial and may in the long term be resisted. Generic anti-discriminatory approaches see the interaction between various oppressions as complex, requiring analysis. However, this presents practical and ideological problems. An agency or workers may specialise in ways which make it impossible for them to accord equal weight to all the oppressions. Needs of clients may present in one area, and they may resist dealing with other areas. Both workers and clients may, at the level of ideas, have difficulty in accepting the equivalence of oppression of, say, ageism or of lesbians and gays with that of, say, race. This may be due to their own prejudice, or to their reasonable assessment that ageism, say, has far less serious consequences for particular clients or in general than racism.

Within social work, anti-racism and anti-discriminatory approaches arose from the needs of agencies and workers facing new ethnic issues, spurring them on to reform by rising conflicts. Feminist approaches grew up much more from an ideological commitment from some women workers and wider social movements in favour of feminism. The development of these approaches may also reflect the failure of radical, class-based approaches to theory to have more than a general influence on ideas of social work. Socialist commitment therefore migrated towards feminist and anti-racist approaches as topical and more broadly acceptable ideas as a way of implementing structural ideas in practice. This has sometimes led to conflict with 'liberal' approaches which do not emphasise structural analysis. The evident oppression and needs of minority ethnic groups, women, disabled and elderly people as they present themselves to the social services have, however, created agency and worker pressures towards responding to these needs without commitment to structural theories. Consequently, there is a literature and approach which seeks to understand and incorporate the needs and perspectives of oppressed groups within treatment-orientated social work (for example, Braye and Preston-Shoot, 1995; Dalrymple and Burke, 1995).

Denney (1983, 1991; Ely and Denney, 1987), Gould (1994), in terms of power, and Jenkins (1988) identify a number of perspectives in anti-racism:

- *Assimilation.* This is an approach which assumes that migrants to a new country will assimilate to the culture and life style of that country. Where there is a native population and dominant incomers, it assumes assimilation to the incomers (for example, in Australia, see LeSueur, 1970). These alternative formulations demonstrate that it is the power of the dominant culture which is at issue, and not who was present first. In Small's (1989) terms, immigrants start from identifying with the culture and life style of their country of origin and *substitute* the new country's culture and way of life. Herberg (1993) describes this as *acculturation.* Social and personal difficulties, like those social workers often deal with, are often interpreted as failures in substitution or acculturation. Alternatively, a *cultural deficit* may be assumed. This view considers that the original culture does not develop the skills and knowledge to cope with the new environment. It might be assumed, for example, that child-care skills are lacking, or that oppression of female members of Muslim families is inappropriate in a Western society. This leads to *pathologising* black people (Singh, 1992), an example of 'blaming the victim'.

Power here is used to remove oppression from the agenda, so that agencies do not recognise the problem. The social work response would be understanding the various stages of acculturation (Herberg, 1993), understanding the cultural origins of the problems and working to change and develop ability to manage in the new society and, in the case of offences, providing training and social control mechanisms to support acculturation.

- *Liberal pluralism.* This view, rather like liberal feminism, focuses on equal opportunities. The concern is that power is used overtly to control decision-making, disadvantaging minorities. We are all entitled to the same treatment on the same terms in a society, whatever our social group. Immigrants and oppressed black groups, such as long-standing black populations deriving from slavery in the United States, suffer multiple deprivations arising from their inferior position in the labour market and their poor wage-earning capacity. Therefore, in the same way that equal opportunities laws are designed to enforce equal treatment in work and housing, social work seeks to provide equal access to services and special help to improve social conditions in compensation for multiple deprivations. This often leads to a *colour-blind* approach (Dominelli, 1988: 36–9), where efforts are made to ensure that minority ethnic groups are treated in the same way as every other group. This is partly designed to avoid a 'white backlash' in which white people react against the perceived unfairness to them of policies for special provision for black or other specific groups (Ely and Denney, 1987: 77). Jenkins (1988) does not distinguish this view from cultural pluralism.

- *Cultural pluralism.* This view accepts that in many societies a variety of ethnic groups exist. Each group maintains to a greater or lesser extent their cultural patterns, and this should be encouraged, and all cultures valued. This leads to a policy of *multi-culturalism*, in which spreading knowledge and experience of different cultures is encouraged. Sanders (1978) defines multi-culturalism as affirming the reality of cultural diversity, allowing individuals to keep much that is distinctive about their cultural traditions and integrating diverse cultural traditions in society, thus opposing a single, dominant culture. Such knowledge makes services more appropriate and responsive.

- *Structuralist.* The assumption of this view is that capitalist societies affect groups within them differently. Traditionally, this was applied to social classes, but ethnic and gender divisions are

increasingly recognised as the basis for economic and social
domination of particular groups by economically and socially
dominant groups in society. Power is exercised by elites so that
society is organised to avoid recognition of oppression of
minorities. Jenkins (1988) regards this as a *conflict* approach,
since it assumes that the central issue will be increasing conflict
between groups for resources and power. Dominelli's (1988) anti-
racist social work, which has a structuralist perspective, requires
acceptance that racism pervades social work ideology, practice and
training. Workers need to explore their own racism, particularly by
exploring who holds power in particular situations. They should be
careful to work with black clients and their families in ways which
accept the families' own social values and expectations of
appropriate family behaviour. A focus on changing their own
agency's and other organisations' racism is necessary. Partly this
will involve moving social work away from controlling towards
supportive mechanisms. Efforts should be made to change social
work practice and values by advocating anti-racist practice, and
confronting and making explicit racism where it is perceived.
Work should be undertaken in alliance with black communities
and organisations and following their priorities.

- *Black perspectives.* These approaches, which are not identified by
  Jenkins (1988), emphasise the requirement to include the point of
  view of black people and communities themselves in
  development of service and practice. They should also be
  involved in actions and practice, which should be constructed
  taking their perspectives as a dominant factor in policy, decision-
  making and practice. Evidence can be disclosed of their real
  contributions to society (for example, black people's contribution
  to the history of social work; Carlton-LaNey, 1994). These may
  have been hidden by racist assumptions which devalue such
  contributions. Narayan (1994) suggests that minority groups have
  an 'epistemic' privilege. That is, they understand more directly
  the lived experience of oppression. However, this does not mean
  that nobody else can understand such experiences, but this is a
  hard struggle. Power is revealed in language and discourses
  which support oppressive assumptions. Ahmad's (1990: 3) view
  of 'black perspectives' requires us to explore black people's
  experience and writing. We should focus on those which express
  and clarify the history of black people's subordination to white
  people, the experience of racism and powerlessness and on those

which focus on attaining the goal of racial equality and justice. Practice should emphasise black people's own understanding of their experience, particularly during assessment phases of social work. This should be interpreted to agencies and more widely within social work. Practice is 'empowering', with references to Solomon's model of black empowerment (see Chapter 12). Resources offered by black workers, the black community and black organisations are relevant sources of change to black people. Workers should also explore and build on legislative provision and policy developments. In this way, the needs of black people and communities can be included in developments, systems and practice. Workers should be sensitive to black perspectives and experiences of the world, and in its attempts to adapt the skills of conventional practice to this perspective. Practice methods can contribute to this. For example, Martin (1995) shows how a process of exploring the 'oral history' of an individual in family and community contexts can include black and community perspectives in professional assessment. Efforts should be made to develop and make use of social science information about black people, which respond to the understandings which black people have about the world (Robinson, 1995). We should avoid assuming that there is only one minority culture, or that each group has a single culture, but explore the range of views in each case (Gross, 1995).

Theoretical approaches in relation to other oppressed groups are less well developed, but it is possible to position them within these perspectives. *Normalisation* (Wolfensberger, 1972, 1984) takes, in many ways, an assimilationist position. This is because it seeks to include people with learning disabilities as far as possible into 'ordinary life' (Towell, 1988), so that their social roles can, as far as possible, be equivalent to widely valued social roles. However, it also has elements of a perspectives position, because it seeks to take up and promote disabled people's own perspectives on their situation. A *social model of disability* view (Oliver, 1990, 1996) is a pluralist position with structural elements arguing that medical models concentrate on disabled people's impairment. Instead, we must recognise that social definitions of what is normal lead to society being organised in ways which create disability. For example, if there were no steps in buildings, a person with a walking impairment would not be disabled. Society should be changed so that all groups can coexist on an equal basis. Recognition of 'communities' among disabled people (such as a Deaf community of people born Deaf whose language and culture derives from sign language) suggests the possibility of a perspectives position as well. A *political economy of ageing* view (Laczko and Phillipson, 1991) is mainly structuralist. It argues that assumptions about ageing derive from the exclusion of older people from the labour market, making them economically and socially dependent. A *disabled living* view (Morris, 1993) is related to perspectives positions. It argues that disabled individuals and communities should direct and manage services designed to support them towards independence.

Thus it is possible to extend the idea of black perspectives towards a concept of 'oppressed groups' perspectives'. Inherent in many of these positions is the achievement of a detailed analysis and understanding of the views and experience of oppressed groups. This is the basis for social work action, and for promoting the involvement of members of those groups in management and development of services.

Because many anti-discriminatory positions contain elements of each of the perspectives outlined above, the strict division and contrasting of each perspective is probably unsustainable. However, the politics of anti-racist theory counterposes structuralist and black perspectives against pluralist perspectives. Singh (1992), in seeing a black pathology view as moving towards a black perspectives view, and Ely and Denney (1987), in proposing a basically historical account, imply that theoretical development is leading towards structuralist and possibly black perspectives positions. Several British writers (for example, Sivanandan; 1991; Husband, 1991; Mullard, 1991) explicitly reject pluralist perspectives, and relate anti-racism to socialist political objectives. Others (such as Ahmed, 1991) comment on the failure of class-based radical structuralist theory to respond to black perspectives, particularly women's perspectives. The essential characteristic of anti-racist practice as against multi-cultural perspectives, according to Naik (1991: 51, emphasis original) is 'to attend to *structural inequalities in society*, …[including] the dynamics of race, economics and political power'. The British anti-racist structuralist emphasis on power derives from the radical structuralist position, considered in Chapter 10. It is subject to the same sorts of criticisms, discussed at the end of this chapter.

The black perspectives position, however, while focusing on the importance of understanding and working with power differentials, values opportunities to achieve power for black perspectives, black participation and black influence and control in services and attitudes. This is also the approach of the disabled living perspective and some aspects of normalisation and ordinary life perspectives, as discussed above, leading us to an oppressed groups' perspective. McNay (1992) argues in relation to feminist practice that the analysis of power relations at individual and societal levels can lead to an approach to helping oppressed clients and groups gain experience of the use of power. This leads several writers, including Dalrymple and Burke (1995), whose work is discussed more fully below, to propose forms of anti-oppressive practice which rely on structuralist analyses of power, while proposing anti-oppressive practice which seeks to be empowering. Strict structuralists would regard such views as naïve in their failure to focus primarily on inequalities of power. Fook (1993: 17), for example, criticises empowerment for not necessarily being informed by or actively opposing structuralist oppression.

American accounts of anti-racism (for example, Pinderhughes, 1988, 1989) similarly attach great significance to power, but see this in relation to its interpersonal effects and consequences for behaviour and experience. Herberg's (1993) Canadian approach, for example, focuses on different value positions in different cultures. Another characteristic of the American literature (for instance, Jacobs and Bowles, 1988; Ryan, 1992; Kim, 1995) is the exploration of detailed information about different minority groups. This appears to be at least partly because of the presence in the United States of large groups of recent migrants raising specific language, cultural and practical issues and indigenous 'Indian' (native American) ethnic groups, whereas in Britain immigration control has reduced concern about cultural differences. Taking a black perspectives position, the American approach contained in work such as Devore and Schlesinger's 'ethnic-sensitive practice' (1991) values and responds to the special demands of minority ethnic groups. In groups, for example, it is necessary to take account of the fact that some ethnic minorities are accustomed to dealing with personal issues in groups, while others are not, and preparation for the group has to be managed accordingly (Davis, 1984). Dungee-Anderson and Beckett (1995) argue that we need to understand other cultures with which we work to avoid mistakes in intervention caused by misunderstanding our own or clients' reactions. Applied to the curriculum, however, such approaches run the risk of multiculturalism, which has been criticised for encouraging white students and practitioners to be interested in the diversity and exotic nature of many different cultures, without coming to grips with the element of discrimination which is crucial to developing an anti-racist stance. Gould (1995) argues that we should develop multi-culturalism to offer a framework for all groups to integrate thinking across cultures. However, as I have argued elsewhere (Payne, 1996a), this runs the risk of subordinating alternative cultures to Western interpretations of them, or simplifying them and denying real philosophical and practical differences in cultural views.

In summary, anti-discriminatory/oppressive perspectives are critical of all social work practice and organisation in its failure to incorporate major social change to achieve equality and social justice for minority and oppressed groups. Within these perspectives, however, we can identify a conflict between radical structuralist and pluralist positions. Simple pluralism in the 'race' field appears to have been defeated by the arguments for a structuralist position, but black perspectives positions include elements of structuralism and pluralism. This is because, although they recognise structural issues about power, they assert the importance of gaining power for black perspectives, and so reject the negative view of empowerment held within a strict structuralist position. Similar disagreements are present within feminism, and in debate about work with other oppressed groups.

In presenting examples of coherent analyses of practice theories, I have reflected some of these political and specialised areas of discussion. Hanmer and Statham (1988) present a socialist view of feminist social work, but I draw attention also to Dominelli and McCleod's (1989) radical feminist text. Dalrymple and Burke's (1995) account of anti-oppressive work is given as an example of a structural analysis allied with a more liberal empowerment perspective. More extensive accounts of empowerment are contained in Chapter 12.

Hanmer and Statham: women-centred work

Hanmer and Statham (1988) present an approach to social work which is not explicitly Marxist, and seeks to be woman-centred and non-sexist rather than feminist. Van der Vlugt (1994), referring to Dutch experience, distinguishes between emancipatory and gender-specific feminist work. Emancipatory work is concerned with consciousness-raising, increasing women's autonomy and reducing power imbalances between women and men. Gender-specific work is concerned with supporting and developing femininity. This distinction is between socialist and radical feminism, respectively.

Dominelli and McCleod (1989) cover similar ground, from a Marxist position.

Gender, in Hanmer and Statham's account, is the basis of important life experiences for women. They are often defined by their gender (for example, as mothers, wives), while men are defined by their status (for instance, by job titles). Yet, women's gender often becomes invisible because they are socially expected to accept certain roles (such as carer of elderly people) which are often expected of women rather than men, but that expectation is unstated. So public policy assumes that informal carers will be the main helpers of people with difficulties, but informal carers are nearly always women.

Women have many things in common – for example, managing both home and job, living with and caring for men, and being mothers and caring for dependants. Important differences between them which lead to diverse experiences and expectations of women are different employment patterns and status, ethnic differences, different experiences of being powerful or feeling powerless. Thus, a white woman in a professional job, with experience of being seen as competent and powerful on occasions, will have a different view of life and different expectations to those of a black woman in a manual job who feels powerless to affect her life. Dominelli and McCleod (1989) make the point that gender cannot be separated from other forms of oppression, and in particular class and ethnic differences, although women often have a special experience of such differences.

Nonetheless, Hanmer and Statham argue that women are treated as dependent on and inferior to men, and share the experience of the expectations that arise from this. Social workers should start from recognising the common experiences of women, and should always move on to examining the diversities between this particular woman and others. Gender, then, is an important theme in defining women in three main ways: women are always expected to be *carers*, to be *subordinate to men*, and for effective work their *personal identity* is crucial to overcoming many problems that they face.

Assessment of women clients should always contain knowledge of life patterns and policies that affect women, and assumptions which often affect how they are assessed. Relevant life patterns include demographic factors, such as the fact that there are increasing numbers of one-parent families, reductions in the number of children in households, increase in divorce and remarriage, and more working mothers. We should not always make assumptions about normal or acceptable behaviour in women without taking these developments into account. Women are often poorer than men, and experience more strongly the effects of poor family income, poor housing and transport. The importance of women's work both to family income and to self-respect is often underestimated by social workers.

Especially important in assessing women clients is their role as carers. Most women have and care for children, and often other dependants at different stages of their lives. Our assessment of their capacity to do so often reflects cultural assumptions, which may be questioned. Different ethnic groups, for example, may expect different kinds of approach to child care. We may also have expectations that might be questioned, such as expecting that clients will always be able to have stable, monogamous relationships with a man, or will be able to care without relief for several young children in a more material and home environment. Because women are assumed to be able and willing to care, their contribution may be taken for granted and they are often given less help than men in similar circumstances. Workers should avoid making resource allocations on such assumptions.

It should not be assumed that women will usually be dependent upon, care for and be subordinate to men. Their status and relationships will be defined by marriage, or the legal consequences of divorce, or the fact that they are unmarried. Their caring role requires skill and commitment, but is often undervalued compared with men's social status defined by their job. Work can usefully focus on promoting women's identity, self-image and self-esteem. Women can be encouraged to see their achievements, to demand support and resources for the important work that they do.

To recognise and share the experiences of women clients in this position, women social workers must recognise power imbalances and unequal treatment that they receive as employees in agencies which are dominated by men and male attitudes. Women are often excluded from promotion and have difficulties in using their perspective in management, which is often defined in male language and expectations. There are a variety of shared and collaborative approaches to dealing with this. Dominelli and McCleod (1989: 76–100) focus on the contribution of feminist work to strengthening women's emotional well-being.

In working with clients, Hanmer and Statham propose strategies for women-centred work, and these are summarised in Table 11.1.

McCleod's (1979) work with prostitutes is an example of feminist social work showing the reality of poverty and their need to maintain their families, which leads them to gain the high material rewards from

Table 11.1 Principles of woman-centred work

Principle	Practice of social worker
preparation	clarify aims, accept writing and recording as helpful in meeting aims rather than feeling disabled by demands for this, check facts and research about women, develop skills and knowledge to be able to challenge from a strong position, take risks to ask for appropriate help, support and resources, define services and policies which are unhelpful to women, keep information on resources for women clients
devise principles for women-centred practice	like and value women, use experience of women as a resource, believe and accept women, share with and learn from clients in non-hierarchical ways, use all-women groups, ensure space for women to get away from caring and dependence on men, avoid using conventional assumptions, which treat women's ordinary behaviour as bad (e.g. sexuality), encourage women to feel in control of their lives and behaviour, use a wide range of social work
make methods relevant to gender	theories and methods, give importance and time to women alone, adapt theories so that they affirm rather than criticise women, avoid stereotyping and sexualising women's behaviour, avoid sexist language, accept oppression and unhappiness, accept disagreement with feminist views, avoid jargon about oppression, aim for success in limited tasks, use groups to stress shared experiences and support, use separate groups because men tend to dominate groups which include both sexes
link clients to agencies specialising in women's needs	generalist agencies may not provide enough help of the right kind
increase resources for women	encourage expression of needs and formalise and gain support for new resources, encourage equal opportunity policies and structures
involve women in decision-making and policy-making of the agency	set up representative arrangements
create a code for feminist practice	establish women's groups and training

Source: Hanmer and Statham (1988).

this work, contrary to the more conventional assumption that they become committed to prostitution through contact with deviant subcultures and personal inadequacies. Donnelly (1986) gives one of a number of accounts of groupwork with women clients, raising the sense of shared experience and understanding of women on a deprived housing estate. Both are aimed in various ways at consciousness-raising, which Longres and McCleod (1980) relate to the conscientisation of Freire (1972), discussed above, and is thus explicitly radical. Not all feminist therapy and social work is radical, however. Their analysis is that consciousness-raising aims to encourage reflection so as to understand dehumanising social structures and action to change such social conditions. It involves dialogue between equals, concern for ideology and how dominant ideologies in society may create misfortune and social problems, mutual and shared exploration and respect for each other's views, and making connections between private troubles and public issues and individual and class interests. Consciousness-raising is best done in groups for mutual support and broader exploration. It may be harder to find the time and commitment in individual work, and harder to empathise where the relationship between an individual client and worker is usually unequal. There needs to be a commitment to action to change situations which are identified in groups, otherwise complaining about the 'system' simply leads to complaining acceptance of it.

Dalrymple and Burke: anti-oppressive practice

Dalrymple and Burke (1995) place many of the ideas discussed here in a comprehensive account of anti-oppressive practice. Their focus is how the legal and professional responsibilities of social workers may be implemented oppressively or in an empowering way. They have thus developed their model in an extremely difficult area for social work – the use of power and authority – in search of protection for both public and clients. It makes their formulation all the more powerful for focusing on an area of social work which seems to conflict with attacking discrimination and developing empowerment for clients.

Their starting point is an assertion that effective anti-oppressive practice requires a clear theoretical perspective to inform a value base which will permit anti-oppressive work. A clear understanding of power and of oppression must also inform the values of practice. Power is seen as concerned with personal and social relationships where one person or group consistently prevents others, who are seen as powerless, from achieving their needs or aspirations. Oppression is understood to be characterised by personal and social relationships based upon the assumption of inequalities of power, so that people internalise acceptance of their own lack of power in their lives. Dalrymple and Burke argue that a clear connection must be seen between an individual's personal social environment which may render them powerless and the wider social system which reinforces and takes for granted the powerlessness of certain groups. Workers must also be aware of agency contexts so that they do not just accept policy issues about service provision as routine constraints, and they must build reflection, involvement and evaluation into everything that they do.

Such principles must be applied in practice to enable workers to understand where they are applying values and legal rights and duties in a liberal rather than radical way. Thus, for Dalrymple and Burke, anti-oppressive practice requires:

- an empowering approach;
- working in partnership with clients;
- minimal intervention.

Workers can use these practices to inform their use of the conventional powers of social work practice and avoid acting oppressively. For example, a worker should not arrange for a home help to assist an elderly lady with the covert aim of checking up on the client's capacity to manage alone. Instead, the worker should discuss with the client openly the risks of managing alone, working with her on a plan to prevent problems arising. This avoids trying to set up a system which takes away too much responsibility for action from the client. Such an approach would mean that she has even less practice in taking responsibility for her own safety.

An empowering approach requires focusing on helping clients to gain more control over their lives, to become aware of and use their own personal resources, to overcome obstacles in meeting their needs and aspirations, to have their voice heard in decision-making and to be able to challenge situations where they experience inequality and oppression. Empowerment requires making links between clients' personal positions and structural inequalities. This involves helping clients understand how things have happened to them and trying to find ways in which they can gain control over at least some aspects of their lives. This reduces their confusion and helps them to feel more in touch with their lives.

For example, Mrs Wilkins is an elderly lady who has saved for most of her life, but now finds she cannot manage on her small pension. This makes her feel incompetent and confused about priorities. The worker helped her to understand that she was affected by poor mobility, so that she could not use cheaper superstores but had to rely on expensive local shops, and by historically poor pension provision, which she had saved to compensate for. She could set priorities for daily expenditure such as food, rent, heating and lighting. This could be made from her pension and then she could feel that she was managing efficiently with that. She could draw from her savings for more major expenditure on clothes and equipment purchases. In this way, she could feel in control of the expenditure from her savings, seeing it as appropriate to what she had saved for, instead of leaking away on the everyday. The worker was also able to get her advice on ways in which she could invest her money to gain a better income. In this case the worker was operating at the interpersonal level to harness the client's own resources and using the agency's knowledge and information resources at the organisational level. In the long run, information from situations such as this can be accumulated to work at a policy level to improve the way pension provision is made.

Dalrymple and Burke work at several different levels:

- *Feelings,* where they try to reduce the effect of the personal experiences which have led to the client feeling powerless. They emphasise, as does Rees (1991 – see Chapter 12) the importance of exploring biography in understanding such personal experiences.
- *Ideas*, where they concentrate on clients' feelings of self-worth and try to strengthen their ability to control their lives, feelings and ability to act. This is similar to ego-supportive work in psychodynamic social work and much of the focus of cognitive theory. The aim here is to lead to a changed consciousness within the client of their capacity.
- *Action*, which is concerned with seeking changes in the agency, social welfare or wider systems which adversely affects clients.

The next aspect of Dalrymple and Burke's anti-oppressive practice involves partnership. One formulation or partnership, identified by Stevenson and Parsloe (1993) from a community care project, requires the following policies:

- only investigating problems with the client's explicit consent;
- only acting where there is clear agreement by the client or an explicit legal requirement;

- basing action on the views and needs of all relevant family members;
- basing action on negotiated agreement rather than on assumptions or prejudices about clients' needs and wishes;
- giving clients the greatest possible degree of choice, even when they must be legally compelled.

Dalrymple and Burke recommend the use of written agreements, produced in circumstances where there is effective communication between worker and client. Also, clients should have access to independent advocates who can represent their views effectively. Written charters or standards of service and explanations of clients' rights create a clear focus for them to be able to understand their entitlement. Partnership involves effective inter-agency work and careful planning of services, so that clients have the widest degree of choice with the minimum of professional and agency barriers to exercise their choice.

Minimal intervention requires workers to be aware of their potential power. This may oppress clients, either leading to excessive or non-participative intervention or to failure to intervene when their use of appropriate powers might assist and protect clients. Workers should prefer to intervene at various levels:

- *The primary level*, to prevent problems arising. Services might be adapted to be appropriate and helpful to clients, community resources mobilised to help them, and the public and people involved given information and education to enable them to manage themselves.
- *The secondary level*, to catch problems and try to deal with them early, before they become serious. This reduces the amount of interference in clients' lives.
- *The tertiary level*, to reduce the consequences for people when something has gone wrong or action has been forced on the agency.

This approach stresses not waiting until the last possible moment, and then being forced into excessive or oppressive action. It is better to intervene at an earlier stage to prevent greater incursions into clients' lives.

A crucial element of Dalrymple and Burke's approach is to link strategies for wider change to everyday action. This avoids oppressing clients by the worker's actions and by the agency's policies and services. A strategic approach to issues involves the following:

- clearly identifying the issue and goals which would resolve it;
- breaking down the issue and goals so that they are manageable;
- setting a time limit or target;
- reviewing and evaluating achievement against the definition and the target;
- making links with others who are working on the same or similar issues.

Commentary

Anti-discriminatory and anti-oppressive theories in social work have had a significant influence in the 1980s and 90s. This is for practical and theoretical reasons. In practice, many societies and agencies have faced pressures from the consequences of population migration through an increasingly global economy and through refugee movements. Moreover, attitudes among groups such as disabled people and among women have become less deferential, and less accepting of present patterns of power, particularly patriarchal power. These theoretical perspectives have helped to analyse and respond to these new social issues. Oppressed groups' perspectives and multi-cultural approaches have also helped workers to put into action new knowledge about the needs of women, various minority ethnic groups and of groups such as disabled and older people in social relations. Feminist and non-sexist work has become important to many women. It also offers lessons to men in understanding and approaching their women clients leading to new and less judgemental approaches to women's sexuality and lives.

Anti-discriminatory and anti-oppressive theories also offer theoretical advantages over other approaches to social work. They develop radical and Marxist approaches to take into account the range of different bases for oppression of groups and for inequalities and divisions in society, and thus provide a more effective account of the issues social work must face. This has also permitted a new and increasingly relevant lease of life for radical approaches within social work. A new focus on oppression has emerged, which has made possible more directed accounts of radical social work such as that of Fook (1993) discussed in Chapter 10, which relies heavily on feminist insights. They draw attention to the weaknesses of many psychological and individualistic theories of social work in dealing with discrimination and the issues facing minority groups and women in present-day society, and offer a way of understanding these issues. They thus strengthen the sociological basis of social work.

Criticisms of anti-discriminatory and anti-oppressive theories depend on the particular perspective taken. Liberal feminist views, and pluralist anti-racist views, are criticised because they accept the present social order and do not adequately recognise differences in interest and power in society which lead to oppression of particular groups. If we accept this kind of criticism, we are led towards taking a structuralist perspective. Radical feminist views and oppressed groups' perspectives may be criticised for failing to take account of institutionalised structural oppression, although they do take account of inequalities of power as they affect and are experienced by individuals and groups.

Particular criticism bears on the structuralist perspective. This presents all the difficulties, referred to in Chapter 10, of structural radical and Marxist perspectives, which may be summarised as follows, but here with relevance to anti-discriminatory and anti-oppressive approaches:

- They focus on general social change and neglect prescriptions and a knowledge base for individual practice. Many structuralist texts (such as Dominelli, 1988) focus on change in social work agencies and training, and in analysis of rather than practice with families and individuals.
- They present significant criticisms of society, and place most action at the societal level, with little hope of successful change, and this stifles optimistic action in individual work. In this way, the approach expresses the concern of all socialist-collectivist perspectives on social work about its individualist focus. It is, even by its name, an *anti* perspective, rather than being *for* something.
- They equate power with control of oppressed people and neglect the possibility of their empowerment. This has led writers concerned with developing practice to focus on empowerment approaches, even though some radical criticism would doubt that empowerment can be adequately combined with a structuralist position. The structuralist view of the immutability of capitalist power relations also contradicts oppressed groups' perspectives, which claim the need and possibility for black and other oppressed groups to gain influence and take control of definitions of the issues affecting them and also achieve control of discriminatory services and organisations.

- They neglect important areas of rights and important human
  problems in favour of a limited set of priorities. It might be
  argued, for example, that responding to poverty and housing
  problems or individual child care and personal mental health
  problems is more important than empowerment in gender or
  disabled roles or against race discrimination. These might be
  related because all such problems derive from structural
  inequality and some might come from social constructions of
  clients' inadequacies due to sexism, disablism or racism.
  Nonetheless, it might be a client's priority and a sensible social
  priority to focus on the economic inequality of poverty and
  housing problems. Focusing on anti-oppressive practice may also
  conflict with other priorities and a social worker's role. White
  (1995), for example, found that committed feminist workers
  found difficulty in applying the assumption that they should work
  on commonalities with women clients. These workers found that
  the authority and power demanded by their official role and the
  social distance between their experience and the needs of their
  clients made such affinities difficult.
- They favour a cooperative and consciousness-raising approach
  which may not respond adequately to the needs of people in
  severe difficulties – they may need personal help, drawing on
  knowledge and expertise.
- They take an ideological stance in which criticism is interpreted
  as acceptance of oppression, which is by definition rejected since
  this is what the approach seeks to overcome. This has been a
  particular issue with anti-racist theory. The structuralist
  assumption that racism is endemic in society leads to a position
  where change is required in social work, agencies and education
  as well as in wider society. Resistance to such change and
  alternative analyses of the issues are rejected as signs of the
  appearance of the endemic racism.

This has been particularly controversial in social work education,
where there is a liberal tradition of criticism and debate, and it has generally been the position of 'academic freedom' that people are free to hold
and argue any point of view. This freedom is rejected by anti-racist
theory, on the grounds that any view which was not explicitly anti-racist
would in itself be an expression of the endemic racism. According to
social work and general social values, racist views or actions should
naturally be rejected. Therefore, there cannot be any case for permitting

any alternative expression or mode of operation. Moves by the British social work education body, CCETSW, to enforce anti-racist policies and curricula on social work courses have led to outbursts of criticism (Jones, 1993). These have been met by the argument that there cannot be any objection to the view that anti-racist policies should be promoted. Since, as we have noted, it is sometimes claimed that such policies are integral with general socialist political views, there has been criticism that they simply implement party political views.

Structural analysis of issues of discrimination and oppression has much to commend it, and has been more successful than the economic and class-based analysis of radical and Marxist perspectives in social work. It has been much more relevant to the issues faced daily by many social workers in practice. However, oppressed groups perspectives and those of black people do not permit a wholly structural response. They require careful attention to be paid to the wishes and needs of the groups affected, in all their variety.

Perspectives approaches reject the alignment of all members of a group together as 'oppressed' or discriminated against, and seek a much more diversified and complex analysis of their needs. This suggests that plural responses will be required, while acknowledging the importance of structural analyses of power as partly conditioning the appropriate response. As a result, a variety of services involving and fitting the needs of particular minorities and oppressed groups would grow up. Multi-cultural approaches, if we take this to imply workers attempting to gain a smattering of understanding of a variety of groups with whom they might be involved, are unacceptable in these perspectives. Instead, there would be a focus on building up a range of workers with detailed and specialised understanding. All workers would take responsibility for a sensitive response to the expressed needs and wishes of people they worked with. If these required specialised understanding, there would be referral to someone with appropriate knowledge and experience.

The remaining weakness of these approaches, if an oppressed groups' and black perspectives approach is taken, is in prescribing practice responses. Wise (1995), for example, claims that feminist practice is often exemplified by work outside the mainstream (for example, in women's refuges) and its impact on conventional social work is uncertain. We have seen that some anti-oppressive theories have sought to develop empowerment approaches to respond to this lacuna, and developments in this area of theory are the subject of Chapter 12.

12

Empowerment and Advocacy

Wider theoretical perspectives

Empowerment seeks to help clients gain power of decision and action over their own lives by reducing the effect of social or personal blocks to exercising existing power, by increasing capacity and self-confidence to use power and by transferring power from the environment to clients. Advocacy seeks to represent the interests of powerless clients to powerful individuals and social structures. In the previous two chapters, we saw that developments in radical and anti-discriminatory theory have used empowerment and advocacy to carry out practical action within their perspective. We also noted some controversy about whether we could always regard empowerment and advocacy as radical or structural in their implied explanations of social and psychological issues. This is partly because these ideas have wider use in non-radical contexts. They are also increasingly being used as a terminology to reflect self-determination and openness in other theories of social work.

Related contexts for empowerment and advocacy include management theory and practice and conservative political ideology. The management view of empowerment (for example, Stewart, 1994) is concerned with motivating individuals and teams to achieve more within organisational objectives by granting them independence from managerial controls. Political empowerment ideology often seeks to place responsiblity on individuals for providing for their own needs, with the covert aim of limiting state services. We need to be cautious about social work implementation of empowerment to avoid similar impositions.

Advocacy has its origins particularly in the legal field. Here, 'advocacy' is the term applied to what lawyers do in the courts and elsewhere in representing their clients. In addition, it is an explicit group of skills, with a literature which forms an important element in legal training. It is used as a skill and value objective in other professions. For example, UK professional codes enjoin nurses to undertake advocacy in the sense of raising problems in the resourcing or management of services which might lead to detriment to their patients.

Connections

Full-blown empowerment and advocacy perspectives are products of the 1980s and 90s. An important forerunner is Solomon's (1976) book (see below). Furlong (1987) sees empowerment as an important goal in casework because it avoids a crude polarisation of social action and individualised perspectives, placing work with individuals and families in a context of concern for social objectives. Russel-Erlich and Rivera (1986) argue that promoting empowerment in oppressed communities is an essential response to trends in political and economic life which add to oppression.

Thus, it has gained importance as an approach in social development (de Graaf, 1986; see also Chapter 9). Anderson *et al.* (1994) present a model of empowerment for social development in Africa concerned with five dimensions of practice: personal, social, educational, economic and political. Seeing these dimensions as interlocking allows people to meet individual needs (personal power), improves their capacity to influence others (interpersonal power), and in turn this creates an ability to influence the distribution of power more widely (political power). Ntebe (1994) argues that the social work profession must develop an advocacy role for oppressed communities as part of empowerment within a radical model of practice.

A comprehensive account of empowerment has emerged from Rees (1991) which particularly focuses on the political role of empowerment in social work. He identifies five essential ideas within empowerment:

1 *Biography* is an easily understood way of analysing experience and understanding about the world. Using it allows us to draw in

a wide range of ideas and theories that we might have come across. It places present struggle in context, allows us to understand the continuity and coherence in people's experience, and helps to identify what prevents people from acting. Exploring a biography raises the potential of changing the way someone participates in future events.

2 *Power* needs to be understood as potentially liberating as well as oppressive. We have already noted that a major difference between empowerment and radical and anti-discriminatory theories is the view of power as something that might be used positively, instead of seeing it always as oppressive. Rees values understanding power as it affects those subject to it. He focuses on politics as a process of getting resources and settling conflicts using influence through power struggles. He emphasises how the use of language expresses power relations.

3 *Political understanding* needs to inform practice, in observing both constraints and opportunities. Social work acts always involve either accepting or seeking to change an existing way of organising power relations. Belief in economic rationalism as the best way of understanding human life is allied to managerial control of agencies and social systems in the cause of 'efficiency and effectiveness'. Setting this against the ideal of social justice shows how managerial purposes express different and more oppressive goals than the justice purposes of social work.

4 *Skills* can empower. Gaining and using skills can be an important way of experiencing liberation.

5 *Interdependence of policy and practice* must be established. This is contrary to convention, which regards the development of policy as outside the role of practitioners and their work with clients.

The basic objective of empowerment, in Rees's view, is social justice, giving people greater security and political and social equality, through mutual support and shared learning building up small steps towards wider goals. Kondrat (1995) argues that empowerment requires us to consider whose knowledge is valuable. We should focus on local knowledge, particularly that gained from clients. Also practice should reject insight and self-awareness as professional and treatment objectives and focus on critical discernment through dialogical processes of power differences and changes. Holmes and Saleebey (1993) argue that only a collaborative approach will remove the power aspects of the traditional medical model in social work. Similarly, Kieffer (1984) argues that empowerment contains elements of achieving a better self-concept and self-confidence, gaining a more critical capacity in relation to our environment and cultivating personal and collective resources for social and political action.

Mullender and Ward's (1991) self-directed groupwork reflects an important development in groupwork in the 1980s. Recent trends are much more towards self-help and client participation through groups, rather than the therapeutic approaches of many other theories. However, all groupwork can be seen as empowering because of its democratic, participative and humanistic values (Pernell, 1985) and the experience it gives in affecting others in a protected environrment (Hirayama and Hirayama, 1985). It can also help overcome the dependency-creating effects of residential care (Coppola and Rivas, 1985). Pinderhughes (1995) usefully points out that dependency is not a preferred option, but is a way of seeking power by being close to the powerful.

Gutiérrez *et al.* (1995) studied workers' views of empowerment in the United States. Their concepts included control over our lives, confidence in our ability to act over issues which are important to us, ability to recognise or develop our own power to act, being aware of and having access to choices and independence from others in making decisions and acting. In another study, Gutiérrez (1995) found that consciousness-raising groups increased the ethnic awareness of people from a minority group; this led them to change their way of understanding their problems and the way they might change their situation. This is likely to make them more politically active in ethnic minority issues. This research gives some support to the assumption that raising consciousness can lead to empowerment.

Rojek (1986) argues that, although closely related to radical and Marxist perspectives, advocacy and empowerment strategies have different objectives. They are rationalist in nature, assuming that changing the environment in clients' favour is possible. Radical approaches are materialist and claim that the social system needs broad change before true empowerment is possible. Radical and Marxist social workers would seek empowerment to create social contradictions leading to eventual change, rather than, as the rationalist would, expecting to change society directly.

A difficult aspect of advocacy is the dual but related meanings of 'representation'. Advocates 'represent', in the sense of acting and arguing for the interests of their clients. But Philp (1979) uses advocacy to imply the aspect of social work that 'represents' in the sense of interpreting or displaying the value of clients to powerful groups in society. So, advocacy can mean a service arguing clients' views and needs, a set of skills or techniques for doing so and the interpretation of powerless people to powerful groups.

Early in its development, advocacy was seen as a service to clients. *Case advocacy* was provided by professionals to enhance their access to provision designed to benefit them. *Cause advocacy* sought to promote social change for the benefit of social groups from which clients came. An important strand of practice lies in *welfare rights*, which is concerned with ensuring that clients benefiting from other welfare services receive their entitlement to other welfare provision. Initially, this term focused on social security benefits, but now has wider application. It is concerned with rights because, unlike many welfare services, such benefits are often founded on legal entitlements. There has been controversy (see Burgess, 1994; Fimister, 1986) about whether such work is integral to social work. This is because it relies on analysis of legal rights and espousal of them in official tribunals rather than on using interpersonal relationship skills with therapeutic aims. However, the boundaries are blurred, since we need relationship skills to work with clients to understand their legal position. Also, we need advocacy skills to act on behalf of clients in other forms of social work. Ensuring that clients receive all their entitlements to other services is an important part of many other formulations of social work. Poverty and economic welfare are important aspects of many clients' problems. An effective response to these issues is integral to most social work, though specialised social security assessment and advocacy may require referral elsewhere by the non-specialist worker. Bateman (1995) develops an account of the skills needed for such work in ways which are widely applicable in social work. He calls it 'principled advocacy', using the British term for the policy of getting as much from the social security system for clients as possible, without colluding with its oppressive aspects. This includes a focus on particular kinds of interviewing, value principles similar to those of social work, except that advocates work only following clients' wishes and instructions. Skills such as assertiveness and negotiation are crucial.

A different form of advocacy work grew up during the 1980s. It started as a process of increasing the capacity of people with mental illness and learning disabilities to manage their own lives. A movement grew up to give them assistance in achieving their civil rights within institutions, and in leaving institutions where they may have been held by compulsion. The following account is based on Brandon *et al.* (1995; Brandon, 1995). This movement started in Scandinavia, grew up in the United States and has moved to the United Kingdom. It has been particularly important in promoting the independence of people with all kinds of disabilities. One area of work lies in helping families of people with disabilities to present the difficulties both of disabled people and the families caring for them. Self-advocacy, mainly for people with learning disabilities, involves helping people speak for themselves. This takes place particularly in official planning processes, such as case conferences or individual programme planning meetings. It is a group activity, where people meet together to discuss their situation, and use this support to present their personal difficulties and wishes within this context. An important organisation is 'People First', an international advocacy group. Citizen advocacy involves volunteers in developing relationships with potentially isolated clients, understanding and representing their needs. Peer advocacy derives from self-help organisations, in which people recovering from difficulties in their lives work together to represent individual needs. It is a short step from all these approaches to more general campaigning in the interests of the group represented.

Normalisation (Wolfensberger, 1972) or *social role valorisation* (Wolfensberger, 1984) is related to this form of advocacy (Brown and Smith, 1992; Ramon, 1991; Towell, 1988). This form of policy and practice seeks to offer people in institutions an environment which gives them valued social roles and a life style as close as possible to those valued by people outside institutions. This is an influential development in the residential care field (Sinclair, 1988). It is also used as a philosophy for people being reintegrated into the community from hospital or residential care. Ramon (1989) argues that it involves attempts at changing attitudes among the general public and among professionals providing services, and at changing people with handicaps and organisations involved with them.

An important area of practice has been to assist self-help groups develop (Jack, 1995a; Wilson, 1995a, b; Thursz *et al.*, 1995). Here, workers have supported groups of clients sharing the same problems to come together to support one another. New responses to and ideas about appropriate services often arise from these groups. The groups either create them themselves, or pressurise agencies to change their practices. Mondros and Wilson (1994: 2–5) classify the theoretical work on these activities into four groups, as follows:

1 theoretical debate about the origins of social discontent;
2 classifications of community organisations;
3 descriptions of poor people's campaigns for power;
4 practice wisdom about organising to help such groups.

Much of this connects to the discussion in Chapter 9 about social and community development.

Jack (1995b) argues that empowerment is paradoxical, because if power is given by an organisation or individual, they must give it from a powerful position. Self-help groups must take power, since there is little mandate in legislation or management of services for empowerment. It should not be confused with enablement, which is what workers do when they help organisations to develop to take power. Oliver (1996) argues that social and political rights drawn from citizenship should form the basis of taking power by groups of disabled people. An important aspect of working in this context is to make the operation of services more participatory (Croft and Beresford, 1994; Shemmings and Shemmings, 1995) thus leading to shared ownership of provision and cultural appropriateness and sensitivity (O'Brien and Pace, 1988). A movement to this effect is connected to the idea of consumerism. This is concerned to promote opportunities for consumers of services to criticise and complain about services which do not suit their needs. Beresford and Croft (1993) take this further, to promote it for seeking changes in services through group activity and campaigning. Such approaches are closely allied both to supporting self-help and social and community development. This is possible even in areas where the law (in the UK, at any rate) is very restrictive, such as child protection (Cloke and Davies, 1995). In child protection, according to Katz (1995a), participation and empowerment can be enhanced by giving access to information, by involvement in decision-making processes and by paying careful attention to clients' views of social work processes. Hegar (1989) argues that empowerment practice with children benefits from children being able to identify with empowered adults, by being part of traditions which value empowerment, by involvement in decisions, and by experiencing supported independence in various activities.

Empowerment may be particularly appropriate with adults such as elderly people (Thursz *et al.*, 1995). This is because mutual support in adulthood allows people to share experiences of stigmatisation and to reduce isolation. Cox (1989), for example, used groupwork to empower elderly people to respond to issues such as income maintenance, elder abuse and health care.

Croft and Beresford (1994) argue that a participative approach is valuable because people want and have a right to be involved in decisions and actions taken in relation to them. Their involvement reflects the democratic value base of social work; it increases accountability, makes for more efficient services and helps achieve social work goals. It also helps challenge institutionalised discrimination. Their view of participatory practice has four elements:

1 *Empowerment* involves challenging oppression and making it possible for people to take charge of matters which affect them.
2 *Control* in defining their own needs and having a say in decision-making and planning.
3 *Equipping people with personal resources* to take power, by developing their confidence, self-esteem, assertiveness, expectations and knowledge and skills.
4 *Organising the agency to be open* to participation.

The practice approach to this, in Shemmings and Shemmings' (1995) view, is to foster mutuality through reciprocity, directness and sensitivity to people's wishes and needs. The worker must also show their trustworthiness, by being even-handed and by acting in ways that clients define as trustworthy.

The philosophy of self-direction, personal responsibility and self-actualisation through empowerment has relationships with cognitive and particularly humanist approaches. They emphasise the process of recognising and building on strengths or competence (Maluccio, 1981a) in clients. Maluccio (1981b) regards this as related to ecological systems theory, since it requires working on the ability of clients to interact effectively with their environment. However, this is equally cognitive, since, as we saw in Chapter 5, it involves working on attribution – that is, how people perceive and interpret information about the environment (Fleming, 1981). The strengths perspective is humanist or constructionist in that it focuses on people's own ability to define their interaction with the environment (Saleebey, 1992). However, empowerment and advocacy give more importance to power differentials, class and oppression as aspects of society which obstruct self-actualisation and need actively to be overcome.

Many of these developments are brought together in the work on advocacy of Rose and Black (1985) describing a project promoting independent living for mentally ill people in the community. They base their approach explicitly on the work of Freire (see Chapter 10), in that they seek to empower people to become subjects rather than objects in their lives, by involving them in the process of advocacy. *Critical debate* with clients enters their present subjective reality and explores objective reality with them. As a result, they can see various situations where their subjective reality limits their control of the environment. Clients are engaged in a *transformation* from dependence to interdependence, with collective networks of social support. Total autonomy is not desirable (or attainable for many people): we are all interdependent with others to some extent.

The work is broadly educational, following Freire's perspective. All social exchanges have a political content in that they either accept or deny the present social order. By *dialogue* in a situation of trust, with people who behave authentically (in humanist terms), clients engage in a *praxis*, acting and experiencing the reality that results from their actions which then affects later actions. Praxis is reflexive in this way. Workers try to get inside and understand clients' reality. Their history in mental hospitals has oppressed them through institutionalisation, poverty and material deprivation. They have taken these experiences into their own view of the world. Self-expression is encouraged, helping them gain vitality and acceptance of their own capacity and worth. *Validation* is the main treatment process, aimed at reconnecting clients to their capacity for self-expression. This is done through trying to understand the reality of their own life history, and rejecting internalised judgements that they are incompetent. Clients become 'producer-participants' in their lives rather than passively consuming services.

In a later formulation, Rose (1990) gives three principles of advocacy and empowerment practice:

1 *Contextualisation* involves focusing on the client's own understanding of their 'social being' rather than the worker's assumptions or policies. This allows a dialogue to develop based on the client's reality. In the dialogue, clients are enabled to express, elaborate and reflect upon their feelings and understandings about life.

2 *Empowerment* is a process through which workers support clients to identify the full range of possibilities which might meet the client's needs. The work centres on helping clients make decisions which affect their lives.

3 *Collectivity* focuses on reducing feelings of isolation and connecting clients to relationships. The experience of this form

of socialisation produces stronger feelings of self-worth among clients. Similarly, an important principle of Moreau's (1990) structural approach to social work (see Chapter 10) is to collectivise rather than personalise experience.

The politics of empowerment and advocacy

Empowerment and advocacy are relatively new concepts. Although they have been available in social work, they have not been at the centre of thinking. Simon (1995) argues that empowerment is a long-standing ideal of American social work. Ezell (1994) claims this for advocacy. However, this seems to reinterpret in modern terminology related historical ideas which do not imply the same objective of political and social change. Nevertheless, Ezell's (1994) study found that most American social workers undertook some advocacy, mainly case-based and internal to their own agencies. Cause advocacy was done on a voluntary basis.

In the 1990s, as we have seen, empowerment and advocacy have become attached to many different sorts of work. In particular, individualised work has been seen as empowering, though many original uses of the word in social work were applied to oppressed groups rather than individuals. The use of empowerment as a fashionable concept creates an idealistic and perhaps misleading objective for practice in a period when financial controls on agency budgets restrict services throughout the world. Equally, it may be used as an objective because provision of comprehensive services is difficult in a restricted financial environment. This is a misuse of the term, since the assumption of empowerment practice is that workers lend their power to the client for a period to assist them to take power permanently through helping them attain control over their lives. Workers need resources to do this. Moreover, we should not mistake empowerment for enablement. Empowerment is not limited, as enablement is, to allowing or assisting people to take actions, but is aimed at relinquishing and transferring to them the power permanently to control their lives.

However, Jack's (1995b) criticism that giving power from a powerful position is impossible seems to go too far. Increasing the total amount of power in use is possible, since not all capacity for power is taken up. Clients often have power which they are unable to use or do not believe they have. Therefore, empowerment is a more positive approach to social work than the traditional radical or anti-oppressive approach which argues that oppressed groups are completely powerless, in the face of structural oppression.

Advocacy is in part an aspect of empowerment, since it can be used to argue for resources, or change the interpretation which powerful groups make of clients. It has a long history as an aspect of welfare rights work, and as an integral aspect of workers' activities on behalf of clients within their own agencies or arguing on their behalf with other agencies. Recent advocacy movements have sometimes led workers to deny their involvement in advocacy, because they believe it can only be practised by client groups themselves, through self- or peer-advocacy. However, as well as taking the traditional professional role of working on behalf of clients, workers can act as formal advocates, by following clients' instructions.

Black empowerment: Barbara Solomon

Solomon's book (1976) applies to all oppressed communities, but she is particularly concerned with black ethnic minorities. We all need personal and financial resources to accept valued identities and roles. Solomon (p. 16) defines *powerlessness* in individuals or social groups as 'the inability to manage emotions, skills, knowledge and/or material resources in a way' that effective performance of valued social roles will lead to personal gratification'.

In some communities, we have valued people negatively so much and for so long that their powerlessness is extensive and crippling. *Negative valuations* occur in practices, organisations and events which discriminate against minority groups and also in language which attaches derogatory words to such groups.

Empowerment aims to use specific strategies to reduce, eliminate, combat and reverse negative valuations by powerful groups in society affecting certain individuals and social groups. Applying it in family work may be useful since mutual support may strengthen the development of capacity among family members, and help to interpret the worker's intervention jointly within the family's culture (Weaver, 1982; Pinderhughes, 1983).

Social workers have difficulties with empowerment strategies because their agencies are part of a social system which routinely devalues certain minority groups. Making equal responses to all people who come to an agency may reduce discrimination. Since negative valuations are so widespread, agencies may unthinkingly implement them. Consequently, we discourage potential clients from using the agency and they do not receive the equal treatment available. Also, agencies may reflect negative valuations in their own organisation through institutionalised racism. For example, they may not employ black people in senior positions or do not have an office in an area with a predominantly ethnic minority population in order to protect staff from potential violence. Negative valuations of minorities (not only ethnic minorities) may be so institutionalised that we may not perceive the problem. Often, therefore, such groups suffer from *power absence* rather than *power failure* (meaning that they have tried to use power and have failed).

An empowerment strategy requires commitment to *both* maintenance and improvement of effective equal services and *also* to confrontation of pervasive negative valuations.

Most people, according to Solomon, move through *three levels of development*. They have:

1 positive experiences in early family life which give them confidence and competence in social interactions, and this
2 reinforces their ability to manage social relationships and use social institutions (such as schools) to gain further competence, with which
3 they can accept and perform well in valued social roles.

Indirect power blocks can affect each level. Negative early experiences (for example, stigma due to race, disability or poverty) reduce confidence in social interaction. This in turn reduces gains made at the second level and so obstructs the growth of capacity to perform valued social roles at the third level. *Direct power blocks* similarly affect each level. Poor services, for example, might mean bad health, retarding early growth; discrimination in education may restrict access to learning and equally may prevent people from taking on valued social roles.

Solomon argues that because social work has concentrated on changing individuals rather than social institutions it is weak at dealing with power blocks.

The *aims* of empowerment are to help clients see

● themselves as *causal agents* in finding solutions to their problems;
● social workers as having knowledge and skills that clients can use;
● social workers as a peer and partner in solving problems;

- the power structure as complex and partly open to influence.

The *model of practice* is as follows:

- Overcome responses among clients that arise from negative valuations so that they see themselves as able to have some impact on their problem.
- Find and remove blocks and find and reinforce supports to effective problem-solving.

Social workers must always be aware of powerlessness. For example, we might see advocacy for a social security allowance as using the worker's skills or as taking away clients' freedom to act for themselves. We should assess these possibilities and their implications for individuals. Workers should also beware of seeing clients as the cause of their problems, simply because they are trying to see clients as causal agents in solving their problems. For example, I worked with a woman who was accused of neglecting her child because she was not developing properly. As part of this, I was trying to help her to see ways in which she could play with the child regularly as part of her day. This is to treat her as a causal agent who can actively do something about her problem, rather than sending the child to a nursery where someone else would take over from her. While doing this, I found myself becoming frustrated and blaming her for her inability to organise her day to make time for the child, and for her lack of creativity in playing with the child, who became bored. This was, wrongly, to see her as the cause of these problems. It was more appropriate to acknowledge that the poverty of her surroundings and the constant struggle to make ends meet took up much of her time and energy. Also, lack of mothering experiences in her own childhood limited her capacity. It was more effective to involve an older woman assistant who could offer her more personal time and help her to plan her domestic responsibilities to make space for the child.

We may extend the characteristics of a non-racist practitioner to apply to work with many oppressed groups. These are:

- the ability to see alternative explanations for any behaviour, and especially those alternatives which we might most want to reject as false;
- the ability to use many cues to choose the alternative explanation which is most relevant to the client;

- the ability to feel warmth, genuine concern and empathy regardless or race or other characteristics;
- the ability to confront clients when they have misinterpreted or distorted true feelings of warmth.

We can also usefully apply Solomon's approach to engaging black client systems in work to a wide range of oppressed groups. The underlying assumption is that most black people coming to social agencies have been sent by others and will not be convinced that workers have anything to offer. We must establish rapport across the racial divide, in spite of a pervasive distrust of white people and of established agencies. We can see these feelings in many other clients of social work agencies. Workers should show familiarity with the communication patterns, life styles and life experience of the client and must present themselves 'authentically' in the humanist sense. It is often important to make clear the helping role of the worker in contrast to experiences that clients may have had of other agencies.

Assessing *motivation, capacity and opportunity* is crucial, since access to services is often obstructed by failings in the way this is done. Our criteria for motivation may be inappropriate, because the worker values things which the client's culture does not value. Knowing appropriate cultural expectations and patterns gives clues about what will motivate clients. We may more accurately assess capacity in settings which are more secure for clients than offices or formal settings. Opportunity needs weighing carefully. This is because clients may be blamed for not taking up opportunities which in reality have not been available, because of various blocks, as with the mother being unable to play with her child. Contracts should always place the client as the main causal agent.

The *workers' roles* which work best in empowerment are as follows:

- as resources consultants linking clients to resources in ways which improve their self-esteem and problem-solving abilities;
- sensitising helps clients gain self-knowledge;
- teaching/training offers processes and skills enabling clients to complete specific tasks.

For example, I worked with an elderly man from an Asian community who was becoming disabled, and was isolated because several friends had returned to Malaysia. Rather than arrange attendance at a day centre, which I thought might be unsympathetic, I suggested that we both investigate various possibilities for social contact through organisations that we knew. We sat down to identify some that we each knew, and he came with me as I approached one organisation that I had not been in touch with before. It proved uncongenial for him. Having had this experience, however, he followed up other contacts for himself; although he did not become involved with these groups for various reasons, he seemed happier to go out more and made one or two contacts in the community. I think this came from the social skills and confidence he acquired and from having learned how to make new approaches.

An important strategy is to help the client to provide services in their family, neighbourhood or community. A more equal relationship between client and worker often results, since both are offering something, and mutuality and complementarity of relationships in the community also improves. For example, helping a woman to improve her child-care skills may improve her self-esteem, give her skills to feed back into the community, improve relationships in the family, and help to prevent the child having poor experiences at the first stage of development.

Mullender and Ward: self-directed groupwork

Mullender and Ward's (1991) account of self-directed groupwork offers a clear view of empowerment theory focused on groupwork settings and processes. They also offer it (p. 2) as a basis for wider forms of social action. They argue that empowering action must be 'self-directed' (that is, by services users) but must also oppose oppression. This is defined as the state of affairs whereby a presumption in favour of dominant groups arises and skews relationships in society so that all social institutions are affected. This includes processes by which this occurs, thus limiting the life opportunities and experiences of people not in dominant groups. Such a definition implies that empowering work must confront the nature of power. It must do so both in its direct exercise and in the way it subsists and persists in social structures, benefiting dominant groups whether or not they have sanctions to back up their influence. This is more important and more generally applicable than radical theories of the state and of class. However, many ideas from feminist and anti-racist work are relevant to self-directed work. It must include analysis of the situation and action to deal with it. This is better done in groups, because in individual and family work, individualisation of private troubles is too powerful to promote shared, social responses. Groups allow people to share resources and initiate and experiment with action jointly.

The model of practice has five stages.

1 *Pre-planning:* find a compatible co-working team, consultancy support and agree on empowering principles.
2 *Taking off:* engage with users as partners and plan the group jointly through 'open planning'.
3 *Group preparation* for action: help the group explore what issues are to be tackled, why these issues exist and how we can produce change.
4 *Taking action:* group members carry out agreed actions.
5 *Taking over:* workers begin to withdraw, and the group reviews what it has achieved, seeing connections between what, why and how. It then identifies new issues, sees links between the issues and again decides what actions to take. This process then continues throughout the group's life.

Co-working is preferred because it offers a richer experience to service users and provides more support for them. Consultancy is needed to question and challenge the workers in helping them to an anti-oppressive perspective. Five important empowering practice principles are:

1 All people have skills, understanding and ability. We must recognise these rather than negative labels.
2 People have rights – especially to be heard, to control their own lives, to choose to participate or not and to define issues and take action.
3 People's problems always reflect issues of oppression, policy, economy and power as well as personal inadequacies.
4 People acting collectively can be powerful, and practice should build on this.
5 Practising what you preach involves facilitating, not 'leading' and challenging oppression.

The empowering approach to starting a group involves workers in the following. Workers must acknowledge and contract to work with an existing group on members' issues. Alternatively, they should get the idea from one or more members and check whether others might join, arranging for members to set the goals. Self-directed groups are not there to meet agency objectives or as workers' pet projects. Membership should not be selected, but should come from wide dispersal of invitations. We should take specific steps to signal to potentially oppressed people, such as black, disabled or elderly people or women, that they will not be oppressed in the group. Workers should accept that voluntary and open-ended membership will lead to fluctuating membership and no minimum or maximum size. The venue should be accessible to people with physical and communication disabilities and those who have caring responsibilities which might prevent attendance. It should be on members' own territory or on neutral ground, and members should make their own way there rather than relying on agency transport. Agreement and mutual convenience of members should decide timing frequency and number of meetings. Members should agree and maintain rules for conduct and recording systems in the group. Worker roles should be clear and distinguished from any other roles that workers have in relation to the service users. The group works on agreed problems, not the individual problems of service users.

In the preparation for the action stage, workers facilitate participants' views of what the problem is. This might include brainstorming, creating an art gallery of individuals' responses to the issue, using films and videos as discussion starters, and using statements on display cards devised by members as discussion starters. The 'why' stage might involve consciousness-raising (see Chapter 11). Workers should help with problem-posing. This involves taking participants through the following stages:

- *Description* – what do you see happening?
- *Analysis* – why is it happening?
- *Related problems* – what problems does it lead to?
- *Root causes* – what leads to these problems?
- *Action planning* – what can we do about it?

Workers will often have to help participants find ways of feeding in information. The group can then move on to a cycle of reflecting (looking, thinking and planning), taking action, seeing the results and then taking in new information to restart the cycle. The 'how' stage involves breaking down issues into component parts, rather like task-centred work. The group can work on grids on blackboards or large sheets of paper. One axis can set out possible actors, another various time-scales for action (now-soon-later). A force-field analysis allows people to evaluate the various pressures for and against particular solutions.

The 'taking action' stage may involve public campaigns, setting up representative systems such as advocacy schemes or promoting influence and action by creating linkages and alliance with other agencies. Communication with and involvement in other groups may be an important strategy. Workers should help groups to dig deeper for the answers to 'why' questions, especially if their first moves are unsuccessful. This often reveals further action to take. Community arts and other techniques for allowing a community's voice (Payne, 1988) to be heard more widely can often be effective. Throughout this stage, as elsewhere, an approach which challenges oppression enables participants to see issues more clearly, particularly where they are obstructed from action. It also helps participants themselves to act less oppressively, rather than learning manipulative power tactics from the process of resolving their problems.

In the final 'taking over' stage, workers help group members to take on some facilitating roles they themselves have fulfilled. Thus, group members learn to challenge and work unoppressively. They gain confidence in working with the media and public and official bodies. Using the experience of the group, they also approach gaining access to information which they can use in future themselves. They can also be helped to learn how to evaluate their own activities, their own performance and the contribution that the workers have made to the group.

Learned helplessness theory

Barber (1986) proposes that learned helplessness theory may be a useful perspective for social work. These ideas are closely related to and offer some research support for ideas of empowerment. Seligman's (1975) theory is based on experiments with animals and humans. If people have important experiences which show that what they do does not affect what happens to them, they form the expectation that their actions will generally not produce any useful results. Their capacity to learn useful behaviour in other situations becomes impaired. People may lose motivation, become anxious and depressed and poor at thinking and learning. This evidence clearly supports some of Solomon's (1976) ideas about powerlessness. People who are powerless throughout their lives would carry a sizeable burden of learned helplessness. The response should be, according to Barber (1986), *environmental enrichment*, by giving such people experience of situations in which they are in control and achieve successful results.

Commentary

Advocacy and empowerment strategies have proved attractive in recent years as a development and implementation of radical social work and as an aspect of anti-discriminatory work. Advocacy has evolved strongly as part of the movement to discharge many people from long-stay institutions in which they would previously have been cared for, and as part of welfare rights work. These approaches are idealistic, but it is a practical idealism, which can be carried out. Some forms of therapy can, if used incautiously, make people dependent on the expertise of the worker. Therefore, it may be argued that advocacy and empowerment represent an ideology of treatment which is radically different, or at least is experienced differently by client and, perhaps, worker. However, power *given* by a worker leaves the power with the worker. Clients must *take* power, and it is the role of social work to organise the institutional response which makes this possible and accepts it when it occurs (see Gomm, 1993).

Like insight therapies, empowerment concentrates on developing clients' capacities and does not seek direct change in oppressive social structures, except by the effects of individual cases through advocacy. Thus it might place responsibility for social change upon clients, who may be strengthened, but still face formidable social obstacles. The practice prescriptions do not address powerless people whose own capacities are inadequate for the assumption of full power over their lives. There is a danger that workers will act as though all clients can achieve a high degree of empowerment. Very damaged, oppressed and institutionalised clients can achieve much greater degrees of self-control and power through such techniques, but this should not exclude therapeutic work for their benefit as well.

Related to this is the role of empowerment, where protection for clients or security for the public is at issue. Ideas such as normalisation and self-advocacy have often become associated with civil liberties perspectives which focus on the need to free clients oppressed by assumptions about their dependence on care. However, it is no empowerment to fail to provide services that clients need. For example, a young man was discharged from a mental hospital, and hostel accommodation was arranged. This was set up to offer a great deal of freedom of action, but there was security through a system where a worker was 'on call'. This was explained to the client, who missed the point of the explanation because he did not understand what 'on call' meant. Then the worker arranged to show him how to use local shops, but failed to check that his social security allowance had arrived or that he had some provisions until it did so. He did not feel he could raise these problems because the worker had already been so helpful, so a later visitor found him completely unable to make a hot drink. It is, therefore, important not to use the idea of empowerment to avoid responsibility for assessing and providing for appropriate care and support. Gray and Bernstein (1994), describing a South African project to help 'pavement people', argue that practical help is an essential part of responding to serious difficulties, but becomes part of empowerment strategies where this develops towards responses to structural oppression.

Another difficulty, where workers deal with individuals, is that empowering individuals may not extend to their wider community or networks. So empowered individuals may be taking power and resources from others in their oppressed environment, to their disadvantage, rather than taking it from wider society. Where social and political resources are limited, empowerment may set oppressed or deprived groups against others, rather than uniting them.

13

Assessing Social Work Theories

Evaluating social work theories

Social work and the theory within it are changing, as they always have changed, in response to the demands made on them by the world in which they operate and in response to their own movements. The demands are effectiveness, legitimacy and coherence, and it is against these that we must assess the value of social work theory. But, we may ask, effectiveness to what ends? legitimacy in whose interests? coherence to what central idea? Any evaluation leads us to ask these sorts of basic questions about the social origins of the values we are placing on particular theories. In the next three sub-sections, I examine each of these issues in turn and see how we can assess social work theories in relation to that issue.

Effectiveness of social work theories

Social work is increasingly seen as effective, according to the research results discussed below. It is increasingly a social success, too, although we must beware of the growth myth that bigger is always better. The evidence, though, is that in many societies it is used for more and more social purposes and the number of countries where it is developing is increasing too. This does not mean that it is without criticism or without its detractors. It is not free from attack, but then neither are doctors, journalists, lawyers, politicians or priests, all of whom are pretty universal. It is a less deferential, more critical age and we are the better for it, because it means we must constantly be alert to improve our performance. So we must see whether our theories are effective as part of that search for improvement. If the research says social work is effective and the evidence around us is of increasing social acceptance, does this mean our theories are accepted as effective? Or is it only some of them? If so, we might select particular theories to practice with, or use them in debate and criticism of other perspectives to improve our overall approach. This aspect of the evaluation of theories is the focus of this sub-section.

Early evaluations of social work in the 1950s and 60s either failed to demonstrate that it achieved the results it set out to achieve, or produced uncertain results (Fischer, 1973, 1976; Mullen *et al.*, 1972; Wood, 1978). In Chapter 2, we noted the development of the American empirical practice movement, which brought together researched ideas about methods from work such as Rogers' associates (see Chapter 8), behavioural methods and other psychological knowledge, such as communication research considered in Chapter 7. A strong focus of this approach, following behavioural models, lies in single-case or single-system research designs (see Chapter 5). These start from a baseline at the beginning of a piece of intervention, and check for improvement in intended directions during and after intervention. Social work objectives became more highly specified and testable, goals were more limited, assessment was more thorough, evaluation gave better feedback to workers, intensive and focused activities were used, clients' rehearsed behaviour instead of just being counselled, special projects were staffed by enthusiasts instead of evaluations being made focusing on routine services, attempts were made to restrict outside interference which limited projects' effectiveness and services were located to encourage clients to come early for help (Sheldon, 1987). All these led to clear evidence, mostly from the United States, that in well-designed agency programmes or individual work demonstrable success was achieved (Reid and Hanrahan, 1982; Rubin, 1985; Videka-Sherman, 1988; MacDonald and Sheldon, 1992). Most interventions were cognitive-behavioural, but about half the investigations of ordinary casework, non-behavioural groupwork and much family therapy were also successful (MacDonald and Sheldon, 1992). American surveys of groupwork (Tolman and Molidor, 1994) and residential care (Curry, 1995) show that research techniques have been less strong in these areas, but some successful results have been achieved. A number of studies have shown that service developments including or focusing on social work have been successful (Goldberg, 1987). This includes some aspects of community social work and case management with elderly people as part of community care services.

From this brief account of research into the effectiveness of social work, there is research evidence to support cognitive-behavioural and like theories, and probably fairly focused practice based on task-centred work. Research is into problems or social programmes (Brawley and Martinez-Brawley, 1988) rather than attempting to validate theoretical approaches (Jenkins, 1987). This may partly be because explicit use of theories is not a characteristic of most social work, hence the use of special projects for evaluative research. In any case, Sainsbury (1987) makes the point that often research does not produce changes in practice because individuals' commitments and political impetus lies behind agency practice. There is also a problem of dissemination between those who generate and those who might use research findings (Brawley and Martinez-Brawley, 1988). Eventually, though, the general professional climate changes, and affects practitioners and students through academic interest in research outcomes. Also, qualitative and practitioner research may generate more relevant results which build up into a bigger picture of success over a longer period of time.

The empirical practice movement (see Chapter 2) argues that practice should be affected by the research outcomes. However, we noted in Chapter 2 that such proposals take for granted the methodology and basic assumptions of the scientific method in generating these results. This means that there are legitimate arguments that wider social purposes, non-therapeutic activities and important aspects of meaning within social work theory cannot be validated by empirical studies. Although this is so, it is important to recognise the guidance that empirical practice offers for selecting appropriate methods where effectiveness is demonstrated and the research is relevant to the practice situation. It also makes it possible to see what kind of methods may be effective in less certain situations.

Legitimacy of social work theories

I commented above on the success of social work as a profession in expanding and taking on additional roles in many societies. We must question whether it does so legitimately and in whose interests. The broad legitimacy question is not the focus for this book. However, some related activity might perform social work's social roles. So, are our practice and our theories of practice truly of social work alone, creating a legitimate, identifiable theoretical base for social work?

I have argued elsewhere (Payne, 1996a) that social work is part of a network of occupations working in a territory or social space concerned with interpersonal and social action. These occupations, such as counselling, nursing, development work, teaching, police work and medicine, have social roles, theories, social, legal and political contexts for their practice, systems of professional organisation and education which may overlap but which also have distinctive features. Professionals may move among these occupations, or stay within the boundaries of one throughout their careers. The boundaries between these groups are more or less permeable, more or less negotiable and shift according to social expectations and preferences as they are constructed within societies.

Therefore, related professions are likely to share some aspects of their theoretical base. For each, this may be strengthening. A social worker in a psychiatric setting, for example, may be supported in daily practice by sharing a theoretical base with a professional colleague. It also helps the colleague. The availability of a range of theoretical perspectives in social work enables appropriately trained workers to work in agencies using specialised techniques, and this helps the penetration of the profession into various settings from which it might otherwise be excluded.

However, we have also seen that there are considerable differences in the use of different theories, and how ideas implemented within social work become distanced from the literature in related professions. Books focusing on counselling or clinical psychology, for example, deal with cognitive, behavioural and psychodynamic theories with virtually no recognition of the social work literature, although some importation from these areas is made into social work literature.

There are also substantial areas of thinking, particularly from sociology, which social work incorporates but which are not represented well in related literatures. Each profession creates its own focus and interpretation of bodies of knowledge. The particular characteristic of social work is to bring together reflexive-therapeutic literature and perspectives, socialist-collectivist objectives and thought and individualist-reformist ideas into a nexus of practice theories. It is this process that we explore in this chapter.

Theoretical coherence

Now we turn to the body of the theory of social work practice. Does it provide a coherent guide to practice? Is it consistent with the aims and values of social work? Is there a pattern and a future to social work theory?

In Chapter 1, I proposed an analysis of social work as a discourse between three views about it: reflexive-therapeutic, socialist-collectivist and individualist-reformist. I said that these views are intertwined in our views of social work. They both criticise and incorporate one another. People sometimes complain that this is confusing and that it makes the nature of social work unclear. I think that the complexity of this idea just reflects the complexity of real life. It is better than an unreal simplification. For me, the point to hang on to is that the view that social work is a discourse among ideas in action alerts us to the importance of looking at the patterns of relationships between theories and their supporters. Our consideration in each chapter of the wider theoretical perspectives, connections with other theories and the politics of theory all point to the need to see particular social work theories as part of a body of interacting and competing ideas, not as completely separate entities.

In Chapter 2, I suggested that all valid practice theories, using the word 'theory' in the loose sense of an organised statement of practice guidance, contained a *perspective* – namely, a view of the world, a *theory* (that is, an explanation supported by evidence about why people act as they do) and a *model* (that is, an organised prescription for action). Particular groups of theories are centred in views of social work and have strengths in their theoretical approach. I provide an analysis of the groups of theories discussed in this book along these lines in Table 13.1

Table 13.1   Analysis of social work theories

Type of theory	Reflexive-therapeutic	Socialist-collectivist	Individualist-reformist
Perspective			
→ Comprehensive	psychodynamic		social development
→ Inclusive	humanistic	radical	systems
Theory	role/communication	anti-oppressive	cognitive-behavioural
Model	crisis	empowerment	task-centred

This table divides perspectives into comprehensive and inclusive categories. *Comprehensive* theories claim to offer a system of thought to cover all the practice that social workers might want to undertake. They do so by offering a view of the world which organises our thoughts and gives us priorities within the range of things that might be possible. These theories are more or less supported by an evidenced body of knowledge, and the extent to which this is so might be disputed. However, the literature about them contains a great deal of commentary, analysis and prescription that is able to form the basis of a social work practice on its own. *Inclusive* theories, while they are comprehensive in this way, also explicitly permit the inclusion within them of other theories and models, provided they are used consistently with the overall outlook of the perspective.

Before looking at trends and types of theory, I want to comment first on how I have allocated theories to different cells in Table 13.1. First, I must emphasise again that the ideas of discourse between views within social work and the need for all theories to have elements of perspective, theory and model within them means that no theory can be allocated wholly to any category. We are talking about centres of focus and strengths, not absolutes. On more specific points, I want to comment on the positioning of social development, radical and anti-oppressive groups of theories. I have placed social development theories as individualist-reformist because they are generally theories which accept the current social order. Some theories of development are socialist and seek radical change, but, generally, *social development practice* theories seek reform or operate on individuals and small groups or communities, rather than seeking radical social change. Radical theories might have been regarded as comprehensive, since some formulations do offer a worked-out practice model and in their own terms are based on a well-constructed and evidenced theory. However, much radical theory is very sketchy in its practice guidance, and leaves workers to include methodologies from anywhere provided they fit with the overall ideology. Also, the theory is more a well-constructed edifice of ideology than a theory evidenced from social science research. Because of these two points, I have preferred on balance to treat it as an inclusive perspective rather than as a comprehensive one. Anti-oppressive theory is strongly supported by evidence of discriminatory social relations and a well-worked-out explanatory account. This makes it, among *socialist-collectivist ideas*, an important explanatory base for action, even though the implications of the structuralist ideology drawn from it are strongly disputed.

I turn now to more general comment on Table 13.1. This analysis groups practice theories in six ways: the downward columns and the rows across. The rows represent the interaction of different 'views' of social work together. That interaction may be one of eclectic integration or, at the other extreme, critical conflict. Thus, cognitive-behavioural ideas may be used integrally as part of anti-oppressive ideas or to alert us to limits and inadequacies in anti-oppressive practice; and vice versa.

The first row of perspective theories contains implementations of some very basic philosophies in social work. Among the ideas that come from them are the importance of considering the origins of human feelings and emotions and the effect they have on our lives (psychodynamic perspectives), the objectives of personal and social fulfilment (humanist perspectives) and social improvement and development (social development), the search for radical social change in pursuit of greater humanity and social achievement (radical perspectives) and ideas about how human life and social environments interact (systems perspectives). They can be, and are, used comprehensively and exclusively by some workers in some settings as explicit models for practice. More likely, though, workers take these basic ideas about how we can intervene in social and personal affairs and incorporate them with personal values to form an approach to their work. They need to do so because in a career in social work we must take into account reflexive-therapeutic, socialist-collectivist and individualist-reformist views. We must, therefore, have theoretical perspectives which enable us to order our thoughts according to such perspectives.

I once worked with a man with a very chaotic household, full of accumulated possessions. He had lost his teaching job because of overwhelming anxiety associated with unresolved depression about the death of his parents. He was isolated from local support systems, taunted and rejected by neighbours, and persecuted by health and housing authorities and utility companies because of unpaid bills. In trying to do this work, I had to be aware of his internal irrational thoughts, emotions and motivation and the need for him to rediscover a fulfilling way of living his life. I was conscious of the need for social changes which would reduce the marginalisation of people like him, and more immediately in the policies of large public and private organisations. I could see the need for local supportive social developments, how he interacted with different social systems in his locality and how he needed to interact more. Since I was working for a local mental health charity with a campaigning focus, some of the broader social objectives could be sought, as well as improvements in the individual situation.

It is hard to see social work in any individual case as isolated from its social aspects. It is hard to focus on social change, without responding to the individual needs in front of us. Perspectives theories give us ideas, which help us understand the broad sweep of the issues we must face. Most of us combine these ideas as we need, and so we find it hard to see a politics in which these ideas are in opposition. A few of us use these perspectives in all their complex detail as a guide to work. The politics here is preference: they choose to focus their understanding in this way, probably reflecting the preferences of their agency setting, other colleagues and personal political and social ideologies.

The second row of theories presents us with bodies of knowledge for the social understanding of action. I conceive them as particularly concerned with social identity. They deal with, reading across the row, the collection of social roles that we inhabit, the language and communication by which we construct ourselves and others, the social structures from which our identification with social groups emerges and the modes of thinking and behaving and how they originate. They say: 'This is how life is, in interpersonal interaction, in our social groups, in our thinking and behaviour. Now we know this, we can do something.' What we might do follows logically. It is a well-worked-out, well-evidenced set of prescriptions in cognitive-behavioural work and in communication theory. The social theories underlying role and anti-oppressive practice lead to less specific practice prescriptions, but they focus our attention on evidence about the social environment which creates the identity of the individuals we work with. They are less the servants of the agency's prescription for service than the other theories in this row. This is needed to counterbalance the highly detailed prescriptions which arise from behavioural and communication knowledge.

The third row represents a series of models for action. I believe they represent current interpretations of the three 'views' of social work which are particularly relevant to modern conditions. Many social workers conceive of the condition of their clients when they present themselves to agencies as in crisis. They perceive their social objective as personal and social empowerment. Task-centred work implements the responsibility to be accountably effective in financially straitened agencies. Modern – that is, current – social work is interpreted in theories which reflect these modern practical needs.

The reflexive-therapeutic column represents the ideas within social work which concern personal development and fulfilment, with an emphasis on emotions and interpersonal responses. It is concerned with personal change. The socialist-collectivist column represents the ideas within social work which focus on its social purposes. It is concerned with social change. The individualist-reformist column represents those ideas within social work which focus on its response to social and political demands for order. It is concerned with maintaining social order.

Theories and social work

What impact do these theories have on social work? I want to consider this question in two different aspects. First, the three groupings of theories set out in Table 13.1 take different views of social work. If we work within a particular group, rather than take ideas from everywhere, this will have consequences for how we understand social work and what we are doing within it. Second, people work within different aspects of social work provision, and I want to consider, briefly, what impact theories have on different types of social work.

Theories and the nature of social work

None of the three 'views' of social work is ultimately capable of providing a complete perspective on social work. As I have indicated, in discussing the interaction of ideas in the rows of Table 13.1, workers are likely to need ideas from other views in at least some of their work. One useful aspect of practice review for any worker, therefore, may be a consideration of the extent to which they do use practice theories outside their conventional view to criticise or integrate with their own position.

Presuming, though, that workers often operate within one or the other view of social work, this naturally has implications for the view they take of their role within social work. In Table 13.2, I examine some aspects of the social context of social work which are often thought important and how they are reinterpreted within each view. I have chosen seven features of social work practice which say something about its socially defined purposes, from different points of view.

The selection of these should not be seen as an attempt to 'define' the character of social work. Indeed, the fact that the table shows how they are interpreted in different ways by different views of social work indicates that such definition depends on our view and interpretation of the world, rather than on any identifiable set of characteristics.

Table 13.2   Common features in the social context of social work

Feature	*Implications*		
	Reflexive-therapeutic perspective	*Socialist-collectivist perspective*	*Individualist-reformist perspective*
Individualisation	Social work aims to help individuals achieve self-fulfilment.	Social work's focus on individuals ignores policy implications of personal problems, and discourages collective responses.	Social work's role treats people as individuals, while bureaucrats treat them as categories of problem.
Use of knowledge	Knowledge allows workers to act skilfully and without risk to clients.	Knowledge should be shared with clients, empowering them to act on their own behalf.	Social work uses psychological and social knowledge, evidence and argument to help clients.
Relationship	Relationship carries communication which influences clients and also creates personal involvement which 'moves' clients to respond.	Relationship with workers can offer experience of cooperative endeavour, but may also lead to manipulation through personal influence.	Social work relationships personalise services and influence clients to change more readily.
Organisational context	Agencies' functions give focus to therapeutic intervention.	Agencies represent the interests of powerful groups in society. They reduce the pressures of an oppressive society and maintain dependence on discretionary services.	The organisational context of practice sanctions social work action on society's behalf and limits and directs social work activity in accordance with socially defined objectives.
Need	Social work identifies and works with the needs that clients exhibit or express.	Social work's role in assessing need may give or deny access to services through resource allocation or rationing.	Social work defines and rsponds to need on society's behalf, ensuring that resources are effectively used.

Feature	*Implications*		
	Reflexive-therapeutic perspective	*Socialist-collectivist perspective*	*Individualisst-reformist perspective*
Maintenance of social institutions	Social work helps clients participate in social structures which give them support and fulfilment.	Social work maintains important social institutions, such as community and family, which support the present social order and limit possibilities of change.	Social work plays an important part in maintaining social institutions which provide stability and continuity for people in society.
Advocacy	Social work helps people gain the personal power to achieve their aims in life.	Social work should create structures for client cooperation to fight for needs.	Social work advocates for clients' needs in agencies and policy changes.

An examination of this table shows that theories included within the different views of social work are likely to include, within those different views, different conceptions of what social work is about. Different groups of theories of social work practice thus prescribe different approaches to the world.

Theories and types of social work

It is customary, particularly in American texts, to distinguish case-work, groupwork and community work as different forms of social work. Some writers also distinguish residential or group care work, possibly management and administration and perhaps social work education as elements of social work. Avoiding argument about whether these may legitimately be separated out, I merely deal with the fact that they sometimes are. Are particular theories relevant to one or the other type of social work as some people distinguish them?

The general approach taken in this book has been to identify examples of applications within groups of practice theories as they have been used in residential or group work. I have not been able to identify a particular 'group' or 'residential' work theory, but I have shown where particular accounts of a theory have focused on group, residential or community work. In the case of community work, I have emphasised its importance in social development theory. This might almost be identified as being basically community work. In Chapter 2,

I gave examples of various analyses of group and community work theories, which allows the possibility of connecting the more detailed examples used in various chapters with an overall account of theory within that type of social work. I have not found such an analysis of residential work, except for the relatively restricted material given in Chapter 2. Examining discussions of management, administration and education within social work, I have found these to be based on more general management and education theories. I have not, therefore, tried to treat these in this book, whose focus is on theories in social work practice. However, I have included some discussion of education theories which may influence social work; for example, Schon's 'reflective' practitioner ideas (see Chapters 2 and 8).

The future politics of social work theory

Social work theory must have a future, because all activities are informed by theory, even if it is covert or inexplicit. What trends, then, can we see?

Modern developments in social work theory are leading in similar directions to a reformation of basic social work ideas. Cognitive theory, from psychodynamic ego psychology, from behaviourist approaches and from existentialism, draws attention to the rational control that human beings have over their environment and their own behaviour. If we accept this movement, it rejects the traditional psychodynamic view that clients are driven by irrational and unreasonable needs. It rejects the traditional radical structuralist view that clients are unable to overcome the oppression which characterises all capitalist societies, or the systems view that energy to make changes in a system must come from external influences. Instead, the client is clearly seen as a crucial actor, even *the* crucial actor, in achieving whatever outcomes are desired in the social work process. Thus, social work must be more participatory, rather than therapeutic. This is the success of task-centred work. Social work must also recognise the particular social and personal characteristics of clients, rather than treating them as all of a kind, or all needing the same model of practice. This is the success of feminist and humanist approaches to social work. It must also recognise the way clients are treated in social systems, without denying the possibility of action. This is the success of anti-oppressive and empowerment approaches to social work.

Social work, therefore, is forming round a new nexus: we can see this from its theoretical movements. It is accepting the reflexive-therapeutic element of itself, but moving towards the reflexive, away from the therapeutic. It is accepting the individualist-reformist element of itself, but the individualism is not of the conservative kind which says that only the individual, not the social, counts. Social work theory is saying that the needs and wishes of the individual served must count in any morally valid practice which intervenes in the social. Social work theory is, finally, accepting the socialist-collectivist part of itself, but with an emphasis on the social and political position of clients within empowering practice, rather than seeking to form their needs into false collective interests.

I have argued in this chapter that social work theory as it enters the twenty-first century accepts the range of perspectives which have informed social work in the twentieth. It seeks to implement the strongest possible base of evidenced theory in its practice. In its models of practice, however, it focuses on the crises in clients' lives, seeks to empower them and society to overcome the blocks to personal and social progress and to implement its practice in a well-organised and practical series of steps implied in theories like task-centred work. Social workers implement in their practice different views of the social role of their profession, implying different analyses of their social world. This book's account and analysis of their practice theories present some of the possibilities for using those theories to draw ideas from various perspectives, explanatory theories and models. Social workers use them either to create an eclectic practice perspective or as a fully formed theoretical practice stance or as a basis for critical debate among the ideas which may be used to inform social work action in a complex social world.

Bibliography

Abatena, Hailu (1995) 'The significance of community self-help activities in promoting social development', *Journal of Social Development in Africa* **10**(1):5–24.

Abrams, Philip (1984) 'Social change, social networks and neighbourhood care', *Social Work Service* **22**:12–23.

Abrams, Philip, Sheila Abrams, Robin Humphrey and Ray Snaith (1989) *Neighbourhood Care and Social Policy* (London, HMSO).

Abrams, Sandra (1983) 'Casework: a problem-solving process', in Carol H. Meyer (ed.) *Clinical Social Work in the Eco-systems Perspective* (New York, Columbia University Press).

Adepoju, Aderanti (ed.) (1993) *The Impact of Structural Adjustment on the Population of Africa: the Implications for Education, Health and Employment* (Portsmouth, NH, Heinemann/UNFPA).

Adibi, Bobbie (1992) 'Religious fundamentalism', in Richard J. Estes (ed.) *Internationalizing Social Work Education: a Guide to Resources for a New Century* (Philadelphia, PA, University of Pennsylvania School of Social Work), 200–3.

Alinsky, Saul D. (1969) *Reveille for Radicals* (New York, Vintage).

Alinsky, Saul D. (1971) *Rules for Radicals* (New York, Random House).

Agere, S. (1986) 'Participation in social development and integration in sub-Saharan Africa', *Journal of Social Development in Africa* **1**(1):93–110.

Ahmad, Bandana (1990) *Black Perspectives in Social Work* (Birmingham, Venture).

Ahmed, Shama (1991) 'Developing anti-racist social work education practice', in CD Project Steering Group (1991) *Setting the Context for Change* (London, CCETSW), 166–82.

Ainsworth, Frank and Leon C. Fulcher (eds) (1981) *Group Care for Children: Concepts and Issues* (London, Tavistock).

Aldgate, Jane (1991) 'Attachment theory and its application to child care social work – an introduction', in Joyce Lishman (ed.) *Handbook of Theory for Practice Teachers in Social Work* (London, Jessica Kingsley), 11–35.

Alexander, K. C. (1994) *The Process of Development of Societies* (New Delhi, Sage).

Alexander, Leslie B. (1972) 'Social work's Freudian deluge: myth or reality?', *Social Service Review* **46**(4):517–38.

Allan, Graham (1983) 'Informal networks of care: issues raised by Barclay', *British Journal of Social Work* **13**(4):417–34.

Allen, Jo Ann (1993) 'The constructivist paradigm: values and ethics', *Journal of Teaching in Social Work* **8**(1/2):31–54.

Anderson, Stephen C., Martha K. Wilson, Lengwe-Katembula Mwansa and Kwaku Osei-Hwedie (1994) 'Empowerment and social work education and practice in Africa', *Journal of Social Development in Africa* **9**(2):71–86.

Arber, Sara and Jay Ginn (1991) *Gender and Later Life: a Sociological Analysis of Resources and Constraints* (London, Sage).

Arnold, Magda B. and J. A. Gasson (1979) 'Logotherapy's place in psychology', in Joseph B. Fabry, Reuven P. Bulka and William S. Sahakian (eds) *Logotherapy in Action* (London, Jason Aronson).

Asamoah, Yvonne W. and Creigs C. Beverly (1988) 'Collaboration between Western and African schools of social work: problems and possibilities', *International Social Work* **31**(3):177–94.

Atherton, Charles R. (1993) 'Empiricists versus social constructionists: time for a cease-fire', *Families in Society* **74**:617–24.

Atherton, Charles R. (1994) 'Atherton's response', *Families in Society* **75**(5):315–17.

Atherton, James S. (1989) *Interpreting Residential Life: Values to Practise* (London, Tavistock/Routledge).

Attlee, Clement R. (1920) *The Social Worker* (London, Bell).

Bailey, Roy and Mike Brake (eds) (1975a) *Radical Social Work* (London, Edward Arnold).

Bailey, Roy and Mike Brake (1975b) 'Introduction: social work in the welfare state', in Roy Bailey and Mike Brake (eds) *Radical Social Work* (London, Edward Arnold).

Bailey, Roy and Mike Brake (1980) 'Contributions to a radical practice in social work', in Mike Brake and Roy Bailey (eds) *Radical Social Work and Practice* (London, Edward Arnold).

Bailey, Roy and Phil Lee (1982) *Theory and Practice in Social Work* (Oxford, Blackwell).

Balgopal, Pallasana R. and Thomas Vassil (1983) *Groups in Social Work: an Ecological Perspective* (New York, Macmillan).

Bandura, Albert (1977) *Social Learning Theory* (Englewood Cliffs, NJ, Prentice-Hall).

Banton, Michael (1987) *Racial Theories* (Cambridge, Cambridge University Press).

Barber, James G. (1986) 'The promise and pitfalls of learned helplessness theory for social work practice', *British Journal of Social Work* **16**(5):557–70.

Barber, James G. (1991) *Beyond Casework* (London, Macmillan).

Barber, James G. (1995) 'Politically progressive casework', *Families in Society* **76**(1):30–7.

Barbour, Rosaline S. (1984) 'Social work education: tackling the theory-practice dilemma', *British Journal of Social Work* **14**(6):557–78.

Barclay Report (1982) *Social Workers: Their Role and Tasks* (London, Bedford Square Press).

Barker, Mary and Pauline Hardiker (eds) (1981) *Theories of Practice in Social Work* (London, Academic Press).

Bateman, Neil (1995) *Advocacy Skills: a Handbook for Human Service Professionals* (Aldershot, Hants, Gower).

Bateson, Gregory, Don Jackson, Jay Haley and J. Weakland (1956) 'Toward a theory of schizophrenia', *Behavioral Science* **1**:251–64.

Batten, T. R. (with Madge Batten) (1967) *The Non-directive Approach in Group and Community Work* (London, Oxford University Press).

Beck, Aaron T. (1989) *Cognitive Therapy and the Emotional Disorders* (Harmondsworth, Middlesex, Penguin).

Becker, Howard (1963) *Outsiders: Studies in the Sociology of Deviance* (New York, Free Press).

Benn, Concetta (1976) 'A new developmental model for social work', in Phillip J. Boas and Jim Crawley (eds) *Social Work in Australia: Responses to a Changing Context* (Melbourne, Australia International), 71–81.

Beresford, Peter and Suzy Croft (1993) *Citizen Involvement: a Practical Guide for Change* (London, Macmillan).

Berger, Peter L. and Thomas Luckmann (1971) *The Social Construction of Reality* (Harmondsworth, Middlesex, Penguin) (original American publication, 1966).

Berglind, H. (1992) 'Action theory: a tool for understanding in social work', *Scandinavian Journal of Social Welfare* 1(1):28–35.

Berlin, Sharon B. (1990) 'Dichotomous and complex thinking', *Social Service Review* 1:46–59.

Berne, Eric (1961) *Transactional Analysis in Psychotherapy* (New York, Grove Press).

Berne, Eric (1964) *Games People Play* (Harmondsworth, Middlesex, Penguin).

Bettelheim, Bruno (1950) *Love is Not Enough* (Glencoe, IC Free Press).

Biddle, Bruce J. and Edwin J. Thomas (eds) (1979) *Role Theory: Concepts and Research* (Huntington, NY, Robert S. Krieger Publishing).

Bion, W. R. (1961) *Experiences in Groups and Other Papers* (London, Tavistock).

Birchwood, Max, Stephen Hallett and Martin Preston (1988) *Schizophrenia: an Integrated Approach to Research and Treatment* (London, Longman).

Birdwhistell, Ray L. (1973) *Kinesics and Context: Essays on Body-motion Communications* (Harmondsworth, Middlesex, Penguin).

Birks, Colin (1987) 'Social welfare provision in France', in Roslyn Ford and Mono Chakrabarti (eds) *Welfare Abroad: an Introduction to Social Welfare in Seven Countries* (Edinburgh, Scottish Academic Press).

Black, Clifford and Richard Enos (1981) 'Using phenomenology in clinical social work: a poetic pilgrimage', *Clinical Social Work Journal* 9(1):34–43.

Blakemore, Ken and Margaret Boneham (1994) *Age, Race and Ethnicity: a Comparative Approach* (Buckingham, Open University Press).

Blom, Björn (1994) 'Relationem socialarbetare – klient ur ett Sartre anskt perspektiv', *Nordisk Sosialt Arbeid* 4:265–76.

Blumer, Herbert (1969) *Symbolic Interactionism: Perspective and Method* (Englewood Cliffs, NJ, Prentice-Hall).

Bocock, Robert (1988) 'Psychoanalysis and social theory', in Geoffrey Pearson, Judith Treseder and Margaret Yelloly (eds) *Social Work and the Legacy of Freud: Psychoanalysis and its Uses* (London, Macmillan).

Booth, Charles (1892–1903) *Life and Labour of the People of London* (vols 1–7) (London, Macmillan).

Booth, David (ed.) (1994a) *Rethinking Social Development: Theory, Research and Practice* (London, Longman).

Booth, David (1994b) 'Rethinking social development: an over view', in David Booth (ed.) *Rethinking Social Development: Theory, Research and Practice* (London, Longman).

Borensweig, Herman (1980) 'Jungian theory and social work practice', *Journal of Sociology and Social Welfare* **7**(4):571–85.

Bowlby, John (1951) *Maternal Care and Mental Health* (Geneva, World Health Organisation).

Bowlby, John (1969) *Attachment and Loss, vol. I: Attachment* (London, Hogarth Press).

Bowlby, John (1973) *Attachment and Loss, vol. II: Separation* (London, Hogarth Press).

Bowlby, John (1980) *Attachment and Loss, vol. III: Loss* (London, Hogarth Press).

Bowser, Benjamin P. (ed.) (1995) *Racism and Anti-racism in World Perspective* (Thousand Oaks, CA, Sage).

Bradford, Kirk A. (1969) *Existentialism and Casework: the Relationships between Social Casework Theory and the Philosophy and Psychology of Existentialism* (Jericho, NY, Exposition Press).

Brager, George and Francis Purcell (1967) *Community Action against Poverty: Readings from the Mobilization for Youth Experience* (New Haven, CT, College and University Press).

Brager, George, Harry Specht and James L. Torczyner (1987) *Community Organizing,* 2nd edn (New York, Columbia University Press).

Brake, Mike and Roy Bailey (eds) (1980) *Radical Social Work and Practice* (London, Edward Arnold).

Brandon, David (1976) *Zen and the Art of Helping* (London, Routledge & Kegan Paul).

Brandon, David (1995) 'Peer support and advocacy – international comparisons and developments', in Raymond Jack (ed.) *Empowerment in Community Care* (London, Chapman & Hall).

Brandon, David, Althea Brandon and Toby Brandon (1995) *Advocacy: Power to People with Disabilities* (Birmingham, Venture).

Brawley, Edward Allan and Emilia E. Martinez-Brawley (1988) 'Social programme evaluation in the USA: trends and issues', *British Journal of Social Work* **18**(4):391–414.

Braye, Suzy and Michael Preston-Shoot (1995) *Empowering Practice in Social Care* (Buckingham, Open University Press).

Breakwell, Glynis M. and Colin Rowett (1982) *Social Work: the Social Psychological Approach* (Wokingham, Berks, Van Nostrand Reinhold).

Brearley, Judith (1991) 'A psychodynamic approach to social work', in Joyce Lishman (ed.) *Handbook of Theory for Practice Teachers in Social Work* (London, Jessica Kingsley).

Brennan, William C. (1973) 'The practitioner as theoretician', *Journal of Education for Social Work* **9**(1):5–12.

Bricker-Jenkins, Mary, Nancy R. Hooyman and Naomi Gottlieb (eds) (1991) *Feminist Social Work Practice in Clinical Settings* (Newbury Park, CA, Sage).

Brigham, Thomas M. (1977) 'Liberation in social work education: applications from Paulo Freire', *Journal of Education for Social Work* **13**(3):5–11.

Brigham, Thomas M. (1984) 'Social work education in five developing countries', in Charles Guzzetta, Arthur J. Katz and Richard A. English (eds) *Education for Social Work Practice: Selected International Models* (New York, Council on Social Work Education).

Brook, Eve and Ann Davis (1985) *Women, the Family and Social Work* (London, Tavistock).

Brown, Allan (1992) *Groupwork,* 3rd edn (Aldershot, Hants, Arena).

Brown, Allan, Brian Caddick, Mike Gardiner and Sylvia Sleeman (1982) 'Towards a British model of groupwork', *British Journal of Social Work* 12(6):587–603.

Brown, Catrina (1994) 'Feminist postmodernism and the challenge of diversity', in Adrienne S. Chambon and Allan Irving (eds) *Essays in Postmodernism and Social Work* (Toronto, Canadian Scholars' Press).

Brown, Hilary and Helen Smith (1992) (eds) *Normalisation: a Reader for the Nineties* (London, Routledge).

Brown, Leonard N. (1993) 'Groupwork and the environment: a systems approach', *Social Work in Groups* 16(1/2):83–95.

Brown, Phil (1985) *The Transfer of Care: Psychiatric Deinstitutionalisation and its Aftermath* (New York, Routledge).

Brown, Robert, Stanley Bute and Peter Ford (1986) *Social Workers at Risk: the Prevention and Management of Violence* (London, Macmillan).

Browne, Elizabeth (1978) 'Social work activities', in DHSS *Social Service Teams: the Practitioner's View* (London, HMSO).

Bryant, Christopher G. A. (1985) *Positivism in Social Theory and Research* (London, Macmillan).

Bryant, Coralie (1985) 'Rural development: Asian lessons and African perspectives', *Indian Journal of Social Work* 46(3):399–409.

Bulmer, Martin (1986) *Neighbours: the Work of Philip Abrams* (Cambridge, Cambridge University Press).

Bulmer, Martin (1987) *The Social Basis of Community Care* (London, Allen & Unwin).

Bundey, Claire (1976) 'Developments in social group work, 1965–1975', in Phillip J. Boas and Jim Crawley (eds) *Social Work in Australia: Responses to a Changing Context* (Melbourne, Australia International), 142–55.

Bunston, Terry (1985) 'Mapping practice: problem-solving in clinical social work', *Social Casework* 66(4):225–36.

Burden, Dianne S. and Naomi Gottlieb (eds) (1987) *The Woman Client: Providing Services in a Changing World* (New York, Tavistock).

Burgess, Paul (1994) 'Welfare rights', in Christopher Hanvey and Terry Philpot (eds) *Practising Social Work* (London, Routledge).

Burgess, Robin, Robert Jewitt, James Sandham and Barbara L. Hudson (1980) 'Working with sex offenders: a social skills training group', *British Journal of Social Work* 10(2):133–42.

Burgoon, Michael, Frank G. Hunsaker and Edwin J. Dawson (1994) *Human Communication,* 3rd edn (Thousand Oaks, CA, Sage).

Burkey, Stan (1993) *People First: a Guide to self-Reliant, Participatory Rural Development* (London, Zed Books).

Burn, Michael (1956) *Mr Lyward's Answer: a Successful Experiment in Education* (London, Hamish Hamilton).

Burrell, Gibson and Gareth Morgan (1979) *Sociological Paradigms and Organisational Analysis* (London, Heinemann).

Bytheway, Bill (1995) *Ageism* (Buckingham, Open University Press).

Canda, Edward R. (1988) 'Conceptualising spirituality for social work: insights from diverse perspectives', *Social Casework* **69**(4):238–47.

Canda, Edward R., Sun-in Shin and Hwi-Ja Canda (1993) 'Traditional philosophies of human service in Korea and contemporary social work implications', *Social Development Issues* **15**(3):84–104.

Cannan, Crescy (1972) 'Social workers: training and professionalism', in Trevor Pateman (ed.) *Counter Course: a Handbook for Course Criticism* (Harmondsworth, Middlesex, Penguin).

Caplan, Gerald (1965) *Principles of Preventive Psychiatry* (London, Tavistock).

Caplan, Gerald (1974) *Support Systems and Community Mental Health: Lectures on Concept Development* (New York, Behavioral Publications).

Caplan, Gerald and Marie Killilea (eds) (1976) *Support Systems and Mutual Help: Multidisciplinary Explorations* (New York, Grune & Stratton).

Carew, Robert (1979) 'The place of knowledge in social work activity', *British Journal of Social Work* **9**(3):349–64.

Carkhuff, Robert R. and Bernard C. Berenson (1977) *Beyond Counseling and Therapy*, 2nd edn (New York, Holt, Rinehart & Winston).

Carlton-LaNey, Iris (ed.) (1994) *The Legacy of African-American Leadership in Social Welfare*. Special issue of *Journal of Sociology and Social Welfare* **21**(1).

Carniol, Ben (1992) 'Structural social work: Maurice Moreau's challenge to social work practice', *Journal of Progressive Human Services* **3**(1):1–20.

Carr, Wilfred (1986) 'Theories of theory and practice', *Journal of the Philosophy of Education* 1 **20**(2):177–86.

Case, Lois P. and Neverlyn B. Lingerfelt (1974) 'Name-calling: the labeling process in the social work interview', *Social Service Review* **18**(2):75–86.

Cavanagh, Kate and Viviene E. Cree (eds) (1996) *Working with Men: Feminism and Social Work* (London, Routledge).

CCETSW (1991) *One Small Step Towards Racial Justice: the Teaching of Antiracism in Diploma in Social Work Programmes* (London, CCETSW).

CD Project Steering Group (1991) *Setting the Context for Change* (London, CCETSW).

Cecil, Rosanne, John Offer and Fred St Leger (1987) *Informal Welfare: a Sociological Study of Care in Northern Ireland* (Aldershot, Hants, Gower).

Chaiklin, Harris (1979) 'Symbolic interaction and social practice', *Journal of Sociology and Social Welfare* **6**(1):3–7.

Chakrabarti, Mono (1987) 'Social welfare provision in India', in Roslyn Ford and Mono Chakrabarti (eds) *Welfare Abroad: an Introduction to Social Welfare in Seven Countries* (Edinburgh, Scottish Academic Press).

Chambers, Robert (1993) *Challenging the Professions: Frontiers for Rural Development* (London, Intermediate Technology Publications).

Chambon, Adrienne S. and Allan Irving (eds) (1994) *Essays on Postmodernism and Social Work* (Toronto, Canadian Scholars' Press).

Chan, Cecilia L. W. (1993) *The Myth of Neighbourhood Mutual Help: the Contemporary Chinese Community-based Welfare System in Guangzhou* (Hong Kong, Hong Kong University Press).

Chan, Cecilia L. W. and Nelson W. S. Chow (1992) *More Welfare after Economic Reform? Welfare Development in the People's Republic of*

China (Hong Kong, Department of Social Administration, University of Hong Kong).

Chan, Peggy Chan-ying (1987) 'Promoting peace in Chinese families of Hong Kong – a multi-faceted approach for social work students', in Yoko Kojima and Tetsuya Hosaka (eds) *Peace and Social Work Education: Developing Human Relations and Social Structures for Peace* (Vienna, International Association of Schools of Social Work), 100–7.

Chandra, Bipan (1987) *Communalism in Modern India*, 2nd edn (New Delhi, Vikas).

Cherniss, Cary (1980) *Staff Burnout: Job Stress in the Human Services* (Beverly Hills, CA, Sage).

Chiu, Thomas L. and Chuck Primeau (1991) 'A psychiatric mobile crisis unit in New York City: description and assessment, with implications for mental health care in the 1990s', *International Journal of Social Psychiatry* **37**(4):251–8.

Chow, Nelson W. S. (1987) 'Western and Chinese ideas of social welfare', *International Social Work* **30**(1):31–41.

Cigno, Katy (1985) 'The other Italian experiment: neighbourhood social work in the health and social services', *British Journal of Social Work* **15**(2):173–86.

Cingolani, Judith (1984) 'Social conflict perspective on work with involuntary clients', *Social Work* **29**(5):442–6.

Clark, Chris (1995) 'Competences and discipline in professional formation', *British Journal of Social Work* **25**(5):563–80.

Clark, David H. (1974) *Social Therapy in Psychiatry* (Harmondsworth, Middlesex, Penguin).

Clarke, Michael (1976) 'The limits of radical social work', *British Journal of Social Work* **6**(4):501–6.

Claxton, Guy (ed.) (1986) *Beyond Therapy: the Impact of Eastern Religions on Psychological Theory and Practice* (London, Wisdom).

Cloke, Christopher and Murray Davies (eds) (1995) *Participation and Empowerment in Child Protection* (London, Pitman).

Clough, Roger (1982) *Residential Work* (London, Macmillan).

Coates, John and Marilyn McKay (1995) 'Toward a new pedagogy for social transformation', *Journal of Progressive Human Services* **6**(1):27–43.

Coburn, Denise Capps (1986) 'Transactional analysis: a social work treatment model', in Francis J. Turner (ed.) *Social Work Treatment: Interlocking Theoretical Approaches,* 3rd edn (New York, Free Press).

Cocozzelli, Carmelo and Robert T. Constable (1985) 'An empirical analysis of the relation between theory and practice in clinical social work', *Journal of Social Service Research* **9**(1):47–64.

Cohen, Stan (1972) *Folk Devils and Moral Panics* (London, Paladin).

Cole, Judy (1990) 'Radical casework in a psychiatric setting', in Jude Petruchenia and Ros Thorpe (eds) *Social Change and Social Welfare Practice* (Sydney, Hale & Iremonger), 126–34.

Coleridge, Peter (1993) *Disability, Liberation and Development* (Oxford, Oxfam).

Collins, Anne H. and Diane L. Pancoast (1976) *Natural Helping Networks* (Washington, DC, NASW).

Collins, Barbara G. (1986) 'Defining feminist social work', *Social Work* **31**(3):214–19.

Compton, Beulah Roberts and Burt Galaway (1994) *Social Work Processes*, 5th edn (Pacific Grove, CA, Brooks/Cole).

Coombe, Vivienne and Alan Little (eds) (1986) *Race and Social Work: a Guide to Training* (London, Tavistock).

Coppola, Mary and Robert Rivas (1985) 'The task-action group technique: a case study of empowering the elderly', in Marvin Parnes (ed.) *Innovations in Social Group Work: Feedback from Practice to Theory* (New York, Haworth), 133–47.

Corden, John and Michael Preston-Shoot (1987a) *Contracts in Social Work* (Aldershot, Hants, Gower).

Corden, John and Michael Preston-Shoot (1987b) 'Contract or con trick? a reply to Rojek and Collins', *British Journal of Social Work* **17**(5):535–43.

Corden, John and Michael Preston-Shoot (1988) 'Contract or con trick? a postscript', *British Journal of Social Work* **18**(6):623–34.

Corner, John and Jeremy Hawthorn (eds) (1989) *Communication Studies: an Introductory Reader*, 3rd edn (London, Edward Arnold).

Corrigan, Paul and Peter Leonard (1978) *Social Work Practice under Capitalism: a Marxist Approach* (London, Macmillan).

Costa, Maria das Dores (1987) 'Current influences on social work in Brazil: practice and education', *International Social Work* **30**(2):115–28.

Cox, Enid Opal (1989) 'Empowerment of low income elderly through group work', *Social Work with Groups* **11**(4):111–25.

Craig, Gary, and Marjorie Mayo (eds) (1995) *Community Empowerment: a Reader in Participation and Development* (London, Zed Books).

Craig, Gary, Marjorie Mayo and Nick Sharman (eds) (1979) *Jobs and Community Action* (London, Routledge & Kegan Paul).

Craig, Gary, Nick Derricourt and Martin Loney (eds) (1982) *Community Work and the State: Towards a Radical Practice* (London, Routledge & Kegan Paul).

Croft, Suzy and Peter Beresford (1994) 'A participatory approach to social work', in Christopher Hanvey and Terry Philpot (eds) *Practising Social Work* (London, Routledge).

Curnock, Katherine and Pauline Hardiker (1979) *Towards Practice Theory: Skills and Methods in Social Assessments* (London, Routledge & Kegan Paul).

Curry, John F. (1995) 'The current status of research into residential treatment', *Residential Treatment for Children and Youth* **12**(3):1–17.

Dalrymple, Jane and Beverley Burke (1995) *Anti-oppressive Practice: Social Care and the Law* (Buckingham, Open University Press).

David, Gerson (1993) 'Strategies for grass roots human development', *Social Development Issues* **15**(2):1–13.

Davies, Martin (1977) *Support Systems in Social Work* (London, Routledge & Kegan Paul).

Davies, Martin (1994) *The Essential Social Worker: a Guide to Positive Practice,* 3rd edn (Aldershot, Hants, Arena).

Davies Jones, Haydn (1994) *Social Workers, or Social Educators? The International Context for Developing Social Care* (London, National Institute for Social Work International Centre).

Davis, Ann (1981) *The Residential Solution* (London, Tavistock).

Davis, Ann (1991) 'A structural approach to social work', in Joyce Lishman (ed.) *Handbook of Theory for Practice Teachers in Social Work* (London, Jessica Kingsley), 64–74.

Davis, Ann, Steve Newton and Dave Smith (1985) 'Coventry crisis intervention: the consumer's view', *Social Services Research* 14(1):7–32.

Davis, Daniel L. and Lucinda H. Broster (1993) 'Cognitive-behavioral-expressive interventions with aggressive and resistant youth', *Residential Treatment for Childen and Youth* 10(4):55–68.

Davis, Larry E. (ed.) (1984) *Ethnicity in Social Group Work Practice* (New York, Haworth).

Davis, Liane V. (1985) 'Female and male voices in social work', *Social Work* 30(2):106–13.

Davis, Liane Vida (1986) 'Role theory', in Francis J. Turner (ed.) *Social Work Treatment: Interlocking Theoretical Approaches* (New York, Free Press).

Davis, Liane V. (1993) 'Feminism and constructivism: teaching social work practice with women', in Joan Laird (ed.) *Revisioning Social Work Education: a Social Constructionist Approach* (New York, Haworth Press).

Davis-Sacks, Mary Lou, Srinika Jayaratne and Wayne A. Cheis (1985) 'A comparison of the effects of social support on the incidence of burnout', *Social Work* 30(3):240–4.

de Graaf, Martin (1986) 'Catching fish or liberating man: social development in Zimbabwe', *Journal of Social Development in Africa* 1(1):7–26.

de Lange, Janice M., Judy A. Barton and Susan L. Lanham (1981) 'The WISER way: a cognitive-behavioral model for group social skills training with juvenile delinquents', *Social Work with Groups* 4(3/4):37–48.

de Maria, William (1992) 'On the trail of a radical pedagogy for social work education', *British Journal of Social Work* 22(3):231–52.

de Maria, William (1993) 'Exploring radical social work teaching in Australia', *Journal of Progressive Human Services* 4(2):45–63.

de Shazer, Steve (1985) *Keys to Solution in Brief Therapy* (New York, Norton).

de Shazer, Steve (1988) *Clues: Investigating Solutions in Brief Therapy* (New York, Norton).

de Shazer, Steve (1991) *Putting Difference to Work* (New York, Gardner).

Dean, Ruth Grossman (1993) 'Teaching a constructivist approach to clinical practice', in Joan Laird (ed.) *Revisioning Social Work Education: a Social Constructionist Approach* (New York, Haworth Press), 55–75.

Denney, David (1983) 'Some dominant perspectives in the literature relating to multi-racial social work', *British Journal of Social Work* 13(2):149–74.

Denney, David (1991) 'Antiracism, probation training and the criminal justice system', in CCETSW, *One Small Step Towards Racial Justice: the Teaching of Antiracism in Diploma in Social Work Programmes* (London, CCETSW).

Denney, David (1992) *Racism and Anti-Racism in Probation* (London, Routledge).

Devore, Wynetta (1983) 'Ethnic reality: the life model and work with black families', *Social Casework* 64(9):525–31.

Devore, Wynetta and Elfriede G. Schlesinger (1991) *Ethnic-sensitive Social Work Practice* (New York, Merrill).

DHSS (1978) *Social Services Teams: the Practitioner's View* (London, HMSO).

Dimmock, Brian and David Dungworth (1983) 'Creating manoeuvrability for family/systems therapists in social services departments', *Journal of Family Therapy* 5(1):53–70.

Dixon, John (ed.) (1987) *Social Welfare in Africa* (London, Croom Helm).

Dixon, John and Robert P. Scheurell (eds) (1989) *Social Welfare in Developed Market Economies* (London, Routledge).

Dixon, John and Robert P. Scheurell (eds) (1995) *Social Welfare with Indigenous Peoples* (London, Routledge).

Doel, Mark (1994) 'Task-centred work', in Chris Hanvey and Terry Philpott (eds) *Practical Social Work* (London, Routledge), 22–36.

Doel, Mark and Peter Marsh (1992) *Task-centred Social Work* (Aldershot, Hants, Ashgate).

Dominelli, Lena (1988) *Anti-Racist Social Work* (London, Macmillan).

Dominelli, Lena (1990) *Women and Community Action* (Birmingham, Venture).

Dominelli, Lena and Eileen McCleod (1989) *Feminist Social Work* (London, Macmillan).

Dominelli, Lena, Lennie Jeffers, Graham Jones, Sakhile Sibanda and Brian Williams (1995) *Anti-Racist Probation Practice* (Aldershot, Hants, Arena).

Donnelly, A. (1986) *Feminist Social Work with a Women's Group* (Norwich, Norfolk, Social Work Monographs).

Dore, Martha M. (1990) 'Functional theory: its history and influence on contemporary social work', *Social Service Review*, 358–74.

Douglas, Tom (1979) *Group Processes in Social Work: a Theoretical Synthesis* (Chichester, Hants, John Wiley).

Douglas, Tom (1993) *A Theory of Groupwork Practice* (London, Macmillan).

Dowrick, Christopher (1983) 'Strange meeting: Marxism, psychoanalysis and social work', *British Journal of Social Work* 13(1):1–18.

Dryden, Windy (1991) 'A brief, highly structured and effective approach to social work practice: a cognitive-behavioural perspective', in Joyce Lishman (ed.) *Handbook of Theory for Practice Teachers in Social Work* (London, Jessica Kingsley), 173–88.

Dungee-Anderson, Delores and Joyce O. Beckett (1995) 'A process model for multicultural social work practice', *Families in Society* 76(8):459–66.

Durkheim, Emile (1938) *The Rules of Sociological Method,* 8th edn, trans. (New York, Free Press).

Edlis, Noemi (1993) 'Rape crisis: development of a center in an Israeli hospital', *Social Work in Health Care* 18(3/4):169–78.

Edwards, Michael and David Hulme (eds) (1992) *Making a Difference: NGOs and Development in a Changing World* (London, Earthscan).

Eisenhuth, Elizabeth (1981) 'The theories of Heinz Kohut and clinical social work practice', *Clinical Social Work Journal* 9(2):80–90.

Elliott, Doreen (1993) 'Social work and social development: towards an integrative model for social work practice', *International Social Work* 36(1):21–36.

Ellis, Albert (1962) *Reason and Emotion in Psychotherapy* (Secaucus, NJ, Lyle Stuart).

Ellis, June (1977) 'Differing conceptions of a child's needs: some implications for social work with West African children and their parents', *British Journal of Social Work* **7**(2):155–72.

Else, John F., Zebbediah M. Gamanya and Kwanele O. Jirira (1986) 'Economic development in the African context: opportunities and constraints', *Journal of Social Development in Africa* **1**(2):75–87.

Ely, Peter and David Denney (1987) *Social Work in a Multi-Racial Society* (Aldershot, Hants, Gower).

England, Hugh (1986) *Social Work as Art* (London, Allen & Unwin).

Epstein, Laura (1992) *Brief Treatment and a New Look at the Task-Centered Approach* (New York, Macmillan).

Erikson, Erik (1965) *Childhood and Society,* 2nd edn (London, Hogarth Press).

Estes, Richard J. (1993) 'Toward sustainable development: from theory to praxis', *Social Development Issues* **15**(3):1–29.

Etzioni, Amitai (1975) *A Comparative Analysis of Complex Organisations: On Power, Involvement and their Correlates* (New York, Free Press).

Evans, Estella Norwood (1992) 'Liberation theology, empowerment theory and social work practice with the oppressed', *International Social Work* **35**(2):135–47.

Evans, Roger (1976) 'Some implications of an integrated model of social work for theory and practice', *British Journal of Social Work* **6**(2): 177–200.

Everitt, Angela, Pauline Hardiker, Jane Littlewood and Audrey Mullender (1992) *Applied Research for Better Practice* (London, Macmillan).

Ezell, Mark (1994) 'Advocacy practice of social workers', *Families in Society* **75**(1):36–46.

Eziakor, Ikechukwu G. (1989) 'Rethinking Third World development: an analysis of contemporary paradigms', *Journal of Social Development in Africa* **4**(2):39–48.

Fairbairn, W. R. D. (1954) *An Object Relations Theory of Personality* (New York, Basic Books).

Feldman, Ronald A. and John S. Wodarski (1975) *Contemporary Approaches to Group Treatment* (San Francisco, Jossey-Bass).

Fimister, Geoff (1986) *Welfare Rights Work in Social Services* (London, Macmillan).

Fineman, Stephen (1985) *Social Work Stress and Intervention* (Aldershot, Hants, Gower).

Fischer, Joel (1973) 'Is casework effective? a review', *Social Work* **18**(1): 5–20.

Fischer, Joel (1976) *The Effectiveness of Social Casework* (Springfield, IL, Charles C. Thomas).

Fischer, Joel (1978) *Effective Casework Practice: an Eclectic Approach* (New York, McGraw-Hill).

Fischer, Joel (1981) 'The social work revolution', *Social Work* **26**(3): 199–207.

Fischer, Joel and Harvey L. Gochros (1975) *Planned Behaviour Change: Behaviour Modification in Social Work* (New York, Free Press).

Fishbein, M. and I. Adzen (1975) *Belief, Attitude and Intention: an Introduction to Theory and Research* (Reading, MA, Addison-Wesley).

Fisher, David D. V. (1991) *An Introduction to Constructivism for Social Workers* (New York, Praeger).

Fisher, Jo (1993) *Out of the Shadows: Women, Resistance and Politics in South America* (London, Latin America Bureau).

Fisher, Robert and Joe Kling (1994) 'Community organization and new social movement theory', *Journal of Progressive Human Services* 5(2):5–23.

Fisher, William H., Jeffrey L. Geller and Janet Wirth-Cauchon (1990) 'Empirically assessing the impact of mobile crisis capacity on state hospital admissions', *Community Mental Health Journal* 26(3):245–53.

Fleming, Ronald C. (1981) 'Cognition and social work practice: some implications of attribution and concept attainment theories', in Anthony N. Maluccio (ed.) *Promoting Competence in Clients: a New/Old Approach to Social Work Practice* (New York, Free Press), 55–73.

Fong, Lina Yuk-Shui and Daya Sandu (1995) 'Cultural value orientation and choice of intervention style for Chinese-American compared to Anglo-American clients', *New Global Development* 11:35–41.

Fook, Janis (1993) *Radical Casework: a Theory of Practice* (St Leonards, NSW, Allen & Unwin).

Forder, Anthony (1976) 'Social work and systems theory', *British Journal of Social Work* 6(1):24–41.

Fortune, Anne E. (1985) *Task-centered Practice with Families and Groups* (New York, Springer).

Foucault, Michel (1972) *The Archaeology of Knowledge and the Discourse on Language* (New York, Pantheon).

Fraiberg, Selma (1978) 'Psychoanalysis and social work: a re-examination of the issues', *Smith College Studies in Social Work* 48(2):87–106.

Franklin, Cynthia (1995) 'Expanding the vision of the social constructionist debates: creating relevance for practitioners', *Families in Society* 76(7):395–406.

Franklin, Marjorie E. (1968) 'The meaning of planned environment therapy', in Arthur T. Barron (ed.) *Studies in Environment Therapy,* vol. 1 (Worth, Sussex, Planned Environment Therapy Trust).

Freedberg, Sharon (1986) 'Religion, profession and politics: Bertha Capen Reynolds' challenge to social work', *Smith College Studies in Social Work* 56(2):95–110.

Freire, Paulo (1972) *Pedagogy of the Oppressed* (Harmondsworth, Middlesex, Penguin).

Friedmann, John (1992) *Empowerment: the Politics of Alternative Development* (Cambridge, MA, Blackwell).

Fulcher, Leon C. and Frank Ainsworth (eds) (1985) *Group Care Practice with Children* (London, Tavistock).

Furlong, Mark (1987) 'A rationale for the use of empowerment as a goal in casework', *Australian Social Work* 40(3):25–30.

Furlong, Mark (1990) 'On being able to say what we mean: the language of hierarchy in social work practice', *British Journal of Social Work* 20(6):575–90.

Galper, Jeffrey (1975) *The Politics of Social Service* (Englewood Cliffs, NJ, Prentice-Hall).

Galper, Jeffrey (1980) *Social Work Practice: a Radical Approach* (Englewood Cliffs, NJ, Prentice-Hall).

Gambrill, Eileen (1977) *Behavior Modification: a Handbook of Assessment, Intervention and Evaluation* (San Francisco, CA, Jossey-Bass).

Gambrill, Eileen (1981) 'The use of behavioural procedures in cases of child abuse and neglect', *International Journal of Behavioural Social Work and Abstracts* **1**(1):3–26.

Gambrill, Eileen (1994) 'What's in a name? Task-centred, empirical, and behavioral practice', *Social Service Review* **68**(4):578–99.

Gambrill, Eileen (1995) 'Behavioral social work: past, present and future', *Research on Social Work Practice* **5**(4):460–84.

Gangrade, K. D. (1970) 'Western social work and the Indian world', *International Social Work* **13**(3):4–12.

Garbarino, James (1983) 'Social support networks: Rx for the helping professions', in James K. Whittaker and James Garbarino (eds) *Social Support Networks: Informal Helping in the Human Services* (New York, Aldine).

Garber, Benjamin (1992) 'Countertransference reactions in death and divorce: comparison and contrast', *Residential Treatment for Children and Youth* **9**(4):43–60.

Gargett, Eric (1977) *The Administration of Transition: African urban settlement in Rhodesia* (Gwelo, Mambo Press).

George, Vic and Paul Wilding (1994) *Welfare and Ideology* (London, Harvester Wheatsheaf).

Germain, Carel B. (1970) 'Casework and science: a historical encounter', in Robert W. Roberts and Robert H. Nee (eds) *Theories of Social Casework* (Chicago, University of Chicago Press).

Germain, Carel B. (1976) 'Time: an ecological variable in social work practice', *Social Casework* **57**(7):419–26.

Germain, Carel B. (1978) 'General-systems theory and ego psychology: an ecological perspective', *Social Service Review* **52**(4):534–50.

Germain, Carel B. (ed.) (1979a) *Social Work Practice: People and Environments – an Ecological Perspective* (New York, Columbia University Press).

Germain, Carel B. (1979b) 'Introduction: ecology and social work', in Carel B. Germain (ed.) *Social Work Practice: People and Environments – an Ecological Approach* (New York, Columbia University Press).

Germain, Carel B. (1981) 'The ecological approach to people-environment transactions', *Social Casework* **62**(6):323–31.

Germain, Carel B. and Alex Gitterman (1980) *The Life Model of Social Work Practice* (New York, Columbia University Press).

Germain, Carel B. and Ann Hartman (1980) 'People and ideas in the history of social work practice', *Social Casework* **61**(6):323–31.

Ghosh, B. (1984) 'Social work contribution to population programme management', *Indian Journal of Social Work* **44**(4):409–18.

Gibbons, Jane, I. Bow, J. Butler and J. Powell (1979) 'Clients' reactions to task-centred casework: a follow-up study', *British Journal of Social Work* **10**(2):203–15.

Gibson, Faith, Anne McGrath and Norma Reid (1989) 'Occcupational stress in social work', *British Journal of Social Work* **19**(1):1–16.

Gilbar, Ora (1991) 'Model for crisis intervention through group therapy for women with breast cancer', *Clinical Social Work Journal* **19**(3):293–304.

Gilgun, Jane F. (1994) 'An ecosystemic approach to assessment', in Beulah R. Compton and Burt Galaway *Social Work Processes,* 5th edn (Pacific Grove, CA, Brooks/Cole), 380–94.

Gilligan, Carol (1982) *In a Different Voice: Psychological Theory and Women's Development* (Cambridge, MA, Harvard University Press).

Gilligan, Carol (1986) 'Reply to critics', in Mary Jeanne Larrabee (ed.) *An Ethic of Care: Feminist and Interdisciplinary Perspectives* (New York, Routledge).

Gingerich, Wallace J. (1990) 'Re-thinking single-case designs', in Lynn Videka-Sherman and William J. Reid (eds) *Advances in Clinical Social Work Research* (Silver Spring, MD, NASW Press), 11–24.

Gingerich, Wallace J., Mark Kleczewski and Stuart A. Kirk (1982) 'Name-calling in social work', *Social Service Review* **56**(3):366–74.

Gitterman, Alex (1983) 'Uses of resistance: a transactional view', *Social Work* **28**(2):127–31.

Glaser, B. and A. Strauss (1967) *The Discovery of Grounded Theory* (London, Weidenfeld & Nicolson).

Glasser, William (1965) *Reality Therapy: a New Approach to Psychiatry* (New York, Harper & Row).

Glassman, Urania and Len Kates (1990) *Group Work: a Humanistic Approach* (Newbury Park, CA, Sage).

Goffman, Erving (1968a) *Stigma: Notes on the Management of Spoiled Identity* (Harmondsworth, Middlesex, Penguin).

Goffman, Erving (1968b) *The Presentation of Self in Everyday Life* (Harmondsworth, Middlesex, Penguin).

Goffman, Erving (1972a) *Relations in Public: Microstudies of the Public Order* (Harmondsworth, Middlesex, Penguin).

Goffman, Erving (1972b) *Interaction Ritual: Essays on Face-to-face Behaviour* (Harmondsworth, Middlesex, Penguin).

Goffman, Erving (1972c) *Encounters: Two Studies in the Sociology of Interaction* (Harmondsworth, Middlesex, Penguin).

Golan, Naomi (1978) *Treatment in Crisis Situations* (New York, Free Press).

Golan, Naomi (1986) 'Crisis theory', in Francis J. Turner (ed.) *Social Work Treatment: Interlocking Theoretical Approaches* (New York, Free Press).

Goldapple, Gary C. and Dianne Montgomery (1993) 'Evaluating a behaviorally based intervention to improve client retention in therapeutic community treatment for drug dependency', *Research on Social Work Practice* **3**(1):21–39.

Goldberg, E. Matilda (1987) 'The effectiveness of social care: a selective exploration', *British Journal of Social Work* **17**(6):595–614.

Goldberg, E. Matilda, Jane Gibbons and Ian Sinclair (1985) *Problems, Tasks and Outcomes* (London, Allen & Unwin).

Goldstein, Eda G. (1984) *Ego Psychology and Social Work Practice* (New York, Free Press).

Goldstein, Howard (1973) *Social Work Practice: a Unitary Approach* (Columbia, SC, University of South Carolina Press).

Goldstein, Howard (1981) *Social Learning and Change: a Cognitive Approach to Human Services* (Columbia, SC, University of South Carolina Press).

Goldstein, Howard (ed.) (1984) *Creative Change: a Cognitive-humanistic Approach to Social Work Practice* (New York, Tavistock).

Gomm, Roger (1993) 'Issues of power in health and welfare', in Jan Walmsley, Jill Reynolds, Pam Shakespeare and Ray Woolfe (eds) *Health, Welfare and Practice: Reflecting on Roles and Relationships* (London, Sage), 131–8.

Gordon, William E. (1983) 'Social work revolution or evolution?', *Social Work* **28**(3):181–5.

Goroff, Norman N. (1974) 'Social welfare as coercive social control', *Journal of Sociology and Social Welfare* **2**(1):19–26.

Gottschalk, Shimon S. and Stanley L. Witkin (1991) 'Rationality in social work: a critical evaluation', *Journal of Sociology and Social Welfare* **18**(2):121–35.

Gould, Ketayun H. (1995) 'The misconstruing of multiculturalism: the Stanford debate and social work', *Social Work* **40**(2):198–205.

Gould, Nick (1994) 'Anti-racist social work: a framework for teaching and action', *Issues in Social Work Education* **14**(1):2–17.

Granger, Jean M. and Doreen L. Portner (1985) 'Ethnic- and gender-sensitive social work practice', *Journal of Social Work Education* **21**(1):38–47.

Gray, Elizabeth (1987) 'Brief task-centred casework in a crisis intervention team in a psychiatric setting', *Journal of Social Work Practice* **3**(1):111–28.

Gray, Marilyn and Andrea Bernstein (1994) 'Pavement people and informal communities: lessons for social work', *International Social Work* **37**(2):149–63.

Greif, Geoffrey L. (1986) 'The ecosystems perspective "meets the press"', *Social Work* **31**(3):225–6.

Greif, Geoffrey L. and Arthur A. Lynch (1983) 'The eco-systems perspective', in Carol H. Meyer (ed.) *Clinical Social Work in the Eco-Systems Perspective* (New York, Columbia University Press).

Greene, Gilbert J., Carla Jensen and Dorothy Harper Jones (1996) 'A constructivist perspective on clinical social work practice with ethnically diverse clients', *Social Work* **41**(2):172–80.

Grimwood, Cordelia and Ruth Popplestone (1993) *Women, Management and Care* (London, Macmillan).

Gross, Emma R. (1995) 'Deconstructing politically correct practice literature: the American Indian case', *Social Work* **40**(2):206–13.

Grosser, Charles F. and Jacqueline Mondros (1985) 'Pluralism and participation: the political action approach', in Samuel H. Taylor and Robert W. Roberts (eds) (1985) *Theory and Practice of Community Social Work* (New York, Columbia University Press), 154–78.

Gulbenkian Foundation Study Group (1968) *Community Work and Social Change* (London, Longman).

Guntrip, Harry (1968) *Schizoid Phenomena, Object Relations and the Self* (London, Hogarth Press).

Gutiérrez, Gustavo (1973) *A Theology of Liberation* (Maryknoll, Orbis Books).

Gutiérrez, Gustavo (1992) 'Poverty from the perspective of liberation theology', in Hubert Campfens (ed.) *New Reality of Poverty and Struggle for Social Transformation* (Vienna, International Association of Schools of Social Work).

Gutiérrez, Lorraine M. (1995) 'Understanding the empowerment process: does consciousness make a difference?', *Social Work Research* **19**(4):229–37.

Gutiérrez, Lorraine M., Kathryn A. DeLois and Linnea GlenMaye (1995) 'Understanding empowerment practice: building on practitioner-based knowledge', *Families in Society* **76**(8):534–42.

Hadley, Roger, Mike Cooper, Peter Dale and Graham Stacy (1987) *A Community Social Worker's Handbook* (London, Tavistock).

Hadley, Roger and Stephen Hatch (1981) *Social Welfare and the Failure of the State: Centralised Social Services and Participatory Alternatives* (London, Allen & Unwin).

Hadley, Roger and Morag McGrath (eds) (1980) *Going Local: Neighbourhood Social Services* (London, Bedford Square Press).

Hadley, Roger, and Morag McGrath (1984) *When Social Services are Local: the Normanton Experience* (London, Allen & Unwin)

Hall, Edward T. (1966) *The Hidden Dimension* (Garden City, NY, Doubleday).

Hall, Nigel (1993a) 'The social workers of tomorrow and fieldwork today: poverty and urban social work in Africa in the 1990s', in Nigel Hall (ed.) *Social Development and Urban Poverty* (Harare, School of Social Work), 7–14.

Hall, Nigel (ed.) (1993b) *Social Development and Urban Poverty* (Harare, School of Social Work).

Hallett, Christine (ed.) (1989) *Women and Social Services Departments* (London, Harvester Wheatsheaf).

Hämäläinen, Juha (1989) 'Social pedagogy as a meta-theory of social work education', *International Social Work* **32**(2):117–28.

Hamilton, Gordon (1950) *Theory and Practice of Social Casework,* 2nd edn (New York, Columbia University Press).

Hamilton, Gordon (1957) 'A theory of personality: Freud's contribution to social work', in Howard J. Parad (ed.) *Ego Psychology and Dynamic Casework* (New York, Family Service Association of America).

Hammersley, Martyn and Paul Atkinson (1995) *Ethnography: Principles in Practice,* 2nd edn (London, Routledge).

Hanmer, Jalna and Daphne Statham (1988) *Women and Social Work: Towards a Women-centred Practice* (London, Macmillan).

Hanson, Barbara Gail (1995) *General Systems Theory: Beginning with Wholes* (Washington, DC, Taylor & Francis).

Hanson, Meredith (1983) 'Behavioral approaches to social work practice', in Carol H. Meyer (ed.) *Clinical Social Work in the Eco-Systems Perspective* (New York, Columbia University Press).

Hanvey, Christopher and Terry Philpot (eds) (1994) *Practising Social Work* (London, Routledge).

Harcourt, Wendy (ed.) (1994) *Feminist Perspectives on Sustainable Development* (London, Zed Books).

Hardiker, Pauline (1981) 'Heart or head – the function and role of knowledge in social work', *Issues in Social Work Education* **1**(2):85–111.

Hardiker, Pauline and Mary Barker (1991) 'Towards social theory for social work', in Joyce Lishman (ed.) *Handbook of Theory for Practice Teachers in Social Work* (London, Jessica Kingsley), 87–101.

Hardiman, Margaret and James Midgley (1980) 'Training social planners for social development', *International Social Work* **23**(3):2–15.

Hardiman, Margaret and James Midgley (1989) *The Social Dimensions of Development: Social Policy and Planning in the Third World,* rev. edn (Aldershot, Hants, Gower).

Harris, Thomas A. (1973) *I'm OK – You're OK* (London, Pan).

Harrison, Diane F., Walter W. Hudson and Bruce A. Thyer (1992) 'On a critical analysis of empirical clinical practice: a response to Witkin's revised views', *Social Work* **37**(5):461–4.

Harrison, W. David (1991) *Seeking Common Ground: a Theory of Social Work in Social Care* (Aldershot, Hants, Avebury).

Hart, John (1980) 'It's just a stage we're going through: the sexual politics of casework', in Mike Brake and Roy Bailey (eds) *Radical Social Work and Practice* (London, Edward Arnold).

Hartman, Ann (1971) 'But what is social casework?', *Social Casework* **52**(7):411–19.

Hartman, Ann (1986) 'The life and work of Bertha Reynolds: implications for education and practice today', *Smith College Studies in Social Work* **56**(2):79–94.

Haworth, Glenn O. (1991) 'My paradigm can beat your paradigm: some reflections on knowledge conflicts', *Journal of Sociology and Social Welfare* **18**(4):35–50.

Hazell, Jeremy (1995) *Personal Relationships Therapy* (London, Jason Aronson).

Heap, Ken (1992) 'The European groupwork scene: where were we? where are we? where are we going?' *Groupwork* **5**(1):9–23.

Hearn, Gordon (1958) *Theory-building in Social Work* (Toronto, University of Toronto Press).

Hearn, Gordon (ed.) (1969) *The General Systems Approach: Contributions toward an Holistic Conception of Social Work* (New York, Council on Social Work Education).

Hearn, Jeff (1982) 'The problem(s) of theory and practice in social work and social work education', *Issues in Social Work Education* **2**(2): 95–118.

Hegar, Rebecca L. (1989) 'Empowerment-based practice with children', *Social Service Review* **63**(3):372–83.

Heineman, Martha Brunswick (1981) 'The obsolete scientific imperative in social work research', *Social Service Review* **55**(3):371–97.

Heisler, Helmuth (1970) 'Social welfare and African development', *Applied Social Studies* **2**(2):81–9.

Herberg, Dorothy Chave (1993) *Frameworks for Cultural and Racial Diversity: Teaching and Learning for Practitioners* (Toronto, Canadian Scholars' Press).

Herbert, Martin (1987) *Behavioural Treatment of Children with Problems: a Practice Manual,* 2nd edn (London, Academic Press).

Hettne, Bjorn (1990) *Development Theory and the Three Worlds* (London, Longman).

Hindmarsh, Jennie Harré, (1992) *Social Work Oppositions: New Graduates' Experiences* (Aldershot, Hants, Avebury).

Hirayama, Hidashi and Kasumi Hirayama (1985) 'Empowerment through group participation: process and goal', in Marvin Parnes (ed.) *Innovations in Social Group Work: Feedback from Practice to Theory* (New York, Haworth), 119–31.

Hofstein, Saul (1964) 'The nature of process: its implications for social work', *Journal of the Social Work Process* **14**:13–53.

Hogg, Michael A. and Dominic Abrams (1988) *Social Identifications: a Social Psychology of Intergroup Relations and Group Processes* (London, Routledge).

Hollin, Clive R. (1990) 'Social skills training with delinquents: a look at the evidence and some recommendations for practice', *British Journal of Social Work* **20**(5):483–93.

Holmes, Gary E. and Dennis Saleebey (1993) 'Empowerment, the medical model and the politics of clienthood', *Journal of Progressive Human Services* **4**(1):61–78.

Holmes, T. and M. Masuda (1973) 'Life change and illness susceptibility', in J. P. Scott and E. C. Senay (eds) *Separation and Depression: Clinical and Research Aspects* (Washington, DC, American Association for the Advancement of Science).

Horowitz, Louis Irving (1972) *Three Worlds of Development: the Theory and Practice of International Stratification,* 2nd edn (New York, Oxford University Press).

Howard, Jane (1971) 'Indian society, Indian social work: identifying Indian principles and methods for social work practice', *International Social Work* **14**(4):16–31.

Howard, Tina U. and Frank C. Johnson (1985) 'An ecological approach to practice with single-parent families', *Social Casework* **66**(8):482–9.

Howe, David (1987) *An Introduction to Social Work Theory* (Aldershot, Berks, Wildwood House).

Howe, David (1994) 'Modernity, post-modernity and social work', *British Journal of Social Work* **24**(5):513–32.

Howe, David (1995) *Attachment Theory for Social Work Practice* (London, Macmillan).

Howe, Michael W. and John R. Schuerman (1974) 'Trends in the social work literature: 1957–72', *Social Service Review* **48**(2):279–85.

Hudson, Annie (1985) 'Feminism and social work: resistance or dialogue?', *British Journal of Social Work* **15**(6):635–55.

Hudson, Barbara L. (1978) 'Behavioural social work with schizophrenic patients in the community', *British Journal of Social Work* **8**(2):159–70.

Hudson, Barbara L. (1982) *Social Work with Psychiatric Patients* (London, Macmillan).

Hudson, Barbara and Geraldine Macdonald (1986) *Behavioural Social Work: an Introduction* (London, Macmillan).

Hugman, Bruce (1977) *Act Natural: a New Sensibility for the Professional Worker* (London, Bedford Square Press).

Hugman, Richard (1987) 'The private and the public in personal models of social work: a response to O'Connor and Dalgleish', *British Journal of Social Work* **17**(1):71–6.

Hulme, David and Mark Turner (1990) *Sociology and Development: Theories, Policies and Practices* (Hemel Hempstead, Herts, Harvester Wheatsheaf).

Husband, Charles (1980) 'Culture, context and practice: racism in social work', in Mike Brake and Roy Bailey (eds) *Radical Social Work and Practice* (London, Edward Arnold), 64–85.

Husband, Charles (1991) '"Race", conflictual politics, and anti-racist social work: lessons from the past for action in the 90s', in CD Project Steering Group (1991) *Setting the Context for Change* (London, CCETSW), 46–73.

Hutten, Joan M. (1977) *Short-term Contracts in Social Work* (London, Routledge & Kegan Paul).

Ilango, P. (1988) 'Existing model of social work education for community development', *Indian Journal of Social Work* **49**(1):21–5.

Illich, Ivan, Irving K. Zola, John McKnight, Jonathan Caplan and Harley Shaiken (1977) *Disabling Professions* (London, Marion Boyars).

Irvine, Elizabeth E. (1956) 'Transference and reality in the casework relationship', *British Journal of Psychiatric Social Work* **3**(4):1–10.

Irving, Allan (1994) 'From image to simulacra: the modern/postmodern divide and social work', in Adrienne S. Chambon and A. Irving (eds) *Essays on Postmodernism and Social Work* (Toronto, Canadian Scholars' Press).

Jack, Raymond (ed.) (1995a) *Empowerment in Community Care* (London, Chapman & Hall).

Jack, Raymond (1995b) 'Empowerment in community care', in Raymond Jack (ed.) *Empowerment in Community Care* (London, Chapman and Hall).

Jackson, Ben (1994) *Poverty and the Planet: a Question of Survival,* rev. edn (London, Penguin).

Jackson, Henry J. and Neville J. King (1982) 'The conceptual basis of behavioural programming: a review with implications for social work', *Contemporary Social Work Education* **5**(3):227–38.

Jacobs, Carolyn and Dorcas D. Bowles (eds) (1988) *Ethnicity and Race: Critical Concepts in Social Work* (Silver Spring, MD, National Association of Social Workers).

Jansen, Elly (ed.) (1980) *The Therapeutic Community Outside the Hospital* (London, Croom Helm).

Jansson, Bruce S. (1994) *Social Policy from Theory to Policy Practice,* 2nd edn (Pacific Grove, CA, Brooks/Cole).

Jarrett, Alfred A. (1991) 'Problems and prospects of the social welfare systems of Sierra Leone and Nigeria', *International Social Work* **34**(2):143–57.

Jayaratne, Srinika (1978) 'A study of clinical eclecticism', *Social Service Review* **52**(4):621–31.

Jayaratne, Srinika, Tony Tripodi and Wayne Cheis (1983) 'Perceptions of emotional support, stress and strain by male and female social workers', *Social Work Research and Abstracts* **19**(Summer):29–37.

Jehu, Derek (1967) *Learning Theory and Social Work* (London, Routledge & Kegan Paul).

Jehu, Derek (ed.) (1972) *Behaviour Modification in Social Work* (Chichester, Hants, John Wiley).

Jenkins, Shirley (1987) 'The limited domain of effectiveness research', *British Journal of Social Work* **17**(6):587–94.

Jenkins, Shirley (1988) 'Ethnicity: theory base and practice link', in Carolyn Jacobs and Dorcas D. Bowles (eds) *Ethnicity and Race: Critical Concepts in Social Work* (Silver Spring, MD, National Association of Social Workers).

John, Lindsay H. (1994) 'Borrowed knowledge in social work: an introduction to post-structuralim and postmodernity', in Adrienne S. Chambon and A. Irving (eds) *Essays on Postmodernism and Social Work* (Toronto, Canadian Scholars' Press), 49–62.

Johnson, Hazel (1992) 'Women's empowerment and public action: experiences from Latin America', Marc Wuyts, Maureen Mackintosh and Tom Hewitt (eds) *Development Policy and Public Action* (Oxford, Oxford University Press), 147–72.

Jones, Chris (1993) 'Distortion and demonisation: the Right and anti-racist social work education', *Social Work Education* **12**(3):9–16.

Jones, David and Marjorie Mayo (eds) (1974) *Community Work One* (London, Routledge & Kegan Paul).

Jones, David and Marjorie Mayo (eds) (1975) *Community Work Two* (London, Routledge & Kegan Paul).

Jones, Howard (1979) *The Residential Community* (London, Routledge & Kegan Paul).

Jones, Howard (1990) *Social Welfare in Third World Development* (London, Macmillan).

Jones, John F. (1981) 'An introduction to social development: an international perspective', in John F. Jones and Rama S. Pandey (eds) *Social Development: Conceptual, Methodological and Policy Issues* (Delhi, Macmillan India).

Jones, John F. and Rama S. Pandey (eds) (1981) *Social Development: Conceptual, Methodological and Policy Issues* (Delhi, Macmillan India).

Jones, John F. and Toshihiro Yogo (1994) *New Training Design for Local Social Development: the Single System Design in Competency-based Training* (Nagoya, Japan, United Nations Centre for Regional Development).

Jones, Maxwell (1968) *Social Psychiatry in Practice: the Idea of the Therapeutic Community* (Harmondsworth, Middlesex, Penguin).

Jordan, Bill (1978) 'A comment on "Theory and practice in social work"', *British Journal of Social Work* **8**(1):23–5.

Jordan, Bill (1987) 'Counselling, advocacy and negotiation', *British Journal of Social Work* **17**(2):135–46.

Kabadaki, Kyama K. (1995) 'Exploration of social work practice: models for rural development in Uganda', *Journal of Social Development in Africa* **10**(1):77–88.

Karger, H. Jacob (1983) 'Science, research, and social work: who controls the profession?', *Social Work* **28**(2):200–5.

Karnik, Sachin J. and Kul Bushan Suri (1995) 'The law of karma and social work considerations', *International Social Work* **38**(4):365–78.

Kassim Ejaz, Farida (1989) 'The nature of casework practice in India: a study of social workers' perceptions in Bombay', *International Social Work* **32**(1):25–38.

Katz, Alfred H. (1983) 'Deficiencies in the status quo', *Social Work* **28**(1):71.

Katz, Ilan (1995a) 'Approaches to empowerment and participation in child protection', in Christopher Cloke and Murray Davies (eds) *Participation and Empowerment in Child Protection* (London, Pitman), 154–69.

Katz, Ilan (1995b) 'Anti-racism and modernism', in Margaret Yelloly and Mary Henkel (eds) *Learning and Teaching in Social Work: Towards Reflective Practice* (London, Jessica Kingsley), 120–35.

Keefe, Thomas (1986) 'Meditation and social work treatment', in Francis J. Turner (ed.) *Social Work Treatment: Interlocking Theoretical Approaches,* 3rd edn (New York, Free Press).

Keenan, Colin (1991) 'Working within the life-space', in Joyce Lishman (ed.) *Handbook of Theory for Practice Teachers in Social Work* (London, Jessica Kingsley), 220–32.

Kelley, Patricia (1994) 'Integrating systemic and postsystemic approaches to social work practice with refugee families', *Families in Society* **75**:541–9.

Kemshall, Hazel (1986) *Defining Clients' Needs in Social Work* (Norwich, Norfolk, Social Work Monographs).

Kennard, David (1983) *An Introduction to Therapeutic Communities* (London, Routledge & Kegan Paul).

Kettner, Peter M. (1975) 'A framework for comparing practice models', *Social Service Review* **49**(4):629–42.

Khandwalla, Pradip N. (ed.) (1988) *Social Development: a New Role for the Organizational Sciences* (New Delhi, Sage).

Kieffer, Charles H. (1984) 'Citizen empowerment: a developmental perspective', *Prevention in Human Services* **3**(1):9–36.

Kim, Yoon-Ock (1995) 'Cultural pluralism and Asian-Americans: culturally sensitive social work practice', *International Social Work* **38**(1):69–78.

Klein, Melanie (1959) 'Our adult world and its roots in infancy', in Hannah Segal (ed.) (1988) *Envy and Gratitude* (London, Virago).

Ko, Eva Li (1987) 'The re-emerging structure of the Chinese family – its role in peace-making', in Yoko Kojima and Tetsuya Hosaka (eds) *Peace and Social Work Education: Developing Human Relations and Social Structures for Peace* (Vienna, International Association of Schools of Social Work), 92–9.

Kohut, Heinz (1978) *The Search for the Self: Selected Writings of Heinz Kohut: 1950–1978,* 2 vols (New York, International Universities Press).

Kolevson, Michael S. and Jacqueline Maykranz (1982) 'Theoretical orientation and clinical practice: uniformity versus eclecticism?', *Social Service Review* **58**(1):120–9.

Kondrat, Mary Ellen (1995) 'Concept, act, and interest in professional practice: implications of an empowerment perspective', *Social Service Review* **69**(3):405–28.

Krill, Donald F. (1969) 'Existential psychotherapy and the problem of anomie', *Social Work* **14**(2):33–49.

Krill, Donald F. (1978) *Existential Social Work* (New York, Free Press).

Krill, Donald F. (1990) *Practice Wisdom: a Guide for Helping Professionals* (Newbury Park, CA, Sage).

Kuhn, Thomas S. (1970) *The Structure of Scientific Revolutions* (Chicago, University of Chicago Press).

Kumar, Hajira (1994) *Social Work: an Experience and Experiment in India* (New Delhi, Gitanjali).

Kurtz, P. David and Eldon K. Marshall (1982) 'Evolution of interpersonal skills training', in E. K. Marshall, P. D. Kurtz *et al., Interpersonal Helping Skills* (San Francisco, Jossey-Bass).

Lacan, Jacques (1979) *The Four Fundamental Concepts of Psychoanalysis* (Harmondsworth, Middlesex, Penguin).

Laczko, Frank and Chris Phillipson (1991) *Changing Work and Retirement* (Buckingham, Open University Press).

Laing, Ronald D. (1965) *The Divided Self: an Existential Study in Sanity and Madness* (Harmondsworth, Middlesex, Penguin).

Laing, Ronald D. (1971) *Self and Others,* 2nd edn (Harmondsworth, Middlesex, Penguin).

Laird, Joan (1995) 'Family-centered practice in the post-modern era', *Families in Society* **76**(3):150–62.

Lane, Helen J. (1984) 'Self-differentiation in symbolic interactionism and psychoanalysis', *Social Work* **29**(3):270–4.

Langan, Mary and Lesley Day (eds) (1992) *Women, Oppression and Social Work: Issues in Anti-discriminatory Practice* (London, Routledge).

Langan, Mary and Phil Lee (eds) (1989) *Radical Social Work Today* (London, Unwin Hyman).

Lantz, Jim (1987) 'The use of Frankl's concepts in family therapy', *Journal of Independent Social Work* **2**(2):65–80.

Lantz, Jim and Richard Greenlee (1990) 'Existential social work with Vietnam veterans', *Journal of Independent Social Work* **5**(1):39–52.

Lappin, Ben (1985) 'Community development: beginnings in social work enabling', in Samuel H. Taylor and Robert W. Roberts (eds) (1985) *Theory and Practice of Community Social Work* (New York, Columbia University Press), 59–94.

Lee, Phil and David Pithers (1980) 'Radical residential child care: Trojan horse or non-runner?', in Mike Brake and Roy Bailey (eds) *Radical Social Work and Practice* (London, Edward Arnold).

Leighninger, Robert D. (1978) 'Systems theory', *Journal of Sociology and Social Welfare* **5**:446–66.

Lemert, Edwin (1972) *Human Deviance, Social Problems and Social Control,* 2nd edn (Englewood Cliffs, NJ, Prentice-Hall).

Lennox, Daphne (1982) *Residential Group Therapy with Children* (London, Tavistock).

Leonard, Peter (1975) 'Towards a paradigm for radical practice', in Roy Bailey and Mike Brake (eds) *Radical Social Work* (London, Edward Arnold).

Leonard, Peter (1984) *Personality and Ideology: Towards a Materialist Understanding of the Individual* (London, Macmillan).

LeSueur, Edwin (1970) 'Aboriginal assimilation: an evaluation of some ambiguities in policy and services', *Australian Journal of Social Work* **23**(2):6–11.

Levy, Allan and Barbara Kahan (1991) *The Pindown Experience and the Protection of Children: the Report of the Staffordshire Child Care Inquiry* (Stafford, Staffordshire County Council).

Levy, Charles S. (1981) 'Labeling: the social worker's responsibility', *Social Casework* **62**(6):332–42.

Lewin, Kurt (1951) *Field Theory in Social Science* (New York, Harper).

Liberman, R. P., L. W. Wing, W. J. Derisi and M. McCann (1975) *Personal Effectiveness: Guiding People to Assert Themselves and Improve their Social Skills* (Champaign, IL, Research Press).

Lindemann, Erich (1944) 'Symptomatology and management of acute grief', in Howard J. Parad (ed.) (1965) *Crisis Intervention: Selected Readings* (New York, Family Service Association of America).

Lishman, Joyce (ed.) (1991) *Handbook of Theory for Practice Teachers in Social Work* (London, Jessica Kingsley).

Lishman, Joyce (1994) *Communication in Social Work* (London, Macmillan).

Loewenberg, Frank M. (1984) 'Professional ideology, middle range theories and knowledge building for social work practice', *British Journal of Social Work* 14(4):309–22.

Loney, Martin (1983) *Community Against Government: the British Community Development Project 1968–1978: a Study of Government Incompetence* (London, Heinemann).

Longres, John F. and Eileen McCleod (1980) 'Consciousness raising and social work practice', *Social Casework* 61(5):267–76.

Lorenz, Walter (1994) *Social Work in a Changing Europe* (London, Routledge).

Lowenstein, Sophie (1985) 'Freud's metapsychology revisited', *Social Casework* 66(3):139–51.

Lukton, Rosemary Creed (1982) 'Myths and realities of crisis intervention', *Social Casework* 63(5):276–85.

Lum, Doman (1982) 'Toward a framework for social work practice with minorities', *Social Work* 27(3):244–9.

Lusk, Mark W. (1981) 'Philosophical changes in Latin American social work', *International Social Work* 24(2):14–21.

Lusk, Mark W. and Marie D. Hoff (1994) 'Sustainable social development', *Social Development Issues* 16(3):20–31.

Lyon, Kate (1993) 'Why study roles and relationships?', in Jan Walmsley, Jill Reynolds, Pam Shakespeare and Ray Woolfe (eds) *Health Welfare and Practice: Reflecting on Roles and Relationships* (London, Sage), 231–9.

MacDonald, Geraldine and Brian Sheldon with Jane Gillespie (1992) 'Contemporary studies of the effectiveness of social work', *British Journal of Social Work* 22(6):615–43.

MacLean, Mary (1986) 'The neurolinguistic programming model', in Francis J. Turner (ed.) *Social Work Treatment: Interlocking Theoretical Approaches* (New York, Free Press).

McAuley, Pat, Mary Louise Catherwood and Ethel Quayle (1988) 'Behavioural-cognitive groups for adult psychiatric patients: a pilot study', *British Journal of Social Work* 18(5):455–71.

McAuley, Roger and Patricia McAuley (1980) 'The effectiveness of behaviour modification with families', *British Journal of Social Work* 10(1):43–54.

McCleod, Eileen (1979) 'Working with prostitutes: probation officers' aims and strategies', *British Journal of Social Work* 9(4):453–70 .

McCleod, Eileen and Lena Dominelli (1982) 'The personal and the apolitical: feminism and moving beyond the integrated methods approach', in Roy Bailey and Phil Lee (eds) *Theory and Practice in Social Work* (Oxford, Basil Blackwell), 112–27.

McCouat, Malcolm (1969) 'Some implications of object relations theory for casework', *Australian Journal of Social Work* 22(3):34–42.

McIntyre, Deborah (1982) 'On the possibility of "radical" casework: a "radical" dissent', *Contemporary Social Work Education* 5(3):191–208.

McNay, Marie (1992) 'Social work can improve relations: towards a framework for an integrated practice', in Mary Langan and Lesley Day (eds) *Women, Opression and Social Work: Issues in Anti-discriminatory Practice* (London, Routledge), 48–66.

Maguire, Lambert (1991) *Social Support Systems in Practice* (Silver Spring, MD, NASW Press).

Maluccio, Anthony N. (ed.) (1981a) *Promoting Competence in Clients: a New/Old Approach to Social Work Practice* (New York, Free Press).

Maluccio, Anthony N. (1981b) 'Competence-oriented social work practice: an ecological approach', in Anthony N. Maluccio (ed.) *Promoting Competence in Clients: A New/Old Approach to Social Work Practice* (New York, Free Press), 1–26.

Mancoske, Ronald (1981) 'Sociological perspectives on the ecological model', *Journal of Sociology and Social Welfare* 8(4):710–32.

Manning, Nick (1989) *The Therapeutic Community Movement: Charisma and Routinisation* (London, Routledge).

Mararike, Claude G. (1995) *Grassroots Leadership: the Process of Rural Development in Zimbabwe* (Harare, University of Zimbabwe).

Marcus, Grace F. (1935) 'The status of social case work today', in Fern Lowry (ed.) (1939) *Readings in Social Case Work, 1920–1938: Selected Reprints for the Case Work Practitioner* (New York, Columbia University Press), 611–19.

Marsh, Peter (1991) 'Task-centred practice', in Joyce Lishman (ed.) *Handbook of Theory for Practice Teachers in Social Work* (London, Jessica Kingsley).

Martin, Ruth R. (1995) *Oral History in Social Work: Research, Assessment, and Intervention* (Thousand Oaks, CA, Sage).

Maslow, Abraham (1970) *Motivation and Personality*, 2nd edn (New York, Harper & Row).

Mattaini, Mark A. (1993) 'Behavior analysis and community practice: a review', *Research on Social Work Practice* 3(4):420–47.

Mead, George Herbert (1934) *Mind, Self and Society* (Chicago, University of Chicago Press).

Meichenbaum, D. (1977) *Cognitive Behaviour Modification: an Integrative Approach* (New York, Plenum).

Meichenbaum, D. (1985) *Stress Inoculation Training* (New York, Pergamon).

Menzies-Lyth, Isabel (1988) *Containing Anxiety in Institutions* (London, Free Association).

Messkoub, Mahmood (1992) 'Deprivation and structural adjustment', in Marc Wuyts, Maureen Mackintosh and Tom Hewitt (eds) *Development Policy and Public Action* (Oxford, Oxford University Press), 175–98.

Meyer, Carol H. (ed.) (1983) *Clinical Social Work in the Eco-Systems Perspective* (New York, Columbia University Press).

Midgley, James (1981) *Professional Imperialism: Social Work in the Third World* (London, Heinemann).

Midgley, James (1984) 'Social welfare implications of development paradigms', *Social Service Review* 58(2):182–98.

Bibliography

323

Midgley, James (1987) 'Popular participation, statism and development', *Journal of Social Development in Africa* 2(1):5–15.

Midgley, James (1989) 'Social work in the Third World: crisis and response', in Pam Carter, Tony Jeffs and Mark Smith (eds) *Social Work and Social Welfare Yearbook 1, 1989* (Milton Keynes, Open University Press), 33–45.

Midgley, James (1993) 'Ideological roots of social development strategies', *Social Development Issues* 15(1):1–13.

Midgley, James (1995) *Social Development: the Developmental Perspective in Social Welfare* (London, Sage).

Midgley, James and Paul Sanzenbach (1989) 'Social work, religion and the global challenge of fundamentalism', *International Social Work* 32(4):273–88.

Milligan, Don (1975) 'Homosexuality: sexual needs and social problems', in Roy Bailey and Mike Brake (eds) *Radical Social Work* (London, Edward Arnold).

Miri, Sujata (1993) *Communalism in Assam: a Civilisational Approach* (New Delhi, Har-Anand).

Mitchell, Juliet (1975) *Psychoanalysis and Feminism* (Harmondsworth, Middlesex, Penguin).

Mondros, Jacqueline B. and Scott M. Wilson (1994) *Organizing for Power and Empowerment* (New York, Columbia University Press).

Moore, Edith E. (1976) 'Eclecticism and social work practice', *Social Worker* 44(1):23–8.

Mor-Barak, Michal E. (1988) 'Support systems intervention in crisis situations: theory, strategies and a case discussion', *International Social Work* 31(4):285–304.

Moreau, Maurice J. (1979) 'A structural approach to social work practice', *Canadian Journal of Social Work Education* 5(1):78–94.

Moreau, Maurice J. (1990) 'Empowerment through advocacy and consciousness-raising: implications of a structural approach to social work', *Journal of Sociology and Social Welfare* 17(2):53–68.

Morén, Stefan (1994) 'Social work is beautiful: on the characteristics of social work', *Scandinavian Journal of Social Welfare* 3(3):158–66.

Morgan, Roger T. T. and Gordon C. Young (1972) 'The conditioning treatment of childhood enuresis', *British Journal of Social Work* 2(4):503–10.

Morris, Jenny (1993) *Disabled Lives: Community Care and Disabled People* (London, Macmillan).

Moyana, Toby Tafirenyika (1989) *Education, Liberation and the Creative Act* (Harare, Zimbabwe Publishing House).

Mullally, Robert P. (1993) *Structural Social Work: Ideology, Theory and Practice* (Toronto, McClelland and Stewart).

Mullard, Chris (1991) 'Towards a model of anti-racist social work', in CCETSW *One Small Step Towards Racial Justice: the Teaching of Antiracism in Diploma in Social Work Programmes* (London, CCETSW), 10–19.

Mullen, Edward J. and James R. Dumpson *et al.* (1972) *Evaluation of Social Intervention* (San Francisco, Jossey-Bass).

Mullender, Audrey and Dave Ward (1991) *Self-Directed Groupwork: Users Take Action for Empowerment* (London, Whiting and Birch).

Mulwa, Francis W. (1988) 'Participation of the grassroots in rural development: the case of the Development Education Programme of the Catholic
Dioceses of Machakos, Kenya', *Journal of Social Development in Africa*
3(2):49–65.

Munson, Carlton E. and Pallassana Balgopal (1978) 'The worker/client relationship: relevant role theory', *Journal of Sociology and Social Welfare*
5(3):404–17.

Muzaale, Patrick John (1988) 'The organisation and delivery of social
services to rural areas', *Journal of Social Development in Africa* 3(2):
33–48.

Muzumdar, Amma Menon (1964) *Social Welfare in India: Mahatma
Gandhi's Contributions* (London, Asia Publishing House).

Mwansa, Lengwe-Katembula (1995) 'Participation of non-governmental
organisations in social development process in Africa: implications',
Journal of Social Development in Africa 10(1):65–75.

Nagpaul, Hans (1972) 'The diffusion of American social work education to
India: problems and issues', *International Social Work* 15(1):3–17.

Naik, Don (1991) 'Towards an antiracist curriculum in social work training',
in CCETSW *One Small Step Towards Racial Justice: the Teaching of
Antiracism in Diploma in Social Work Programmes* (London, CCETSW),
50–7.

Nanavatty, Meher C. (1981) 'Rural development and social work', *Indian
Journal of Social Work* 42(3):265–72.

Narayan, Uma (1994) 'Working together across differences', in Beulah
R. Compton and Burt Galaway *Social Work Processes* (Pacific Grove, CA,
Brooks/Cole), 177–88.

Nartsupha, Chatthip (1991) 'The community culture school of thought', in
Manas Chitakasem and Andrew Turton (eds) *Thai Constructions of Knowl-
edge* (London, School of Oriental and African Studies, University of
London).

Neary, M (1992) 'Some academic freedom', *Probation Journal* 39(8):200–2.

Neill, A. S. (1964) *Summerhill* (London, Victor Gollancz).

Neimeyer, Greg J. and Neimeyer, Robert A. (1993) 'Defining the boundaries
of constructivist assessment', in Greg J. Neimeyer (ed.) *Constructivist
Assessment: a Casebook* (Newbury Park, CA, Sage), 1–30.

Neimeyer, Robert A. (1993) 'Approaches to the measurement of meaning', in
Greg J. Neimeyer (ed.) *Constructivist Assessment: a Casebook* (Newbury
Park, CA, Sage), 58–103.

Nelsen, Judith C. (1980) *Communication Theory and Social Work Practice*
(Chicago, University of Chicago Press).

Nelsen, Judith C. (1986) 'Communication theory and social work treatment',
in Francis J. Turner (ed.) *Social Work Treatment: Interlocking Theoretical
Approaches* (New York, Free Press).

Nelsen, Judith C. (1990) 'Single-case research and traditional practice: issues
and possibilities', in Lynn Videka-Sherman and William J. Reid (eds)
Advances in Clinical Social Work Research (Silver Spring, MD, NASW
Press), 37–47.

Nkunika, Adam I. Z. (1987) 'The role of popular participation in programmes
of social development', *Journal of Social Development in Africa*
2(1):17–28.

Norman, Alison (1985) *Triple Jeopardy: Growing Old in a Second Homeland* (London, Centre for Policy on Ageing).

Norton, Dolores G. (1978) *The Dual Perspective: Inclusion of Ethnic Minority Content in the Social Work Curriculum* (Washington, DC, Council on Social Work Education).

Ntebe, Ann (1994) 'Effective intervention roles of South African social workers in an appropriate, relevant and progressive social welfare model', *Journal of Social Development in Africa* 9(1):41–50.

Nuttall, Kathryn (1985) *The Place of Family Therapy in Social Work* (Norwich, Norfolk, Social Work Monographs).

O'Brien, Daniel and Jacqueline Pace (1988) 'The role of social work development theory in informing social work degree programs for indigenous native people: a critique of the Canadian experience', in Charles Guzzetta and Florence Mittwoch (eds) *Social Development and Social Rights* (Vienna, International Association of Schools of Social Work), 89–99.

O'Connor, Ian and Len Dalgleish (1986) 'Cautionary tales about beginning practitioners: the fate of personal models of social work in beginning practice', *British Journal of Social Work* 16(4):431–47.

O'Connor, Margaret (1992) 'An Adlerian approach to casework in a hospital setting', *The Social Worker* 60(2):121–2.

O'Hagan, Kieran (1986) *Crisis Intervention in Social Services* (London, Macmillan).

O'Hagan, Kieran (1991) 'Crisis intervention in social work', in Joyce Lishman (ed.) *Handbook of Theory for Practice Teachers in Social Work* (London, Jessica Kingsley), 138–56.

O'Hagan, Kieran (1994) 'Crisis intervention: changing perspectives', in Christopher Hanvey and Terry Philpot (eds) *Practising Social Work* (London, Routledge), 134–45.

Ohri, Ashok, Basil Manning and Paul Curno (1982) *Community Work and Racism* (London, Routledge & Kegan Paul).

Oliver, Michael (1990) *The Politics of Disablement* (London, Macmillan).

Oliver, Michael (1996) *Understanding Disability: From Theory to Practice* (London, Macmillan).

Olsen, M. Rolf (ed.) (1978) *The Unitary Model: Its Implications for Social Work Theory and Practice* (Birmingham, BASW Publications).

Olssen, Eric (1993) ' "Naiv teori" i socialt behandlingsarbete', *Nordisk Socialt Arbete* 2(1):3–17.

Onokerkoraye, Andrew G. (1984) *Social Services in Nigeria: an Introduction* (London, Kegan Paul International).

Osei-Hwedie, Kwaku (1990) 'Social work and the question of social development in Africa', *Journal of Social Development in Africa* 5(2):87–99.

Osei-Hwedie, Kwaku (1993) 'The challenge of social work in Africa: starting the indigenisation process', *Journal of Social Development in Africa* 8(1):19–30.

Owusu-Bempah, J. (1994) 'Race, self-identity and social work', *British Journal of Social Work* 24(2):123–36.

Paiva, J. F. X. (1977) 'A conception of social development', *Social Service Review* 51(2):327–36.

Paiva, J. F. X. (1993) 'Excuse me, I wish to be unboxed...', *Social Development Issues* 15(1):22–3.

Pandey, Rama S. (1981) 'Strategies for social development: an analytical approach', in John F. Jones and Rama S. Pandey (eds) *Social Develpment: Conceptual, Methodological and Policy Issues* (Dehli, Macmillan India), 33–49.

Papell, Catherine P. and Beulah Rothman (1966) 'Social group work models: possession and heritage', *Journal of Education for Social Work* 2(2):66–73.

Parad, Howard J. (1958) *Ego Psychology and Dynamic Casework* (New York, Family Service Association of America).

Parad, Howard J. (ed.) (1965a) *Crisis Intervention: Selected Readings* (New York, Family Service Association of America).

Parad, Howard J. (1965b) 'Introduction', in Howard J. Parad (ed.) *Crisis Intervention: Selected Readings* (New York, Family Service Association of America).

Parad, Howard J. and Roger Miller (1963) *Ego-oriented Casework: Problems and Perspectives* (New York, Family Service Association of America).

Parad, Howard J. and Libbie G. Parad (1990a) *Crisis Intervention Book 2: the Practitioner's Sourcebook for Brief Therapy* (Milwaukee, WI, Family Service America).

Parad, Howard J. and Libbie G. Parad (1990b) 'Crisis intervention: an introductory overview', in Howard J. Parad and Libbie G. Parad *Crisis Intervention Book 2: the Practitioner's Sourcebook for Brief Therapy* (Milwaukee, WI, Family Service America).

Pardeck, John T., John W. Murphy and Woo Sik Chung (1994) 'Social work and postmodernism', *Social Work and Social Sciences Review* 5(2):113–23.

Parkes, Colin Murray (1972) *Bereavement: Studies of Grief in Adult Life* (Harmondsworth, Middlesex, Penguin).

Parton, Nigel (1994) 'The nature of social work under conditions of (post) modernity', *Social Work and Social Sciences Review* 5(2):93–112.

Parton, Nigel (ed.) (1996) *Social Theory, Social Change and Social Work* (London, Routledge).

Patel, Diana (1988) 'Some issues of urbanisation and development in Zimbabwe', *Journal of Social Development in Africa* 3(2):17–31.

Patel, Naina (1994) 'Establishing a framework for anti-racist social work education in a multi-racial society – the UK experience from a statutory body, CCETSW', in Lena Dominelli, Naina Patel and Wanda Thomas Bernard *Anti-Racist Social Work Education: Models for Practice* (Sheffield, University of Sheffield Department of Sociological Studies), 7–21.

Patterson, C. H. (1986) *Theories of Counselling and Psychotherapy*, 4th edn (New York, Harper and Row).

Payne, Chris (1977) 'Residential social work', in Harry Specht and Anne Vickery (eds) *Integrating Social Work Methods* (London, Allen & Unwin), 195–216.

Payne, Chris (1994) 'The systems approach', in Christopher Hanvey and Terry Philpot (eds) *Practising Social Work* (London, Routledge).

Payne, Malcolm (1986) *Social Care in the Community* (London, Macmillan).

Payne, Malcolm (1988) 'How can we hear the community voice? Responding to community participation at consumer feedback' *Practice* 2(1):74–84.

Payne, Malcolm (1992) 'Psychodynamic theory within the politics of social work theory', *Journal of Social Work Practice* **6**(2):141–9.

Payne, Malcolm (1993) Routes to and through clienthood and their implications for practice', *Practice* **6**(3):169–80.

Payne, Malcolm (1995) *Social Work and Community Care* (London, Macmillan).

Payne, Malcolm (1996a) *What is Professional Social Work?* (Birmingham, Venture).

Payne, Malcolm (1996b) 'The politics of social work theory and values', in IASSW (ed.) *Proceedings of the 27th Congress* (Hong Kong, IASSW).

Pearson, Geoffrey (1975) *The Deviant Imagination: Psychiatry, Social Work and Social Change* (London, Macmillan).

Pearson, Geoffrey, Judith Treseder and Margaret Yelloly (eds) (1988) *Social Work and the Legacy of Freud* (London, Macmillan).

Pepper, David (1991) *Communes and the Green Vision: Counterculture, Lifestyle and the New Age* (London, Green Print).

Perlman, Helen Harris (1957a) *Social Casework: a Problem-Solving Process* (Chicago, University of Chicago Press).

Perlman, Helen Harris (1957b) 'Freud's contribution to social welfare', *Social Service Review* **31**(2):192–202.

Perlman, Helen Harris (1968) *Persona: social role and personality* (Chicago, University of Chicago Press).

Perlman, Helen Harris (1970) 'The problem-solving model in social casework', in Robert W. Roberts and Robert H. Nee (eds) *Theories of Social Casework* (Chicago, University of Chicago Press).

Perlman, Helen Harris (1979) *Relationship: the Heart of Helping People* (Chicago, University of Chicago Press).

Perlman, Helen Harris (1986) 'The problem-solving model', in Francis J. Turner (ed.) *Social Work Treatment: Interlocking Theoretical Approaches,* 3rd edn (New York, Free Press).

Perls, Frederick, Ralph F. Hefferline and Paul Goodman (1973) *Gestalt Therapy: Excitement and Growth in the Human Personality* (Harmondsworth, Middlesex, Penguin) (original American edition, 1951).

Pernell, Ruby B. (1985) 'Empowerment and social group work', in Marvin Parnes (ed.) *Innovations in Social Group Work: Feedback from Practice to Theory* (New York, Haworth), 107–17.

Phillips, David R. and Yola Verhasselt (eds) (1994) *Health and Development* (London, Routledge).

Phillips, Helen U. (1957) *Essentials of Social Group Work Skill* (New York, Association Press).

Phillipson, Chris (1982) *Capitalism and the Construction of Old Age* (London, Macmillan).

Philp, Mark (1979) 'Notes on the form of knowledge in social work', *Sociological Review* **27**(1):83–111.

Philpot, Terry (ed.) (1986) *Social Work: a Christian perspective* (Tring, Herts, Lion Publishing).

Pilalis, Jennie (1986) '"The integration of theory and practice": a re-examination of a paradoxical expectation', *British Journal of Social Work* **16**(1):79–96.

Pincus, Allen and Anne Minahan (1973) *Social Work Practice: Model and Method* (Itasca, IL, Peacock).

Pincus, Lily (1976) *Death and the Family* (London, Faber & Faber).

Pinderhughes, Elaine B. (1983) 'Empowerment for our clients and ourselves', *Social Casework* **64**(6):331–8.

Pinderhughes, Elaine B. (1988) 'Significance of culture and power in the human behavior curriculum', in Carolyn Jacobs and Dorcas D. Bowles (eds) *Ethnicity and Race: Critical Concepts in Social Work* (Silver Spring, MD, National Association of Social Workers), 152–66.

Pinderhughes, Elaine B. (1989) *Understanding Race, Ethnicity and Power: the Key to Efficacy in Clinical Practice* (New York, Free Press).

Pinderhughes, Elaine B. (1995) 'Empowering diverse populations: family practice in the 21st century', *Families in Society* **76**(3):131–40.

Pithouse, Andrew (1987) *Social Work: the Social Organisation of an Invisible Trade* (Aldershot, Hants, Gower).

Pitman, Elizabeth (1982) 'Transactional analysis: an introduction to its theory and practice', *British Journal of Social Work* **12**(1):47–64.

Pitman, Elizabeth (1983) *Transactional Analysis for Social Workers* (London, Routledge & Kegan Paul).

Pitts, John (1992) 'The end of an era', *Howard Journal of Criminal Justice* **31**(2):133–49.

Piven, Frances and Richard O. Cloward (1977) *Poor People's Movements: Why They Succeed, How They Fail* (New York, Vintage).

Pizzat, Frank J. (1973) *Behaviour Modification in Residential Treatment for Children: Model of a Program* (New York, Behavioral Publications).

Poertner, John (1994) 'Popular education in Latin America: a technology for the North?', *International Social Work* **37**(3):265–76.

Pollio, David E. (1995) 'Use of humor in crisis intervention', *Families in Society* **76**(6):376–84.

Polsky, Howard (1968) *Cottage Six: the Social System of Delinquent Boys in Residential Treatment* (Chapel Hill, NC, University of North Carolina Press).

Popple, Keith (1995) *Analysing Community Work: Its Theory and Practice* (Buckingham, Open University Press).

Preston-Shoot, Michael and Dick Agass (1990) *Making Sense of Social Work: Psychodynamics, Systems and Sense* (London, Macmillan).

Pringle, Keith (1995) *Men, Masculinities and Social Welfare* (London, UCL Press).

Pugh, Richard (1996) *Effective Language in Health and Social Work* (London, Chapman & Hall).

Ramon, Shulamit (1989) 'The value and knowledge bases of the normalization approach: implications for social work', *International Social Work* **32**(1):11–23.

Ramon, Shulamit (1990) 'The relevance of symbolic interaction perspectives to the conception and practice construction of leaving a psychiatric hospital', *Social Work and Social Sciences Review* **1**(3):163–76.

Ramon, Shulamit (ed.) (1991) *Beyond Community Care: Normalisation and Integration Work* (London, Macmillan).

Ramon, Shulamit and Maria Grazia Giannichedda (eds) (1988) *Psychiatry in Transition: the British and Italian Experiences* (London, Pluto Press).

Raynor, Peter and Maurice Vanstone (1994) 'Probation practice, effectiveness and the non-treatment paradigm', *Britsh Journal of Social Work* **24**(4):387–404.

Raynor, Peter, David Smith and Maurice Vanstone (1994) *Effective Probation Practice* (London, Macmillan).

Redl, Fritz (1959) 'Strategy and techniques of the life space interview', *American Journal of Orthopsychiatry* **29**:1–18.

Rees, Stuart (1991) *Achieving Power* (Sydney, Allen & Unwin).

Reid, William J. (1978) *The Task-Centered System* (New York, Columbia University Press).

Reid, William J. (1985) *Family Problem-solving* (New York, Columbia University Press).

Reid, William J. (1990) 'An integrative model for short-term treatment', in R. A. Wells and V. Gianetti (eds) *Handbook of Brief Psychotherapies* (New York, Plenum).

Reid, William J. (1992) *Task Strategies: an Empirical Approach to Clinical Social Work* (New York, Columbia University Press).

Reid, William J. (1994) 'The empirical practice movement', *Social Service Review* **68**(2):165–84.

Reid, William J. and Ann W. Shyne (1969) *Brief and Extended Casework* (New York, Columbia University Press).

Reid, William J. and Laura Epstein (1972a) *Task-centered Casework* (New York, Columbia University Press).

Reid, William J. and Laura Epstein (eds) (1972b) *Task-centered Practice* (New York, Columbia University Press).

Reid, William J. and Patricia Hanrahan (1982) 'Recent evaluations of social work: grounds for optimism', *Social Work* **27**:328–40.

Rein, Martin and Sheldon H. White (1981) 'Knowledge for practice', *Social Service Review* **55**(1):1–41.

Resnick, Rosa Perla (1976) 'Conscientization: an indigenous approach to international social work', *International Social Work* **19**(1):21–9.

Rex, John and David Mason (eds) (1986) *Theories of Race and Ethnic Relations* (Cambridge, Cambridge University Press).

Reynolds, Jill (1993) 'Feminist theory and strategy in social work', in Jan Walmsley, Jill Reynolds, Pam Shakespeare and Ray Woolfe (eds) *Health Welfare and Practice: Reflecting on Roles and Relationships* (London, Sage).

Rhodes, Margeret L. (1985) 'Gilligan's theory of moral development as applied to social work', *Social Work* **30**(2):101–5.

Richardson, Ann and Jane Ritchie (1989) *Developing Friendships: Enabling People with Learning Difficulties to Make and Maintain Friends* (London, Policy Studies Institute).

Richmond, Mary (1917) *Social Diagnosis* (New York, Free Press).

Righton, Peter (1975) 'Planned environment therapy: a reappraisal', *Association of Workers with Maladjusted Children Journal*, Spring 1975; reprinted in Peter Righton (ed.) *Studies in Environment Therapy*, vol. 3 (Toddington, Glos, Planned Environment Therapy Trust).

Roan, Sylvia Sui-Feng (1980) 'Utilizing traditional elements in the society in casework practice', *International Social Work* **23**(4):26–35.

Roberts, Albert R. (1990) 'An overview of crisis theory and crisis intervention', in Albert R. Roberts (ed.) *Crisis Intervention Handbook: Assessment, Treatment and Research* (Belmont, CA, Wadsworth), 3–16.

Roberts. Albert R. (1991) *Contemporary Perspectives on Crisis Intervention and Prevention* (Englewood Cliffs, NJ, Prentice-Hall).

Roberts, Albert R. (ed.) (1995) *Crisis Intervention and Time-Limited Cognitive Treatment* (Thousand Oaks, CA, Sage).

Roberts, Albert R. and Sophia P. Dziegielewski (1995) 'Foundation skills and applications of crisis intervention and cognitive therapy', in Albert R. Roberts (ed.) *Crisis Intervention and Time-Limited Cognitive Treatment* (Thousand Oaks, CA, Sage).

Roberts, Richard (1990) *Lessons from the Past: Issues for Social Work Theory* (London, Tavistock/Routledge).

Roberts, Robert W. and Robert H. Nee (eds) (1970) *Theories of Social Casework* (Chicago, University of Chicago Press).

Roberts, Robert W. and Helen Northen (eds) (1976) *Theories of Social Work with Groups* (New York, Columbia University Press).

Robinson, Lena (1995) *Psychology for Social Workers: Black Perspectives* (London, Routledge).

Rodger, John J. (1991) 'Discourse analysis and social relationships in social work', *British Journal of Social Work* 21(1):63–80.

Rogers, Carl R. (1951) *Client-centered Therapy: Its Current Practice, Implications and Theory* (London, Constable).

Rogers, Carl R. (1961) *On Becoming a Person: a Therapist's View of Psychotherapy* (London, Constable).

Rogers, Carl R. (1977) *Carl Rogers on Personal Power* (London, Constable).

Rogers, Carl R. and Mary Strauss (1967) *Person to Person: the Problem of Being Human* (London, Souvenir Press).

Rojek, Chris (1986) 'The "Subject" in social work.' *British Journal of Social Work* 16(1):65–77.

Rojek, Chris and Stewart Collins (1987) 'Contract or con trick?', *British Journal of Social Work* 17(2):199–211.

Rojek, Chris, and Stewart Collins (1988) 'Contract or con trick revisited: comments on the reply by Corden and Preston-Shoot', *British Journal of Social Work* 18(6):611–22.

Rojek, Chris, Geraldine Peacock and Stewart Collins (1989) *Social Work and Received Ideas* (London, Routledge).

Ronen, Tammie (1994) 'Cognitive-behavioural social work with children', *British Journal of Social Work* 24(3):273–85.

Ronnby, Alf (1992) 'Praxiology in social work', *International Social Work* 35(3):317–26.

Rooney, Ronald H. (1992) *Strategies for Work with Involuntary Clients* (New York, Columbia University Press).

Rose, Melvyn (1992) 'The design of atmosphere: ego nurture and psychic change in residential treatment', *Residential Treatment for Children and Youth* 10(1):5–23.

Rose, Sheldon (1991) 'Cognitive behavioural modification in groups', *International Journal of Behavioural Social Work and Abstracts* 1(1):27–38.

Rose, Stephen M. (1990) 'Advocacy/empowerment: an approach to clinical practice for social work', *Journal of Sociology and Social Welfare* **17**(2):41–52.

Rose, Stephen M. and Bruce L. Black (1985) *Advocacy and Empowerment: Mental Health Care in the Community* (Boston, Routledge & Kegan Paul).

Rosenfeld, Jona M. (1989) *Emergence from Extreme Poverty* (Paris, Science and Service Fourth World Publications).

Ross, R. R. and E. A. Fabiano (1985) *Time to Think: a Cognitive Model of Delinquency Prevention and Offender Rehabilitation* (Johnson City, Canada, Academy of Arts and Sciences).

Ross, R. R., E. A. Fabiano and C. D. Ewles (1988) 'Reasoning and rehabilitation', *International Journal of Offender Therapy and Comparative Criminology* **32**(1):29–35.

Ross, R. R., E. A. Fabiano and R. Ross (1989) *Reasoning and Rehabilitation: a Handbook for Teaching Cognitive Skills* (Ottawa, The Cognitive Centre).

Rothman, Jack and Mayer N. Zald (1985) ' Planning theory in social work community practice', in Samuel H. Taylor and Robert W. Roberts (eds) *Theory and Practice of Community Social Work* (New York, Columbia University Press), 125–53.

Rowe, William (1986) 'Client-centered therapy'. in Francis J. Turner (ed.) *Social Work Treatment: Interlocking Theoretical Approaches,* 3rd edn (New York, Free Press).

Rubin, Allen (1985) 'Practice effectiveness: more grounds for optimism', *Social Work* **30**:469–76.

Ruckdeschel, Roy A. and Buford E. Farris (1982) 'Science: critical faith or dogmatic ritual?' *Social Casework* **63**(5):272–5.

Ruddock, Ralph (1969) *Roles and Relationships* (London, Routledge & Kegan Paul).

Russel-Erlich, John L. and Felix G. Rivera (1986) 'Community empowerment as a non-problem', *Journal of Sociology and Social Welfare* **13**(3):451–65.

Rutter, Michael (1981) *Maternal Deprivation Reassessed* (Harmondsworth, Middlesex, Penguin).

Ryan, Angela Shen (ed.) (1992) *Social Work with Immigrants and Refugees* (New York, Haworth Press).

Ryan, Peter (1979) 'Residential care for the mentally disabled', in J. K. Wing and Rolf Olsen (eds) *Community Care for the Mentally Disabled* (Oxford, Oxford University Press).

Ryant, Joseph C. (1969) 'The revolutionary potential of social work', *Social Worker* **37**(3):151–6.

Ryder, Eleanor L. (1976) 'A functional approach', in Robert W. Roberts and Helen Northen (eds) *Theories of Social Work with Groups* (New York, Columbia University Press).

Sainsbury, Eric (1987) Client studies: their contribution, and limitations in influencing social work practice', *British Journal of Social Work* **17**(6):633–44.

Saleebey, Dennis (1992) *The Strengths Perspective in Social Work Practice* (New York, Longman).

Saleebey, Dennis (1993) 'Theory and the generation and subversion of knowledge', *Journal of Sociology and Social Welfare* **20**(1):5–26.

Salole, Gerry (1991a) 'Not seeing the wood for the trees: searching for indigenous non-government organisations in the forest of voluntary self-help associations', *Journal of Social Development in Africa* **6**(1):5–17.

Salole, Gerry (1991b) 'Participatory development: the taxation of the beneficiary', *Journal of Social Development in Africa* **6**(2):5–16.

Salzberger-Wittenberg, Isca (1970) *Psychoanalytic Insights and Relationships: a Kleinian Approach* (London, Routledge & Kegan Paul).

Sanders, Daniel S. (1978) 'Multiculturalism: implications for social work', in IFSW *Social Work and the Multi-cultural Society* (Geneva, International Federation of Social Workers), 33–41.

Sanders, Jacquelyn (1993) 'Culture and residential treatment', *Residential Treatment for Children and Youth* **10**(3):337–48.

Satir, Virginia (1964) *Conjoint Family Therapy* (Palo Alto, CA, Science and Behavior Books).

Satir, Virginia (1972) *Peoplemaking* (Palo Alto, CA, Science and Behavior Books).

Satyamurti, Carole (1979) 'Care and control in local authority social work', in Noel Parry, Michael Rustin and Carole Satyamurti (eds) *Social Work, Welfare and the State* (London, Edward Arnold).

Sayers, Janet (1986) *Sexual Contradictions: Psychology, Psychoanalysis and Feminism* (London, Tavistock).

Sayers, Janet (1988) 'Feminism, social work and psychoanalysis', in Geoffrey Pearson, Judith Treseder and Margaret Yelloly (eds) *Social Work and the Legacy of Freud: Psychoanalysis and its Uses* (London, Macmillan).

Scheflen, Albert E. (1972) *Body Language and Social Order* (Englewood Cliffs, NJ, Prentice-Hall).

Scheflen, Albert E. and Norman Ashcraft (1976) *Human Territories: How we Behave in Space–time* (Englewood Cliffs, NJ, Prentice-Hall).

Schenk, Quentin F. and Schenk, Emmy Lou (1987) 'Ethiopia', in John Dixon (ed.) *Social Welfare in Africa* (London, Croom Helm).

Schiele, Jerome H. (1994) 'Afrocentricity as an alternative world view for equality', *Journal of Progressive Human Services* **5**(1):5–25.

Schlesinger, Elfriede G. (1995) *Social Work with Minority and Ethnic Groups*, special edition of *Journal of Sociology and Social Welfare* **22**(1).

Schön, Donald A. (1983) *The Reflective Practitioner: How Professionals Think in Action* (New York, Basic Books).

Scott, Jan J., Mark G. Williams and Aaron T. Beck (1989) *Cognitive Therapy in Clinical Practice: an Illustrative Casebook* (London, Routledge).

Scott, Mike (1989) *A Cognitive-behavioural Approach to Clients' Problems* (London, Tavistock/Routledge).

Scott, Michael J. and Stephen G. Stradling (1991) 'The cognitive-behavioural approach with depressed clients', *British Journal of Social Work* **21**(5):533–44.

Scott, Michael J. and Windy Dryden (1996) 'The cognitive-behavioural paradigm', in Ray Woolfe and Windy Dryden (eds) *Handbook of Counselling Psychology* (London, Sage).

Secker, Jenny (1993) *From Theory to Practice in Social Work: the Development of Social Work Students' Practice* (Aldershot, Hants, Avebury).

Sedgwick, Peter (1972) 'R. D. Laing: self, symptom and society', in Robert Boyers and Robert Orrill (eds) *Laing and Anti-psychiatry* (Harmondsworth, Middlesex, Penguin).

Seebohm Report (1968) *Report of the Committee on Local Authority and Allied Personal Social Services* (Cmnd 3703) (London, HMSO).

Seed, Philip (1990) *Introducing Network Analysis in Social Work* (London, Jessica Kingsley).

Seligman, M. E. P. (1975) *Helplessness: on Depression, Development and Death* (San Francisco, Freeman).

Sefansky, Susan (1990) 'Pediatric critical care social work: interventions with a special plane crash survivor', *Health and Social Work* 15(3):215–20.

Sheldon, Brian (1978) 'Theory and practice in social work: a re-examination of a tenuous relationship', *British Journal of Social Work* 8(1):1–22.

Sheldon, Brian (1982) *Behaviour Modification: Theory, Practice and Philosophy* (London: Tavistock).

Sheldon, Brian (1984) 'Evaluation with one eye closed: the empiricist agenda in social work research – a reply to Peter Raynor', *British Journal of Social Work* 14(6):635–7.

Sheldon, Brian (1986) 'Social work effectiveness experiments: review and implications', *British Journal of Social Work* 16(2):223–42.

Sheldon, Brian (1987) 'Implementing findings from social work effectiveness research', *British Journal of Social Work* 17(6):573–86.

Sheldon, Brian (1995) *Cognitive-behavioural Therapy: Research, Practice and Philosophy* (London, Routledge).

Shemmings, David and Yvonne Shemmings (1995) 'Defining participative practice in health and welfare', in Raymond Jack (ed.) *Empowerment in Community Care* (London, Chapman & Hall), 43–58.

Shulman, Lawrence (1991) *Interactional Social Work Practice: Toward an Empirical Theory* (Itasca, IL, F. E. Peacock).

Sibeon, Roger (1982) 'Theory–practice symbolisations: a critical review of the Hardiker/Davies debate', *Issues in Social Work Education* 2(2):119–47.

Sibeon, Roger (1990) 'Comments on the structure and forms of social work knowledge', *Social Work and Social Sciences Review* 1(1):29–44.

Silavwe, Geoffrey W. (1995) The need for a new social work perspective in an African setting: the case of social casework in Zambia', *British Journal of Social Work* 25(1):71–84.

Simon, Barbra Levy (1995) *The Empowerment Tradition in American Social Work: A History* (New York, Columbia University Press).

Simpkin, Mike (1989) 'Radical social work: lessons for the 1990s', in Pam Carter, Tony Jeffs and Mark Smith (eds) *Social Work and Social Welfare Yearbook 1, 1989* (Milton Keynes, Open University Press), 159–74.

Sinclair, Elma (1988) 'The formal evidence', in National Institute for Social Work *Residential Care: a Positive Choice* (London, HMSO).

Singh, Gurnam (1992) *Race and Social Work from 'Black Pathology' to 'Black Perspectives'* (Bradford, Yorkshire, The Race Relations Research Unit, University of Bradford).

Sinha, Durganand and Henry S. R. Kao (eds) (1988a) *Social Values and Development: Asian Perspectives* (New Delhi, Sage).

Sinha, Durganand and Henry S. R. Kao (1988b) 'Introduction: values– development congruence', in Durganand Sinha and Henry S. R. Kao (eds) *Social Values and Development: Asian Perspectives* (New Delhi, Sage).

Siporin, Max (1975) *Introduction to Social Work Practice* (New York, Macmillan).

Siporin, Max (1980) 'Ecological systems theory in social work', *Journal of Sociology and Social Welfare* 7(4):507–32.

Sivanandan, A. (1991) 'Black struggles against racism', in CD Project Steering Group *Setting the Context for Change* (London, CCETSW), 28–45.

Skeith, Paul (1992) 'Liberation theology and social development', in Richard J. Estes (ed.) *Internationalizing Social Work Education: a Guide to Resources for a New Century* (Philadelphia, PA, University of Pennsylvania School of Social Work), 262–6.

Skenridge, P. and I. Lennie (1971) 'Social work: the wolf in sheep's clothing', *Arena* 5(1).

Small, John (1989) 'Towards a black perspective in social work: a transcultural exploration', in Mary Langan and Phil Lee (eds) *Radical Social Work Today* (London, Unwin Hyman), 279–91.

Small, Neil (1987) 'Putting violence to social workers into context', *Critical Social Policy* 19:40–5.

Smalley, Ruth E. (1967) *Theory for Social Work Practice* (New York, Columbia University Press).

Smalley, Ruth E. (1970) 'The functional approach to casework practice', in Robert W. Roberts and Robert H. Nee (eds) *Theories of Social Casework* (Chicago, University of Chicago Press).

Smid, Gerhard and Robert van Krieken (1984) 'Notes on theory and practice in social work: a comparative view', *British Journal of Social Work* 14(1):11–22.

Smith, Carole R. (1975) 'Bereavement: the contribution of phenomenological and existential analysis to a greater understanding of the problem', *British Journal of Social Work* 5(1):75–94.

Smith, Carole R. (1982) *Social Work with the Dying and Bereaved* (London, Macmillan).

Smith, David (1987) 'The limits of positivism in social work research', *British Journal of Social Work* 17(4):401–16.

Smith, Gilbert (1980) *Social Need: Policy, Practice and Research* (London, Routledge & Kegan Paul).

Smith, Leo and David Jones (eds) (1981) *Deprivation, Participation and Community Action* (London, Routledge & Kegan Paul).

Solomon, Barbara Bryant (1976) *Black Empowerment: Social Work in Oppressed Communities* (New York, Columbia University Press).

Solomon, Barbara Bryant (1985) 'Community social work practice in oppressed minority communities', in Samuel H. Taylor and Robert W. Roberts (eds) *Theory and Practice of Community Social Work* (New York, Columbia University Press), 217–57.

Solomos, John (1993) *Race and Racism in Britain,* 2nd edn (London, Macmillan).

Specht, Harry (1986) 'Social support, social networks, social exchange and social work practice', *Social Service Review* 60(2):218–40.

Specht, Harry and Riva Specht (1986a) 'Social work assessment: the route to clienthood – part 1', *Social Casework* 67(9):525–32.

Specht, Harry and Riva Specht (1986b) 'Social work assessment: the route to clienthood – part II', *Social Casework* 67(10):587–93.

Specht, Harry and Anne Vickery (eds) (1977) *Integrating Social Work Methods* (London, Allen & Unwin).

Spybey, Tony (1992) *Social Change, Development and Dependency: Modernity, Colonialism and the Development of the West* (Cambridge, Polity).

Starak, Yaro (1988) 'Hong Kong: a model of "social happiness" for the new China', *International Social Work* **31**(3):211–17.

Statham, Daphne (1978) *Radicals in Social Work* (London, Routledge & Kegan Paul).

Stenson, Kevin and Nick Gould (1986) 'A comment on "A framework for theory in social work" by Whittington and Holland', *Issues in Social Work Education* **6**(1):41–5.

Stern, Richard and Lynne Drummond (1991) *The Practice of Behavioural and Cognitive Psychotherapy* (Cambridge, Cambridge University Press).

Stevenson, Olive and Phyllida Parsloe (1993) *Community Care and Empowerment* (York, Joseph Rowntree Foundation).

Stewart, Aileen Mitchell (1994) *Empowering People* (London, Pitman).

Strean, Herbert S. (1971) 'The application of role theory to social casework', in Herbert S. Strean (ed.) *Social Casework: Theories in Action* (Metuchen, NJ, Scarecrow Press).

Strean, Herbert S. (1979) *Psychoanalytic Theory and Social Work Practice* (New York, Free Press).

Sucato, Vincent (1978) 'The problem-solving process in short-term and long-term service', *Social Service Review* **52**(2):244–64.

Sullivan, Michael (1987) *Sociology and Social Welfare* (London, Allen & Unwin).

Sutton, Carole (1994) *Social Work, Community Work and Psychology* (London, British Psychological Society).

Swartz, Sue (1995) 'Community and risk in social service work', *Journal of Progressive Human Services* **6**(1):73–92.

Taylor, Patricia (1995) 'Power and authority in social work', in Patricia Taylor and Catherine Daly (eds) *Gender Dilemmas in Social Work: Issues Affecting Women in the Profession* (Toronto, Canadian Scholars' Press).

Taylor, Patricia and Catherine Daly (eds) (1995) *Gender Dilemmas in Social Work: Issues Affecting Women in the Profession* (Toronto, Canadian Scholars' Press).

Taylor, Samuel H. (1985) 'Community work and social work: the community liaison approach', in Samuel H. Taylor and Robert W. Roberts (eds) *Theory and Practice of Community Social Work* (New York, Columbia University Press), 179–216.

Taylor, Samuel H. and Robert W. Roberts (eds) (1985) *Theory and Practice of Community Social Work* (New York, Columbia University Press).

Tenaw, Shimelles (1995) *Time is for All* (Helsinki, Institute for Cooperative Studies, University of Helsinki).

Thomas, Alan (1992) 'Non-governmental organizations and the limits to empowerment', Marc Wuyts, Maureen Mackintosh and Tom Hewitt (eds) *Development Policy and Public Action* (Oxford, Oxford University Press), 117–46.

Thomas, Edwin J. (1968) 'Selected sociobehavioural techniques and principles: an approach to interpersonal helping', *Social Work* **13**(1):12–26.

Thomas, Edwin J. (1971) 'The behaviour modification model and social casework', in Herbert S. Strean *Social Casework: Theories in Action* (Metuchen, NJ, Scarecrow Press).

Thompson, Neil (1992) *Existentialism and Social Work* (Aldershot, Hants, Avebury).

Thompson, Neil (1993) *Anti-Discriminatory Practice* (London, Macmillan).

Thompson, Neil (1995a) 'Men and anti-sexism', *British Journal of Social Work* 25(4):459–76.

Thompson, Neil (1995b) *Theory and Practice in Health and Social Welfare* (Buckingham, Open University Press).

Thursz, Daniel, Charlotte Nusberg and Johnnie Prather (1995) *Empowering Older People: an International Approach* (London, Cassell).

Thyer, Bruce A. (1987) 'Contingency analysis: toward a unified theory for social work practice', *Social Work* 32:150–7.

Thyer, Bruce A. (ed.) (1989) *Behavioral Family Therapy* (Springfield, IL, Charles C. Thomas).

Thyer, Bruce A. (1993) 'Social work theory and practice research: the approach of logical positivism', *Social Work and Social Sciences Review* 4(1):5–26.

Thyer, Bruce A. (1994) 'Empiricists versus social constructionists: more fuel on the flames', *Families in Society* 75(5):308–12.

Thyer, Bruce A. and Walter W. Hudson (1987) 'Progress in behavioral social work: an introduction', *Journal of Social Services Research* 19(2/3/4):1–7.

Timms, Elizabeth (1983) 'On the relevance of informal social networks to social work intervention', *British Journal of Social Work* 13(4):405–16.

Timms, Noel (1964) *Psychiatric Social Work in Great Britain* (1939–62) (London, Routledge & Kegan Paul).

Titmuss, Richard M. (1963) *Essays on 'The Welfare State'*, 2nd edn (London, Allen & Unwin).

Titmuss, Richard M. (1968) *Commitment to Welfare* (London, Allen & Unwin).

Tolman, Richard M. and Christine E. Molidor (1994) 'A decade of social group work research: trends in methodology, theory, and program development', *Research on Social Work Practice* 4(2):142–59.

Towell, David (ed.) (1988) *An Ordinary Life in Practice* (London, King Edward's Hospital Fund for London).

Truax, Charles B. and Robert R. Carkhuff (1967) *Toward Effective Counseling and Psychotherapy: Training and Practice* (Chicago, Aldine).

Tully, J. Bryan (1976) 'Personal construct theory and psychological changes related to social work training', *British Journal of Social Work* 6(4):480–99.

Turner, Francis J. (1983a) 'Directions for social work education: the challenge of developing a comprehensive, coherent and flexible integrating network of theories', in Louise S. Bandler (ed.) *Education for Clinical Social Work Practice: Continuity and Change* (Oxford, Pergamon), 125–42.

Turner, Francis J. (ed.) (1983b) *Differential Diagnosis and Treatment in Social Work,* 3rd edn (New York, Free Press).

Francis J. Turner (ed.) (1986) *Social Work Treatment: Interlocking Theoretical Approaches,* 3rd edn (New York, Free Press).

Ukpong, Ebebe A. (1990) 'A quest for self-glory or self-reliance: upgrading the benefits of community development programmes', *Journal of Social Development in Africa* 5(2):73–85.

UNDP (United Nations Development Programme) (1994) *Human Development Report 1994* (New York, Oxford University Press).

Van der Vlugt, Ineke (1994) 'Female social work or gender-specific social work with women and girls?', in Karl-Ernst Hesser and Wibo Koole (eds) *Social Work in the Netherlands: Current Developments* (Utrecht, SWP), 18–23.

Van Elst, Ton (1994) 'Gender-specific social work with men and boys', in Karl-Ernst Hesser and Wibo Koole (eds) *Social Work in the Netherlands: Current Developments* (Utrecht, SWP), 24–34.

Verma, Ratna (1991) *Psychiatric Social Work in India* (New Delhi, Sage).

Vickery, Anne (1974) 'A systems approach to social work intervention: its uses for work with individuals and families', *British Journal of Social Work* 4(4):389–404.

Videka-Sherman, Lynn (1988) 'Meta-analysis of research on social work practice in mental health', *Social Work* 33:325–38.

von Bertalanffy, Ludwig (1971) *General System Theory: Foundations, Development, Application* (London, Allen Lane).

Wadia, A. R. (1961) 'Ethical and spiritual values in the practice of social work', in A. R. Wadia (ed.) *History and Philosophy of Social Work in India* (Bombay, Allied Publishers Private).

Wakefield, Jerome C. (1995) 'When an irresistible epistemology meets an immovable ontology', *Social Work Research* 19(1):9–17.

Wakefield, Jerome C. (1996) 'Does social work need the eco-systems perspective? Part 1: is the perspective clinically useful?' *Social Service Review* 70(1):1–31.

Walker, Barbara G. (1994) 'Science: feminists' scapegoat?', *Research on Social Work Practice* 4(4):510–14.

Wallen, JoAnne (1982) 'Listening to the unconscious in case material: Robert Langs' theory applied', *Smith College Studies in Social Work* 52(3):203–33.

Walrond-Skinner, Sue (1976) *Family Therapy: the Treatment of Natural Systems* (London, Routledge & Kegan Paul).

Walter, John L. and Jane E. Peller (1992) *Becoming Solution-focused in Brief Therapy* (New York, Bruner/Mozel).

Walton, Ronald G. (1975) 'Welfare rights and social work: ambivalence in action', in Howard Jones (ed.) *Towards a New Social Work* (London, Routledge & Kegan Paul), 102–21.

Walton, Ronald G. (ed.) (1986) 'Integrating formal and informal care – the utilization of social support networks', *British Journal of Social Work* 16 (Supplement).

Walton, Ronald G. and Medhat M. Abo El Nasr (1988) 'Indigenization and authentization in terms of social work in Egypt', *International Social Work* 31(2):135–44.

Ward, Liz (1980) 'The social work task in residential care', in Ronald Walton and Doreen Elliott (eds) *Residential Care: a Reader in Contemporary Theory and Practice* (Oxford, Pergamon).

Watson, David (1980) *Caring for Strangers* (London, Routledge & Kegan Paul).

Weaver, Donna R. (1982) 'Empowering treatment skills for helping black families', *Social Casework* 63(2):100–5.

Webb, David (1981) 'Themes and continuities in radical and traditional social work', *British Journal of Social Work* 11(2):143–58.

Weber, Max (1930) *The Protestant Ethic and the Spirit of Capitalism* (London, Allen & Unwin).

Weick, Ann (1981) 'Reframing the person-in-environment perspective', *Social Work* 26(2):140–3.

Weick, Ann (1983) 'Issues in overturning a medical model of social work practice', *Social Work* 28(6):467–71.

Weick, Ann (1986) 'The philosophical context of a health model of social work', *Social Casework* 67(9):551–9.

Wells, Richard A. (1982) *Planned Short-term Treatment* (New York, Free Press).

Wenger, G. Clare (1984) *The Supportive Network: Coping with Old Age* (London, Allen & Unwin).

Wenger, G. Clare (1994) *Understanding Support Networks and Community Care: Network Assessment for Elderly People* (Aldershot, Hants, Avebury).

Werner, Harold D. (1982) *Cognitive Therapy: A Humanistic Approach* (New York, Free Press).

Werner, Harold D. (1986) 'Cognitive theory', in Francis J. Turner (ed.) *Social Work Treatment: Interlocking Theoretical Approaches,* 3rd edn (New York, Free Press).

Westcott, Helen L. (1992) 'The cognitive interview – a useful tool for social workers', *British Journal of Social Work* 22(5):519–33.

Whang, In-Young (1988) 'Social services programmes for the poor in a newly industrialising country: experience in South Korea', in Dennis A. Rondinelli and G. Shalikin Cheema (eds) *Urban Services in Developing Countries: Public and Private Roles in Urban Development* (London, Macmillan).

White, M. and D. Epston (1990) *Narrative Means to Therapeutic Ends* (New York, Norton).

White, Shirley A., K. Sandandan Nair and Joseph Ashcroft (eds) (1994) *Participatory Communication: Working for Change and Development* (New Delhi, Sage).

White, Vicky (1995) 'Commonality and diversity in feminist social work', *British Journal of Social Work* 25(2):143–56.

Whiteley, J. Stuart (1979) 'The psychiatric hospital as a therapeutic setting', in Peter Righton (ed.) *Studies in Environment Therapy,* vol. 3 (Toddington, Glos, Planned Environment Therapy Trust).

Whittaker, James K. (1974) *Social Treatment: an approach to interpersonal helping* (Chicago, Aldine).

Whittaker, James K. (1981) 'Major approaches to residential treatment', in Frank Ainsworth and Leon C. Fulcher (eds) *Group Care for Children: Concepts and Issues* (London, Tavistock), 89–127.

Whittaker, James K. and James Garbarino (eds) (1983) *Social Support Networks: Informal Helping in the Human Services* (New York, Aldine).

Whittaker, James K. and Elizabeth M. Tracy (1989) *Social Treatment: an Introduction to Interpersonal Helping in Social Work Practice* (New York, Aldine de Gruyter).

Whittington, Colin and Ray Holland (1985) 'A framework for theory in social work', *Issues in Social Work Education* 5(1):25–50.

Wignaraja, Ponna (ed.) (1993) *New Social Movements in the South: Empowering the People* (London, Zed Books).

Wikler, Meir (1986) 'Pathways to treatment: how orthodox Jews enter therapy', *Social Casework* **67**(2):113–18.

Wilkes, Ruth (1981) *Social Work with Undervalued Groups* (London, Tavistock).

Williams, G., J. Mark and Stirling Moorey (1989) 'The wider application of cognitive therapy: the end of the beginning', in Jan Scott, J. Mark, G. Williams and Aaron T. Beck (eds) *Cognitive Therapy in Clinical Practice: an Illustrative Casebook* (London, Routledge).

Willmott, Peter (1986) *Social Networks, Informal Care and Public Policy* (London, Policy Studies Institute).

Willmott, Peter (1989) *Community Initiatives: Patterns and Prospects* (London, Policy Studies Institute).

Wills, David (1973) 'Planned environment therapy – what is it', in Hugh Klare and David Wills (eds) *Studies in Environment Therapy*, vol. 2 (London, Planned Environment Therapy Trust).

Wills, W. David (1964) *Homer Lane: a Biography* (London, Allen & Unwin).

Wilson, Elizabeth (1980) 'Feminism and social work', in Mike Brake and Roy Bailey (eds) *Radical Social Work and Practice* (London, Edward Arnold).

Wilson, Judy (1995a) *How to Work with Self-help Groups: Guidelines for Professionals* (Aldershot, Hants, Arena).

Wilson, Judy (1995b) 'Self-help groups as a route to empowerment', in Raymond Jack (ed.) *Empowerment in Community Care* (London, Chapman & Hall), 77–95.

Wilson, Maureen G. and Elizabeth Whitmore (1994) 'Gender and international development praxis', *Social Development Issues* **16**(1):55–66.

Winkels, Dorine (1994) 'Social work and community development work', in Karl-Ernst Hesser and Wibo Koole (eds) *Social Work in the Netherlands: Current Developments* (Utrecht, SWP), 105–11.

Winnicott, Donald W. (1964) *The Child, the Family and the Outside World* (Harmondsworth, Middlesex, Penguin).

Wise, Sue (1995) 'Feminist ethics in practice', in Richard Hugman and David Smith (eds) *Ethical Issues in Social Work* (London, Routledge), 104–19.

Witkin, Stanley L. (1989) 'Towards a scientific social work', *Journal of Social Service Research* **12**(2):83–98.

Witkin, Stanley L. (1991) 'Empirical clinical practice: a critical analysis', *Social Work* **36**(2):158–63.

Witkin, Stanley L. (1992) 'Empirical clinical practice or Witkin's revised views: which is the issue?', *Social Work* **37**(5):465–8.

Witkin, Stanley L. and Shimon S. Gottschalk (1988) 'Alternative criteria for theory evaluation', *Social Service Review* **62**(2):211–24.

Wolfensberger, Wolf (1972) *The Principle of Normalisation in Human Services* (Toronto, National Institute on Mental Retardation).

Wolfensberger, Wolf (1984) 'A reconceptualization of normalisation as social role valorization', *Mental Retardation* **34**:22–5.

Wong, Stephen E., James E. Woolsey and Estrella Gallegos (1987) 'Behavioral treatment of chronic psychiatric patients', *Journal of Social Services Research* **10**(2/3/4):7–36.

Wood, Gale Goldberg and Ruth R. Middleman (1989) *The Structural Approach to Direct Social Work Practice in Social Work* (New York, Columbia University Press).

Wood, Katherine M. (1971) 'The contribution of psychoanalysis and ego psychology to social work', in Herbert S. Strean (ed.) *Social Casework: Theories in Action* (Metuchen, NJ: Scarecrow Press).

Wood, Katherine M. (1978) 'Casework effectiveness: a new look at the research evidence', *Social Work* **23**:437–58.

Woodroofe, Kathleen (1962) *From Charity to Social Work* (London: Routledge & Kegan Paul).

Woods, Mary and Florence Hollis (1990) *Casework: a Psychological Process*, 2nd edn (New York, Random House).

Wright, Nancy A. (1995) 'Social skills training for conduct-disordered boys in residential treatment: a promising approach', *Residential Treatment for Children and Youth* **12**(4):15–28.

Yasas, Frances Maria and Vera Mehta (eds) (1990) *Exploring Feminist Visions: Case Studies on Social Justice Issues* (Pune, India, Streevani/Ishvani Kendra).

Yelaja, Shankar A. (1970) 'Toward a conceptualization of the social work profession in India', *Applied Social Studies* **2**(1):21–6.

Yelloly, Margaret A. (1980) *Social Work Theory and Psychoanalysis* (Wokingham, Berks, Van Nostrand Reinhold).

York, Alan S. (1984) 'Towards a conceptual model of community social work', *British Journal of Social Work* **14**(3):241–55.

Young, Katherine P. H. (1983) *Coping in Crisis* (Hong Kong, Hong Kong University Press).

Zimmerman, Jerome H. (1989) 'Determinism, science and social work', *Social Service Review* (1):52–62.

Author Index

Subject Index